IP92 45—

40—

RS

POPPIES,
PIPES,
and PEOPLE

POPPIES, PIPES, and PEOPLE

Opium and Its Use in Laos

Joseph Westermeyer
Foreword by Peter G. Bourne

University of California Press
Berkeley   Los Angeles   London

University of California Press
Berkeley and Los Angeles, California

University of California Press, Ltd.
London, England

Copyright © 1982 by The Regents of the University of California

Library of Congress Cataloging in Publication Data

Westermeyer, Joseph.
  Poppies, pipes, and people.

  Includes bibliographical references.
  1. Opium habit—Laos.   2. Opium trade—Laos.
I. Title
HV5816.W47   394.1   81–21995
ISBN 0–520–04622–6   AACR2

Printed in the United States of America

1 2 3 4 5 6 7 8 9

To Rachel Moga Westermeyer, for her
Competence as sometimes solo parent
Consistent support and occasional patience
Adaptiveness to motorcycles, jeeps, and ancient aircraft
Courage through coup, flood, and war
Affection for Laos, its people, and their ways.

Contents

CONTENTS

CONTENTS

CONTENTS

Foreword

With the exception of certain Eskimo groups, virtually every culture has at some stage in its history discovered and utilized mind-altering substances. While alcohol, an almost inevitable find of any grain-consuming society, by far heads the list of most widely used psycho-active substances, the resourcefulness of many cultures in identifying the obscure roots or leaves in their environment that produce an intoxicating effect is quite extraordinary. The ubiquitous nature of drug and alcohol use suggests the existence of a powerful human need that is being met by these substances. Despite this near universality in the desire to alter mental states pharmacologically, however, almost all scientific research in the field has been curiously ethnocentric. In part this is because a primary concern with regard to the use of drugs in a culture is what effect that use, especially if widespread and excessive, will have on the social fabric of that particular society. When the concern has been so highly culture-specific there has been little motivation to uncover what may be the fundamental issues relating to the interaction between the individual and society affecting the use and abuse of drugs, something that can only be done by a careful cross-cultural analysis free from the biases of any one society. The study reported in this volume represents a unique attempt to provide such a cross-cultural perspective, a perspective substantially enhanced by the author's multidisciplinary approach.

Early observations of the phenomenon of drug use and addiction were largely confined to autobiographical accounts by various figures in Europe and North America in the eighteenth and nineteenth centuries describing their personal encounters with drugs. Even when the effects had been quite destructive to the authors, their intimate descriptions of their experiences resembled the numerous accounts by explorers of that era of their travel to distant parts of the earth. These recountings of the drug experience were aimed as much at entertaining their audiences as providing useful scientific information. De Quincey's *Confessions of an English Opium Eater*, Coleridge's accounts, and even Freud's *Cocaine Papers* provided an interesting window on the lives of drug users but offered little in the way of hard scientific data. Descriptions alone of the effects of the drugs on the human mind were considered fascinating enough for most authors and readers.

With the development of psychology as an accepted science, attention was inevitably focused on the problem of drug addiction and particularly on the psychological factors that led one individual, but not another, to become addicted. Since this was a time when personality theory was dominating the thinking in the field, it is not surprising that the early considerations given to addiction should focus on what was identified as the "addictive personality." In what now seems like an extraordinarily narrow view of the phenomenon, addiction was seen to be solely a result of intrapsychic factors derived almost entirely from childhood experiences. It implied in many ways a sense of predestination suggesting that the "addictive personality," irrevocably created in early life, virtually guaranteed a decline into some form of degradation no matter what society or the individual might do to try to prevent it. At the time this theory helped explain to theorists why, among those who started using narcotics for medical purposes, some became addicted while others did not.

The idea that drug addiction resulted from some form of character disorder received strong reinforcement in the United States during the first half of this century due to the split between the medical community and law enforcement agencies. The management of addicts was clearly regarded as a responsibility of the medical profession during the first twenty years of this century, with morphine maintenance clinics established around the country under the direction of physicians to provide humane care for opiate addicts. The passage of the Harrison Narcotic Act in 1915, however, while ostensibly establishing the legitimacy of the maintenance clinics, became the basis for the gradual encroachment of the federal law enforcement system into the field of addiction. Eventually the Harrison Narcotic Act was used to justify the closing of all the maintenance clinics, and there began a period of thirty to forty years during which governmental concern with addiction was exclusively in the hands of law enforcement agencies. Their view of addiction was that the addict was a criminal who had transgressed against the mores of society, a perspective that was quite compatible with the psychological notion of the "addictive personality." Both views held that while the individual could not be held entirely accountable for his condition, he was afflicted with something that was irreversible and unresponsive to clinical intervention. Forceful control of the addict was therefore in his interests as well as those of society. By contrast in Europe, especially in Britain, the addict, while still viewed as intractable to any useful clinical intervention, was nevertheless regarded as better managed in a medical rather than a criminal setting.

Eventually in the United States, a moderation occurred in this view of addicts as inherently criminal, and federal facilities that were essentially combined hospitals and prisons were established in Lexington, Kentucky and Fort Worth, Texas. Studies conducted at these facilities, along with a changing emphasis in the study of human behavior away from the intrapsychic model, opened the door for consideration of an expanding range of factors that might affect the addictive process.

It became clear that social environment played a major role in whether individuals not only became addicts but also whether they were able to overcome their addiction. The highly pleasurable, positive reinforcement provided by heroin suggested a behavioral model in which addiction could be a learned phenomenon quite apart from any psychic predisposition an individual might have. The level of availability of drugs, especially heroin, could clearly transcend all other factors in determining the incidence of addiction in a community. And as American society became concerned about the traditional debasement of blacks, the possibility of the social oppression of minorities as a contributing factor was raised.

Widespread use of drugs in the United States beginning in the late 1960s opened up a whole range of other possibilities concerning the social and psychological etiology of drug use and addiction. Alienation and the use of drugs as forbidden substances as a form of protest were discussed. Heavy use of drugs by soldiers in Vietnam was attributed to the stresses of combat (ignoring the fact that drug use was higher in support units than combat units). The massive increase in tranquilizer prescribing by the medical profession suggested strongly to many people that drug taking, legal or illegal, was an inevitable result of the pressures of modern living. Physicians with backgrounds in medical epidemiology began to look at the explosive increase in heroin use in some communities and found that addiction could be closely compared with infectious disease in terms of its pattern of epidemic spread. Others observed that

nationwide efforts to prevent drug abuse by educating vulnerable populations about the potential hazards served only to pique interest and had
the reverse of the intended effect, being in many respects a campaign
that promoted drug use rather than prevented it. Studies of the families
of heavy drug users indicated that where there was heavy parental
use of alcohol and cigarettes, especially by mothers, the children were
much more likely to become regular drug users than children in families
where the use of alcohol and cigarettes was minimal or nonexistent.
Some surveys among young drug users from affluent backgrounds even
suggested that boredom alone could be a significant contributing factor
in drug abuse.

Intensified interest in drug abuse and addiction generally led to
greater concern on the part of medical scientists to elucidate the basic
biochemical and neurophysiological pathways by which addiction
occurred in the human brain. Opiate receptor sites were identified,
and naturally occurring opiatelike substances labeled endorphins were
identified in the brain. Various workers suggested that a genetic compo-
nent might contribute to the development of addiction in some individuals, as it was clearly shown that it was possible to breed strains of
mice with a predilection for alcohol.

The emergence of such a wide range of perspectives on the process
of addiction reflects the markedly enhanced sophistication with which
the issue has been addressed in the United States in recent years. It also
suggests the extraordinary complexity of entwined elements at many
different levels that influence drug use and addiction in the individual
and in the society at any given time in history. At the same time, the
importance of many of the identified factors may well be specific to
the cultural and social setting of the United States during the last twenty
years, and there is little way of determining what their importance might
be with regard to addiction in other cultures.

What is quite remarkable is that despite the substantial interest in
addiction in the United States and Western Europe in the last twenty
years and despite the significant increase in drug use in those regions
and elsewhere in the world, there have been almost no studies of the
phenomenon outside the industrialized nations. The possibility of getting
beyond the inherent cultural biases of studying addiction in only one
setting and thereby addressing some of the universal, cross-cultural
determinants of the process has largely been ignored by researchers.
For these reasons the studies described in this book are not only unique
but offer a very important contribution to our overall understanding
of addiction. What is also of interest is that the author was able to

study not only addicts indigenous to the Lao culture but also a significant number of Caucasians, most of whom had an addiction problem that had started in Asia. While this is obviously a group that is in many ways highly self-selected and representative neither of the general populations nor necessarily of the addict population in their homeland, it does offer a fascinating view of the cross-cultural interplay around the drug issue.

The observations that the author makes predictably call into question many of the assumptions made about narcotic addiction by researchers who have worked exclusively within the United States. In so doing, he leads us to recognize the exceptional cultural bias that most of us bring to our perspective on addiction. In particular, the opportunity afforded in Laos of comparing opium addiction with heroin addiction within the same cultural setting raises interesting new questions about the presumed relative perniciousness of the latter. At the same time the description of the treatment of addiction by a Buddhist monk at Wat Tan Kha Bok is, despite all of the differences in cultural context and style, very reminiscent of many residential therapeutic community programs in the United States, suggesting that certain fundamental elements in therapy can well be transposed from one cultural setting to another.

Perhaps the most important lessons from this study relate to the remarkably adverse impact of various foreign policy decisions made in the United States that were based in part on misinformation and misunderstanding, geared toward dealing with the drug problem as it affected Americans, and had very little regard for the impact they might have in Laos. The author clearly and persuasively shows that the decision to try to reduce both the flow of opium from Laos and the use of opium there influenced opening the way for heroin use in that country. Historically, United States narcotics policy has centered on an effort to keep drugs out of America. That we cared little about the impact of that policy on the rest of the world was of limited concern to us until relatively recently. In a world of steadily increasing interdependence, that is a matter we can no longer ignore, particularly when, as this book shows us so well, the impact is probably not in our own best interests in the long run.

In a world that is steadily shrinking, however, there will no longer be isolated tribal groups with traditional opium cultivation and use. Those few areas of the world where opium is now still grown are becoming increasingly integrated into a worldwide system of control and monitoring. Over the next few years that control is likely to increase, particularly as improved satellite technology allows for the detection and measuring of opium crops anywhere in the world. Greater strength of central governments in developing countries will likely lead to diminished tolerance for minorities to cultivate and traffic in opium outside the legitimate economy. The political developments in Laos over the last ten years are ample testimony to this trend. I deplore the ill-conceived and misdirected efforts of the United States to influence opium cultivation and use in Laos; this crop and its consumption is clearly the inevitable victim of international political pressures. The assumption of total power in Laos by the Pathet Lao resulted in a major move against the cultivation of opium and an abolition of the treatment program. After a period under American influence, during which an effort was made to deal with addicts in Laos as people with a medical problem in need of treatment, they are now regarded as criminals, which is reminiscent of the attitude that prevailed in the United States fifty years ago.

One aspect of this book that is unique is that it serves as a detailed record of a situation that has now vanished. As such it is a most important historical record. This will become increasingly true as the traditional tribal cultivation of opium disappears in the few areas where it still remains, primarily in Thailand, Burma, and Afghanistan. Urbanization, political change, and general economic development of rural areas all doom the existence of traditional opium cultivation. At the same time, heroin use, traditionally favored only in developed nations, has become widespread in such major Asian cities as Bangkok, Hong Kong, and Rangoon as well as in many smaller communities. The factors leading to the switch from opium to heroin, described so well in this book, have operated similarly elsewhere. But with a large demand for heroin created in developing countries at the same time that the traditional quasi-legitimate cultivation of opium is in decline, there is every reason to expect that a completely illicit system of supply will be created. Opium will cease to be a subsistence crop for poor farmers and become an entirely illegal commodity grown by entrepreneurs for quick profits. The pattern we saw during the 1970s in northern Mexico, where opium was grown expressly to meet the heroin demands in the United States, is likely to be repeated elsewhere. Perhaps a concerted worldwide effort to monitor and suppress such cultivation will be successful, with the only legitimate cultivation being for the international pharmaceutical market. If this is the case, and if as a result illicit heroin can be made relatively unavailable throughout the world, then perhaps mankind will be better off. But the evidence to date as well as the immense financial profits available from heroin trafficking make such worldwide control seem out of reach at the present time.

In recent years the infectious and parasitic diseases that afflict the populations of most developing countries and that have been primarily responsible for high infant mortality rates and low life expectancy have begun gradually to be brought under control. Increasingly in the future the health problems of developed and developing countries are likely to be very much the same. We are already beginning to see, however, that the current major causes of death and disability among young adults in the United States, mainly life-style problems such as alcoholism, cigarette smoking, obesity and hypertension, suicide, and automobile accidents, are now replacing infectious diseases as the primary causes of mortality in developing countries. Dr. Halfdan Mahler, the Director-General of the World Health Organization, recently stated that alcohol and tobacco would pose the greatest health threats to the population of the developing world over the next fifty years. He might equally well have included drug abuse. An enormous market for psychoactive substances is now mushrooming in the developing world. Pharmaceutical products in this category are pouring into developing countries usually without even the limited controls that exist in Europe and North America. We can anticipate a continuing major expansion in the use and abuse of these substances. Particularly in cultures where there is not the constraining influence of the Protestant ethic or other religious forces such as the Moslem faith, the potential for widespread psychoactive drug consumption is alarming. This is even truer with the breakdown of the traditionally prescribed social patterns of drug use in indigenous cultures as described in this book. Urbanization, social and political dislocation, and the ready availability of potent, imported synthetic drugs create a most volatile mixture. So far it would seem that we have seen only the tip of the iceberg with regard to the very serious problems we will encounter in the future.

One of the great weaknesses of the discipline that concerns itself with the problems of substance abuse is that there is a strong tendency to ignore both the cross-cultural experience and the historical data that are available. As a result there is a tendency to interpret aspects of alcohol and drug abuse as though they were unique and to repeat regularly the errors of the past in the establishment of policies and programs for dealing with the problem. A better education for workers in the field about experiences other than those they are immediately dealing with would greatly contribute to solving this problem. This book offers a great deal in that respect. While there are the obvious lessons and conclusions that the author draws, the book also provides a microcosm of information that cannot help but immeasurably broaden the perspective of anyone working in this field.

Peter G. Bourne

Preface

This book is meant for the reader interested in opium and its uses, benefits, and consequences among the people in Laos. It is based primarily on my experiences as a physician, public health worker, and researcher there between 1965 and 1975. Research work of others conducted in Asia and my own work elsewhere in Asia and in the United States supplement these firsthand observations from Laos.

Several different research methodologies were employed to examine opium, its uses, and its effects. To begin with, I focused on ecological, sociocultural, and agroeconomic issues. Later my efforts focused on lengthy interviews with addicts and their families. Several epidemiological surveys were undertaken in different communities, utilizing several methods of case finding. Addicts and their families were studied in general medical settings, as well as in special treatment facilities for addicts. Folk treatment methods for addiction were described, along with the milieu, inhabitants, and functions of opium dens. Treatment outcome for addicts was evaluated, with a comparison of a Buddhist monastery program and a multimodality medical program. In recent years I have had the opportunity of studying former addicts from Laos who are now in the United States as refugees.

The diversity of these experiences and observations presents certain inherent advantages and disadvantages for the reader. On the beneficial side, numerous facets of opium and its uses are presented, as opposed to a single social, medical, or economic focus. It is hoped that this will allow the reader to see the complexity of the issue, the desirable as well as undesirable aspects of this widely praised and widely condemned substance. But there is a disadvantage as well. If I have done my task as I set out to do it, this book will be read by people from a diversity of backgrounds who have a common interest in this topic. It is expected that readers will include physicians, social and behavioral scientists, epidemiologists, a few pharmacologists, a historian or two, and perhaps even a legislator or government official. Therein has lain a special obstacle for me, since each of these various groups employs terms or jargon that are not mutually intelligible to the others. Even worse, a term that has quite precise, denotative meaning to those in one field (e.g., "addiction" for physicians and pharmacologists) may have highly subjective, connotative meaning to those in other fields (e.g., "addiction" for most social scientists and legislators). There is the additional difficulty that those in different fields do not always know how those other than themselves go about their work. For example, anthropologists and epidemiologists tend to know little or nothing of one another's research techniques, even though both often undertake research in communities (as opposed to laboratories or hospitals).

I have tried to handle this problem in several ways. First, there is a glossary that includes many terms that may not be clear to all readers. Reference to the glossary is made in the first few chapters so that the reader can become familiar with it. Second, the sampling methods, research techniques, and data collection instruments are presented in somewhat greater detail than usual, rather than using the usual shorthand descriptions that most of us use when writing for people from similar backgrounds. (Some of this is located in the footnotes.) And third, I have elaborated some of the common philosophical and epistemological issues in certain fields as they touch on these data. All of these three means of handling the basic communication problem will undoubtedly assist the reader at some points, while causing some frustration with overly elementary descriptions or explanations at other points. I ask the readers' indulgence when this occurs and suggest reading rapidly through such paragraphs until the material becomes engaging again.

Acknowledgments

As with any research effort spanning a fifteen-year period, many people played key roles in facilitating this work. Before it began, Dr. Neil Gault and Professor Perti Pelto provided support and direction in undertaking cross-cultural research. Later assistance in the analysis and interpretation of these data came from Professor Robert Kiste, Drs. Fuller Torrey, Patrick Hughes, Peter Bourne, and Edward Kaufman, and Mrs. Grace Peng. For subsequent discussions and meetings that have helped focus my thoughts on this topic, I am indebted to Drs. Awni Arif, Charas Suwanwela, Vichai Poshyachinda, Visut Navaratnam, and David Feingold.

Numerous people in Laos provided critical help in undertaking the clinical and field studies. Their assistance included logistical support, contacting subjects, entrees into villages and treatment settings, translation, and critique of written materials. Among the Hmong, I am grateful to Messrs. Tou Fu Vang, Vang Geu, Her Tou (deceased), and Moua Lia and Mesdames Choua Thao, Gaohli Lyfong, and Xiong Chao Beeson. The Iu Mien, Messrs. Chao Mai (deceased) and Chao La, as well as "the old tasseng" and "Robert," made studies and surveys in this population possible. Among Lao people I thank Drs. Chomchanh Soudaly, Phim, Khamleck Vilay, and Khammeung Tounalom and Messrs. Adul Keomahathai and Phimpha (deceased). Various staff members of the Ministries of Public Health and Social Welfare also provided invaluable support and information. In Thailand, Abbott Phra Chamroon Parcharn of Wat Tan Kha Bok was most cordial. Among North Americans in Laos whose friendship and interest helped greatly in conducting this work, I count Ambassador and Mrs. William Sullivan, Dr. Charles (Jigs)

Weldon, Dr. Patricia McCreedy, Dr. Frank Becker, Larry Berger, Joe Kerch, Fred and Millie Michaels, Don and Minh Dougan, Marge and Frank Manley, and the Reverend Lucien Bouchard. Without the continued patience and friendship shown by each of these individuals, the work could not have been completed.

This attempt to distill the fieldwork of a decade, with its cognitive, emotional, and experiential aspects, was not easily accomplished. In this difficult task I received support from several quarters. Anthropologists Linda Bennett and Barbara Pillsbury made excellent suggestions regarding means for organizing the data and presenting them in a reasonably coherent fashion. Reviewers for the University of California Press recommended several useful modifications. Peter Bourne and Rachel Westermeyer similarly helped with their editorial comments. And finally, the persistence and patience of Gloria Wolf in typing several revisions was a key factor in finally completing this work, started and abandoned on several occasions.

The efforts of both colleagues and family members permitted me to devote the time and effort necessary to these studies. Here in the Department of Psychiatry, at the University of Minnesota, I am especially indebted to Drs. Burtrum Schiele, Donald Hastings, Richard Anderson, Floyd Garetz, William Hausman, James Stephans, and Elke Eckert. Their covering of my clinical and academic responsibilities permitted me to conduct field studies during the period 1965 to 1975. My family tolerated extensive periods away from home that, on the installment plan, amounted to about a year and a half. In addition to the joys and excitement of work in an exotic setting, they shared the pains, boredom, and tragedies associated with residence in that time and place. Reveries from my wife's childbirth under the most primitive of conditions, my daughter's Honda burn while accompanying me on an interview (at age four years), and my son's forebearance during lengthy visits to opium dens (at the same age) remind me of their personal contributions to this volume.

J.W.

Minneapolis, Minnesota
September 4, 1981

I

Introduction

Learning Addiction Hmong Style. Northern Laos 1965, three in the morning. A flashlight glaring in my face chases sleep away. *"Thān-maw—Doctor,"* she begins hesitantly. "A very sick man has just come to the hospital. Would you see him?"

Jacket and pants on, feet jammed into a pair of thongs, and at least my body is on the move—my mind is still half-asleep. Gao Xiong, the Hmong nurse, leads the way along the sloping laterite path with her flashlight. Pit vipers and scorpions often seek the retained warmth of such paths on cold, damp nights. That thought arouses me a bit more. We can see our breath as we exhale, and fog shrouds the hospital only a few hundred feet away.

As the low frame buildings emerge from the mist, we hear loud groaning. Not the weak muffled groans of the wounded or the typhoid afflicted, nor the sharp screeching of a fearful child or a hysterial adult. Rather something in between. The groans now become louder with each step. My teenaged guide speaks above the wailing: *"Khanoy seah chai, Thān-maw—*I'm sorry, Doctor. It's been like this the last two hours. He's awakened everyone in the whole hospital."

All the beds are occupied, some with two patients in one bed. Apparently they've put the new man out on the veranda; we're climbing the stairs in that direction. Yes, that's right, the sounds are coming from one of the cots on the triage porch. There's our man by the wall—old, he looks—moaning loudly, almost wailing, in a repetitive sing-song "oh yaw—oh yaw—oh yaw." Not only moaning; rocking slightly, gently with each "oh-yaw" as he lies there on his right side.

1

It looks like his abdomen hurts. His legs are flexed up almost to his rib cage. Both arms are crossed on his belly, and each hand grasps the opposite flank. "*Nyā-paw, pen nyang*—Venerable father, what is the matter?" I ask in Lao. He responds only with moans. One of two men on the porch (both about my age) steps into the flashlight's penumbra and responds in Hmong, "*Meu plaa*—belly pain." Good. We've got a historian for the man and his problem. The Hmong nurse takes my questions in Lao, passes them on in Hmong, and brings the responses back to me in Lao.

All three men are from a refugee encampment about a day's . walk in the northeast mountains. A few days ago the old man, father of the two others, first developed the symptoms of a cold: runny nose and eyes, sneezing. Within hours, he ached all over, felt weak, and refused even rice gruel. Last night he turned definitely for the worse: vomiting at intervals, diarrhea, and constant abdominal cramps. The family held a meeting. If the old man died, his departing ghost would leave the world happier if he died at home; but then again maybe the hospital could help him. His sons started for the hospital aₜ dawn this morning, taking turns carrying him on their backs.

A good, succinct account of his sudden illness—accurate, detailed, precisely stated. The cause of his symptoms still escapes me; perhaps I've not been listening closely enough. A good physical exam should easily unravel the problem. By now my mind is alert enough to perceive what eye, ear, nostril, and hand have to tell about the old man and his malady.

Skin pale and clammy. Eyes glazed, lids drooping half shut. Thin, clear discharge from the nose. Tongue caked and dry. Pulse rapid and thready. And no more. Surely there has to be more. But a recheck of the eye grounds, the heart, the lungs, the abdomen confirms the first exam: here indeed is a critically ill man with no evident cause for his malady. No lobar pneumonia, no malaria, no typhoid, no ruptured appendix.

Back to more history. The young woman dutifully passes on the questions: recent illnesses in the family? recent deaths in the village? similar episodes in the man's past life? Still no leads. The nurse reads my perplexed frown. "*Thān-maw,*" respectfully, lowering her eyes and her voice, "*Than-maw, phu ne phen khon tēt dyā-fēn*—Doctor, this man is one addicted to opium."

A few more questions confirm the nurse's diagnosis. The man is indeed an opium addict; and yes, he ıs in opium withdrawal. According to his sons, the old man smoked opium daily since their childhood—

at least twenty years. During most of this time he smoked a little opium each morning and more each evening—not so much that he couldn't farm and hunt. Over the last several years he has gradually used more opium, especially during the cold season when the joints of his legs and arms ached severely. In the last few months he has smoked opium so heavily and so often (five and six times a day) that he has become incapable of sustained productive work.

Were it not for his four sons, the old man would have been destitute. Among themselves they provided enough opium from their own poppy crops to keep him supplied. Recent military incursions had brought on the present crisis. Forced to leave their homes and fields, the family had not planted an opium crop this last year. The old man's opium supply had run out last week. Unable to purchase more, he had gone into withdrawal.

So here he was in one of the worst cases of narcotic withdrawal I'd ever encountered. On top of it all, severely dehydrated and not young (though his sons said he was more like fifty-five than the seventy he appeared to be). We'd better get going before he lost more ground.

A quarter grain of intramuscular morphine and rapid intravenous fluids for starters. Twenty minutes later his groaning is louder and his see-saw rocking more vigorous, so he isn't going to die tonight any-way. Pulse is still rapid but not so thready. Asked if he feels any better, he replies that he doesn't. Another quarter grain of intramuscular morphine. And two more over the next few hours.

By dawn it's evident that he will survive: more luster to his eyes, some moisture now on his tongue, less clawing at his abdomen. But what about our morphine supply? At this rate, the old man will require almost as much morphine a day as we are using for all the wounded and postoperative cases in a hospital of over a hundred beds. A purple glow from the eastern sky lights my way back to the one-room shack. Don't remember even climbing into my mummy bag.

By rounds next morning the word is out. The *Thān-maw* missed a diagnosis last night. And such a simple one at that—any mother's child would have readily identified the problem. Coy, knowing smiles from all the teenaged nurses. Indirect, but more overt comments from the older medics.

Moua Geu, the head medic, agrees to instruct me on the nuances of opium addiction during rounds that morning. First the skinny man with pneumonia and malaria: "See the small kerosene lamp by his bedside, the tarry black substance under the nail of his little finger? Note that his wife has no silver around her neck. Smell his breath and clothes while you listen to his chest with the stethoscope—that sharp, musky smell of opium is like no other, wouldn't you say?''

On to the teenaged boy with the shrapnel wounds in his legs. The dull one with the blank stare. "Not him," I insist. "He's mentally retarded." "Ask him some questions," responds Moua Geu. We do and he's right—not retarded. The lad relates that both his parents are addicts, and they do not object to his smoking opium once or twice a day. He's the youngest, the only son, their support for their old age. Since he is an addict, no woman wants to marry him. And he enjoys his pipe more than women, anyway. So everyone in the family triad appears to benefit.

"Look again at the old man who came to the hospital last night," suggests Moua Geu. Ah yes, once instructed, the scales fall from my eyes. The old man's hands and fingers are long and thin, none of the usual roughened skin and callouses. His skin has a sallow, yellowish white tone rather than the usual ruddy brown of most Hmong men. His gums and lips have a purplish cyanotic tinge, his teeth are loose, and he has marked pyorrhea. Unlike the average ascetic mountaineer, he complains of minor discomforts and begs at each nurse's passing for more sedative and analgesic medication. His clothes are shoddy, and soot is embedded in every crease and pore of his body.

Within a few days I begin testing my new skill with Moua Geu. "That one, Moua Geu, she smokes opium once or twice a day." "Yes, *Thān-maw,* that's right." "That one, Moua Geu, he is a *khon khē dyā fēn*—an opium sot who smokes all day long." "Yes, *Thān-maw,* that's right."

With such informed and patient teachers, I learn rapidly.

BACKGROUND

My first two-year sojourn into Laos began with elements having nothing to do with Asia or opium. Rather its origins were in my own home town (St. Paul, Minnesota) and in my work as a general physician. I practiced in a clinic that served several ethnic populations: Catholic Irish and Germans and Poles; upwardly mobile Chicanos; a group of Baptist Scandinavians; and some Italians (many unable to speak English). An occasional Chippewa, Jewish, or Anglo patient added to the diversity. These diverse peoples had disorders and played out their sick roles in ways that were often quite different.

Like most young physicians, I was first interested in adding to my knowledge of illness and my clinical skills. Fairly soon it became evident that economics had predetermined certain limitations to expanding these. In a city the size of St. Paul, specialists resisted incursions by generalists into their rice bowl—the care of the simpler, common procedures and disorders that supported them. At hand lay the opportunity for a way out of my frustration: the sociocultural diversity among my patients. I enrolled in a freshman anthropology course to gain the concepts for understanding and the tools for studying these people and their ailments.

To my surprise, the anthropologists seemed pleased to have me. Coming on the heels of rejection by my medical and surgical colleagues, that was a breath of fresh air. Over the next two years I took evening courses and seminars during my off-duty afternoon, while still practicing. It was a chance suggestion by a former physician-teacher, Dr. Neil Gault, that led to the next step. He mentioned, after learning of my cultural interests, that I might consider working in another society— much as he had done in Korean villages as that country was developing a rural health care system. He recommended that I contact the United States Agency for International Development (AID).

In 1964, AID did have available rural health work with refugees in Indochina. Mid-1965 found me in Laos where, over the next two years, my practice consisted mostly of wartime surgery, tropical disease, nutritional deficiencies, obstetrical complications (midwives did the normal deliveries), and various public health tasks. Among the episodic crises of battles, epidemics, flood, supply shortages, and budgetary revisions, there were also some evenings, weekends, and idle afternoons for collecting data. Even my medical, surgical, and public health work provided opportunities to acquire cultural information not otherwise accessible.

Originally my plans were to study psychosomatic disorder (an area of general medical interest during the mid-sixties) and to compare refugees with those in settled villages. Practical considerations prevented this, since the work load during refugee moves was too great. Serendipity intervened in the guise of the old man just described, the brightly colored poppy patches on the hills all about me, and the pungent tar-balls that were sold in markets and that fellow passengers sometimes carried onto trucks, boats, and planes. As pointed out later by Hughes and Crawford (1974), communities with a high prevalence of narcotic addiction—such as those in Laos—provide a superb opportunity to study the addictive phenomenon and conduct experiments to reduce that prevalence. My plans changed to the study of opium, its roles and functions in this society, its uses, its advantages and problems.

THE RESEARCH HYPOTHESES

In the Western world (and even in much of the Eastern world) opium is viewed as an unalloyed evil. With the possible exception of its medical use, there is little good that is said of it. And to some extent, that is true. A brief saunter through the wards of Sam Thong Hospital (as you took with me a few paragraphs back) would provide ample evidence for that. Illness, poverty, family discord, malnutrition, isolation and alienation, loss of social standing and self esteem—all were there to see.

But there was also another side. A village health worker at whose home I stayed, as industrious and responsible as most health workers, had a pipe every night and was not addicted. Honest, hard-working farmers worked as diligently and as proudly on their poppy crop as they did at the care of their rice and corn fields. Parents of the nurses and medics at the hospital, when they came from their more remote villages for a visit to their children, often financed their journey southward by bringing a few kilograms of opium and returning northward with a few bolts of cloth and a few transistor radios. Any balanced understanding of opium in the context of Laos required a recognition of both aspects: that is, the problems, the devils in this substance, and the advantages, the monetary and comforting sides of it.

In order to comprehend these diverse facets, the general topic of opium must be broken down into subtopics. Within each subtopic, questions can be asked or hypotheses posed that can be answered or tested within a research format. At the outset broad, general hypotheses were based on the conventional wisdom available in Laos (although these sometimes contradicted each other).

My initial hypotheses posed during these studies and addressed in the body of this book were as follows:

1. Opium can, like alcohol, be used as a recreational intoxicant or folk medication without addiction.
2. Opium is consumed primarily by wealthy men, most of whom are elderly and ill.
3. Poppy is raised primarily as a cash crop and can readily be supplanted by other cash-producing crops, animals, or labor.
4. Ethnicity is a prime determinant of opium use, with the more Sinitic peoples (i.e., Chinese, Iu Mien, Hmong, Vietnamese) consuming more than the Thai-Lao and Mon-Khmer peoples (i.e., Lao, Thai, Cambodian, Khamu, Tai Dam).

5. Heroin is more addictive and more pathogenic than opium and leads to higher rates of addiction where it is used.

6. Opium addiction has no effect on economic productivity, and it may even enhance productivity.

7. Opium addiction has been traditionally viewed in Asia as a habit rather than as an illness; the latter conceptual framework is an imported, Western one.

8. There is no natural course of opium addiction. This is a perversion of the infectious-disease model of medicine.

9. Treatment of opium addiction is not necessary, effective, or cost-efficient.

10. If a country wishes to eliminate opium addiction, the most effective and cost-efficient means involves legislation and law enforcement, such as was done in China.

METHODS

Times and Places

These data were collected over a ten-year period, from mid-1965 to early 1975. During this period I made seven trips to Laos and spent a total of three years there. Between 1976 and 1982, opium addiction elsewhere in Asia was assessed during five additional trips. In addition, the movement of Southeast Asian refugees to the United States provided the opportunity to study former Hmong, Lao, and Vietnamese opium users and addicts in an opium-free environment. Dates, funding sources, locations, and roles for my Asian trips were as follows:

Date	Funding source	Location(s)	Role(s)
July 1965 to June 1967	USAID	Laos	General physician, Public health officer
February–April 1971	International Programs Office, University of Minnesota	Laos	Researcher
November 1971	USAID, Ministry of Public Health	Laos	Consultant

7

March–April 1972	USAID, Ministry of Public Health	Laos	Treatment planner, Researcher
March–April 1973	USAID, Ministry of Public Health	Laos	Teacher, Researcher
January– March 1974	USAID, Ministry of Public Health	Laos	Evaluator, Researcher
February–April 1975	International Programs Office, Minnesota Medical Foundation	Laos	Researcher
October– November 1977	Office of Drug Abuse Prevention, White House	Philippines, Singapore, Indonesia, Malaysia, Burma, Thailand, Hong Kong	Consultant
July 1979	World Health Organization, Drug Abuse Division	Hong Kong	Consultant
October– November 1979	World Health Organization, Drug Abuse Division	Hong Kong, Thailand	Consultant, Teacher
August 1981	World Health Organization, Drug Abuse Division	Malaysia	Consultant
January 1982	World Health Organization, Drug Abuse Division	Thailand	Consultant

Map 1. Laos: Provinces and Major Towns. (From Whitaker, D. P., Barth, H. A., Berman, S. M., et al. Area Handbook for Laos, Washington, D. C. U. S. Govt. Printing Office, 1972.)

During 1965 to 1975, forty-four different sites were visited in all of the provinces of Laos (see map 1), with the exception of Phong Saly in the far north and Champassak in the far south. Duration of time in these various sites, among various ethnic groups and in various provinces, was as follows:

9

a. Duration of visit and number of sites

8–24 hours:	31 sites	
2–7 days:	23 sites	(average approximately 5 days)
8–21 days:	8 sites	(average approximately 15 days)
8 months:	1 site	(Sam Thong Valley, including several nearby villages)
1.5 years:	1 site	(Vientiane Prefecture, including several districts and approximately 20 villages)

b. Predominant ethnic group in each location and time

Lao	19.5 months
Hmong	12.0 months
Iu Mien (Yao)	1.5 months
other tribal groups	1.5 months
expatriate Asians	1.0 months
expatriate Caucasians*	0.5 months

c. Provinces and time

Vientiane	20.0 months
Xieng Khouang	10.5 months
Houa Kong (also called Nam Tha)	1.0 months
other	4.5 months

As noted above, from 1965 to 1967 I was a general physician in the Public Health Division of AID/Laos. One-third of this time was spent as a general physician and surgeon, in periods lasting from a few to several weeks. This occurred at a small hospital in a remote Hmong village in northern Laos (sixty beds in 1965, 100 beds by 1967). Another one-third of this time was spent in villages and refugee camps assessing health problems, supervising, and rendering medical assistance. These efforts were almost exclusively among indigenous people, and Lao was our common language (with bits of French and English depending on speakers and context). The remaining one-third of the period 1965 to 1967 was spent with the following: (1) administrative responsibilities with AID; (2) liaison work and program planning with the Health Ministry of the national government and the World Health Organization (WHO); (3) survey activities to supply public health information to the host government, WHO, and AID; and (4) instruction of nurses

*This reflects the time devoted to studying expatriate Caucasian addicts, not time spent in working and socializing with expatriate Caucasians.

and medics for village health work. These latter responsibilities were undertaken primarily at the capital city, Vientiane, and involved frequent contacts with health professionals and government leaders. Data collected during this time were the basis of an anthropology thesis and scientific reports on opium addiction (see the list of references for further details).

The second visit in early 1971 was funded by University of Minnesota research funds within the Office of International Programs. Having completed training in anthropology, psychiatry, and public health during the years 1967 to 1970, I returned to conduct an intensive case study of forty Laotian opium addicts. Sampling method was by community survey.

Four annual visits were subsequently made from late 1971 to early 1974. They involved consultation to the Ministry of Public Health and the Ministry of Social Welfare of the Royal Lao Government regarding the growing social and health problem presented by refugee opium addicts. The first visit was to consider what programs might be undertaken to deal with the problem. Of some twenty alternatives, each ministry chose one. The second visit four months later was to assist new staff members with the planning of these programs. The following year, a third visit was primarily a consultation regarding the inevitable difficulties after staff members had several months' experience in treating addicts. During a final consultation in 1974, the programs were evaluated. Between these visits, training opportunities were arranged for several Lao staff members in Bangkok, Hong Kong, and the United States. My consultations were paid by AID, while the programs were funded by a consortium of the Lao national government, AID, WHO, a Buddhist women's auxiliary, the Asia Foundation, and various local charitable and social action groups.

A final research trip to Laos in 1975 was for the purpose of collecting data on mental illness. This was funded by two research foundations at the University of Minnesota (i.e., the Minnesota Medical Foundation and International Programs Office). Further data on opium addicts were collected during this visit.

Sampling and Research Methods

These are described in greater detail later in each of the chapters. Briefly, several research methods were employed during these visits. First, observations were made regarding poppy growing, opium commerce, opium use, and opium addiction. Since prior to 1971 there were no laws against opium production or use, these studies could be con-

11

ducted fairly easily once rapport was established and reasons given for the information being sought. Interviews were also obtained with poppy farmers and with merchants who bought and sold opium. The focus of this phase was to understand the social and economic concomitants of opium. My many friends, colleagues, associates, and acquaintances acquired over the years in Laos facilitated this process.

Next, several community surveys were conducted to study addicted persons in Hmong, Iu Mien (Yao), Lao, and Khamu villages. Addicts were also studied in a general hospital (in Xieng Khouang), in a medical treatment program for addicts (in Vientiane), and at a Buddhist temple (in Thailand) where addicts received care and exhortation. An addict registry provided information on addicts for Vientiane Prefecture. Data varied from simple demographic background (i.e., age, sex, ethnicity) to detailed drug use information and extensive life histories. Several individual addicts were followed over periods of one to ten years. The purpose was to learn about addicts, the natural history of addiction, and the prevalence of addiction in various settings.

Several smaller investigations were initiated to answer specific questions regarding addiction. Data on folk therapies were collected from addicts. Visits were made to several opium dens, and addicts there were interviewed. An outcome study of treated addicts was conducted to assess those factors that favored subsequent abstinence.

My observations on addicts from Asia continue. Data are being collected on former opium users and addicts here in the United States. This takes place in weekly clinics that I have conducted over the last five years for Hmong, Lao, Vietnamese, and Cambodian refugees in the United States. I have also been a consultant to the World Health Organization from 1978 to 1982 regarding the epidemiology and treatment of drug addiction in Asia.

THE WRITING

The results of these studies have been published in scientific journals over the years (see the references at the back of the book). Five coauthors have collaborated in these publications. One of these is Peter Bourne, M.D., who was deputy chief of the White House Special Action Office for Drug Abuse Prevention. Dr. Bourne served as a special consultant to the State Department regarding American assistance for treatment of opium addicts in Laos. Larry Berger, formerly a Peace Corps worker in Thailand, served as an administrative liaison to the treatment program in Laos. Berger, now a hospital administrator, and I published two papers regarding Caucasian addicts in Laos. Grace Peng, a native of China and later Taiwan, a statistician and a computer expert, played a key role in the analysis of these data. Peng and I also published two papers together. And a single paper was published with Dr. Chomchan Soudaly, director of a treatment program for addicts in Laos, and Dr. Edward Kaufman, editor of the *American Journal of Alcohol and Drug Abuse*, who visited Dr. Soudaly's treatment facility in Laos. These published reports have permitted neither the presentation of a global overview nor an analysis of the numerous and complex factors involved in opium production and use. This book has been written to fill that gap.

In writing such a book, my goal has been to discern and present general principles. This is not a journalistic effort to titillate the reader with a few esoteric cases or events. The presentation of only general characteristics and common manifestations inevitably leads, however, to a loss of the unique, the specific, the complexity of events and behavior. In an effort to lend some flesh to these statistical bones, case vignettes have been included in selected portions of these chapters (as in the opening paragraphs of this chapter). Vignettes run the risk of disrupting the flow of the reading. At the same time I believe they serve as a touchstone to the reality of these findings in the lives of the people who served as informants, subjects, and coparticipants with me in this study.

II

The Country and Its People

GEOGRAPHY AND CLIMATE

Laos, a landlocked country, is bounded by China, Vietnam, Cambodia, Thailand, and Burma. Its area covers 91,000 square miles, slightly larger than Minnesota or Great Britain. Population estimates over the last few decades have ranged from 2.5 to 3.3 million, but no careful census has been conducted. Two major topographical features dominate the landscape: the Mekong River and the Annamite chain of mountains, both of which originate in Tibet and course southeastward to the South China Sea (see map 2).

These two geographic characteristics have their ecological and cultural parallels. The Mekong River flood plain, with its tributaries and valleys, is inhabited by Lao people. Here they live in permanent villages, raise paddy rice, and engage in fishing. Riverine commerce vies with ox carts as the primary means of transport. In the forested mountains of the Annamite Chain, covering perhaps 90 percent of the terrain, live the diverse tribal peoples who comprise about half the population. Rice remains the staple crop, but it is raised without irrigation on hillsides and mountain slopes. Game supplants fishing here; travel afoot or by horseback replaces the lowland pirogue and sampan.

A cycle of rains alternates with a dry season, each lasting about six months. Southwest winds bring showers (the mango rains) and thunderstorms in late April/early May. These diminish to steady rains in July and August. Daytime temperatures range in the eighties during this May-to-October rainy season. The northeast monsoon ends the wet weather. The first half of the dry season is cool, with daytime tempera-

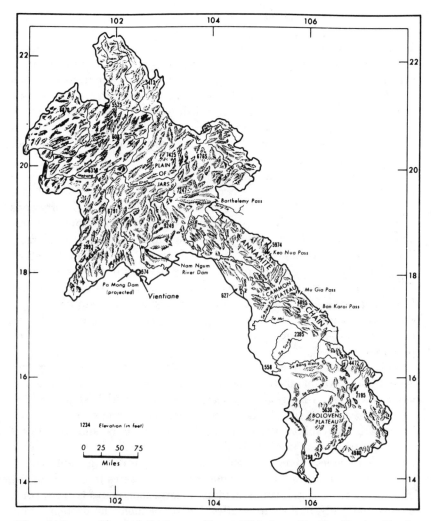

Map 2. Laos: Physical Features. (From Whitaker, D. P., Barth, H. A., Berman, S. M., et al. Area Handbook for Laos, Washington, D. C. U. S. Govt. Printing Office, 1972.)

tures generally in the fifties to seventies (down to the thirties and forties at night in the high northern mountains). This gives way to a hot, dry season with daytime temperatures into the nineties. Average rainfall ranges around fifty to ninety inches, although some areas receive 120 to 200 inches.

Natural resources have not been extensively developed. The first major hydroelectric development opened in the early 1970s in northern Vientiane province (the Nam Ngum Dam). Local topography and abundant rain provide the potential for extensive hydroelectric and irrigation projects in the future. Adequate salt for local consumption is mined locally.* At one time the French mined tin in southern Laos. Deposits of several minerals exist in Laos, but their extent and value are unclear. In recent decades the flora and fauna of Laos have provided the most valuable exports: opium poppy, tropical hardwoods (e.g., rosewood, teak), and stic-lac for shellac manufacture.

The vegetation in Laos is that of a tropical and subtropical environment. In forest areas some hardwood trees tower to 80 or 100 feet tall, with trunks several feet in diameter. Other hardwoods and softwoods rise forty to sixty feet high, many with lovely seasonal flowers. Parasitic vines and orchids lend a lush, colorful density to jungle areas. Tropical palm, coconut, mango, and similar trees are found in the settled lowlands, while there are large stands of pine trees in the more remote hills. Over a score of different bamboo species grow in dense patches. Luxuriant grasses, thorned bushes and scrub trees shoot up from abandoned farm plots. Areas of grassy savanna predominate on the Plaine de Jarres and are found scattered here and there throughout all of the provinces.

For such a relatively small area the large number of animal species is impressive. Mammals there include several species of smaller wildcats, leopards, tigers, a few kinds of bear, gaur (wild cattle), small barking deer to large Asian elk, rhinoceroses, elephants, several species of monkeys, gibbons, rabbits, squirrels, and ubiquitous mice and rats. Pheasants, partridges, many songbird species, migrating ducks, and some hawks and eagles inhabit the airways, while cobras, poisonous kraits, crocodiles, and diverse lizards crawl the earth. Insect life is perhaps the most diverse. It ranges from scorpions as large as a man's fist, to scores of seasonal grubs and flying beetles that supplement the protein intake for villagers and townspeople alike. (The latter are definitely an acquired taste, but they do go well with beer or locally made rice wine.)

HISTORY AND GOVERNMENT

Archaeological and historical information indicates that most of the people now in Laos (i.e., the Tai-Lao, Hmong-Yao, and Tibeto-Burmans)

---

*I had the opportunity to initiate the iodization of salt for refugee consumption in 1966. Congenital cretinism and goiter were endemic in the iodine-poor hills of Laos.

migrated from the north out of China. Certain tribal peoples (i.e., Proto-Malay, Malayo-Polynesian) had been there previously or perhaps had migrated from further south. Much village life strongly resembles the Sinitic culture from the north. Village organization, house types, many common words (e.g., chicken, rice), common implements, folk medicinal practices, commerce, and other familiar features of everyday life are similar or identical to those in parts of China. These ancient technologies and mores comprise the basis of society in Laos. In contrast, much of the more recent and sophisticated aspects of Lao culture have come westward from India by way of Burma, Thailand, and Cambodia. These are reflected in the state religion (Theravada Buddhism, rather than any of the Chinese sects), the Pali language of Lao Buddhism, the Sanskritic writing system used by the Lao (rather than Chinese ideographs), central government organizations, and many of the more sophisticated or abstract terms in the Lao vocabulary. This Indian-Sanskritic veneer on a strong Sinitic core makes for an interesting, sometimes confusing, but usually attractive and pleasing society for the foreign visitor.

Ascendancy of the Lao peoples in eastern and southeastern Asia has waxed and waned over the centuries. Myth, archeology, and history all point toward a number of feudal Lao kingdoms in what is now southern China. One of these areas, the Sip Song Phan Na (the Twelve Thousand Rice Paddies), is still known by that name today. External pressures from the Mongols under Kublai Khan and later the Han Chinese forced migrations southward into what had been the Khmer empire. About six centuries ago the Lao kingdom of Lan Xang (a Million Elephants) included land tracts now occupied by its neighbor-nations, from Burma to Vietnam and from Thailand to China. This grand and powerful kingdom gradually became eroded until, by the nineteenth century, only three small principalities remained. France declared them a protectorate in 1892, made them a member of the French Union in 1949, and accorded the country its independence in 1953.

Laos participated in the French-Vietminh struggle from 1946 to 1954, primarily on the side of the French. Between 1954 and 1973 there ensued a war that was in small part a civil war between native-born Laotians, and in large part a foreign invasion. Since most indigenous Laotian peoples supported the central government or remained neutral, there were never sufficient pro-Vietnamese forces to topple the Vientiane government. Vietnamese military units began to make forays against the Laotian government early in the 1960s, gradually increasing their incursions over the subsequent decade. By the later 1960s, Thai volunteers and American air support joined unsuccessfully against the Vietnamese.

Withdrawal of American forces from Vietnam, with subsequent victory of communist forces there, led swiftly to a communist assumption of power in Laos.

Numerous government changes have occurred between 1953 and this writing. For almost two decades the Royal Lao Government was a constitutional representative government with a symbolic hereditary king. Leadership changed several times during this period by force of arms, negotiated consortium, and, toward the end, popular election. From 1973 to 1975 there was a coalition government, in which each high-level post was occupied by a centralist member and a communist member. This changed abruptly in 1975 when the Neo Lao Hak Sat (Pathet Lao or communist side) took over the government by force, albeit with relatively little bloodshed, at least initially. (See Burchett 1967, Dommen 1965, LeBar and Suddard 1960, Langer and Zasloff 1970, Na Champassak 1961, Zasloff 1973 for further information.)

THE LAO

Cultural Background

The Lao are sedentary wet-rice farmers who migrated out of South China about 800 years ago. Over the centuries they have influenced and been influenced by the Indians, Chinese, Thai, Vietnamese, and—in recent decades—the French, Japanese, Americans, and Russians. They are related culturally, linguistically, and racially to the Shan of Burma, Thai of Siam (Thailand), Lu or Liu of China, and the White Tai and Black Tai of Vietnam.

These subsistence farmers profess the Hinayana Buddhist religion, also referred to as Theravada or Lower Vehicle Buddhism. Their Buddhist tenets overlay a still ubiquitous and ancient spirit religion. Until recent decades, a celibate clergy and an extended royal family were the only classes that could be readily distinguished from the villager-peasants and artisan-laborers. A middle class composed of teachers, health workers, technicians, and bureaucrats has appeared and grown since World War II.

While basically a monosyllabic tonal language, Lao contains many polysyllabic words borrowed from Pali, an ancient Indian Sanskritic dialect. Literature and history have been recorded in a phonetic system of writing also obtained from India. Even remote villages had a monastery or *wat* with its temple and living quarters, where all Lao boys were expected to study Buddhism, learn meditation, and acquire basic literacy.

Technology

Virtually all village men assume such tasks as clearing new land from the forest, hunting and fishing, building the house and granary, and caring for the larger farm animals. A man might also seek to become a village chief, musician, healer, blacksmith or tinsmith, boat or wagon maker, merchant, or boatman. Money might be made by selling bamboo, firewood, charcoal, pottery, rice whiskey, a farm animal, or rice not needed by the family. Village women tend children, clean house, gather firewood, cook, sew, and keep the garden and small farm animals. A woman might aspire to become a midwife, animistic priestess,* weaver, singer, dancer, basketry maker, or merchant for fruits or vegetables in a nearby market. Men and women work together in planting, tending, and harvesting most field crops.

Lao people comprise the majority population in the central provinces that have extensive plains suitable for paddy rice culture. Typical examples are Vientiane and Savannaket provinces (see map 3). They are, however, a minority people in the provinces of the north and south where paddy rice can be raised only on a narrow strip of land along the Mekong River and in some of the broader mountain valleys.

Their settled life in the lowlands depends on paddy rice, which is the dietary staple and sometimes the farmers' primary cash crop. Limited irrigation is provided by damming nearby streams. Fertilization is accomplished by loosing buffalo or cattle into the fallow rice paddy. Permanent villages permit extensive use of tropical fruit trees such as areca palm, coconut palm, many varieties of banana, orange, papaya, pomelo, mango, mangosteen, custard apple, and litchi. A wide variety of fruits and vegetables are grown (including cucumbers, tomatoes, peppers, various beans, garlic, eggplant, lettuce, sugar cane, pineapple, various gourds, yams, melons, and peanuts). Cash crops in particular regions are coffee, cotton, mulberry for silkworms, tobacco, and hemp. Some limited foraging from nearby wooded areas occurs; and fishing in nearby streams, rivers, and irrigation ditches (for catfish, carp, perch, and some larger bottom feeders) is a popular activity. Cattle, water buffalo, pigs, chickens, and—more recently—pigeons and turkeys provide domestic meat. Eggs are also consumed, but there is no tradition for milk products.

Bamboo of many kinds serves as food containers, fish and animal traps, walls and floors of houses. Iron implements, such as knives and cooking utensils, as well as pottery are purchased from merchants in

*While male monks held the major leadership roles in formal Buddhism, women often had leadership roles in the village-based animism religion. The *Phi Nang Tiem* animistic cult was almost exclusively composed of women.

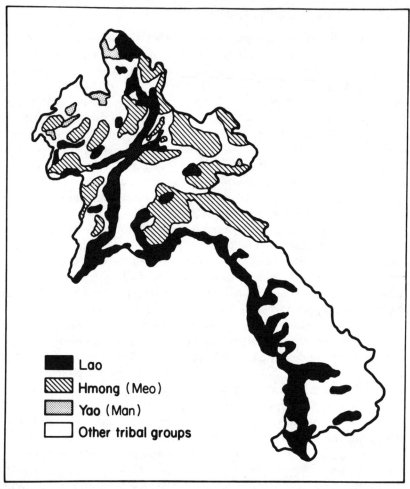

Map 3. Laos Ethnolinguistic Groups. (From Whitaker, D. P. Barth, H. A., Berman, S. M. et al. Area Handbook for Laos, Washington, D. C. U. S. Govt. Printing Office, 1972, p. 39.)

town. Lao build their homes of wood frameworks set several feet off the ground on stilts. Thatch roofs have gradually given way in a few areas to tin-iron or zinc-iron roofing sheets. Beasts of burden assist the farmer in two ways: the water buffalo pull his plow through the paddy, and the Asian ox pull his large-wheeled cart to market and back. The sarong functions as the basic traditional item of clothing, although pants for men and fitted shirts for both sexes have been widely worn since the 1950s.

Social Organization

Lao trace kinship through both their father and their mother, but they are not especially concerned with lineage. Family names did not exist until the French colonizers insisted upon them. There is a weak preference for marriage with distant cousins. The wedding ceremony takes place at the bride's home, and bride price is exchanged. The wealthy sometimes practice polygyny;* divorce (with sequential monogamy) occurs infrequently among the less well-to-do. Matrilocal residence is traditionally preferred. While individual homes center about a nuclear family, a variety of relatives—young and old, single and married—annex themselves to many homes for varying lengths of time. Though inheritance is flexible, the family house site commonly goes to one or another of the daughters (usually the youngest daughter, who has cared for the parents in their senescence).

The extended family has certain political as well as social functions. It is concentrated into several adjacent houses in an area of the village (the *mū bān*, or group of homes), and one older male acts as its spokesman. On the village level, a popularly chosen *naiban* (village head) leads, rather than rules, the 200 to 300 villagers. Consensus and not simply a majority vote decides important matters. Up to a dozen villages within a day's walk are united under a *tasseng*, a man locally chosen but subject to approval by the central government. This *tasseng* organization settles matters of mutual interest, such as road maintenance or bridge building. The national government until recently was led by a hereditary king and his prime minister, who appointed provincial rulers (called *chao khouang*). These *chao khouang* then appointed regional rulers (called *chao mouang*), who supervised the *tassengs*. A standing army, taxation, and use of money were conventions long present in Lao culture.

Ecology

Most Lao live 200 to 500 meters above sea level. Rivers and streams provide the main routes of communication and transportation since there are no railroads and roads are often impassable due to rain or dust. The mountains to the north and east have served as a barrier to military invasion and cultural influence from Vietnam and China. (The Sinitic influences of the Lao probably originate from the time when the Tai-Lao people lived in what is now the Canton area of China.) On the contrary, the Mekong River has promoted cultural and economic contacts with adjacent areas of Thailand.

*See Glossary.

The Lao ecological niche offers, on the one hand, certain natural advantages. Tropical climate and topography favor intensive agriculture of rice, fruits, and vegetables. A modicum of foresight and intensive seasonal labor by Lao farmers give reasonable assurance of survival from year to year. The village itself is usually located on moderately dry land near seasonally inundated paddy land. Drinking water comes from dug wells. Neighboring woodlands supply firewood, bamboo, hardwood, small game, and certain wild fruits and vegetables. Insects are both a supplementary source of dietary protein and a cash crop in the form of stic-lac. Each village has either a navigable stream or an oxcart road leading to a larger village or town.

On the other hand, this country possesses some liabilities. Roads and navigable rivers have historically exposed the Lao to foreign invasion. Located at the crossroads of Southeast Asia and surrounded by large, powerful neighbors, their country has been repeatedly invaded. Tropical diseases—while a scourge from one point of view—have probably served as a valuable ally against stronger enemies. Endemic infectious diseases include malaria, several different dysenteries, cholera, typhoid, typhus, plague, diphtheria, lung and liver flukes, tuberculosis, leprosy, and several types of parasitic worms.

Psychosocial Characteristics

In Lao society, a wide range of acceptable lifestyles and occupations is available to the individual, as compared to adjacent ethnic groups. From childhood the Lao learn to avoid stress whenever possible both within themselves and with other people. (Of course, this is a virtual impossibility, but the ideal is there nonetheless.) Ideally one blends with nature and the cosmos, flowing along peacefully in the mainstream of Lao life. Frequent festivals and religious holidays offer entertainment and respite from hard seasonal labors.

A fundamental goal in life (beyond obtaining basic material needs) is the accumulation of spiritual merit (or *boun*) for the next reincarnation or life-after-death. Lao culture has traditionally stressed spiritual values above material values. Hard work and wealth are not highly valued or esteemed as ends in and of themselves (although most Lao work hard to make ends meet, and wealth is not avoided). Truth is important, but that which offends or disturbs the listener should not be spoken. Honesty is also valued, but possession of adequate material things to meet the standard of living appropriate to one's class sometimes transcends the means for obtaining them.

Family organization is loosely structured to minimize conflicts, allowing individuals (even children) to switch households in order to resolve discord. The strong expression of one's feelings and opinions to another, especially if such expression might prove stress-producing to others, is countermanded. Hinayana Buddhism supports this norm by teaching that extinction of the passions and the attachments to this life leads to nirvana. A cultural imperative is the maintenance of *yen chai* (literally "cool heart").

In home life, quietude and peacefulness are valued. Children are more apt to be pampered or coaxed or patiently instructed rather than ordered or struck. In marital conflict, charms and prayers are invoked to bring the souls of the couple to discuss and settle the problem while they sleep. A family elder or monk would always counsel a couple separately rather than together. At funerals the publicly sanctioned emotion is constrained happiness at the good fortune of the departed who has, it is hoped, advanced to a higher state. This is not to say that marital arguments or grieving at funerals does not occur but rather that they occur outside of the ideal norms.

Solutions to problems outside the home are also handled indirectly. Third-person negotiations prevail in marriage arrangements, business, and politics. In group discussions, Lao seek a general consensus rather than a majority vote; compromise resolutions are traditional. A direct face-to-face conflict or affront grievously offends the recipient, who may be expected to return injury for insult when an appropriate occasion arises. Assassination or amoklike violence, while not everyday occurrences, may follow episodes of *seah nā* (literally, "lost face").

Village and Town

Two separate geographic foci, the town and the village, exist within Lao culture. While the social, economic, and technological elements in the village are much as they have been for centuries, these same elements in the town have been changing rapidly. Japanese imports, Thai mass media, Chinese merchants, Christian missionaries, and various relief and aid personnel were concentrated in the towns (at least until 1975). The influx of money brought by these various endeavors attracted tens of thousands of unskilled people from villages into several large towns. Expansion of the national army to about 50,000 men brought many rustics into the Lao town-culture. Students by the thousands—tribal as well as Lao—came to towns for high school, technical training, and teacher training.

Industrial manufacture of cigarettes, soft drinks, and matches appeared in the 1960s. Cottage industries in metal working, pottery, cloth, and whiskey grew to meet expanding town demand. Small businesses included shops specializing in photography, dining, motorcycle and bicycle repair, dental and health services, tailoring, furniture, and jewelry. Neolocal* residence, increasingly popular, began to undermine the influence of the extended family in towns.

Those several towns whose populations exceeded 5,000 were mostly located along the Mekong River. Refugee movements had given rise to a few large inland towns prior to 1975. Even the largest towns could be more accurately described as collections of villages rather than as cities. Many people in urban households raised their own food in nearby gardens or paddies, while engaging simultaneously in commerce or working in salaried positions. To facilitate such subsistence activity, Lao towns extended longitudinally along the Mekong River or its tributaries. Having extended itself several miles along the Mekong, Vientiane had grown inland along several roads coursing through paddy fields.

Daily face-to-face relationships in a single static social group inevitably expose village dwellers to chafing social controls and emotional inbreeding. To handle these problems, village society has had centuries to develop modes of adjustment. In contrast, the recent glut of villagers into the larger towns has brought them suddenly into a radically changing milieu. Among these altered conditions are impersonal relationships with police, government officials, merchants, neighbors, and employers. Mass media expose them to nationalism, modern influences, and international developments. In place of cooperation, they find that competition is rewarded. While the village is predominantly a one-class society, the town was (up to 1975) a multiclassed entity in which peasants had neither assets for advancement nor much control over their society. Viewing those who could afford the trappings of modern living inevitably engendered in villagers a sense of inferiority and of being deprived of their due.

Faced with such frustrations, the transplanted peasant also lacks traditional sources of psychological support. Magicoreligious beliefs and practices that had previously sustained them no longer thrive in the town's secular environment. The identity previously felt with family is partially left behind in the village; the economic help expected from relatives remains there as well. (See Halpern 1961, 1961–63, 1964; Langer and Zasloff 1970; LeBar and Suddard 1960; Meeker 1959; Westermeyer 1971a, 1972b; Zasloff 1973 for further information.)

*See Glossary.

THE HMONG (MEO) AND IU MIEN (YAO)

Cultural Background

Two ethnic groups in Laos, the Hmong (also called Meo or Miao) and the Iu Mien (also called Yao) comprise the Lao Sūng or High Lao. These peoples raise most of the poppy in Laos. Other groups occasionally work for the Hmong and Iu Mien in raising it or grow poppy themselves on a limited scale. The Hmong and Iu Mien bear many similarities to each other racially, historically, linguistically, and in their material culture. Yet while occupying a similar ecological niche, their areas of greatest population concentration are in different provinces of northern Laos: the Iu Mien in Houa Kong (also called Nam Tha); the Hmong in Luang Prabang, Sam Neua, and Xieng Khouang. Intermarriage between them is infrequent. The loose confederations within each group are separate. Only the Hmong, the larger of the two groups, will be described here; but their characteristics are more or less typical of the Iu Mien. The population of the Iu Mien in Laos at the time of this study was estimated at 30,000 to 50,000.

The Hmong are one of the largest tribal groups in Asia, numbering in the millions. They have gradually migrated southward out of western China in recent centuries and possess many Chinese racial and cultural traits. Although the majority of Hmong still live in China, many also inhabit the mountains of northern Burma, northwestern Thailand, northern Vietnam, and northern Laos. Estimates as to their population in Laos during the early 1970s ranged up to 200,000. They were rarely found below 1,000 meters above sea level before 1970, when military pressure then forced them lower.

Hmong speak in a monosyllabic multitonal language that sounds more like Cantonese and other Sinitic dialects than the Tai-Lao languages. No system of writing was developed prior to contact with Euroamericans, although European missionaries have developed a Latinized script and the Neo Lao Hak Sat have developed a Sanskritic script. The men, especially, often learn the lingua franca* of the area (i.e., Lao in Laos) in order to facilitate communication and business transactions. Over the last decade, many Lao, Thai, French, and English words have crept into daily Hmong usage.

Technology

Their staple foods consist of upland rice and corn raised on mountain slopes by slash-and-burn agriculture. Garden vegetables and some

*See Glossary.

25

fruits are available in season. Hunting and foraging of flora from the forest frequently supplement the daily fare, especially during travel and refugee moves or after a poor harvest. The Hmong exercise particular skill in raising chickens, pigs, cattle, and water buffalo, which might be either sold or slaughtered on ceremonial occasions. Mountain ponies are used for transport over the steep winding paths that join village and lowland town.

Hmong people raise one predominant cash crop in Laos: opium. Except for limited sales of vegetables or meat to lowlanders in certain areas, opium is the one salable commodity available to trade for iron and silver bars. Iron bars obtained by barter are worked into blades of all sizes, pots, and even flintlock rifles by local blacksmiths. Silver bars are obtained in the same manner and worked into a variety of decorative pieces.

At some unknown time in the past, the Hmong came to depend on iron. They wield iron machetes to clear the forest for swidden agriculture, to cut wood for homes and firewood, and to harvest rice. Each man carries his machete with him as protection against pythons, bears, and large jungle cats. Hmong blacksmiths forge flintlock rifles, with a distinctive pistol grip, for hunting and for defense. They make iron pots for cooking, for distilling whiskey from corn mash, and for preparing smoking opium from crude opium. Although the Hmong have come to rely on iron, they do not mine it. They are entirely dependent on trade for this important commodity in their lives.

Social Organization

Since the Hmong practice subsistence farming,* one might expect that silver would not be a central element in Meo life. On the contrary, silver is used as bride price, as an indication of social status by women, as social security, and for barter. Each family's silver is worn mostly by women and, to a lesser extent, by children and men. Intrafamily relations are intimately bound up with silver: a man must decide which of his female relatives receives newly acquired silver as a necklace. Besides needlework (by women) and music (by men), silverwork provides one of the few Hmong art forms.

The entire Hmong people are divided into exogamous* kin groups that reckon descent through males.† Cross-cousin marriage (to one's maternal uncle's offspring) is desirable but not mandatory. While mar-

*See Glossary.

†Clan names common among the Hmong in Laos were Lee (Ly), Xiong, Moua, Yang,

riages are usually arranged formally by parents, the couple ordinarily selects each other. Elopement (often referred to as bride-theft) is an alternative should either family not approve the union. Bride price payment eventually legitimizes most such marriages. Should the husband die, the wife and her children become the responsibility of the husband's clan— in particular the husband's younger brothers. In case a man takes more than one wife, it is preferred (but not required) that he marry his wife's sister or cousin. A judicious man seeks his wife's approval and participation in selecting a minor wife. All the wives typically sleep under the same roof in polygynous households.

The primary socioeconomic unit is the household, usually a nuclear family but sometimes an extended one. Newly married men and their brides ordinarily spend their first year with the husband's parents and then build their own home nearby. Grandparents, older widowed aunts and uncles, orphaned children, and traveling clansmen join the family circle for varying lengths of time. Men work as farmers, hunters, and housebuilders; they also tend the large farm animals. Some have additional roles, including elected village leader, shaman, musician, silversmith, or ironsmith. Women, who are virtually all married, care for children, do housework, cook, gather firewood, tend gardens and smaller farm animals, pound and winnow rice, sew clothing, and do lovely embroidery. Older women may pursue such additional special roles as midwife, shaman, or herbal healer.

Sociopolitical organization among these animist people is simple. Autonomous villages number from fifty to 200 people. Various subgroups of the Hmong have developed over time in various places. Costume distinguishes the subgroups from each other, whence comes their various names: the Blue, White, Green, Striped, Multicolored, and Flowered Hmong. Other subgroup differences involve small variations in floor plan of the house, ceremonial dress, and self-ascribed characteristics (e.g., "we are more clean" or "we are more industrious" or "we are more honest."). In any one village, the members usually all belong to the same subgroup. Most marriages occur within rather than between such groups. During episodic warfare, either against or in alliance with adjacent cultural groups, military organization transcends clan, village, and subgroup divisions.

Vang (sometimes divided into two groups according to burial practice), Kha, Kuh (Keu), Hang, Thao, Chang (or Cha among the White Hmong), Fang (or Fa among the White Hmong) Kong, Lo, Vuh (Vue), and Hauh (Heu or Her). Extended families might designate themselves by a grandfather's name, such as Lee-fong of the Lee clan.

Ecology

Survival in the forested mountains of northern Laos demands considerable, almost daily effort from the Hmong. Since mountain agriculture is done by the slash-and-burn method and a newly cleared field can be used for only a few to several years, preparation of new fields recurs in a never-ending cycle. Tigers, mountain leopards, poisonous snakes, and aggressive bears pose greater threats to both children and adults than in the more densely populated lowlands. Even the climate is more stressful on these mountaineers than it is on the lowlanders. While summer brings tropical temperatures and heavy rain, winter imposes drought, high winds, freezing temperatures, frost, and sometimes snow or hail. Near or at the top of their mountains and ridgebacks, the Hmong have a constant problem with their water supply. Villagers often have to carry water from several hundred to a few thousand meters to their village, sometimes up a steep slope.

Shunning the ill health, bigotry, and "unfriendly spirits" that trouble them in the lowlands, Hmong people seldom descend from their mountain villages located 1,000 to 3,000 meters above sea level. Isolation at these altitudes prevents cash cropping in bulk edibles or extensive animal husbandry. Even if transportation were available to ship farm produce, the great effort and extensive land use involved in slash-and-burn agriculture would prevent extensive cereal production. Exceptions have occurred in areas where a population center was close to their homeland hills and mountains. For example, prior to 1960 the Hmong near the Xieng Khouang provincial capital raised fruit, vegetables, and pigs for the town market; and about 1970 the Hmong practiced truck farming around the Hmong military-refugee centers at Long Cheng in Xieng Khouang province and at Ban Son in northern Vientiane province.

Despite the several disadvantages of the Hmong environment, it is perfect for producing opium. Poppy is an ideal cash crop for the ambitious and industrious Hmong people. Every child learns the intricacies of poppy raising and opium extraction as part of his or her basic education. Their sparsely populated, remote mountains also favor military defense. In them the Hmong have survived centuries of warfare with the Chinese and, more recently, with the lowland peoples of Southeast Asia. They are the dominant tribal power in the mountainous areas they inhabit. (The recent genocidal employment of aerial and chemical warfare against them may be changing this.)

Psychosocial Characteristics

Hmong people grow up and live in a tightly integrated society that imposes many demands and expectations on its members yet also provides a strong identity and powerful social resource. The hierarchy of family obligations is clearly known, and a distinct social locus exists for each individual. Prolonged separation from one's proper family household is not lightly undertaken.

Vocational choices, especially for young rural adults, virtually do not exist. Beginning in their mid-teens, Hmong women become wives and subsequently mothers. All men are farmer-hunters and, as necessary, warriors. Women must assume the role of Hmong women; men must behave as Hmong men. A man should be brave, strong, clever, and ambitious after wealth. A woman should be industrious, loyal, fecund, and maternal. There is little hedging or questioning the boundaries. Social status is primarily attained according to one's ability to meet ideal Hmong norms. Birthright is of secondary importance but can play a limited role in political leadership.

Wealth in the form of silver is very important in Hmong society. Next to maintaining one's good name and the well-being of the family, wealth seeking (i.e., silver seeking) occupies a large portion of Hmong time and attention. Since wealth seeking and the struggle to survive (both related to some extent) require hard work, everyone past early childhood works each day of the year except for several days of holiday at Hmong New Year. Clever bargaining is an adjunct to opium as a means for obtaining wealth. Honesty in business dealings is mandatory, and theft and dishonesty are harshly proscribed. A promise imposes a high obligation, and a Hmong person's word is seldom given unless fulfillment is virtually assured.

The same rigid standards apply to sexual relationships. Discovery of a Hmong wife's extramarital relations exposes her to possible death at her husband's hands or at least to expulsion from her family and separation from her children. Except for grave cause, a woman cannot leave or divorce her husband. Similarly, a man is obligated to support and care for his wife, even if she is ill, lazy, or antagonistic. Prostitution and venereal disease are absent from village Hmong society.

It is not the path of least resistance that children learn but rather the correct Hmong way. Its rules—expressed in folklore, proverbs, and day-to-day gossip—cover all areas of behavior and are clearly defined. Adherence to this right path can lead to personal problems or to interpersonal conflict, but this is viewed as acceptable so long as one persists steadfastly in following the proper way. Acting in a non-Hmong way risks expulsion from family, village, and clan—tantamount to a death sentence in the harsh mountain environment. Nonconformity to Hmong norms is often equated with insanity, witchcraft, or possession by bad spirits. Conversely, self-assurance in the Hmong way of life and stubborn persistence are highly valued characteristics.

Despite the many stresses (both environmental and psychosocial) inpinging on individual Hmong, there exist many modes for expression of thoughts and feelings. Women can and do yell at or argue with their husbands within the home (and vice versa, although less often and more quietly, or so it seems to me). Children can be yelled at loudly for misbehavior or tapped lightly on the head (a gesture of insult) or spanked if they behave mischievously. In return, some Hmong children indulge in loud, screaming temper tantrums that are usually ignored. Men express joy by whooping loudly and discharging their flintlock rifles into the air. Severe pain, anguish, or grief (as following a death) is accompanied by loud moaning or sing-song wailing by men and women.

The Hmong legal code allows, and even prompts, full vent of emotions in problems between neighbors or business partners. A mutually accepted judge presides over a formal hearing. Such judicial sessions can last several hours or many days. Both parties present their side of the story with many supporting arguments, often entailing lengthy high oratory. Witnesses, usually friends or relatives on one side or the other, give elaborate testimony. While the Hmong sometimes criticize themselves for partaking too frequently in such legal theatrics and for wasting both time and wealth on them, they nonetheless indulge in them with great zest.

Short of legal proceedings, fairly free exchange of opinion occurs within this egalitarian society. Even the lowliest man or woman can talk frankly or heatedly to a renowned Hmong leader. Politicking is a favorite pastime, and most men engage in it to some greater or lesser degree. While the woman's place is acknowledged to be lower than the man's outside the home, women within the home do not hesitate to take issue with men where the family's, their own, or their children's welfare is concerned. Married men represent the family in village meetings, but women participate freely in discussions within the family.

A ritual or ceremony exists for every crisis, every life change, and for seasonal changes during the year. Each ceremonial event takes place within a social context, knitting relatives to relatives, neighbors to neighbors, and friends to friends. They provide a means of emotional support through illness and death, a means of sharing joy at birth and marriage, and a means of celebration at harvest and the New Year.

It is important to note that emotion and ideas can be readily expressed in Hmong society when they reflect Hmong norms and attitudes. Expression of nonconformist attitudes or feelings, such as by the young woman who might not want to accept her parents' choice of a husband or by the young man not devoted to courageous acts or industrious labors, are not condoned. Such a person then possesses a two-fold problem: having a nonconformist attitude or feeling, and not being able to express or act upon the attitude or feeling for fear of expulsion and probable death. (See Barney 1967, Bernatzik 1970, Garrett 1974, Geddes 1976, Gray 1977, LeBar and Suddard 1960, Lemoine 1967, Long 1952, Marks 1973, Miles 1979, Osborn 1975, J. T. Ward 1967, Westermeyer 1971b, Wolfkill 1966, Yang 1975, Yih-fu 1962, and Young 1962 for further information.)

THE LAO THEUNG

Literally scores of tribal groups comprise the Lao Theung, or the Lao-on-Top, who live between the lowland ethnic Lao on one hand and the mountaineer Lao Sūng on the other. Numbering well over a million people, they occupy the hills, plateaus, and mountainsides that lie between the other two groups.

Some Lao Theung came from further north and west, some from the south and east, and some may have been aboriginal peoples. Their physiognomic features vary from fair to brown skinned, from almond to round eyed. Linguistic groups include Tai, Tibeto-Bruman, Mon-Kmer, and Malayo-Polynesian or proto-Malay speakers. Individual tribal groups number from only five thousand to perhaps twenty times that number. Lao people sometimes refer to them derisively as the *kha* (slave) since they had once been a source of slave labor for the Lao, Thai, and Cambodians. Upland rice, grown by slash-and-burn agriculture, is their staple food. Cash crops include coffee, tobacco, and cotton. Weaving of cloth, bamboo, and straw mats also brings limited cash income. While some Lao Theung living near the Lao have been converted to Buddhism, most are animists. In recent decades a few have become Christians.

Among the Lao Theung tribes, one of the most numerous is the Khamu who inhabit the northern provinces of Laos. A Mon-Khmer

31

group, they are materially poorer than the Lao and the Hmong. Fragmented politically, they often assume a client relationship with nearby ethnic groups; Khamu villages of 40 to 100 people act as a labor pool for nearby Hmong villages. They also barter for trade goods with their well-known bamboo mats. Some have virtually no iron goods, relying mainly on stone, wood, and bamboo implements.

Perhaps the smallest tribe in Laos, about 4,000 to 5,000 Nya Heun people live on the Bolovens Plateau in southern Laos. Surrounded by other Lao Theung groups, they have no contact with the Hmong or Yao and very little contact with the Lao. A Mon-Khmer linguistic group, their values, dress, and many rituals differ from those of nearby groups, although their tools, homes, and agricultural practices closely resemble those of other peoples in Laos.

Several Tai peoples living in northern Laos are designated according to their dress or location (e.g., Black, White, Red, Northern, or Forest Tai) or by terms indicating their Lao-like characteristics (e.g., Lao Khai Puan) or origins elsewhere (e.g., Lu from China). They raise either paddy or upland rice or both, depending on local topography. Despite linguistic, cultural, racial, and historical ties with the Lao, each group discerns itself as a separate entity. Among these, the Tai Dam (or Black Tai) are especially distinctive. Inhabiting several areas in Sam Neua and Xieng Khouang provinces, they are known for their industriousness, independence, frankness, and honesty—characteristics more those of mountain tribal peoples than of lowland Lao and Thai peoples. As indicated in the 1966 census, 4,955 Tai Dam live in Vientiane Prefecture, refugees from the Dien Bien Phu area of North Vietnam. Formerly allies of the French against the Vietminh, they had left Vietnam in the mid-1950s. Many had been members of a burgeoning educated middle class and a traditional ruling hierarchy. They entered urban occupations in Laos as barbers, tailors, waiters, merchants, cooks, chauffeurs, soldiers, janitors, and maids. (See Burchett 1967, LeBar and Suddard 1960, Long 1952, Osborn 1975, Srisavasdi 1963, Wall 1975, J. T. Ward 1967, and Young 1962 for further information.)

EXPATRIATE ASIANS

Probably the largest expatriate group in Laos is the Chinese, some coming directly from Yunnan but most arriving by way of Vietnam and Thailand. Every small town throughout Laos has a Chinese shop selling dry goods, buying cash crops, lending money, and sometimes serving food and drink. They play a major role throughout the country in commerce, banking, construction, and small industry. Most repair shops, movie theaters, restaurants, and jewelry stores are owned and operated by Chinese. There were 5,910 Chinese in the 1966 census of Vientiane Prefecture.

While the Chinese started coming to Laos centuries ago and continued to arrive until 1975, the Vietnamese came primarily in two waves. The first group was brought by the French prior to World War II to run the government offices, utilities, and larger business concerns. A second wave came when the Vietminh defeated the French in 1954, forcing many Vietnamese merchants, Catholics, and members of the intelligentsia to leave North Vietnam. Concentrated in a few of the larger Lao towns, the Vietnamese run private schools, money changing establishments, restaurants, night clubs, and hotels. They work as tailors, cooks, waiters, and waitresses. A 1966 census showed that 9,170 Vietnamese were living in Vientiane Prefecture.

Thai people have come to Laos in large numbers only in the last few decades, although some movement back and forth across the Mekong River has occurred traditionally. Attracted by relatively high salaries, young, educated graduates of Bangkok technical schools and universities came to work for various American, Australian, and European aid programs. Another large group came to work as maids and gardeners for Caucasians. Unlike their Vietnamese predecessors, most Thai are able to speak English and can adjust to comprehending Lao (a mutual dialect to Thai) in a short time, but they are not establishing homes or raising families in Laos like the Chinese and Vietnamese. They hold temporary work cards and usually return to Thailand weekly or monthly to be with their families. In 1966 there were 14,270 Thai people in Vientiane Prefecture.

Like the Thai, Indian and Pakistani people have come to Laos for financial and employment opportunities. They sell cloth goods and also provide tailoring and sewing services. In Vientiane they also run dry goods stores of various types and descriptions. A small educated and professional group work for the United Nations, the World Health Organization, a health team provided by the Indian government, and various foreign aid groups. The 1966 census indicated 307 Indians and 61 Pakistanis in Vientiane Prefecture.

Small groups of Cambodians live in Mekong River towns upstream as far as Vientiane. Their predominant occupations are boatmen and truck drivers engaged in both licit and illicit trade among Laos, Thailand, and Cambodia. A few political refugees work at miscellaneous occupations. In 1966 there were 123 Cambodians in Vientiane Prefecture.

(For further information on these Asian expatriates, see Dommen 1965; Halpern 1964a, b; LeBar and Suddard 1960; Long 1952; Meeker 1959; Osborne 1967; Skinner 1957, 1958; Westermeyer 1978a; Young 1962.)

THE CAUCASIANS*

Of several thousands Caucasians in Laos, the largest group from 1965 to 1975 was European. Among these, by far the most numerous were French (827 residents of Vientiane Prefecture in 1966). The next largest group was Americans (86 residents of Vientiane Prefecture in 1966). Others included Britishers, Australians, Canadians, Russians, Germans, and Poles, each group ranging from a few to a few score in Vientiane Prefecture.

Most expatriate Caucasians in Laos worked for one or another governmental agency, either as a diplomat, military attaché, foreign technical advisor, or medical or refugee worker. The United Nations, World Health Organization, UNESCO, Red Cross, Colombo Plan, and several other international organizations also employed many of these people. Some were religious missionaries (especially Roman Catholics and the Christian Missionary Alliance). There were several private philanthropic groups, such as the Asia Foundation, Dooley Foundation, and CARE.

Relatively few Caucasian expatriates survived as entrepreneurs in Laos. There were, however, a few score French hoteliers, restauranteurs, mechanics, and sales representatives. Some French functionaries and soldiers had returned to Laos for their retirement. One lone American has successfully run a sales representative business for two decades.†

---

*There were some non-Caucasian Americans in Laos during the time that I conducted this research. About ten black Americans served as AID consultants, technicians, and teachers for several different ministries and programs. Paul White and Juan Manning worked among the Hmong. Paul worked there for several years and was held in very high regard by them. Juan took a bullet in the chest from ambush but survived to return home. Edward Caeser worked among the Lao for a decade. Two Native Americans also worked in Laos and were highly esteemed by all who knew them. One, a pilot from Hawaii, was held captive for a time. The other, chief marine of the embassy guard, was a Navaho. They are not dealt with separately here, in part due to their small number, and in part because none of these exemplary non-Caucasian Americans were opium users, addicts, or substance abusers.

†As of this writing, Frank Manley is the one American outside the diplomatic corps still living and working in Laos—a tribute to his industriousness and his survival instincts.

A new group of Caucasians (and some expatriate Asians as well) appeared in the larger Mekong River towns in the early 1970s. They were latter-day world travelers, men and women predominantly in their twenties. Spurred on by low airline fares, relatively inexpensive room and board, good economic times, and an international focus on Indochina, they came to see and experience Laos for themselves.

(See Berger and Westermeyer 1977; Dommen 1965; LeBar and Suddard 1960; Meeker 1959; Na Champassak 1961; Osborne 1967; J. T. Ward 1967; Westermeyer and Berger 1977; Wolfkill 1966 for further background information.)

COMMENT

These geographic and ethnic data are key elements for understanding the data presented in subsequent chapters. Information on the various ethnic groups demonstrates the diversity of cultural characteristics in Laos. These groups will be considered later on as we examine the production, transport, and use of opium as well as other recreational and addictive substances.

Agroeconomics of Poppy and Opium

Opium Origin Myths. This story on the origin of opium was told by some Hmong of Xieng Khouang province, Laos:

> A long time ago, when the Hmong came down from China, they didn't know how to grow opium. As they were passing through the Burmese side of what is called the Golden Triangle, they saw that the Burmese* vigorously cultivated this crop but that they didn't tend their fields well. Even at that, opium gave the Burmese a good income. Seeing that it was a profitable crop, the Hmong learned to grow poppy from the Burmese. At first, the Hmong worked just as carelessly as the Burmese, but later on as they were moving into Laos, they learned to develop better ways of growing. They perfected the cultivation when the French encouraged it about a decade before World War II.

A common story told by many Hmong from all over Laos contains this basic theme:

> A long time ago, while still in China, a Hmong leader had a beautiful daughter. Unfortunately she had a bad odor, so no one would marry her. As a result, she died in despair. After she was buried, poppy plants grew out of her grave. Its flowers were, like the girl, so beautiful and delicate that people took the seeds and began to grow them. The seeds were delicious. And when the sap was extracted for smoking, it produced a yearning to smoke again. One actually yearned for that sap, the opium, like one yearned for a girl. Since then, it has been grown widely among the Hmong.

*They probably meant the Shan or Karen people.

36

Even more frequently heard than the latter tale is a story in which a Hmong man and woman were lovers. She is often depicted as a "white woman" of albino or Caucasian coloration (there are some fair-skinned, light-haired Hmong). Then a problem develops (they cannot marry because their parents do not approve, or he mistreats her), and she dies. He is heartbroken and his grief cannot be assuaged. Then out of her grave grows the poppy. Some story tellers say only that the flower came from "her body," but others specify that it grew from her breast or her vagina. In any event, the sap of the poppy is sweet, like she was, and relieves his great sorrow.

Political themes often intertwine through these myths. One relates that the reason Hmong live now in Laos is because jealous Chinese farmers, unable to grow poppy as well as the Hmong, cut their poppy flowers. Another attributes widespread Hmong addiction to the North Vietnamese, who taught the Hmong how to make and use the opium pipe.

Anthropologist J. M. McKinnon told me a story that he obtained from the Lisu in Thailand. It has parallels to these from Laos:

> An English girl in Burma had a Chinese boyfriend. She died suddenly of a fever, and he was sorely grieved. Then, out of the soil heaped on her grave, grew the poppy. The dead English girl sent it to provide comfort for her bereaved Chinese lover.

AGRICULTURAL TECHNOLOGY

Mountaineer farmers learn as children to raise poppy. Discussions with them on poppy culture can fill hours, with descriptions of the days and months of labor, the failures and successes over the years—much like discussions among physicians regarding their cases or craftsmen regarding their projects. I have found poppy farmers to be enthusiastic teachers, willing to share their extensive knowledge and experience.

The Site and Soil

Choice of a field involves considerable judgment. Poppies are better grown in dark soil, the same as that which would favor a vegetable garden or a corn field. Red, tan, or grey soil will suffice; but their productivity is less, and the quality of the opium produced by them is said to be less. Southerly and westerly exposures are preferred to take advantage of maximal sun exposure. Too much water run-off can wash away the young plants, so the slope and water run-off must be assessed. Stiff mountain winds can blow away seed or stunt the growing plant, so the location must not be too exposed to the wind. Shading from nearby trees, protection from animals and man, and distance from the village are additional factors. The decision is made by the male head of the family after careful deliberation, family discussion, and sometimes consultation with more experienced villagers.

Political and geographic factors also play a role in the selection of a field. Among the upland tribespeople, land ownership is not permanent. This is due in large part to the type of agriculture practiced there. Mountaineer peoples of Southeast Asia practice shifting agriculture, also referred to as swidden or slash-and-burn agriculture. That is, they farm a field for a few to several years until its fertility is exhausted. Then they move on to another field. Fallow fields are then returned to forest for some decades until another migratory group of mountaineers lays claim to it. Land is thus owned only so long as someone is currently using it (and, in some cases, so long as one has the power to protect it against usurpers or invaders). Members of the same village decide among themselves who will occupy which plots of land, a process in which negotiating skills, social stature, reciprocal obligation, kinship, and other social realities are important. As the nearby fields are spent, new fields are developed in an ever-widening circumference around the village.

Eventually, the trip out to the fields requires too many hours for practical commuting back and forth within a day. In addition, fields are then too distant to provide protection against large animals and man, either of whom might deprive the farmer of the fruits of his labor. The villagers then select a new site and move to it, taking their personal belongings, their aged and their young, their remaining rice and corn, their animals, seeds for the next year's crop, their iron pans and farming implements, and sometimes even the wooden frames and slats from their houses. A migration might be only to an adjacent mountain ridge, or it could cover scores of kilometers across entire provinces or into an entirely different country. Selection of a new village location depends on numerous factors—security, land availability, and quality of soil being among them. For example, the soil in Sam Neua and northern Xieng Khouang provinces is said to be better than that in central and southern Xieng Khouang. Certain mountains and hills have reputations for better productivity or higher quality opium.

Size of the field cleared depends primarily on the number of people available to work in the poppy field. Older children, men and women, and sometimes hired hands from other households or tribes are figured into this calculation. A typical nuclear family raises about three-fourths to one acre of poppy per year (1 acre equals 0.4 hectares or 2.5 rai). If an extended family were large and vigorous or if a relatively wealthy man could hire help, a field might be two, three, or several times that size. Or if only a husband could work the field, due to small children or a pregnant wife, it might be a half or a fourth of an acre. Should the soil be especially poor or land scarce, perhaps only a fourth or an eighth of an acre might be cultivated for local consumption and barter.

Clearing and Planting

Land must be cleared of brush, vines, and trees, a task usually done during March. Men fell larger brush and trees, although women and children sometimes participate in clearing underbrush. Some lumber might be used for firewood or house construction, but most large tree trunks are left in place to be burned where they lie. Gradients on these slopes are usually 20° or 30° but could be almost flat or as steep as 40° or 50°. While the work of clearing does not take many days, it is difficult work done under a bright sun with temperatures in the eighties or nineties.

Felled at the end of the dry season, the flora is fairly dry. It is left on the ground for some days to dehydrate even further in the hot sun. Then, on a day when the wind conditions are right, the field is set afire. This must be done properly to avoid spreading the fire unnecessarily and to prevent injury to oneself. Once the fire roars to life in the dry brush and timber, it creates a fire storm of its own with drafts and heat dangerous to man and the nearby forest. In April before the monsoon, such fields by the hundreds of thousands all over Southeast Asia are set ablaze. A foggy, yellow haze hangs for weeks over the entire region, reducing visibility across hundreds of miles. Up in the highlands, its density blocks out the sun and stings the eyes.

In August or September, toward the end of the monsoon, the field is prepared for planting. Farmers break up the soil with a short-handled hoe and then further reduce the large clumps to a fine texture. Weeds and stones are tossed aside, and the ground is carefully leveled. On a day in September or October, the small dark seeds are broadcast by hand and then carefully mixed in with the soil—sometimes after waiting a few days. Tobacco, beans, or cotton are sometimes grown among the poppy.

Mountaineer farmers attribute various qualities to different subtypes of poppy. This one grows tall, that one is more drought-hardy, others give a higher quality or larger yield of opium. Such character-istics are reportedly associated with the color of the petal, whether white, red, purple, or variegated, but it is difficult to know whether this is farmers' myth or wisdom. Selection of seed type differs with topography of site, anticipated weather conditions, seed on hand, and the farmer's personal preference.

Maintaining and Harvesting

When the poppy is several inches to a foot high, the plants are thinned so they do not impede each other. At this stage, the leaves are eaten as a salad. Weeding takes place at the same time. Like hoeing, this is a laborious task requiring some days of constant bending and stooping. A second and possibly a third weeding are necessary. Some pruning of the poppy plants is performed at this time.

During this period the poppy is subject to many of nature's whims. A succession of overcast or cloudy days at the wrong time can stunt the flowers' growth. An episode of heavy rain late in the monsoon can wash the crop down the hillside. A hail storm in mid-season can smash the delicate flower buds. Excessive cold or early frost can stunt or kill them. Forest animals pose a danger to the poppy field: elephants, rhino-cerous, gaur, Asian elk and deer, tigers, various wildcats, and bears can destroy the crop within minutes should they select the poppy patch as a place to eat or to attack one another (either as food or in a mating battle).

At about four months after planting, in late December to early February, the poppy is ready to harvest. By this time it averages about four feet tall, plus or minus a foot. Bulbs range in size from a golf ball to a tennis ball, depending on the season's growing conditions. Around the time the petals begin falling off, the poppy is ready for harvest.

The harvest work is done by the men, women, and older children of the family. Unless the poppy field is only a short walk from the village, the workers sleep in a shelter at the field. These small shelters are made of nearby materials and may have a wood frame, split bamboo walls, a roof of broad leaves, and a floor of tamped earth. Residence at the poppy field continues throughout the time of the harvest. This requires a few weeks, more or less, depending upon the size of the field and the number of workers. Meals are prepared and eaten at the shelter.

Harvest work is exacting. Vertical incisions are made, usually on one or two sides of the bulb.* Hmong farmers use an instrument com-

*Statuary from prehistoric Crete contains headdresses with poppy capsules on which the incisions were similarly vertical. In recent historical times, however, poppy farmers from the Middle East have used horizontal incisions.

posed of a wooden handle and three or four small blades of iron, brass, or glass splinters. A resinous material slowly oozes out of these incisions. If scoring is done too early in the season, the resin runs thin and drains down the stem to the ground. Late scoring reduces the yield.

Scoring the bulbs is done late in the day, so that the resin continues to ooze from the bulbs overnight. Should the resin dry out in the sunlight, it will coagulate over the incision and the resin will not continue to ooze. Resin left on a bulb for more than several hours in the sun dries to a fine powder and is blown away even by gentle winds. Early on the day after incising the bulbs, before the sun has risen high enough to dry the resin and it is still moist, the harvester returns to the field. Opium resin is harvested by scraping a bladed instrument—a splinter of bamboo, a flat piece of metal, a blade, a broken glass or pottery shard—along the incisions made the previous day. The harvester then scrapes the resin from the bladed instrument into a container—variously made of bamboo, wood, metal, or glass—that hangs from the neck. Some days later the bulbs are incised a second time, along one or two quadrants at an angle to the original incisions. If the bulbs are large and the resin is copious, the bulbs might be incised a third, fourth, or even a fifth time.

This phase of production, while requiring neither the effort necessary for clearing the field nor the constant bending necessary for weeding, still demands long, repetitive, boring hours in the field. It is the most time-consuming step in the entire process. Harvesting crews get up before sunrise to collect the resin from the previous day's incisions. Before the sun rises, in the cold mornings of winter, a damp chill hangs in the air. At times there is frost on the ground, and ice must be broken on the surface of the water containers before drinking. It is a time when one longs to linger in a warm bed until mid-morning. Poppy culture permits no such luxuries: harvesters hurry to their task without even a warm breakfast. By the time the sun has burned off the morning fog and risen to its highest point, the harvesters have collected the day's resin. They can then rest for an hour or two, eat the midday meal, carry water to the harvest site, and look after infants and children (if they are along). By mid-afternoon everyone returns to the field, again incising the bulbs for the next day's harvest. This work continues into dusk, so that the main meal is not taken until dark. That finished, sleep beckons. The first week rolls into a second and possibly a third week before the harvest is finished.

If fields reach the point of harvest at different times, fellow villagers sometimes provide exchange labor for one another, each assisting the other in return for labor in their own fields. When the soil is good and the harvest abundant, the poppy farmer might hire people from adjacent ethnic groups (frequently addicts) to aid in the harvest. Hired addicts are typically not trusted to harvest opium. Instead they perform menial tasks such as carrying water and hauling firewood.

ECONOMICS OF OPIUM

Productivity

How much opium can the average household produce in one season? That simple question is not simply answered. Opium resin starts to dehydrate from the moment it exudes from the bulb. While the rate of dehydration decreases with time, lost moisture alone could account for a 5 to 10 percent difference in weight. In addition, poppy farmers in Laos often make prepared or raw opium into smoking opium (also called cooked opium in Laos or *chandu* elsewhere in Asia) before selling it. This involves dissolving the opium in hot water, straining it through cotton cloth, and then boiling off the water. Removal of dirt, fiber, and other sediments on the cotton filter further lessens the weight.

An average annual yield reported by poppy farmers in Laos is about ten kilograms of smoking opium, ranging down to five kilograms in a poor year or up to fifteen or twenty kilograms in a good year. It should be emphasized that there is a tradition for underestimating amounts. This is in part to hide the extent of one's wealth. It also is probably in part because a tax was once paid on opium under the French, and people have since become quite secretive about their productivity. In any event, I did not collect careful data on annual range of amounts, so these estimates should be considered as tentative.

Several outstanding anthropologists have studied opium productivity among the tribespeople of northwest Thailand (see Dessaint 1971 and 1972, Durrenberger 1976, Feingold 1975, Geddes 1976, McKinnon 1978, and Miles 1979). Sizes of poppy fields among the Hmong and Yao there are similar to those observed in Laos. Reported amounts produced annually vary widely in their reports, however. Anthropologist Anthony Walker, in an unpublished United Nations study, has cited weights of opium per hectare similar to the estimates above from Laos. Amounts recorded by anthropologist William Geddes (1976) from Thailand begin at these levels but run up to twice as high. Doug Miles, an anthropologist who has done extremely detailed work on opium production right at the point of harvesting the poppy, has reported a productivity ranging from the upper limits reported from Laos to amounts four times greater. The opium weighed by Miles appears to have been raw opium, which may have inflated his figures to some degree. Taken as a whole, these data suggest that future researchers studying amounts should (1) specify how long ago the weighed opium was collected, (2) specify if it has been "cooked" into smoking opium, and (3) not rely on verbal accounts from poppy farmers. Other work by Walker among the Lahu in Thailand, a people comparable in many respects to the Khamu in Laos, shows that—compared to the Hmong and Iu Mien—few households choose to raise poppy, their poppy patches are small (0.82 hectares on the average), and their productivity per hectare is relatively low (about 4.2 kilograms per hectare).

Income

The amount of labor involved in producing opium has also been well documented by these same anthropologists in Thailand. Their combined reports show that the man-days of work spent to farm a hectare of poppy are much greater than those for a hectare of rice or corn. In addition, the monetary return for a man-day of labor from poppy consistently exceeds that from rice or corn. Thus, poppy requires greater efforts but returns greater rewards. That is not to say that mountaineer farmers easily acquire great wealth from poppy. Daily returns on poppy cultivation vary from under $1.00 up to $2.50 per day (i.e., about 10¢ to 25¢ per hour at mid-1970s dollar values). Producing a kilogram of opium entails between 240 and 500 man-hours of labor.

In 1966 and 1967, most Hmong farmers in Xieng Khouang and Sam Neua provinces earned between $100 and $250 per year from opium (although there were reports of up to $600 per year by large families close to ready markets). At that time a *pong* of smoking opium (a little less than a pound; 2.6 pong = 1 kilogram) cost $19 retail in the city of Luang Prabang and $20 retail in Vientiane, while farmers received as little as $10. By early 1971, prices had gone up. A pong of smoking opium in Vientiane cost $22, while remote farmers received only about $14 per pong.

The amount of money made by poppy farmers in Laos was small in absolute terms but large in relative terms. The per capita income during 1969 for Laos was estimated at $70.00 (Population Reference Bureau). Some typical 1966 prices in Xieng Khouang province were as follows:

chicken—$0.50 to $1.00

water buffalo, average size—$30

mountain pony—$70 to $300

trained elephant—$800 to $1200

bride price—$40 to $200

rice (if available)—$0.20 per kilogram

Alternatives and Advantages

To reach a market, any produce in mountainous northern Laos must travel over great distances and extremely difficult terrain. Most of this region lies from scores to hundreds of miles away from truck-bearing roadways. Fifty miles on a map may actually be 100, 200, or even 300 miles of steep trails winding up mountainsides, down into gorges, around waterfalls, and through mountain streams and rivers. Such terrain can currently be traveled only by man, mountain ponies, mules, and helicopters. Under such conditions, the ideal cash crop must be compact and light so that it can be carried on the back of a man, mule, or mountain pony. It should be capable of surviving rugged travel over a period of many weeks or months after it is harvested. And it should be relatively impervious to broad climatic changes, ranging from dry winds to torrential downpours, from temperatures below freezing to temperatures over 90°F. Opium meets these unique and demanding criteria.

Poppy has several further advantages in this milieu. It is grown at a time when rice and corn are not being raised. Since rice and corn are staples and themselves require considerable effort, a cash crop should be raised principally during the dry season. Poppy does not deplete the soil of its nutrients as rapidly as does rice, corn, or vegetables, so it can be grown for many years on the same plot. (Reports of ten or even twenty years on one site are heard.) Unlike coffee or fruit, poppy produces income in the first year that it is planted—an important consideration for ever-migratory peoples.

Poppy growers readily abandon this cash crop when other financial opportunities are available. Hmong people in the hills around the capital of Xieng Khouang province, and later around refugee centers at Sam Thong, Long Cheng, and Ban Son, readily switched to producing chickens, pigs, truck garden vegetables, and bananas, doing hourly wage work, and assuming salaried positions.

Iron and Silver

Opium is essential for the acquisition of these two key metals in the uplands. Both iron and silver bars are obtained from merchants. Once a sufficient number of bars is acquired, the farmer then goes to a silversmith or an ironsmith with an order for this or that object. A price is negotiated for the object. A time for its manufacture must also be decided, for the smith is also a farmer-housebuilder-hunter whose other obligations vie for his time.

Iron serves many functions for the poppy grower. It is used for machetes, chopping and harvesting instruments, flintlock rifles, cooking pans and holders, hoe heads, axe heads, and certain opium smoking pieces. Poorer tribal peoples have to rely on wooden instead of iron hoes, crossbows instead of flintlocks, and pottery and bamboo tubes for cooking instead of iron pots. Since iron implements have much greater durability than wood and pottery implements, they are a considerable advantage in easing life and raising the standard of living among the Hmong and Iu Mien, who are more wealthy in such durable goods than nearby Lao and Lao Theung farmers. Poppy has been the key to their prosperity.

Silver is similarly paramount to several aspects of Hmong and Iu Mien culture for both practical and symbolic reasons. It is an art form and a means of decoration, for people as well as objects. Women in particular glory in wearing many pounds of it even while going about their daily tasks, for social status is to some extent proportional to the weight of silver possessed by a person or family. Silver adorns such implements as flintlock rifles, opium pipes, or the tack for a favorite pony. It is intimately bound up with family relationships: a man shows his affection for a wife or daughter by giving her a silver necklace or bracelet, and parents decorate their children's clothes with silver coins or give them silver earrings. Along with music and song, silver is a principal medium for creating beauty. Silver pieces are carefully tended by their owners and kept polished with a mixture of water and wood ash. In addition to its role in social status, interpersonal relations, art, and decoration, silver has practical functions. Silver bars or jewelry are used as currency. Payment of any considerable sum, such as bride price or the purchase of an expensive animal, is done in silver. It acts both as a savings account and as social security. Should a crop fail or a long migration be necessary, rice is purchased in the valleys or on the plains with silver. In one's advanced years, possession of much silver ensures a comfortable and honored place in a relative's home rather than a dutiful pittance from grudging kin. As with iron, these central functions of silver in mountaineer culture depend upon opium.

Other items are also purchased with poppy proceeds. In Laos these tended to be viewed more as luxuries than as necessities, since people could either produce their own (such as homespun and home-woven cotton cloth) or get on acceptably well without them. Nonetheless, access to these items added to one's ease, pleasure, comfort or social stature. Items observed in northern villages during 1965 to 1975 included the following:

wearing apparel: black, red, and green cloth for sewing clothes; needle and thread; scissors; men's berets; canvas shoes with rubber soles; rubber thongs; blankets;

household items: soap, mirror, kerosene lantern and stove, kerosene, tin pots and pans, drinking glasses, tin tablespoons, tin plates, table cloths;

food: salt, sugar, tea, coffee, Ovaltine, sweetened condensed milk, fish sauce, canned milk, canned sardines;

religious and ceremonial items: joss sticks, brightly colored paper, tin foil, funeral shoes (a special cloth shoe for the Hmong dead to speed them on their aerial trip to the next world);

school supplies: pencil, pen, paper, ruler, eraser, pencil sharpener;

miscellaneous: matches, cigarettes, candy, sweet crackers, soft drinks, beer.

These sundries came from many parts of the world. Most originated in Thailand, Japan, Hong Kong, Taiwan, China, and Singapore, with a few items from Denmark, Holland, Switzerland, Germany, the United States, and France.

People are also recompensed for their services with silver. Those providing special services in Hmong culture are the spirit healer, herbal healer, blacksmith, silversmith, midwife, and musician. Anybody requesting these services is indebted to the one who provides them. Recipients might eventually return the favor by helping with farm work or in some other way. In most cases, however, immediate payment of silver, opium, or an animal (such as a chicken or pig) is expected. Manual labor is also repaid by exchange labor, silver, or opium.

Poppy farmer. As far back as he could trace, Geu Pao's father's fathers had been farmers. From childhood his own father taught him to raise upland rice, corn, and the opium poppy. Besides hunting, it was all he knew to support himself and his family.

As a child Geu Pao had lived in northern Laos, in Sam Neua province, where the brown-black earth favored poppy culture. Southward migrations of people from China and military incursions out of Vietnam had forced him and his clansmen further south into Xieng Khouang province. In the northern part of that province the soil had been fairly fertile. For several years, he raised profitable poppy crops, with only one poor year because of bad weather. Since then his further migration into southern Xieng Khouang and later southward migration into northern Vientiane province had made farming more difficult. Soils there contained either too much sand or too much clay. The press of many refugees into the same small area made shifting slash-and-burn agriculture impossible since tracts could not lie fallow while the soil replenished itself.

For Geu Pao, opium was not bad, or even neutral, but rather was good in itself. He subscribed to the old Meo adage, "Every prosperous home must have opium," although he did not use it himself. Even when his relatives or acquaintances enjoyed an opium pipe or two socially, Geu Pao declined.

He avoided opium, he told me, because one of his grandfathers was *neeng hao yeeng*—Hmong for "opium addict." Geu Pao was fearful that if he used opium he also might become addicted. Were he severely ill, with a harsh cough or severe diarrhea, he said that he might use opium. Or, if severe arthritis in the damp mountains prevented his working to support his family, he would use opium to work. But, simply for enjoyment or social relaxation, he refused to take the risk of becoming an opium addict. As a proper Hmong host, though, he always kept opium on hand for unexpected visitors.

For Geu Pao the main importance of opium was economic. It enabled his family to purchase goods and services that he considered necessary. Iron goods, integral to the survival of the Hmong, depleted only a portion of the $150 to $250 per year that the family received from a good opium crop. More of the family income went for purchases that had become necessities in recent times (having previously been considered luxuries) or that contributed to the family's security, prestige, or ease: silver, cloth, rubber thongs, a kerosene lamp, matches.

In earlier days, when he was a boy in Sam Neua province and when his grandfather lived in southern China, the Hmong grew their own cotton and wove their own cloth. Now their cloth was purchased (mostly from mills in Taiwan or Korea). Formerly the Hmong went barefoot; now they wore thongs and canvas shoes from Japan, Taiwan, and China. Geu Pao's wife had come to rely on such manufactured goods as needles and thread, matches and cooking pots. Since his children went to school, unlike their illiterate father, he must purchase paper and pencils as well as candles for them to study by at night.

More and more in recent years prestige among the Hmong was accrued according to what one could purchase rather than to what one could do or make by one's own hand. Geu Pao and his family were proud of the few drinking glasses, the kerosene lantern, and the several metal spoons and plates in their home. A visitor of note was sure to receive some of the family's carefully hoarded coffee, Ovaltine, or sweetened condensed milk, all purchased with opium profits. As the family prospered, so did the family spirits: joss sticks from China and tinfoil from Europe adorned the family shrine.

And there was silver. Silver hung about the necks of Geu Pao's wife and their two daughters. Geu Pao's accumulated wealth adorned his family as they went about their daily activities. Besides demonstrating prestige, silver served as Geu Pao's savings account and social security. In the event of sickness, a funeral, a wedding, an enforced migration, travel to a distant family gathering, or a crop failure, the expenses were paid with the family's silver.

OPIUM COMMERCE

Once produced, how did opium reach the consumer? This topic will be considered in two categories: commerce within Laos and export.

In-Country Trade

Some opium was consumed within the village where it was produced, either by the farmer who grew it or by others who worked for him or purchased it. Some might also be sold locally to nearby Lao Theung or Lao people. While certain observers in Laos and Thailand have reported that such local consumption accounts for little of the total crop, others have said it accounts for most of it, and yet others have adhered to a half-and-half school of thought. I suspect they are all correct, depending on time and place. In a fairly settled village where (1) much poppy is raised, (2) some rice is purchased with opium profits, and (3) there are few addicts, then relatively little opium out of the annual crop might be used locally. At another time and place where (1) comparatively little land is committed to poppy, (2) no rice is available for purchase, and (3) many addicts live nearby, then most of the opium would be consumed locally. Villages between these extremes would strike a balance of use and sale to the outside.

There were two methods by which opium traditionally made its way from the Laotian mountains down to the lowlands. First, one or a few farmers might bring their crop down to a merchant in a town. They would bargain for the best price, purchase various items from the merchant, and carry their profits by backpack or pony up to the village. This was a viable approach for farmers within a few day's walk of a northern town. More common in remote areas of northern Laos was the other method in which the merchant went up to the village. Caravans of mules, ponies, drivers, and guards would wend their way from village to village, exchanging silver, iron, and other items for opium. Some caravans were led by Chinese, and others by Hmong or Iu Mien. Regardless of method (i.e., farmer to merchant or merchant to farmer), a fairly stable patron-client relationship developed over time. A central figure was the lowland merchant, usually ethnic Chinese, who purchased goods from elsewhere for sale to the mountaineers and purchased opium from the mountaineers for sale elsewhere.

Iu Mien people in Laos employed a variant of this model that contributed greatly to their social organization. In Xieng Khouang and Sam Neua provinces there were plenty of Chinese and Hmong merchants willing to venture up into the mountains and trade for opium. It was relatively safe for small entrepreneurs to proceed on their months-long journey among the tribal peoples of Laos. Prior to World War II they had only to guard against roving bandits from Yunnan province in northern China. Security was not so assured in the more desolate western areas toward Burma. Here large groups of organized armed men might intercept and rob a small pack train with impunity. Flintlocks carried by the small merchants were no match for the high-powered modern weapons of the opposing groups (Chinese Haw from Yunnan, Shan tribesmen from Burma, and Karen tribesmen from Burma and northern Thailand). To defend against these strong forces, Iu Mien tribesmen united their resources. Chao Mai, a traditional chief with whom I was acquainted, was the bargaining agent for virtually the entire Iu Mien opium crop. For this he kept a large herd of about forty mules. In addition to the animals, he had sufficient capital and credit to purchase goods needed by the Iu Mien farmers. Thus, he was able to assure the farmers a good price for their crops. Relatively little of the profit went to Chao Mai himself, who lived a modest life in a remote Iu Mien village. Most of the profits were returned to the Iu Mien in the form of Chinese and Shan teachers for Iu Mien primary schools, school supplies, the support of orphans and widows, armaments for self-defense, and the support of a small parttime hierarchy of leaders and administrators. Since Chao Mai depended on the good will of his followers, much like a traditional Plains Indian chief, he worked in close concert with local leaders in purchasing the crop and dispensing the profits. Given the economic base of the opium consortium, he was also able to represent the people politically—a situation that, in the hands of a benevolent and wise leader, worked to the benefit of the people. The Iu Mien leader Chao Mai (now deceased) sold his opium to people in northeast Thailand, not through people in Laos.

While the Hmong had both a rudimentary military and a civilian organization in Laos during 1965 to 1975, their functions were more a response to military incursions against them rather than an economic and developmental scheme like that of the Iu Mien. This is not to say that agriculture, commerce, education, mass media, and other advancements did not occur among the Hmong (because they did) but rather that they developed subsequent to the creation of a military structure to meet an external threat. To my knowledge, Hmong involvement in opium commerce during these years remained entrepreneurial and extragovernmental.* That cannot be said of all Lao leaders, however.

Lao participation in the opium trade did involve a small number of army officers, at ranks up to general-of-the-army. Army officers were often billeted to remote northern posts for years. Consequently, for the first time they had more ready access to opium stores than did the lowland Chinese merchants, many of whom no longer made forays into remote areas because of poor security. Lao officers sometimes also had access to transportation when helicopters or planes brought in supplies. It was possible for them to bring in iron, silver, and consumer goods and to transport opium out of the mountains. While generally this served both the need of the tribespeople and the purse of the army officers (albeit corrupting the latter), this was not always the case. For example, following the death of the Iu Mien leader Chao Mai in the late 1960s, a Lao army colonel inserted himself for a time in the Iu Mien commercial system, requiring that all local opium be sold through him. As one might expect, there was a senior Lao general involved in this network. When foreign pressures mounted to suppress the opium trade in the early 1970s, this man admitted his former role and pledged to help purge

---

*I have heard both public and private accusations that high-level Hmong leaders were involved closely with the opium trade over the 1965 to 1975 period. Despite my proximity to several high-echelon Hmong leaders, their families, and their communities over that time, I have no data to support these allegations.

opium from the land (a brilliant move that saved his status, wealth, and job). He announced publicly that he had received his authority to oversee the opium trade from the right-wing leader of Laos in 1962 (see Rachikul 1970).

During the early 1970s, intensified war and refugee movements greatly increased the north-south movement of people and goods. As mentioned above, many lowland people in military and government positions were sent to mountainous areas. Similarly, many upland tribespeople came down to the valleys and plains because of refugee moves or for education, training, or medical care. Secondary to these population shifts was extensive travel back and forth for funerals, weddings, vacations, and family visits. These travels could often be financed in whole or part by bringing a kilogram or two of opium down from the mountains and returning with a transistor radio, a few bolts of cloth, or some canned sardines. Profits were made in each direction.

This use of opium to finance travel received considerable attention in the American press in about 1972. Three of the American air transport companies in Laos (Air America, Continental Airlines, and Bird and Sons) were accused of actively participating in the opium commerce there. Charges hurled in one direction accused American air companies and airmen of personal collusion in transporting opium. Responses from the airlines denied that even a gram of opium ever saw the inside of an American plane. Insofar as I am aware, both statements are poppycock. American-owned airlines never knowingly transported opium in or out of Laos, nor did their American pilots ever profit from its transport. Yet undoubtedly every plane in Laos carried opium at some time, unknown to the pilot and his superiors—just as had virtually every pedicab, every Mekong River sampan, and every missionary's jeep between China and the Gulf of Siam.

Opium Export

While it is a simple matter to follow the trail of opium from the hills down to the lowland towns, the trail from lowlands to other countries grows suddenly quite dim. The trail is lost at the point of the Chinese merchant or the army officer, who would report selling it but would not specify to whom. With due respect for my own safety, I never pursued these secret dealings. At this point then, I can no longer report on the basis of my own observations or firsthand information obtained from participants. Such information continues to be available from time to time in Thai newspapers when drug busts are made near their borders. In one such case from the mid-1960s, three Frenchmen coming from Laos were caught with a carload of opium on the road to Bangkok. (French people in Laos often implicated the Corsican-French among them as being in the opium trade.) A Lao acquaintance of mine, when he had been a soldier, was paid a handsome fee to guard at the Vientiane airport a military DC-3 plane that contained tons of opium on its way south. (Rumor had it that much of the transport south was by way of airplane, into remote airstrips or for airdrops near boats in the Gulf of Siam.) In the early 1970s the Lao ambassador to France, formerly the vice president of the Laotian National Assembly, was arrested at Orly Airport in Paris with sixty kilograms of high grade heroin in his luggage. Upon his immediate deportation to Laos, this princely member of the royal family was not arrested or even prosecuted.

The reformed Lao general previously active in the trade wrote the following with regard to opium commerce out of Laos:

> When the opium merchants buy opium from upcountry merchants, the opium merchants must know the requirements for each country: South Vietnam requires refined opium, so they have to boil and dry the opium; Singapore, Malaysia and Indonesia require raw opium.
>
> Most of the Lao opium merchants sell to Saigon, South Vietnam, because he [the Vietnamese addict] needs refined opium. In one month they can sell 1,200 kilos [of] refined opium or 2,400 kilos of raw opium. Some years if the weather is bad, the opium merchants do not have enough opium to sell (Rachikul 1970).

Opium Merchant. Before the political instability of the 1960s and 1970s, Tu Lee Huah had been a parttime farmer and a parttime merchant. Each year he would leave his home in the foothills east of the Plaine de Jarres (Xieng Khouang province) to head north into the mountains. He took his own four mountain ponies and four mules borrowed from a Chinese merchant further down on the Plaine. Three or four of his relatives and a few hired men accompanied the pack train. The men carried their flintlocks and machetelike knives to protect their commodities—and themselves.

At each Hmong village they stayed at the home of a Huah clansman or at the home of the village leader. The first day and evening were filled with greetings, eating, drinking, and gossip late into the night. The next day bargaining began. Tu Lee brought out the black beret hats preferred by the men, the luminescent green and red cloth fancied by the women, candles, iron and silver bars, salt, sugar, and sometimes even a few canned goods. Haggling was sharp and active.

Their business done, merchants and villagers spent another evening eating and drinking. Written and verbal messages were entrusted to Tu Lee for relatives and friends at a distance. Next morning they and their pack animals, now laden with opium, trekked over to the next mountain ridge.

Before settling the purchase, Tu Lee would look at the opium carefully. He would smell it and taste a bit of it. Though he was not a regular opium smoker (and rarely took opium for either medicinal or social purposes), he might smoke a bit of the opium if he had any questions about its quality. Mostly he knew by the locale and by the village which opium was the best.

On rare occasions a dishonest man might try to sell Tu Lee opium cut with *paum* (any substance added to the opium to dilute it). Anybody adding *paum* to opium hoped to profit from the venture. Over the long run, the maneuver worked against anyone attempting it. Tu Lee did not purchase opium from anybody known to have ever added *paum* to it.

For thirty years Tu Lee went up into the mountains for three or four months out of each year. These trips were difficult, and the responsibility great. Before he could see a profit from his toil, he had to pay the caravan members and the Chinese merchant who supplied him with goods and mules and then sell his opium. But he had become adroit at his occupation, as evidenced by his four wives (two now dead) and eleven living children.

COMMENT

1. The primary function of opium in Laos was an economic one. It served as the primary cash crop for most Iu Mien and Hmong farmers and for a few farmers from other ethnic groups as well. It stimulated the general economy, since it permitted the import of foreign currency and various trade goods into a country with very little else to export.

2. Opium permitted the Hmong and Iu Mien to become full participants in the Iron Age, while some other tribal groups had limited access to iron tools.

3. Growing poppy was a laborious and risky undertaking. Given the opportunity to turn the same or greater profit on any other work or crop or on animal husbandry, tribespeople readily abandoned poppy culture.

4. There is currently no other cash crop or industry that can meet the stringent commercial requirements of a profitable enterprise in that area. Considerable expenditures toward building a political and/or commercial infrastructure would be necessary to alter these ecological considerations.

5. Opium has contributed to the economic prosperity of specific groups within Laos. For example, it permitted a system of social security, the educational system, and the central organization of the Iu Mien in Laos. It once contributed to the prosperity of Chinese merchants in Laos. For a brief time it enriched (but also compromised) a segment of the Lao military up to the highest echelons.

IV

Using Opium

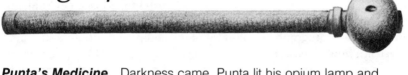

Punta's Medicine. Darkness came. Punta lit his opium lamp and beckoned me over to him. With a smile, he unfolded a paper and in it were some rose-colored crystals. He pointed to the crystals and then pointed to his stomach, said something in Meo and nodded benevolently, to indicate that the rose-colored crystals were good for the stomach. He mixed them with some opium, went through the elaborate process of rolling and inserting the opium into the pipe, and swung the mouth of the pipe towards me. I lay on my side and smoked. He insisted that I smoke four pipes. My nerves and muscles dangled loose as a marionette. I slept.

I woke in the morning immediately aware that I had not risen once during the night to defecate. At morning grub I was able to eat a little more than usual; most important, I had no battle with the impulse to regurgitate.

Elation swept over me. I was cured! Punta's medicine had cured me.

> Grant Wolfkill, *Reported To Be Alive*
> (An autobiography of his incarceration
> by the Pathet Lao in Laos.)

TECHNIQUES FOR USING

Smoking Opium

Several different devices are used to smoke opium in Laos. The most common of these has a wooden or pottery bowl at the end of a hollow bamboo segment. Bowls are inserted at the end of the bamboo or perpendicular to it. The bowl cools the smoke, and a powdery resin accumulates within the bowl over time. This powder might be subsequently mixed with smoking opium or sold as *khe dya-feen,* opium tailings, to destitute addicts.

Infrequently, opium might be smoked with a water pipe, which consists of a thicker piece of bamboo having an inch or two of water through which the smoke passes. This also cools the smoke; but the tailings collect in the water, which does not readily permit its being collected and used at another time. Elsewhere in the world opium pipes resemble tobacco or hashish pipes but have much smaller orifices for the opium. I only once in Laos did observe a water pipe being used for opium smoking, although they were often used for tobacco or cannabis smoking.

In the photograph of opium smoking equipment (pl. 3), both upper pipes are bowl types. That at the top was used by a Hmong family for over a century. The bowl is of pottery and has a Chinese character imprinted in it. At one point it had broken into two pieces and had been repaired with clay and a copper wire. The bamboo shaft has a fine dark patina from daily use over many decades. Such fine family heirlooms were virtually impossible to purchase (this one was a gift to me from a Hmong friend). The second pipe was made within the last decade by a Lao craftsman, who hammered a bas relief design into the silverware used to attach the bowl to the bamboo. The motif is traditional: the three-headed elephant (or Erawan) representing the Kingdom of Laos, along with decorative flora. The bowl and both ends of the pipe are rosewood. Silver bands fix the rosewood ends to the hollow bamboo. Fancier pipes sometimes had ivory inserts on both ends of the pipe. The third pipe, smoked with a few inches of water in the bamboo barrel, could be used with tobacco, cannabis, opium, or a tobacco-opium mixture. It is a simple device that almost any villager of Laos might make from readily available materials.

Cigarette smokers have their lighters, cases, and holders; pipe smokers, their pipe racks and humidors; and betel chewers, their elaborate brass or silver sets. Similarly, even the humblest opium smoker has certain paraphernalia. The set shown in plate 3 belonged for decades to a Hmong addict who had, with treatment, ceased his opium use and made a gift of it to me. The wooden tray, carved from a solid piece of wood, provided a platform for preparing the pipe. Opium sufficient for a few days was placed in the small wooden container (the main supply was kept wrapped in banana leaves and sawn-off cartridge cases). From the small container the smoker removes as much opium as will be used in a single sitting. Small balls are then separated and rolled by hand, each spherule representing a single pipeful of opium. Experienced smokers line up the opium balls, whether there are two or twenty of them, before proceeding further.

Next, a source of heat is necessary. This could be the family hearth, if a fire were going, or a small lamp or candle for this specific purpose. Regular opium smokers usually had a small glass kerosene lamp, although older Hmong said that a lamp of pig fat was decidedly superior. Each ball of opium is placed on a small iron skewer and heated over the flame. As it begins to bubble and fume, it is deftly placed in the small aperture of the pipe. The smoker then places the pipe in his mouth as the flame is applied to the opium wad. With an opium lamp, this process is facilitated by reclining on one's side and holding the pipe so the aperture is horizontal to the ground. If the flame comes from the hearth, the smoker holds a piece of burning wood to the pipe. At the moment when the opium volatilizes from the heat, the smoker inhales deeply. Experienced users then contract their chest, abdominal, and diaphragmatic muscles against a closed glottis so as to realize an optimal effect. This operation, called the Val Salva maneuver by physiologists, increases the intrapulmonary pressure and facilitates the rapid absorption of active opiate compounds across the pulmonary membranes directly into the blood stream. These compounds can be absorbed only from the pulmonary alveoli, not across the trachea and the bronchial tree.

Duration of smoking depends on the number of pipefuls and the smoker's skill. A few pipes could be prepared and consumed in less than five minutes. Even an experienced addict required twenty to thirty minutes to finish twenty pipefuls. No signs of intoxication might be present after one or two pipes or even after several pipes in the case of an addict. But more opium produced lethargy, slurred speech, and difficulty walking. Even long-addicted persons would fall into deep slumber if they smoked an amount greater than their usual dosage.

Opium was sometimes administered to infants in its volatilized form, especially among the people who raised poppy. It was given as a medication for such symptoms as fever, diarrhea, irritability, or cough. An adult inhaled the fumes from a pipe, then quickly exhaled the opium smoke under a blanket held tentlike over the sick infant. The infant then simply inhaled the opium-rich air under the tent. This process was repeated until the infant rested quietly.

Experienced users generally preferred smoking opium to eating it.

This is because with smoking, there is a more rapid and powerful onset of drug effect. Smoking gives a peak effect almost immediately, while the effect from eating is delayed an hour or two and is more gradual.

Eating Opium

While opium smoking was perceived as more satisfying, efficacious, or pleasurable, it is also more wasteful as compared to opium eating. Perhaps 80 to 90 percent of the active compound is lost from fumes going directly from the pipe into the atmosphere and from the exhaling of unabsorbed compounds out of the physiologic dead space in the respiratory system (i.e., that portion of the oropharynx, trachea, and bronchial tree through which drugs cannot be absorbed). Experienced smokers enhanced absorption by delaying exhalation and by the Val Salva maneuver. Unlike smoking, eating allows virtually all of the active alkaloid compounds in opium (particularly morphine and codeine) to be absorbed through the gastrointestinal tract (see Gilman, Goodman, and Gilman 1980).

Users cease smoking and begin eating opium if their access to it is diminished. Reduced availability had several causes. It might occur as a result of decreased opium production, increased cost of opium, or reduced disposable income. A smoker embarking on a long trip might prefer to eat rather than smoke so that the bulky smoking equipment could be left behind and only a relatively small amount of opium need be brought along. Some addicts would eat in the morning to stave off withdrawal, avoid intoxication, and not waste the cool early morning hours (a good time for hard work) in preparing the pipe. They would then smoke in the evening when they could relax, enjoy the smoking process, and sleep off their intoxication during the night (not unlike many alcoholics who drink more heavily late in the day). Oral opium was also given as a medication to children or to adults unable to tolerate the inhalation of smoke.

Opium is also administered in small pill-like pellets or dissolved in warm water. Either crude opium (directly from the plant) or smoking opium (cooked opium or *chandu*) could be used for this purpose. Especially among the Lao and Chinese, opium is sometimes added to rice whiskey (along with various herbs) as a medication.

Opium could be dried and taken intranasally as a snuff. While I encountered only one such case, some Lao women reportedly consumed opium as a snuff in order to avoid the telltale signs of opium use (i.e., the smoking apparatus and the characteristic odor of opium that clung to clothes and hung around the smoking place). Opium could also be taken by rectum, either as an enema or a suppository, but I never observed this mode of administration in Laos (except as I used it medically: I gave tincture of opium by this means to a few seriously ill patients unable to swallow when I had no injectable morphine or codeine). As a raw plant compound, opium could not be injected.

Other Drugs

Some opium addicts smoked tobacco, either along with their opium or after the opium. They said the tobacco caused the effect from the opium to be heightened and prolonged. It is difficult to explain this pharmacologically (see Gilman, Goodman, and Gilman 1980). Nicotine and the opiate alkaloid compounds do not produce cross-tolerance, so their effect would not likely be additive. Use of tobacco actually reduces the effect of some psychotropic substances, such as phenothiazines, presumably by inducing enzyme systems that enhance metabolism of the drug. It may simply be that some users like the combined effect of the two drugs, just as some drug users enjoy the combined use of a depressant and a stimulant (such as a barbiturate and an amphetamine) rather than either drug alone.

In lowland Lao towns, many addicts were said to have formerly been regular or heavy cannabis smokers. While this is plausible, the continued heavy use of cannabis with opium addiction was not common. The same was true of alcohol.

Drs. Charas Suwanwela and Vichai Poshyachinda have told me that tribal addicts in Thailand often add aspirin to their smoking opium. I have not observed this in Laos, but aspirin has not been a widely available commodity in rural Laos.

Heroin was introduced into Laos in 1972 following the passage of an antiopium law in 1971. In Asia some heroin is combined with barbiturates (a particularly dangerous combination, since severe seizures can result from the barbiturate withdrawal of an addicted person). All heroin use that I observed in Laos, however, involved only pure heroin.

I encountered three cases of addiction to pharmaceutical opiates in Laos. One was a *medizin assistant* (a physician's assistant) with the Ministry of Public Health and two were former army corpsmen. All injected themselves, mostly with meperidine (Demerol) that they obtained from medical supplies or private pharmacies. As in many places of the developing Third World, drugs could be readily obtained from pharmacies in Laos without prescription.

REASONS FOR USING

A Caveat

Why do people smoke opium? Rephrased in a broader perspective, why do people do any of the things that they do? This question has preoccupied humankind in all cultures down through the ages. There is no end to the possible theories: gods, the stars, spirits in nature, existence in a previous life, childhood experiences, parents, society, culture—to name only a few. The latter-day response to this question is we behave as we do in response to motivation.

Using this concept of motivation to study human behavior in the complex settings of the real world is not so simple as the theory itself. How do we assess motivations? Do we rely on what people say about themselves and how they explain their own behavior? We have great difficulty explaining our own behavior privately, even secretly, to ourselves—given our penchant for rationalizing, suppressing, repressing, denying, projecting, and so forth. Or do we rely on the scientist, the external observer of behavior, to tell us why we have done a certain thing? This method has its flaws as well, since the observer may try to explain all behavior from a narrow theoretical perspective (be it behavioral, psychological, social, cultural, political, economic, psychoanalytic, etc.). Our external observer is also influenced by such personal characteristics as being an optimist or a pessimist, a fundamental religionist or an agnostic, a humanist or a reductionist, politically leftist or rightist, and so forth.

As you have probably concluded by this point, I am not at all sanguine about the reliability, much less the validity, of examining why people decide to use opium. While some of this doubting stems from epistemological issues, much of it is also the result of personal experience. I have seen addicts, and myself as well, change their reasons for this or that behavior in fairly short order. Nevertheless, the question of the reasons for using opiates warrants examination, if only because it is currently so popular an issue. The reader should take these impressions with a large dose of salt, however. I would suggest interpreting these data not as factual information about motivation but rather as indicators of social norms, values, and ideals.

Motivations and Phases of Use

It appears useful to distinguish the various phases of opium use when considering purported motivation. Before a person has any personal experience with opium use, his or her reasons (or rationalizations) for first using opium are probably not the same as those of the person who has used it on ten occasions. Similarly, the physiologically addicted person who has used opium 10,000 times over ten years may be making decisions on grounds far different from either of the former two people. So we will consider motivational factors at three different points: prior to use, during episodic or moderate (i.e., nonaddictive) use, and after the onset of addictive use (i.e., physiological dependence).

This approach to considering motivation is not so different from what occurs in other realms of life. The motives for which one person marries another change during the process of being married, so the reasons for selecting a spouse differ from the reasons for staying married through the first anniversary. And it is likely that the former reasons differ from those at the twentieth anniversary. Similarly, people first aspiring to be plumbers, scientists, or physicians would modify their expectations after two years of training or education. They would modify them again after a decade of actual experience in their chosen field. Yet, the married couple persists in the same relationship, as do the workers in their respective occupations (at least in many cases). I believe it is useful to consider opium consumption in a similar light, looking for a change in motivation despite a persistence in the stereotypic behavior. This approach may help us to understand why many never use opium, some decide not to use it and later change their minds, others try it but abandon it, some become committed to its daily use as a major feature in their lives, and others abandon it after having pursued its effects with vigor over a long period.

I am suggesting here a process model of addiction rather than the stochastic model usually employed in pharmacological and psychological theories of addiction. The former suggests a dynamic process occurring over time, multifactored in its origins, and influenced by incidents and sequences that are pharmacological, psychological, historical, social, economic, political, and perhaps even spiritual (at least from the point of view of the person experiencing them). The stochastic approach implies an immutable process, occurring in a stereotypic fashion and not affected by change over time. It implies that the sequence or historical timing of numerous causal factors is unimportant. Each of our various fields of scientific endeavor are replete with examples of this: addiction is attributed only to the development of tolerance or to fixation at an oral stage in development or to social deprivation or to genetic factors or to endorphine imbalance—rather than to an interaction of these factors and others as well.

61

The Naive Phase

1. Curiosity. Many addicts and nonaddicts, when asked why they first tried opium, responded with comments such as "I wanted to see what it was like" and "I heard about it and I wanted to try it myself." Among 498 addicts voluntarily admitted to the Narcotic Detoxification Center in Laos, 259 of them (52 percent) gave such answers. There was, however, a marked ethnic disparity in the popularity of this response. Most of those responding thus were ethnic Lao and expatriate Asians (i.e., Chinese, Vietnamese, and Thai). Tribal poppy farmers seldom gave such reasons, perhaps because they were well aware of opium and its effects. It would hold no connotations for them as an exotic or foreign substance.

Even within an ethnic group, the sampling method for obtaining subjects may influence the purported motivation. For example, ten Caucasian users interviewed at large in the community gave markedly different reasons from fifty-six Caucasian addicts treated in a program for addicts. The ten Caucasian subjects who tried opium (only one of whom was my patient) all reported curiosity as the primary reason for using it. None of them had previously been dependent on drugs, nor were they especially devoted to seeking chemical experiences. Of these eight men and two women, three became addicted and seven did not. The three who became addicted were a behavioral scientist, a refugee relief worker, and a government office worker. Occupations of those who did not become addicted included physician, administrator, engineer, teacher, and housewife. Their adventure is nicely exemplified by Meeker's description (1959, pp. 133–134) of his sojourn into a Bangkok opium den during a respite from his toils in Laos:

> One [opium den] down the street was open twenty-four hours a day, and resembled nothing so much as a ramshamble warehouse. I went along one day with one of the senior nurses from Johns Hopkins, thinking I would be in safe hands. Splashing red characters on milk glasses announced the equivalent of "Opium Den" in Chinese. This was perfectly legal, for opium was still a government monopoly, controlled by the police, and a flurry of exhortations and announcements that the government was to abandon its interests in narcotics had to be postponed because of the needs of internal revenue. So I found myself with a nurse in attendance reclining on a porcelain pillow in a cubicle, smoking two pipes of opium in an opium den. This was equivalent to two good, sucking, bubbly whiffs, after an attendant had prepared the pipe each time, turning a little nubbin of opium at the end of a needle in the flame of a small, thick, cutglass lamp before

inserting the smoking gum in the long pipe. I waited for something to happen. Nothing happened. The nurse seemed to be in complete control of herself, though she declined more than one pipe. A number of infants, several small boys, and an assortment of neighbors gathered in front of the cubicle to see what the foreign devils were up to. Nothing happened. Then there was a hiss, a couple of fingers poked through the split bamboo matting separating our cubicle from the next one. This was followed by a nose, and a mysterious voice said, "I speak English, I lived in Chicago."

At the other end of the spectrum, among fifty-six expatriate Caucasians seeking help at the Narcotic Treatment Center, only ten out of fifty-two (19 percent) reported curiosity as a reason for first trying opiate drugs. The majority of these were world travelers, people currently unemployed and passing through Laos as transients.

Curiosity is a motivational concept not readily tested scientifically. It may involve shades of related motivations, such as risk-taking, adventure, bravado. Further, curiosity does not necessarily occur as a pure strain detached from a panoply of other factors enumerated below.

A sense of adventure-seeking may also be a part of such curiosity. Undertaking an adventure often relieves boredom and can lead to increased well-being. Soldiers surviving battle and women surviving childbirth commonly experience increased self-confidence and self-esteem. Similar feelings may accompany the experience of having exposed oneself to the risk of addiction, not having succumbed to it, and thus having shown strength of character and self-control.

2. Peer Pressure. Some users report that they initially had no particular interest in opium and had no plans to try it. They first consumed opium in a social context where one or more other people were using opium, and they were invited or challenged to try it.

Peer pressure played a relatively minor role among Asian addicts, according to the 498 patients admitted to treatment. Only 15 percent reported that friends, relatives, or family members had induced them to try opium. Among these seventy-five people, those reporting influence by friends were four times more numerous than those reporting influence by relatives or family. This proportion was similar to that recorded in a community survey of forty addicts, among whom four (i.e., 10 percent) reported friends or relatives as a primary reason for first experimenting with opium (Westermeyer 1974c).

Addicted world travelers from Europe, North America, and Australia ascribed their opiate initiation to friends more often than did any other group. Among fifty-six addicts seeking treatment, thirty-three of them (59 percent) said they had first used narcotic drugs simply because their companions were using them. There was no influence by family members or relatives in this sample.*

Everybody influenced by peers to try opium does not inevitably become addicted. The journalist Wolfkill, whose book is quoted at the beginning of this chapter, was a prisoner of the Pathet Lao in Laos. Along with three other Americans, he became friends with a Hmong prisoner who was addicted to opium. (Interesting enough, the Pathet Lao allowed the Hmong prisoner's wife to bring him a regular supply of opium.) One day, after the four Americans and the Hmong shared secrets and laughter together, "We suddenly became a close group of five. That evening, as if to seal a pact of friendship among us, Mac, Ed and I each smoked a pipe of opium; Roger smoked two" (p. 262). Among this group of five, only the Hmong addict and Wolfkill (so long as he had dysentery) continued to smoke opium.

Undertaking such an adventure with others may enhance the bonds among friends, as it did for Wolfkill and his four companions. Sharing any risky venture, even of another sort, might accomplish the same end. This may in part explain why so few addicts initiate usage in the company of relatives, since such shared experiences are not ordinarily needed as a means for enhancing or intensifying kin relationships.

The Lonely School Teacher. Moua Tsai was a Hmong elementary school teacher, an acquaintance with whom I had regular contact in 1965 and 1966. Stationed as a head teacher in a small, remote school, he always came to chat and to ask of news from the outside world during my visits to the small medical unit nearby. As a result of his education at the Teacher's Training School near Vientiane, he had become enchanted with plumbing, bicycles, newspapers, and the cinema. He did not like returning to a remote mountain village with his new bride. The proximity of his school to the Plaine de Jarres and its North Vietnamese military units further disturbed him.

As chance would have it, I was temporarily stranded by poor flying weather at Tsai's village on the first day of the Hmong New Year in early 1966. He invited me to celebrate with his friends and family. Late that afternoon and into the evening we feasted on chicken, pork, sweet rice, cabbage soup with hog back, and several rounds of corn

---

*Infrequently, family members did introduce Caucasians in Asia to the use of opiate drugs. In Laos I encountered an addicted American wife introduced by her European husband to opiates and an American teenager introduced by his older brother.

whiskey. That night a few men at the party joined in opium smoking. They urged Tsai, as the host, to accept a pipeful of opium in his honor. Moderately intoxicated on alcohol and chided by his companions, he impulsively decided to try the pipe.

When we met a year later, Tsai had been promoted to a minor administrative position in a provincial town. He told me how he had come to smoke at shorter and shorter intervals with other young men in the village. In recent months, he was smoking three or four pipes every night. Opium helped him sleep, and he had grown less lonely and fearful in his mountain village. He felt better and believed he had become a better teacher and administrator. Although he was no longer isolated in the mountains, he had no desire to stop smoking opium.

Our paths did not cross again for five years. By then Tsai had been trasnferred to a more responsible post in Vientiane. At that time he was taking opium three times a day: morning, early afternoon, and before bed. The father of three children, he complained of his unhappy marriage. Half of the family income was going for opium, and his wife had begun to nag him about it. It was also clear that his supervisor was not satisfied with his industriousness, or lack of it. Opium now provided a solace from these harangues at home and at work, as it had previously moderated his loneliness, insomnia, and fear.

3. Medication. Opium is an excellent antidote for pain, agitation, insomnia, cough, and diarrhea. All of these symptoms occurred often in Laos, especially in the mountains. Common causes of diarrhea were the bacillery dysenteries, typhoid, cholera, amebiasis, and various parasitic infestations. Tuberculosis, pulmonary flukes (*Paragonimus westermani*), and chronic complications of untreated pneumonia (e.g., bronchiectasis, abscess, pleural effusion) produced chronic cough. Acute and chronic pain resulted from trauma, malaria, infections, and arthritis. Anxiety and depression were no less frequent than in other societies. The prevalence of such illnesses, combined with the relative absence of medical facilities, greatly favored the medicinal use of opium. Since its beneficial effects were well known in the areas where opium was grown and used, one might expect that medication would be a common reason for initiating its use.

As with the former reasons for using opium, groups varied in their reporting medicinal use of opium. None of the fifty-six expatriate Caucasian patients gave illness as a reason for beginning opiate use. In the event of physical symptoms, those in this group sought medical treatment rather than dose themselves symptomatically with opiate drugs.

Wolfkill did use opium as a medicine but under extraordinary circumstances. He was a prisoner of the North Vietnamese and Pathet Lao in a remote area, with life-threatening diarrhea and no access to medical care.

Among the 498 Asian addicted patients, only 143 (29 percent) said they started using opium because of its medicinal properties. These were predominantly indigenous tribal peoples from the northern mountains. By contrast, in the community survey (mostly of tribal people), thirty-three out of forty addicts (83 percent) gave this as a reason. These differing percentages (29 percent and 83 percent) appeared related to the low percentage of mountaineers in the former sample and the high percentage in the latter sample.* It appears that Lao people were less apt than mountain tribespeople to take opium as a medicine. The total absence of opium from Sassady's compendium of Lao folk nostrums (1962) supports this viewpoint.

The Diligent Soldier. Shai Yang, a nineteen-year-old single Hmong man, first began using opium while he was a soldier fighting the Vietnamese in northern Laos. A mortar man, he had to carry a pack of twenty-five kilograms during a forced march over several days, though he weighed only about fifty kilograms himself. On the second day of his march, under battle conditions in mountainous country, bright red blood appeared in his urine accompanied by considerable pain in his flanks, lower abdomen and, when he urinated, his urethra.† Because he felt the mortar piece was urgently needed by the column in case of ambush, he wanted to continue carrying the piece and so did not bring his malady to his commander's attention. A fellow trooper, an opium user, offered him a way out of his dilemma: opium to relieve the pain. He ate the opium on that occasion and again whenever forced marches were necessary. At that time he did not become physiologically addicted to it (that is, he never experienced withdrawal symptoms once he discontinued use after a few days).

---

*The two different sampling methods—one a clinical survey of patients and the other a community survey of addicts not seeking treatment—could also account for this difference. I believe, however, that the reason stated in the text is more likely.

†It is likely that his symptoms were the result of red blood cells being damaged by the combined heavy weight and severe muscle exertion—a well-known medical condition. The release of hemoglobin into the blood stream produces flank pain and red urine as the hemoglobin and damaged red cells accumulate in the kidneys and then appear in the urine.

In his third year of soldiering, he stepped on one of the small antipersonnel landmines so widespread in Laos at the time. It blew his foot apart up to the ankle, and he had to have his leg amputated below the knee. He was soon fitted with a prosthesis, though with some discomfort around the stump (common in the early weeks of wearing a prosthesis until toughened skin and callus builds up). In addition, he was separated from the unit with which he had lived the previous four years, as well as from his family. He had to remain in Vientiane close to the Ministry of Veteran Affairs in order to receive his pension regularly. Before many months elapsed, he began smoking opium, which, according to him, controlled the pain in the amputation stump. It also served to relieve his acute loneliness and the anguish he felt at not being able to return to his former life as a farmer and hunter. Along with his smoking he experienced fellowship and relief of his isolation at the den. Within several weeks he was addicted to opium.

The Early-Experienced Phase

1. Loss of Initial Reasons for First Use. Curiosity ceased to be an explanation at this phase. For many whose original motivation began with curiosity and who had no reason or wish to continue, the matter ended there. This appears to be particularly true of those visitors to Laos who were in a stable job, were involved in stable relationships, had no inordinate life stresses or changes at the current time, and would return to an environment that lacked available opium. For others, curiosity regarding the unknown was replaced by seeking after the known effects of opium. The same was true of those initial users experiencing peer pressure or seeking relief from an acute illness.

2. Recreational Intoxication. After a brief period of learning to use opium, some enjoyed both the drug experience and the context of use. A young man enjoyed smoking occasionally with his favorite uncle and older men in the village. A wife found it easier and more pleasant to join her husband in his evening pipes than to oppose his smoking. A solitary world traveler appreciated the instant companionship surrounding heroin use in a group of like sojourners. A young soldier, away from home for the first time and frightened, enjoyed the relaxation and the fellowship among his comrades during their sharing an opium pipe together.

Opium smoking probably induces its many desirable effects on biological, psychological, and social levels. Biochemical research has demonstrated the existence of opiatelike neurotransmitter substances (called enkephalins or endorphins). These substances elicit repeated behaviors in animals; that is, they are rewarding or pleasurable. If opiate compounds mimic these naturally occurring compounds, one would expect two possible effects. First, repeated exposures to the drug effect might be sought by those who experience such extraordinary relief or enjoyment from it as to overcome any hesitancy about its continued use (i.e., the unconditional response). And second, events associated with the pleasurable drug effect (such as entry into a particular den, or the feel of a familiar pipe, or the company of fellow smokers) might continually be sought and become enjoyable in themselves (i.e., the conditioned response).

The common pharmacological effects of opium include sedation, relaxation, and relief of anxiety. Those in psychological distress—from loss, grief, fear, dysphoria, or unacceptable anger*—would find relief. Socially, opiate use could serve as a ticket into a group whose identity was focused on the drug experience. Lonely or alienated people could find instant acceptance by such a group, in which the criteria for inclusion are not based on birth, age, occupation, social status, or accomplishment.

3. Medication for Chronic Illness. Some people in Laos refused to use opium, even for life-threatening or incapacitating illness. Others used it only if death threatened or if opium use would permit continued work despite pain or other disability. Chronic anxiety or depression, arthritis, pulmonary disease, and other maladies could be relieved to the point that an individual might resume a productive life—at least for a time. In the early stages of addiction, opium often enhanced the productivity or the enjoyment of life for some users.

Chronic opium users did not ordinarily stop using opium even when to do so would have no objective detrimental effects on their health. This was true even though the original problem might have been resolved or become quiescent. Addicts often reported their belief that the illness would return or they would die if opium were discontinued, despite the absence of any basis for this belief.

The Refugee Village Chief. Lee Tou was a fifty-three-year-old married Hmong farmer, the father of eight children. Prior to his addiction he

---

*By "unacceptable anger" I mean anger that the person does not or cannot accept in himself or herself. This is not an unusual circumstance among many Asian ethnic groups to whom the open display of anger is strongly proscribed by childhood conditioning and/or religious stricture.

had been a village chief for several years. He was known as a hard worker and was a highly respected man in his village. No one in his immediate family (including his parents, siblings, and children) had ever used opium. In the mid-1960s he and his village made three refugee moves, from Dong Don on the Plaine de Jarres, to Pha Don, in the mountains north of the Plaine, and then to Pha Khao west of the Plaine.

Following the last of these moves he became profoundly ill with severe abdominal pain and fever. During this time there was an outbreak of typhoid fever that ranged through numerous Hmong refugee groups throughout Xieng Khouang province. It is likely that this was Lee Tou's problem. When it appeared after a few weeks that death might ensue shortly, he began smoking opium. For some months he remained markedly weak and thin, and his hair fell out. Slowly, however, he got better.

As he recovered from his illness, he did not cease using opium. Rather, his dosage increased from once a day up to a steady routine of three doses a day. He maintained that rate of smoking from the age of forty-six until interviewed seven years later.

After his illness and his addiction, he no longer served as village chief, although his village had remained intact through the three refugee movements. At the time of interview he was working hard at farming and entirely raised his own opium supply. Unlike many addicts, his family had not suffered materially as a result of his addiction. His wife still kept her silver ornamentation, his children did not want for clothes or other material requirements, and he always constructed a good house for the family. Yet both he and his wife were fearful that as he became older and less productive, his opium habit would make them destitute.

The Late Chronic Phase

1. Avoiding Withdrawal. Continued heavy doses over some weeks led to physiologic dependence on the drug. That is, the addict now took the drug not only for its beneficial effects but to avoid its agonistic effects (i.e., withdrawal). In the case of those who had been taking smaller doses, their withdrawal lasted a few to several days and consisted of symptoms like those of a cold or influenzal infection (e.g., runny nose, sneezing, anorexia, malaise, insomnia, piloerection or "goose flesh"). With larger doses, the withdrawal syndrome lasted a few weeks and included both the milder symptoms as well as more severe signs and complications (e.g., diarrhea, vomiting, tremulousness,

dehydration, secondary infections, vascular collapse). Virtually all addicts had some experience of withdrawal. They feared it and cited it as a major reason not to discontinue opium.

2. Fear of Death. Certain physical problems often developed after years of opium smoking. These included chronic bronchiolitis, chronic bronchitis, emphysema, pulmonary hypertension, and cor pulmonale. These problems primarily affected older or debilitated people who had been addicted for a few decades. They were not present among a high percentage of addicts at any one point in time, nor did they ensue shortly after beginning addiction. Consequently, their relationship to addiction was not clearly established in the conventional wisdom of the people. As a result, these complications did not deter people from becoming addicted (any more than the risk of lung cancer deters young cigarette smokers).

Sudden withdrawal of opiates could exacerbate any of the chronic cardiopulmonary problems associated with chronic opium smoking. Addicts were sometimes known to die in withdrawal (although these were mostly elderly ones, a fact not part of the folk knowledge on the subject). Appreciation of possible death during withdrawal did not serve as a reason for preventing people from first trying opium, although it was a common reason for not trying to stop it later.

The Arthritic Farmer. Chan Prasert was a sixty-two-year-old Lao farmer. He lived with his wife and two children in one of the valleys of northern Laos (Xieng Khouang province). During his thirties he began to be bothered by episodic pain in his back and extremities. Heavy work of any kind tended to exacerbate his symptoms, causing him to have stiffness in the morning and exquisite tenderness in his joints. Nonetheless, he was able to continue work and provide for his family.

Beginning about age forty, his pain became more severe and occasionally his joints became swollen. At times he was unable to do heavy work. Over a two-year period, more and more of the heavy work fell to his two children and his wife. At the point when Chan was disabled more often than he was productive, he and his wife discussed his trying opium. They finally agreed that he should begin taking it, although neither he nor any immediate members of his family had ever used opium before.

He began smoking opium twice a day and maintained exactly that schedule with very little change in dosage for the next twenty years. With opium, he could work productively and, indeed, was still working actively in his early sixties when I interviewed him. On several occasions he had attempted to discontinue opium but had found the withdrawal symptoms (abdominal cramps, diarrhea, bodily aching, heavy perspiration) so noxious that he always resumed it again after two or three days. At the time of the interview Chan had gone from smoking opium to eating opium because of the increasing cost of opium. For the previous ten years there had been no signs of arthritis, chronic or acute, that would indicate the need for continued pain relief.

Deterioration or Recovery Phase

Chronic, stable opium use could continue for years, even decades. Unless the person died prematurely of some cause not related to addiction, it was likely that certain problems would eventually ensue. These included not only the health problems described above but work, financial, family, and social difficulties. Once these problems began to accumulate with increasing severity and frequency, they tended to exacerbate each other. (This point in the process could be delayed by those around the addict if they facilitated his or her addiction, or it could be precipitated earlier by those around the addict if they confronted the situation. The addict's tolerance or intolerance to accumulating problems and his or her ability to cope with them also played a role.) Around this time there occurred a fork in the road, with a trend either toward recovery or toward further deterioration. The costs of addiction began to rise as the benefits fell. Addicts rarely linked the tragedies befalling them (i.e., poverty, weakness, ill health) to their addiction but rather gave these tragedies as an excuse for continuing or increasing their opium use. Conversely, awareness of the link between these problems and their own addiction might lead to efforts at controlling opiate consumption. Should these attempts at control be met with repeated failures, the addict might give in to the deterioration phase (or in rare cases, commit suicide). More information regarding the nature of addiction-related problems and factors favoring recovery or deterioration will be presented in subsequent chapters.

DEMOGRAPHIC CHARACTERISTICS OF OPIUM USERS

Neonates, even hours or days old, might receive opium as a nostrum for vomiting, diarrhea, or cough. During the first several months of life, administration consisted of the blanket-and-smoke method described previously. Older children were given oral preparations. It should be emphasized that many poppy farmers would never think of giving opium to their sick children because of the moral strictures they placed against its use. Lowland farmers would not consider it (unless they lived close to the northern poppy fields) as it was not a part of their folk pharmacopoeia.

In rare instances, children began using opium regularly as young as eight years. I encountered several addicts in Laos who were addicted during their later childhood or early adolescence (i.e., eight to fifteen years of age).* All of them had at least one addicted parent, and many had both parents addicted. Their parents had first given them opium, or they had taken it themselves while their parents were absent or stuporous on opium. Their source of opium supply during their youth was their parents: either the parents gave it to them openly or the child stole it from them. Since they lived in small villages, their addiction eventually became publicly known. They were considered as undesirable choices for a spouse; only one of this small group was able to marry. At first I mistook a few of them as mentally retarded, since they were passive, socially isolated, blank-looking, slow moving, and slow to learn (not unlike those exhibiting the so-called amotivational syndrome recently associated with chronic cannabis abuse among the young in North America).

Adults of any and all ages used opium. As the vignettes so far have indicated, opium smoking was not the exclusive domain of a few elderly men, as is frequently depicted in both Western and Oriental literature. And as we shall see in subsequent chapters, addiction was even less prevalent among the elderly as compared to the middle-aged. Older adolescents and young adults were not immune, and first experimentations with opium commonly occurred at this phase of life.

Stereotypes of Asian opium smokers always depict them as men. To be sure, men were more apt to be observed smoking in a recreational context, and more men were addicted. But many women also used opium, especially those among the tribal poppy farmers. Addicted women often had an addicted husband or used opium to relieve painful menses, pain following childbirth, or chronic pelvic infections.

As we will see in later chapters, opium smoking and eating occurred most often amid circumstances in which availability was high and cost low. All classes and types of people could be found using opium. A

*This circumstance may sound so extremely unusual as to be bizarre. In the United States, however, I have encountered about a dozen cases of alcoholism among children and among teenagers whose regular drinking started in childhood. The family circumstances were remarkably similar to those of the childhood opium addiction cases from Laos.

prominent member of the king's family was an addict. One of my research subjects was a sister of a former cabinet-level officer of the
government. Addicts included illiterate farmer-hunters, literate artisans
and merchants, teachers, and health workers. The range of nationalities
and religions was just as diverse: Asian, European, Australian, and
American; animist, Buddhist, Moslem, Catholic, Protestant, Jew, agnostic, and atheist. Opium cut across these class and cultural boundaries
as did air, water, food, speech, recreation, and sex.

The Hmong raised opium, had it available in their homes at all
times, and used it for barter and as a cash crop. Yet many of them had
never used opium and said that they would refuse to use it under any
circumstances. This attitude is not easy to understand, since opium was
the one folk medication available to them that was highly effective.
Why not use it as a means for relieving severe symptoms, perhaps even
prolonging life? The response of the Hmong to this inquiry was always
the same. Those who would refuse to use the opium ascribed their fear
to becoming "one who is addicted to opium" (*khon tēt dya fēn* in Lao
or *neeng hao yeeng* in Hmong).

PATTERNS OF USE

Addictive use of opium will be considered at greater length in subsequent chapters. Here we will cover only the nonaddictive use of opium
and its use as a means of suicide.

Nonaddictive Use

Unlike the highly regularized addictive use of opium, nonaddictive
use varies widely. Some subjects reported having used it only once or a
few times, years or even decades previously. Others used it a few or
several times in their lives, during particular illnesses (e.g., diarrhea,
a severe bee sting), or in a special social context (such as visiting old
friends or distant relatives). Still others took it more often because of
frequent illness or frequent social occasions where most others were
smoking. A few subjects took it in a highly regular fashion for years
(e.g., one pipe at bedtime or two pipes per day during menses for
dysmenorrhea) without becoming addicted. This variability in nonaddictive use greatly complicated the collection, tabulation, and analysis
of data on the nonaddictive use of opium.

Conducting a study of addicts was a fairly straightforward, albeit
time-consuming process. This was not true of investigating nonaddictive

use. A person might have received opium for an illness during childhood but have no memory of it. Or someone who experimented with a few pipes decades ago might not want to recall the fact or discuss it—especially if his or her attitude toward such youthful adventures had changed. More regular users might be quite private about their use, fearing that social opprobrium might result. Gaining access to such information was more difficult than uncovering addictive use. Over the years a score of people—some patients, some acquaintances and friends, some research subjects—have instructed me regarding their nonaddictive use of opium. But these disclosures have involved a higher degree of confidentiality and trust as compared to the fairly ready responses of the publicly known addict. In addition, there was no reliable sampling method for obtaining these data as the information was often revealed incidentally rather than systematically.

How much nonaddictive use was actually preaddictive use? That is, what was the risk that the first use of opium would lead to eventual addiction? I have no way of knowing that, given the difficulty in counting nonaddicted users in a population and in following them over time. In addition, even prolonged nonaddictive use was no guarantee against subsequent addiction. As we will see, most addicted people in Laos became addicted within a year or two of first using opiate substances. But there were a few who did not become addicted for several years or even a few decades after their first usage.

Nonaddictive doses were usually small, although dosage schedules were widely variable. In its simplest form, a dose of opium consisted of either a small spherule taken orally or smoked in a pipe. For either therapeutic or recreational purposes, one pipe might be all that was prescribed or taken. From there, the doses ranged up to three or four pipes a day. These might be spread throughout the day or taken together at bedtime. In a social context, opium smoking ordinarily took place in the evening and might be repeated over a few to several days during a visit or a festival such as the Hmong New Year. Similarly, therapeutic regimens consisted of a solitary dose or repeated doses over a few days or a few weeks. Most people understood that longer usage carried the risk of addiction.

Excruciating Menses. For Blea Ly Hang, the age of fifteen brought many changes in her life. Early in that year she had her menarche (first menstrual period). Shortly thereafter she married, and by the end of that year she had given birth to her first and only child, a son. She was pleased to be married and to have her own home. Since her father had died (when she was about six years old), she had never felt at home as a child. She was always being shuttled around to live with various relatives, as her stepfather never accepted her and her seven siblings.

From the very beginning Blea had pain with her menstrual periods. Her discomfort was relieved somewhat by the birth of her child, but then the pain gradually began to get worse. Three years after the birth of her child, the pains were severe enough to incapacitate her for several days each month. Within another year the pain continued for even a few days after her menses. Although she had tried to become pregnant during the interim, she was unable to conceive.

Around this time, when she was about twenty years of age, her father-in-law suggested that she smoke opium during her menses. After considerable family discussion, it was decided she should smoke during the painful times of her periods. She began to take between six and nine pipes on the most painful day of her flow (usually the second) and fewer on the other days. She did not take it during every one of her menses, since there was less pain when her periods flowed freely and were of red blood and had no odor; but she did need it during most of them. Her monthly opium smoking continued for about thirteen years, until she left Laos as a refugee. She had never become addicted during that time.

I first saw Blea as a patient in Minnesota when she was about thirty-four years old. At that time she had come to join the growing Hmong community there. Bereft of her opium, she had again become disabled each month during her menses. Consultation with a gynecologist revealed that she had numerous large myomata (benign tumors) in her uterus. Although further diagnostic tests and possible surgery were recommended, Blea made the rounds of various clinics and doctors until she found the kind of relief that she favored. For her, remission lay in a medication similar to that which had given her relief in Asia. A physician prescribed Fiorinal with Codeine #3, a combination of 200 milligrams aspirin, 50 milligrams butalbital (a barbiturate), 30 miligrams codeine (a derivative of opium), 40 milligrams caffeine, and 130 milligrams phenacetin. As with the opium, she consumed generous amounts on the painful days of her flow (up to six tablets a day). Despite the addictive nature of this drug, she took it only during her periods. It enabled her to continue an active life as a factory worker, housewife, grandmother, and herbal healer.

Use In Suicide

Opium overdose was a form of suicide practiced among the Hmong and Iu Mien.* It was well known among them that a large oral dose of opium could be counted on as a highly effective and relatively comfortable means of ending one's life. The one person in Laos to commit suicide while a patient under my care employed this method.

An Opium Suicide. Vuh Shai was twenty-two years old, a Hmong soldier who had been involved in a major battle with the North Vietnamese. Nepalm had been dropped on the enemy despite the proximity of the two forces. As a result Vuh Shai received extensive third- and fourth-degree burns on both legs (about 35 percent on his total body surface). He survived the initial shock and fluid loss and, over the next two weeks, received daily attention to his burns.

The care of these burns caused considerable discomfort for him. To make matters worse, there were inadequate supplies of morphine and Demerol to relieve his pain. It became evident that he would, at best, be crippled. It was also likely that he would lose parts of both lower extremities, since parts of his toes and feet were becoming gangrenous.

One evening a Hmong nurse, a Lao physician,† and I discussed the matter with him. We told him parts of both feet would have to come off if he were to live, and we proposed transplanting some skin from his trunk to his legs in order to save of them what we could. Vuh Shai said he would think about it and tell us his decision the next day. None of the three of us anticipated the eventual outcome from his immediate response, which was measured and accepting.

That night Vuh Shai paid a Hmong hospital assistant to purchase some opium under the guise that he would need it over the next month or so to relieve the pain from his surgeries. The next morning during rounds we found him dead, his pupils pin-point sized, and most of the opium gone. As he had promised, he had given us his decision.

---

*Opium overdose was not the most common method of suicide, however. Men tended to commit suicide with guns and grenades and by hanging. Women mostly used toxic drugs, such as chloroquin (an antimalarial drug) or a toxic leaf that produced death in about half of those who consumed it.

†Dr. Khammeung Tounalom, a respected colleague and good friend, is both a highly skilled physician and an outstanding humanitarian. He is ethnic Lao, and his wife is Hmong.

COMMENT

1. Opium eating requires relatively little in the way of apparatus or technique. On the contrary, opium smoking entails not only a certain level of skill but also a certain minimum of paraphernalia. The latter might be simple and inexpensive or quite elaborate. Opium eating is not so popular with addicts as is opium smoking. The latter provides a rapid onset of pharmacological effect and is more wasteful of the drug. Using powdered opium as snuff was rare in Laos, as was the injection of opiate drugs.

2. Purported reasons for first using opium varied among different ethnic groups. Tribal addicts often specified illness, lowland Asian addicts usually gave curiosity, and Caucasian addicts cited peer pressure as major motivations for their use of the drug. Once addiction was established, the reasons for continuing opium tended to become more uniform. To continued opiate use was ascribed recreational enjoyment or pleasure or effective medication for chronic, disabling somatic or emotional problems. Even when opium no longer provided pleasure, social companionship, symptomatic relief for illness, or enhanced productivity, it was nonetheless continued to avoid withdrawal symptoms and to ameliorate fear of death from withdrawal.

3. Opium users in Laos did not fit a single pattern. They ranged from children to the elderly and included men and women, all religions and most ethnic groups, and the entire spectrum of occupations and social class.

4. Nonaddictive use of opium is considerably more difficult to study than addictive use. In part this is owing to the extreme variability in nonaddictive use as compared to the more stereotypic addictive use. Some nonaddictive use is actually preaddictive use. Some people do persist in regular but nonaddictive use of opium over prolonged periods, but they appear to be few in number.

5. Although it is an effective, relatively painless means of committing suicide, opiate overdose was far less popular than other methods in Laos.

V

Natural Courses
of Addiction

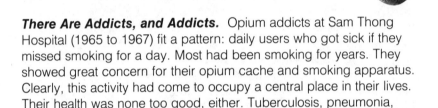

There Are Addicts, and Addicts. Opium addicts at Sam Thong
Hospital (1965 to 1967) fit a pattern: daily users who got sick if they
missed smoking for a day. Most had been smoking for years. They
showed great concern for their opium cache and smoking apparatus.
Clearly, this activity had come to occupy a central place in their lives.
Their health was none too good, either. Tuberculosis, pneumonia,
malaria, and malnutrition befell those improverished by their addiction.

Such was the stereotype taught by hospitalized addicts. Then
early in 1966 I began to stay in villages and refugee settlements. I
visited the homes of Hmong friends and coworkers. In those places I
learned a different perspective on opium addiction.

Luh Je's mother-in-law particularly surprised me. A vigorous
woman of some fifty years, she was well muscled and alert. She
worked harder than any two women in Je's extended family. And she
enjoyed conversation as much as she appeared to enjoy work. At
first I took little notice that she chewed something every morning—
small, black spherules. But the persistence of this daily ritual piqued
my interest, as did the fact that she didn't like the taste. (She screwed
up her face, prunelike, each time she washed them down with her
morning tea.) Finally, curiosity got the best of me, and I asked her what
it was. She assured me off-handedly, "It's to give me strength for the
morning's labor."

Finally one evening I lingered long after supper in conversation
with Je. As various family members were performing their preslumber
ablutions, Je's mother-in-law joined us by the fire with opium-smoking
apparatus. She handily polished off several pipes like an old pro.

Some days later, in fractured French (so as to keep our conversation private from her) Je and I discussed his mother-in-law's habit. He affirmed that the morning pepper-upper was opium, also. As we lazily switched to our more familiar Lao, speckled with some French and Hmong terms, she was delighted to hear that we were gossiping about her. "Yes, I cannot get anything done without my morning opium. My strength goes away, I don't want to do anything, and I have no appetite. A little opium, and strength flows into my arms, my mind becomes sharp and quick, and my food tastes good. It's been like that for the last few years."

The medic Tu Yeu added to the enigma. His dispensary was well ordered, his reports and supply requests clear. Yet every night, when we were all finally abed in his one-room home, Tu Yeu sat by the fire and smoked his pipeful of opium.

By then I had become thoroughly confused. Addicts back at the hospital looked like wrecks of the Hesperides. Those with whom I worked, their relatives, and some other addicts in the village seemed to be getting along fairly well. Out of this puzzlement evolved the several studies detailed in this and subsequent chapters.

RESEARCHING ADDICTION

The first step is to ask the researchable question. No end of interesting and useful questions might be asked. But if there is no way of answering them, the asking becomes a parlor game rather than a serious endeavor. Rephrased as statements, such questions become hypotheses. A few of my early questions about opium addiction in Laos were as follows:

> Are opium addicts mostly elderly men, as is often stated in the literature on Asia?
>
> Are there different kinds of addicts, so that some become impoverished and incapacitated while others do not? Or are there merely different phases, with little or no disability in early stages and increasing disability later?
>
> Are ethnic Chinese more prone to addiction than others, as averred by the Lao?
>
> How common is opium addiction?
>
> Why do some people become addicted to opium while others do not?

As we shall see, other questions appeared as the studies progressed and new data became available (an inevitable consequence of research—an addicting characteristic, if you will).

Definitions

Addiction is one of those terms like *alcoholism, extramarital sex, money lending, socialism,* or *religion* that possesses ethical connotations and about which most of us have strongly held beliefs or values. Meanings can vary widely from person to person. By the same token, each term also has highly specific characteristics when used by researchers.

But researchers can also differ in their use of these terms. As a case in point, several social scientists familiar with Asian opium users have told me that the following man is *not* an addict:

> a prosperous, married farmer who smokes eight pipes of opium three times a day, has been smoking thus for three years, and becomes seriously ill with diarrhea, vomiting, sleeplessness, and bodily aches when he tries to stop smoking for a few days;

and that the following man *is* an addict:

> an impoverished, unmarried, unskilled laborer, with no permanent place of residence, who smokes one pipeful of opium in an opium den every evening and has no illness when he discontinues smoking for a few days.

It is apparent that these scientists were attending to the social characteristics of these two men rather than to their drug use and its pharmacological consequences. Indeed, there is much value in attending to such social characteristics irrespective of drug use. But nondrug terms such as *lower socioeconomic class* (or similar phrases) would be more appropriate to describe or label the sociological characteristics of the second person described above. We are not likely to learn much about drug use per se if variables such as dose, duration and frequency of use, and presence of withdrawal signs are ignored in favor of social characteristics. This is the same problem that attends the term *alcoholic*. Although only about 5 percent of all people with physiological and psychological dependence on alcohol live in Skid Row settings, the popular concept of an alcoholic is the economically destitute drinker—who may or may not be alcohol-dependent.

Here we will be using pharmacological concepts in regard to drug use, just as sociological concepts will be used concerning socioeconomic status. Standard national and international pharmacological definitions regarding narcotic drugs are described in the next chapter. Less technical definitions are also presented in the glossary. It is important to note that drug use and addiction is less like cancer (you either have it or you don't) or like being pregnant (you are or you aren't) and more like hypertension or depression (there are obvious, severe cases and border-line cases as well).

With pharmacological concepts in mind, the following can be said about the prosperous farmer described above:

> *He is addicted, with physiological dependence. Tolerance to opium has developed, and a withdrawal syndrome appears when he tries to stop smoking. He may or may not show any intoxication.*

And we can state the following about the impoverished laborer:

> *He demonstrates psychological dependence but no physiological depen-dence, tolerance, withdrawal, or addiction. He may show some mild intoxication after one pipeful of opium but would show definite intoxica-tion after four pipes and severe intoxication on eight pipes.*

Another important consideration lies in emic versus etic perspec-tives—sociocultural concepts. The former is that of the cultural insider or subject, the folk classification. The latter is that of the cultural out-sider or researcher, the scientific classification. Fortunately, the two were virtually identical in the case of opium use and addiction in Laos. A person who used opium daily and became ill when opium was dis-continued was called "a person attached or connected to opium" (*khon tēt dyā fēn* in Lao, *neeng how yeeng* in Hmong). Merely smoking opium, but without daily use and a withdrawal illness, did not confer a special social identity. Rather it was described as "smoking opium" (*sup dyā fen* in Lao, *how yeeng* in Hmong). There is a derogatory term in Lao that recognizes the special status of the destitute, impoverished addict: *khon khē dyā fēn. Khē* is a vulgar term for filth or excrement, so the term could be translated as "filthy opium person." There is a play on words here in that *khē dyā fēn* also refers to sediment left on the filter when smoking opium is prepared or to the sediment left inside the bowl of an opium pipe. Destitute addicts often purchased such opium sedi-ment in order to eat it, since it was comparatively inexpensive. In my experience, virtually every person identified (either by him/herself or by others) as *khon tēt dyā fēn* was or had been physiologically addicted to opium. Unlike many psychological, social, and cultural phenomena, the gap between emic and etic concepts in the pharmacological arena was minimal.

Sampling

As indicated in the opening remarks to this chapter, the manner in which subjects are obtained can greatly influence the data. In general hospitals, the addicts were ill—and often quite ill. In rice fields, they were bending to their task, sweating and productive. In dens, they were preparing their pipes and slumbering. In homes, they were preparing foods, repairing. In a local shop, they were chatting over tea with their companions. So depending on when and where they were encountered, addicts could be typified as sick, industrious, lazy, responsible, self-centered, withdrawn, or sociable.

To gain a balanced perspective, the investigator should sample (i.e., obtain as subjects) addicts in a variety of settings. Ideally also, they should be contacted when they are new to addiction, as well as years and even decades later. A variety of addicts should be sought: young and old, male and female, those who started early in life and those who started late, poor and wealthy, conformers and deviants, sick and healthy, den attenders and home smokers.

Over ten years and several trips to Laos, I used several sampling methods to study addicts. Initially addicts were observed in the Sam Thong Hospital, located in a remote area of Xieng Khouang province. Next I got to know addicts through work associates and friends who had addicted relatives, neighbors, and friends. Repeated visits were made over time to several opium dens, where addicts were interviewed. Consultation with the Ministry of Social Welfare provided the opportunity to study several hundred addicts who received treatment for addiction at a Buddhist temple. Collaboration with the Ministry of Public Health similarly allowed me to conduct various epidemiologic studies of addiction in several different communities, to study addicts in a medical treatment facility, and to evaluate the effects of treatment in a follow-up study. Since 1975 I have treated a number of former opium users and addicts (and their families) who have come to the United States as refugees. Each of these approaches has opened a new window, cast a different light on the enigma of addiction. None has fully explicated the phenomenon, but each has supplied a different piece to the puzzle. Taken as a whole, they furnish some order for often confusing and contradictory aspects of addiction.

Instruments

This imposing bit of jargon refers to the means for collecting data, once the willing subject has been obtained. It originates from actual instruments, such as rules, scales, and microscopes. At times I did employ some tools-of-the-trade that would be immediately recognized as instruments: stethoscope, ophthalmoscope, blood pressure cuff, camera, tape recorder. Primarily though, my instruments were those of the social scientist and the psychiatrist: open-ended interviews, questionnaire-type formats, and clinical rating scales. Reliability was sought by interviewing the relatives, friends, and fellow villagers of my subjects. Validity was pursued by observing addicts and their families over hours, days, months, and years, in their homes, dens, and places of work, to compare what they did with what they said they did.

Popular notions about addicts insist that they are unreliable, lie about anything, and should not be trusted as sources of valid, or even reliable data. Careful research has indicated that this is not true under the following circumstances. First, rapport must be established between the addicted person and the skilled, nonjudgmental interviewer. Second, the subject must feel assured regarding the confidentiality of the information and regarding guarantees of anonymity. And third, there must be no anticipation that the information will have an adverse influence on the person's life, such as leading to incarceration or expulsion from a hospital. Under these circumstances most addicted people enjoy talking about themselves and educating the researcher, whether in North America or Asia. (See Luetgert and Armstrong 1973, Maddux and Desmond 1974, Cox and Longwell 1974.)

Conducting a Study. In early 1971, with the help of Laotian friends and associates, forty addicts were contacted—mostly the clansmen, neighbors, and friends of my associates. All the addicts were volunteers, living and functioning in their society; they weren't a patient population. An attempt was made to obtain a representative sample of addicts by contacting them initially at various sites: ten at opium dens, ten at various public places (village squares, tea shops), and twenty in their homes. Everyone contacted agreed to participate. Since all the interviews were held within a family or neighbor group context, there were ample opportunities for consensual validation or invalidation of the addicts' accounts.

Subjects were contacted at sites in Vientiane province, where numerous addicts were known to live (the Na Hai Deo district of Vientiane city and refugee villages in Vientiane province). We spoke mainly in Lao, the lingua franca of the area, with occasional forays into Hmong, English, and French as necessitated by the conversation and the linguistic abilities of those present. All the subjects were active opium addicts who had experienced withdrawal symptoms. With one exception, they had come as refugees from the mountainous provinces to the north where opium was grown.

One does not simply sit down and begin asking personal questions of people anywhere. In Laos, this dictum was especially apt, the more so among opium addicts who understood the general bias against addiction and were not anxious to discuss their habit with just anybody. So, except with the few addicts I already knew, an associate —personally known to the addict as well as to me—would explain who I was, my past medical work in Laos (important in setting a social role for me that people could understand), and my interest in opium addiction. It was stressed that I wanted to learn about opium use and opium users and that no names would be recorded or used in any fashion. That settled, we would meet at a location of their choosing (usually their home).

One does not get down to business rapidly in Laos, especially at first meeting. First, we would exchange the usual trite pleasantries about the weather or current events. Some household member would appear with tea. During pouring and serving, again more pleasantries. Ordinarily we would gently slip into an interview *by* the addict *of* me: where I had worked in Laos, mutual friends whose acquaintance we might share, narcotic addiction in the United States (it never failed to amaze them that addicts might want to inject a derivative of opium into their skin). At some point, my honorable host (and subject) would let me know in some direct or indirect fashion that I could proceed to interview him or her.

While a format for certain specific data was always before me, I let the conversation flow as it would rather than chopping it up repeatedly with interrupting questions and forced change-of-topic. Not only was this proper form in Laos (where conversation was a highly developed art, perhaps because mass media had only recently appeared) but this approach also led to information about which I would not have thought to ask. Questions left unanswered were left to the end of the interview. Generally the interview ran about two-and-a-half to three hours. In several cases, we met on more than one occasion. Ongoing contacts with a few of these addicted persons continued over a period of years.

Synchronic Versus Diachronic Studies

Phenomena that change over time can be studied in two general ways. The first method is to examine a number of cases at one point in time, the synchronic or cross-sectional approach. Examples of this method are surveys regarding the prevalence of certain disorders, studies of patients in hospital settings, or post-mortem examinations. The other approach consists of studying the cases over a long period of time, the diachronic, longitudinal, or follow-up method.

Each approach has its relative advantages and disadvantages. Cross-sectional studies demand less effort, allow collection of data on a greater number of subjects, cost considerably less, and are completed more rapidly. Longitudinal studies require years and even decades to complete and are extremely difficult to do because people move, change identities, or die in the interim or the investigator might lose interest or die. These studies cost more, and results can be delayed interminably. Sometimes interest in continuing a longitudinal study wanes, especially when effective methods evolve for treating the disorder, thus greatly influencing the natural course of the disorder (such as the discovery of isoniazid and streptomycin for tuberculosis or chlorpromazine for schizophrenia). The inevitable loss of some subjects to follow-up also introduces a bias.

Some of the longest and most detailed longitudinal studies are biographies or autobiographies. The works by and about Samuel Taylor Coleridge, an addicted English author of the late eighteenth and nineteenth centuries, offer many insights into the phases of early narcotic use, eventual addiction, subsequent loss of friends and family, financial ruin, eventual recovery but an early death from addiction-associated health problems. Hahn (1969) similarly captures insights from her own foray into opium smoking in China. The one- and two-decade follow-up studies by Vaillant (1973) on heroin addicts in the United States are outstanding examples of critical information that can be gleaned in no other way besides longitudinal studies.

Most of the information presented in this book is based on cross-sectional studies. Several addicts, however, were followed over periods ranging up to five years, and one for ten years. Several dozen addicts were followed over periods ranging from several months to a few years. These longitudinal cases provided rich detail about opium addiction in Laos. A combination of both methods provides an effective means for describing the natural course of addiction.

PREADDICTIVE USE

Most addicts in Laos were introduced to opium use by people of about the same age—friends, coworkers, a spouse, or fellow villagers. This generally took place in a recreational or social setting. As a rule, they were curious about the effects of opium but did not think that they personally would become addicted. Men tended to introduce both other men and women to opium smoking, while women seldom did so. Most addicts first tried opium in their twenties, thirties, or forties. Addiction ensued within a few months to a few years of first smoking opium. While later opium experiences were usually enjoyable, the first few intoxications on opium were often accompanied by nausea, lightheadedness, constipation, or similar unpleasant effects. Exceptions to all of these trends occurred irregularly: older family members or relatives taught some addicts; medicinal usage was the original reason for many tribespeople; some women learned from other women; a few people first tried opium in their childhood while others first became addicted in their senescence; and occasional smokers reported profound pleasure from their first experience. These latter circumstances, however, were exceptions to the customary situation described above.

Addicts in virtually all cases were reliably able to recall two specific dates, at least within a few to several months of accuracy. First, they knew the time at which they first began to use opium, and second, the point at which they knew they were addicted because of withdrawal symptoms.* Among the 503 addicts surveyed at the National Narcotic

*The whole issue of ages, years, dates, and time is not a simple one for the researcher in village Laos. With the exceptions of most Caucasians and a few Catholic Vietnamese, people did not celebrate birthdays. (Even the thought of doing so seems narcissistic to me when I assume my "village Laos" world view.) Moreover, villagers, who were usually illiterate, had no reason to fill out a never-ending series of governmental or employment forms stipulating their date of birth, as do inhabitants of literate, industrialized societies (another virtue of that period and lifestyle). Villagers similarly had little interest in either the Gregorian or Buddhist calendar. Much more, they did know, however, times of significant local events, such as when the last few great floods from the Mekong River occurred, the times when the Japanese first entered Laos during World War II and later when they left, the last time a tornado went through their region, the year of a certain local battle, and so forth. People could then relate their own life events to these historical

Detoxification Center in Laos, data on initial use were obtained from 489 people. Their age at first using narcotic drugs ranged from the early teens to the early eighties, with a mean age of 33.8 years (standard deviation 11.3 years). The duration of use prior to addiction varied from only a few weeks up to 38 years, with a mean of 1.2 years (standard deviation 2.4 years). Half of these patients were addicted within one year, and 85 percent within two years.

Preaddictive use did not differ among the various ethnic groups with the single exception of the Hmong. Data from the Detoxification Center showed that, on the average, the Hmong first started using narcotic drugs several years earlier than the others, with a mean age of 27.2 years compared to means of about 35 years for the other groups. The duration of their preaddictive usage was several months shorter than for the other groups, with a mean of 0.4 years as compared to 1.0 to 1.6 years. For both of these variables, the Hmong addicts differed significantly from the other Asian addicts (significance level < .005, Student "t" test). The specific figures underline this marked difference:

Ethnic group	Number	Mean age (and standard deviation) at first use	Duration (and standard deviation) of preaddictive use
Lao	308	35.5 years (11.3)	1.4 years (2.8)
Expatriate Asians*	75	34.5 years (10.7)	1.0 years (1.6)
Hmong	81	27.6 years (9.3)	0.4 years (0.8)
Other tribal groups†	25	35.9 years (10.9)	1.6 years (2.2)

*Chinese, Vietnamese, Thai, Indian, Pakistani
†Tai Dam, Khamu, Iu Mien

The earlier age of first opium use and the shorter period of preaddictive use among the Hmong were probably related to the ready

---

milestones. For example, a respondent might say "I was born three years before the Japanese came." Family history was sometimes a guidepost, such as "I started smoking the year my son was born and he is now eight years old." To interpret the latter, however, one would need to know that the Chinese and sometimes the Vietnamese counted from the time of conception rather than from birth and assigned to the newborn the age of one year. Such practices did not make the discovery of age and time durations impossible but did make them difficult. Of course, there were some people more oriented to time spans who could give age and duration without recourse to these local calendrical events.

availability of opium in their homes, a factor that we will consider again in subsequent chapters. Sampling did not appear to be an influential factor, since Hmong addicts obtained in a community sample also had brief preaddictive use and early onset of addiction.

ADDICTIVE USE

Onset of Addiction

As their opium doses gradually increased, addicts at some point noticed that a runny nose, sneezing, loss of appetite, body aching, irritability, and malaise occurred following a period of heavy opium use. A few knew exactly what it was; others believed that they had a respiratory illness such as a cold (*pen vat* in Lao). Generally another addict, bemused at this naiveté, explained that the cure lay in the cause of the symptoms: more opium. At this point, each addicted person knew that he or she was addicted. This universal experience served as a rite of passage of sorts into addiction. There then ensued a period of months or years in which the narcotic experience was pleasurable and accompanied by few untoward consequences—a time nicely referred to by Hendler and Stephens (1977) as the honeymoon period.

Addicted people were able to recount when they became addicted, often by relating it to some other personal, historical, or climatic event that occurred in the same year. Age at onset of addiction in the 489 Asian addicts at the National Narcotic Detoxification Center ranged from the teens to the eighties, with a mean age of 35.0 years (standard deviation 11.3). Only 5 percent were addicted before age 20 years, and 3 percent after age 60. These figures were similar to those among a group of 1,192 addicts from Laos treated at a Buddhist monastery in Thailand. Age at onset among 1,133 of them varied from later childhood to senescence, with an average of 33.8 years (standard deviation 10.6).

In a community survey of 40 addicts, the mean age at onset ranged from 16 to 49 years, with a mean of 30.8 years. This younger mean age was due to the relatively high proportion of Hmong people in this sample (i.e., 28 out of 40, or 70 percent). In the treatment groups described above, the Hmong comprised less than 20 percent of the total. In all of the samples, Hmong people became addicted at a mean age of 27 to 28 years, while the mean age for others was 34 to 36 years. The consistency of these findings regardless of sampling method points toward their being valid observations.

Dose, Frequency, and Cost

The pattern of opium use was studied among 431 opium addicts at the Narcotic Detoxification Center in Vientiane. Most addicts were taking opium two or three times a day at the time of admission. Daily frequency was related to cost (or equivalent market value, for those who raised their own opium). Those taking more doses of opium per day required slightly higher doses of methadone in the first twenty-four hours of treatment. Specific figures in 1972 United States dollars were as follows:

Daily doses	Number of subjects	Average daily cost (U.S. $)	Average methadone dose in first 24 hours
1	14	0.43	22.9 mg.
2	265	1.20	28.0 mg.
3	141	2.05	31.0 mg.
4 or 5	11	2.93	31.1 mg.

As one might anticipate, opium eaters spent the least amount per day on opium: $1.07. Those who smoked all their opium spent the most: $1.84 per day. People who both smoked and ate their opium were intermediate: $1.35 per day.

While daily frequency varied little, amount spent daily showed tremendous variation. Addicts spent as little as $0.25 and as much as $9.25 per day on opium (or smoked equivalent market values from their own crop). Almost 80 percent of them, however, spent between $0.50 and $2.50 daily. On the average, men spent more on their daily opium dose than did women (statistically significant at the .005 level of probability).

Phases of Addiction

During habitual, preaddictive usage and during early addictive usage, most opium smokers felt well and looked strong and healthy. If they had been ill with diarrhea or chronic cough or had been depressed, their symptoms often improved and their work output increased. Physically they could not be readily distinguished by the naive observer from their nonaddict peers. In this phase they generally consumed opium once or twice a day. They perceived that opium during this time enhanced their life over what it had been previously. This honeymoon period might last months or decades, but usually it persisted for several months to a few, sometimes several years. Relatively few addicts presented themselves for treatment within the first year of addiction, indicating the relative rarity of untoward consequences during this early phase. Of 489 addicts at the Detoxification Center, only 2 percent had been addicted for a year or less—about one-fourth to one-sixth the expected number based on those coming for treatment during their second year of addiction or later.

A phase of deterioration gradually ensued after a few to several years of addiction (sometimes sooner, sometimes later). Shoddy dress, an odor of opium smoke, weight loss, and cyanosis of the lips and gums disclosed their addiction. While they still performed work and often supported their own opium habit, their ambition and energy became dulled. They manifested more concern for their opium cache and smoking equipment than for their family and other responsibilities. An apathetic appearance, lax facial muscles, sagging posture, slowed gait, and glassy-eyed stares persisted for an hour or two after heavy smoking. In advanced cases their skin became pale, dry, and thin. As they increasingly ignored their appearance, their hair became long and disheveled. Men often ceased shaving. Women usually had no jewelry, having sold it to buy opium; generally their menses ceased. Addicts' children were poorly cared for, often with evident malnourishment and inadequate dress. At this stage addicts generally took opium two or three times a day, by smoking or eating or both.

Incapacitated addicts ate or smoked opium three to five times a day and performed little or no work. Preparation of the opium pipe and deep inhalations from it alternated with periods of stupor. These few addicts, mostly older men, were totally dependent on others for their opium supply. If the incapacitated addicts were Hmong, a large portion of the family's cash crop was consumed by them. Some of these addicts resorted to begging in order to supply themselves with opium. They could readily be identified by the thin and uncalloused condition of their hands. Untreated withdrawal from opium was prolonged and severe for these addicts: they showed inability to eat, insomnia, diarrhea, dehydration, and almost incessant whining over a period of a few weeks. Their mortality during withdrawal was high. This was not a numerous group: I encountered only one of them during two field surveys in which seventy-two addicts were interviewed. They were encountered more frequently in the hospital setting (the case described in the first chapter is an example).

CONSEQUENCES

The consequences of addiction, like the courses of addiction, were tremendously variable. One person might encounter more consequences in a year than another person in a decade. While the consequences might be related in a general way to dose, frequency, and duration of use, there was no one-to-one relationship. On the contrary, a given dose, frequency, and duration of addiction might devastate one person's life, while leaving another relatively untouched. Nonetheless, there were modal consequences that affected most addicts over time. You will note the absence of quantitative data. This resulted from the difficulty of defining "family problems" or "economic deterioration" in researchable terms that have acceptable reliability and validity, particularly in the context of village life in Southeast Asia.

Economics

As indicated above, addicts reported a wide range of daily expenditures at the time of admission to the National Detoxification Center. Some of the variation represented the ordinary fluctuation in dosage practiced by many addicts. Doses went up for several reasons: more money, a recent poppy harvest, not much work to do, increased stress, or a recent loss. Addicts might similarly take less opium for similar reasons: little money, depletion of opium reserves around the time prior to poppy harvest, a long trip, or much work to be done. A few addicts compulsively kept their dose at very steady levels, day in and day out, over many years.

On the average, opium addicts treated at the Detoxification Center in Vientiane were spending $1.58 per day on opium at the time of admission (standard deviation 1.70). While 88 percent spent $0.50 to $3.50 per day, there was a skew to the right with some addicts spending several dollars a day.

The reader might presume that narcotic addiction would not comprise much of an economic burden in Laos, since these costs were so minimal by comparison to the price of narcotic drugs in North America and Europe. Around the time of the study, however, the per capita national income for Laos was estimated at $80 per year. An average daily salary for an unskilled workman was $1 per day, and most literate civil servants only earned $30 to $40 per month. So these daily expenditures on narcotic drugs, minimal by certain other standards, were a tremendous economic burden for most addicts and usually for their extended family also.

The most common reason given by addicts for seeking treatment at the Narcotic Detoxification Center in Vientiane related to "economic problems" and "economic pressures," accounting for 48 percent of reasons. Many of the early social consequences of narcotic addiction (e.g., family discord) were secondarily related to the cost of maintaining addiction. Doses that previously provided relaxation and pleasure no longer did so as tolerance for the drug developed. Larger and larger doses were required to obtain the desired feeling, to relieve insomnia, to provide relaxation, or to attain whatever other particular effect the addicted person sought. Some addicted poppy farmers consumed their entire cash crop, with none left over for sale. Addicted peasants, laborers, civil servants, and merchants had to work harder or use more of their income to purchase the drug. This usually happened in degrees, gradually and insidiously, over months and years.

Lifestyle

Eventually many addicts had to make choices about selling their favorite possessions or family heirlooms. Jewelry, Buddha statues, or spirit drums that had been in the family for generations, furniture, wristwatches, a favored horse or mule, or a pirogue would be sold to purchase opium. Typically the addict scrimped in myriad ways on daily necessities to subsidize the addiction: making last year's clothes last another year; buying thongs this year instead of shoes and next year going barefoot altogether; selling the pigs and chickens and giving up eating meat; then giving up eating fish; then not buying a diversity of fruits and vegetables. The addict's clothes began to look shabby. He or she became thinner and eventually blatantly malnourished. As money and resources flowed away from the family, sometimes other members of the family began to dress in old, shabby clothes and became thinner and vitamin deficient.

Addicts eventually spent so much time in taking the drug and in intoxication afterward that there was not time in the day to attend to myriad formerly essential rituals. These activities became unnecessary details: taking a bath, washing clothes, brushing teeth, communicating with family members. In line with these fundamental changes in daily life, the second most common reason given at the National Narcotic Detoxification Center was under the general heading "distaste for present life circumstances" and "wanting to seek a new life-style." These comprised 34 percent of the reasons for seeking treatment.

Family

Known opium addicts, if single, had great difficulty obtaining a marriage partner. Especially if they had been addicted for a year or more, their addiction was usually known socially. This ruled them out as potential spouses for anyone except other opium addicts. One Haw man of my acquaintance (from Yunnan province in China) withdrew himself from opium during his youth while he courted and married a Hmong woman—then later resumed opium smoking.

Family discovery of a member's addiction gave rise to a family crisis, unless virtually everyone in the family was already addicted. Relatives tried tears, arguments, pleadings, exhortations, threats, but typically to no avail. Separation or divorce might take place, but this was unusual. Generally family members stayed together and made accommodations.

Initially these adjustments were not too large or difficult. Family members might then be reassured. Perhaps things would not be so difficult after all, they thought. Perhaps their addicted relative would have only a small habit. Or perhaps the opium smoking would stop. After all, such things did happen. So the family made numerous, small, incremental, partial adaptations to the opium smoking and to the economic burden presented by it. And they hoped for improvement.

Less than 5 percent of addicts gave family pressure as a reason for seeking treatment. This reflects the acceptance, albeit with reluctance, of the typical Asian family to opiate addiction.

Identity and Self-Esteem

At the same time that the family was making economic and interpersonal adaptations, the addict was making psychological accommodations. In the first few months, even for the first year or two, the addicts' surreptitious opium use allowed them to maintain their former self-image and social role. Family discovery greatly encroached on this former self-image. They came to have a special identity in the family as an addicted person. Once this fact was accepted, it was ordinarily not a large step toward allowing neighbors and clan members to know. Usually by that time a few close friends (especially fellow opium smokers) knew anyway.

It should be emphasized that the crises of family discovery and community discovery followed on an earlier crisis: self-discovery. The first appearance of withdrawal, the morning use of opium to stem the withdrawal illness, the struggle to give up opium, the collapse of these struggles, the surrender to daily opium use—all these had preceded the social crises and prepared the way for them. The survival of this earlier crisis, and the continued opium smoking despite it, made it easier to survive the subsequent family and community crises.

These discoveries had their consequences, nonetheless. Family members, relatives, and neighbors gradually stopped trusting the addicted person with money. Addicts were progressively left out of important decisions regarding the family or village. Their opinions carried less and less weight. They received less emotional support from others, despite their increased need for it as their finances and health deteriorated. These served as countervailing forces upon the addict to give up addiction.

Although loss of identity and self-esteem was not frequently given as a reason for seeking treatment, it often was an important conscious element in the addict's maintaining abstinence after treatment.

Health

Major physical consequences of opium addiction did not occur until after some years or even a few decades of addiction. Most prevalent health problems were malnutrition, muscle wasting associated with protein deficiency (from poor diet), anemia associated with iron and vitamin deficiency (again from poor diet), and various other manifestations of vitamin deficiency (e.g., cheilosis or sores at the mouth, keratitis or softening of the cornea). Dermatitis, skin ulcers, and skin abscesses were common, probably due to a combination of poor nutrition, infrequent bathing and grooming, loss of skin thickness, and pressure sores from prolonged stupor. Gingivitis was almost routinely present, with pyorrhea in those addicted for a longer period. Many who became addicted in their twenties had lost all of their teeth by their mid-thirties or early forties. Among older people in their forties to sixties, addicted for twenty years or more, chronic obstructive lung disease was frequent, sometimes associated with cor pulmonale. Similar observations have been made about opium smokers in Singapore (Leong, Poh, and Grandevia 1970, DaCosta, Tock, and Boey 1971 and 1972). Death during acute narcotic withdrawal occurred primarily among these older addicts with cardiopulmonary conditions. Dehydration due to vomiting and diarrhea also frequently preceded death in older addicts.

A Vietnamese Patriarch. Tran Van Nguyen was born outside of Hanoi in Vietnam. A Catholic and a merchant, he decided to emigrate in 1954 when the Vietminh gained control of North Vietnam. He came to Laos where, in his late forties, he began to rebuild his business.

Tran Van had several factors in his favor. He was hard working and intelligent. One-quarter Chinese, he spoke Mandarin and could thus deal with the Chinese businessmen already in Laos. Educated in the French system, he spoke fluent French and could also deal effectively with Lao bureaucrats and the Lao elite. He had ties to French and other European suppliers and was able to obtain credit based on his former reputation. And he had several industrious sons and sons-in-law who loyally followed his firm but wise leadership as patriarch.

Prior to his arrival in Laos, Tran Van had never smoked opium. On the occasion of closing a business deal with a Chinese man in northern Laos, however, an opium pipe and cigarettes were brought forth. Accustomed to such business rituals with wine or rice whiskey, Tran Van did not want to offend. He had never smoked opium and so was also a little curious about it. So he took a pipeful but felt nothing. Offered a second pipe, he took that and noticed a strange and para-doxical effect: a relief of his tension and strain yet at the same time a new energy and strength. The effect pleased him. Before going off to sleep in the merchant's home that evening he had a third and a fourth pipe.

To understand this coincidental event, you should know more about Tran Van's life at that point. He had been in Laos for a year. All of his children and their families had come safely to Laos, and his business was building well. But his life, as he perceived it, was filled with sorrow. Whereas before he had lived in a large villa with servants, here his family was cramped into a Vietnamese ghetto consisting of wooden shacks built over a mosquito swamp. In Vietnam he lived among his siblings, cousins, and their familes, and he had an important political role in the community. Here he had no contact with his ex-tended kin (some of whom he knew to be in Vietnamese prisons), and he had to kowtow to even minor Lao officials. His wife, formerly an able and productive administrator of the household, was depressed.

Unaccustomed to cooking and housework, she cried bitterly every day and talked of suicide. His children could not thrive economically without his leadership, a burden he felt keenly.

Tran Van did not link his enjoyment from the opium with these circumstances in his life. He only knew that he liked the effect. Provided with other opportunities to smoke with friends or business associates, he readily grasped them. Within a year he had his own smoking paraphernalia and was smoking on Sundays, as well as at other times when he felt too tense to relax during the evening. Another six months and he was addicted.

By 1974 Tran Van Nguyen had been addicted for over fifteen years, smoking three times a day. Still successful in business yet aging, he had gradually shifted the leadership for his business to his eldest daughter's husband. He had planned to slowly retire, smoking opium in his waning years. But recent events interfered with that plan. Formerly opium had been relatively inexpensive, and his dose had been small. Now, because of refugee moves out of the poppy-growing areas, the cost had more than doubled; and his daily dosage of opium had quadrupled from what it had been. His monthly opium bill had come to exceed the total living expenses of his extended family. Another factor was the political change occurring in Laos. He had seen the rise to power by the Communist party in Vietnam, and he discerned the same signs now in Laos. The family had discussed this and decided they must acquire as much capital as possible to finance a move to Thailand, or possibly France, if the political winds should blow against them. Patriarch Nguyen's addiction interfered seriously with these plans.

Persuaded by his family and by his own logic of the need to stop opium, Tran Van decided to do it in his own way. He had never gone to doctors and did not plan to start now. When he had an obstacle to overcome, such as his move to Laos, he accomplished it by willpower and on his own. So he announced that in one week, after he had rested, reduced his opium doses somewhat, and made appropriate offerings and prayers at the Catholic church, he would stop opium.

His first day off opium was not too bad: some weakness and loss of appetite, but he could move around and discuss business matters. The second day was much worse: his bowels had become loose, and he could not take food. By the third day, he could barely sit without help and at night he tried to stifle his moans so as not to alarm his family. But the next day they were alarmed anyway. Tran

Van could not keep down even rice gruel or weak tea, and he was too weak even to attend to his own urinations. Water flowed from his bowels, and the dry heaves appeared. By the fifth day, his wife and children were asking him if he would not go to a doctor or a hospital. He refused adamantly, insisting that after another few days of illness he would recover. By the seventh day, he lay immobile and confused. Not having taken any fluids for forty-eight hours, his cheeks and belly were badly sunken. He had not urinated during the previous twenty-four hours.

The family tearfully decided to take him to the Detoxification Center, figuring they would rather cope with his wrath later than lose him. They barely had him through the front door when Tran Van suddenly stopped breathing. The staff at the Center tried unsuccessfully to resuscitate him. The family would have no wrath to face, only their own grief.

ADDICTS' ATTEMPTS AT STOPPING ADDICTION

Attempts at Self-Control

Most addicts eventually tried to stop using opium on their own or at least to cut back on their dosage. Reasons given were similar to those for entering treatment. In 1971 I surveyed forty addicts who had never formally been in treatment for addiction. The decision to stop opium involved finances for a few of them:

> *"Opium was too expensive, so I decided to quit."*
>
> *"I used to raise my own opium. When we had to leave the mountains (as refugees) I used up all of my money buying opium from others."*

For others the reason was declining enjoyment from opium use:

> *"I did not enjoy opium anymore as I did in the past."*
>
> *"Years ago the opium was strong and pleasant. The stuff today is weak and no good."*

Some realized that they had become alarmingly thin and unhealthy looking, that they were an economic burden and a drain to their family, that they could no longer participate in communal activities of the village, or that their social reputation had declined.

"You don't consume the opium. It consumes you. It takes away your money, your health, your friends."

While one or another of these factors was paramount with different people, many times they simply comprised a growing composite list of reasons urging the addicted person to stop opium.

Counteracting these motivations were the repeated failures that addicts experienced in trying to stop on their own, the cramps and aching during withdrawal, and the difficulties that they found in readjusting to the abstinent state. A frequent comment volunteered by opium addicts was, "I would like to stop, but I'm afraid I would die."

Among these 40 nonpatient addicts, all of whom were interviewed at length, 29 (73 percent of the total) had made concerted efforts to withdraw themselves from opium. These efforts continued over days, weeks, or months. Eleven others had never made attempts lasting any more than a day or two. Those who had made more serious attempts to withdraw themselves had a longer mean duration of addiction (18.3 years). Those who had not persisted in their brief attempts to withdraw had a shorter mean duration of addiction (8.1 years), although there was overlap between the two groups. Among the 29 addicts who made longer lasting attempts at withdrawal, 9 resumed opium use within the first month following withdrawal (range: 4 to 20 days). Twenty other addicts were more successful, achieving abstinence for just under six months on the average (range: 1 to 12 months). Half of these 20 subjects had two or more successes—followed each time by a recurrence of their habit. A return to the opium pipe was usually laid to some physical cause, often the same symptoms that accompanied the original addiction. A few people stated frankly that the addiction recurred at times of health when they had no apparent problems, such as the Hmong woman who reported the following:

> But then [some months after withdrawal on two occasions] others with me would start smoking. I would smell the opium and see them enjoying smoking. So I would plan to take only one pipe, so I could enjoy it too. But each time I started smoking again every day, and soon I was addicted like before.

Despite their manifest low success and high recurrence following attempted withdrawal, many addicts nonetheless showed considerable interest in discontinuing opium use. Over half of these 40 addicts in the field survey spontaneously asked during the interview if other treatments might be successful.

Seeking Treatment

Similar reports were obtained from addicts seeking treatment for addiction. Most had withdrawn themselves only for periods lasting days, weeks, or months before resuming opium use. A small percentage returned to addiction after longer periods of abstinence lasting two or three years and, in one case, seven years.

Duration of addiction among those voluntarily seeking treatment also gives some indication of the length of time that it took before an addict perceived that the disadvantages outweighed the advantages of opium. Duration of addiction was the time lapse between onset of addiction and the time that the person sought treatment (or was counted in a community survey). Among 503 addicts admitted voluntarily to the Detoxification Center in Laos, 491 were able to report their duration of addiction. This ranged from a few months to over half a century, with a mean of 13.2. years (standard deviation 10.7). One 83-year-old Lao man had been addicted for 59 years; during that time he had withdrawn himself once and remained abstinent for a year. Average duration of addiction among the various ethnic groups at the Center was as follows:

Ethnic group	Number of subjects	Mean duration	(and standard deviation)
Lao	309	14.3 years	(10.9)
Expatriate Asians	76	12.8 years	(11.5)
Hmong	81	11.6 years	(9.0)
Other tribal groups	25	9.7 years	(8.4)

There was no statistically significant difference in duration of addiction among these ethnic groups. This suggests that, despite considerable intraethnic variability, opium addiction tended to produce problems at about the same rates irrespective of ethnic group or age at addiction.

Of further interest, the duration of addiction was similar among the Center addicts and a group of addicts surveyed in the community. Among the 40 addicts referred to above, the duration of addiction ranged from 3 to 35 years, with a mean of 15.5 years. Thus, the difference in sampling methods did not lead to a significant difference in addiction characteristics, as one might have anticipated that it would. This was probably due to the unwillingness of recently addicted persons to seek treatment during the honeymoon phase and the surreptitious nature of their early opiate use.

COMMENT

1. The natural course of a phenomenon such as addiction is best studied by employing a variety of sampling methods, a variety of research instruments, and both cross-sectional and longitudinal approaches. Biological, psychological, and sociocultural aspects must be considered, since addiction crosses these disciplinary boundaries. Especially when considering a value-laden concept like addiction, social criteria must not be substituted for pharmacological criteria. By the same token, the presence of certain pharmacological characteristics should not lead to a presumption of social characteristics.

2. Most addicts used opium over a period of several months to a few years before becoming addicted. Only infrequently did people become addicted within weeks of beginning opium. Prolonged, regular non-addictive usage extending over several years or even a few decades occurred, but this was infrequent. Ready availability of opium, as among the Hmong, reduced the age at addiction and the duration of preaddictive use.

3. During early addiction there was a honeymoon period in which narcotic use generally enhanced the person's life in some way. This enhancement could be relief from pain, physical or emotional symptoms, or boredom; or it may have enabled the individual to work harder, to function better socially, or to obtain more zest out of life.

4. Eventually opium smoking led to certain untoward consequences for the addicted person and for the family as well. Often the first problem involved the increasing amounts of money spent on the drug as tolerance developed. Other dilemmas included distaste for the opium-related life-style, deteriorating interpersonal relationships within the family, diminished social prestige, and decreasing self-esteem. A major family problem was the nutritional, educational, and emotional neglect of the addicted person's children.

5. Physical complications of opium smoking occurred later, after years or even decades of addiction. These included malnutrition, abscesses and inflammation of the skin, intercurrent infections, chronic obstructive lung disease, and (especially in the older addict) sudden death during withdrawal.

6. After some years of addiction, many addicts tried to withdraw themselves from the drug. Recurrence, when it took place, usually occurred within a year.

VI

Epidemiology of Addiction

Clinicians and epidemiologists study the same disorders but from two different perspectives. Clinicians approach illness as it exists within individuals. Epidemiologists are concerned with distribution of illness in populations.

SPECIAL PROBLEMS OF ADDICTION EPIDEMIOLOGY

What is a Case?

The first task in epidemiology lies in defining a case of the disorder under consideration. Ideally, case assignment is an all-or-none phenomenon. That is, any given person can be readily designated as a case or not a case. Unfortunately, it can sometimes be difficult to make such arbitrary assignments. This is especially true for many chronic disorders, such as arthritis, schizophrenia, chronic bronchitis, and substance abuse.*

Case assignment in narcotic addiction could theoretically be difficult for a number of reasons. First, addiction is a spectrum disorder rather than an all-or-none disorder. For example, during the early phases it is often difficult to distinguish the heavy, regular, but nonaddicted user from the mildly addicted person. During advanced stages of addiction the diagnosis of addiction can usually be made quite easily. Second,

---

*Examples of diagnoses in which case assignment is more readily made include pregnancy, cancer, malaria, long bone fracture, and death. But as any clinician, medical researcher, epidemiologist, or malpractice attorney can attest, there are gray areas here also. The problem of case definition is always eased when investigative methods exist that are inexpensive, easily undertaken, and produce few false negatives and false positives.

an addict, even after many years of addiction, may resume nonaddictive use or become an abstainer, for either a brief or a prolonged period. One must then decide whether to categorize that individual as an addict, nonaddicted user, or abstainer. Third, certain criteria for narcotic addiction can be quite useful in the clinical context but may be almost useless for epidemiologic survey purposes. These include such relatively nebulous criteria as compulsive usage or obsessive thinking about drugs. Application of these concepts involves individual judgment, and they may be difficult to apply in early cases of addiction or outside of the clinical setting.

Despite the difficulty of the task, considerable effort has been directed toward developing criteria for addiction. The World Health Organization in its technical report series (No. 116, 1957) lists the following characteristics:

1. psychological dependence: emotional and cognitive influence from the drug, such as obsessive thinking about the drug, emotional discomfort if the drug cannot be obtained, extremely high valuation of the drug experience, decision to continue using the drug even in the face of untoward consequences;

2. physiologic dependence: control of the drug over various biochemical and psychologic functions, such as neurotransmittor balance, pupil size, sleep, psychoendocrine function;

3. withdrawal syndrome upon discontinuation of the drug: onset of illness within six to forty-eight hours consisting of toxic effects on vital signs, appetite and sleep disturbance, bodily aching, and autonomic nervous system disturbance.

The American Psychiatric Association has more recently (1980) attempted to set more specific diagnostic criteria for opioid abuse as follows:

1. pattern of pathological use: inability to reduce or stop use; intoxication throughout the day; use of opioids nearly every day for at least a month; episodes of opioid overdose (intoxication so severe that respiration and consciousness are impaired);

2. impairment in social or occupational functioning due to opioid use: e.g., fights, loss of friends, absence from work, loss of a job, or legal difficulties (other than due to a single arrest for possession, purchase, or sale of the substance);

3. duration of disturbance of at least one month.

Opioid dependence involves the above factors, plus opioid tolerance and/or withdrawal:

4. tolerance: need for markedly increased amounts of opioid to achieve the desired effect, or markedly diminished effect with regular use of the same amount;

5. withdrawal: development of at least four of the following symptoms due to recent cessation or reduction in opioid use following prolonged heavy use of an opioid: lacrimation, rhinorrhea, pupillary dilation, piloerection, sweating, diarrhea, yawning, mild hypertension, tachycardia, fever, insomnia; none of these symptoms should be due to any other physical or mental disorder.

Substances besides opiates that can cause addiction include alcohol and the barbiturate-sedative drugs.

False Positives and False Negatives

In conducting epidemiologic studies, one must be alert to false negative cases (i.e., addicts who are identified as nonaddicts) and false positive cases (i.e., people identified as addicts who are not addicted). Research experience with addicts in Laos indicated two primary sources for false negative cases. First, there was a trend for persons addicted for less than a year or two not to be identified. There were exceptions to this, so that some addicts appeared in surveys and in clinical studies who had first begun daily use of opium and had experienced withdrawal in previous months. Another source of false negatives included addicts who had temporarily ceased their opium use for some period, usually for a few weeks or months, rarely for some years, and were currently abstinent. (One might legitimately classify this group as abstainers from a cross-sectional perspective, but as addicts from a longitudinal perspective.) At any one point in time, it is not likely that false negative subjects from either group comprise more than 5 percent of all addicts. While one would expect a larger number of false negatives in clinical populations than in community surveys, a comparison of the two approaches in Laos (Westermeyer 1981) indicated that the reverse may be true. That is, closet addicts* may be more willing to identify themselves to a treatment facility than to a community survey. The number of false negative cases in case registers can range even higher, as we will see later.

*Those not known to friends and relatives as addicts.

False positive cases did not appear in any community surveys in Laos, but they did infrequently appear in clinical populations. These were people who had been on heavy doses of opium but who had decided to give up their addiction. They had reduced their consumption to relatively small, once-a-day doses that were too small to produce physiological addiction. Their repeated attempts to cut that small dose had often been unsuccessful, usually leading to a cyclic resumption of higher, then lower doses. In clinical populations these people comprised less than 1 percent of addicts seeking treatment.

Methods of data collection also influenced the rate of false negatives and false positives. While the above comments from Laos relate to data obtained by interviewing, Suwanwela et al. in Thailand have compared urine analysis and interviewing data among the Hmong subjects in a community survey. They noted many false positive urine tests because of (1) use of poppy seeds as a condiment, (2) use of poppy seed oil for cooking, and (3) cooking in and eating from utensils that had been employed for opium collection. Conversely, they encountered only one false negative urine test, a recently addicted person who had initially denied opium use until confronted with his urine findings.

Reliability of Interview Data

Another issue regarding case definition is the reliability of data obtained from interviews with narcotic addicts. Much useful information concerning addiction originates from self-reports by individual addicts themselves, since (as indicated above) relatively limited data can be obtained from methods such as urine screening. Studies of interviews among narcotic addicts in the United States have generally shown a high degree of reliability, especially when confidentiality or anonymity is assured (Leutgart and Armstrong 1973, Cox and Longwell 1974, Maddux and Desmond 1975). Similar studies of cigarette smoking and alcoholism have shown high reliability when confidentiality or anonymity is assured, no loss of status follows from accurate reporting, and rapport between interviewer and addict has been established; reliability is poor when any one of these elements is absent (Williams et al. 1979, Sillett et al. 1978, Annis 1979). Highly reliable data could be obtained from narcotic addicts in Laos when a local person served as an investigator's entree to the addict. That is, some third individual who knew both the investigator and the addict made introductions, explained the reasons for the interview, and responded to the subject's further questions. Inclusion of family members and/or acquaintances in interviews also provided collateral data when the addict's memory or denial impeded accurate reporting (such as regarding the amount of family resources spent on opium). In all interviews, I devoted considerable time in establishing rapport— showing respect, building trust, opening two-way communication, setting informants at ease, and providing them with a sense of participation in the conversation.

Case Finding

Case finding is second in importance only to case definition in epidemiology. The epidemiologist must strive to include all cases of a given disorder represented in the study sample. If all cases are not included erroneous conclusions can be drawn regarding the people with the disorder.

Case finding presents special problems for the epidemiologist studying narcotic addiction. Those recently addicted may be denying to themselves that they have become addicted, still defining themselves as opium users rather than as opium addicts. Opium addicts have reasons to hide their addiction from family members and their community. In Asia there is social opprobrium connected with the addict status: addicts have more difficulty obtaining a spouse, borrowing money, making contracts. Addicts are unwilling to report themselves if they fear possible untoward consequences from doing so, such as pressure from the police.

Case finding in the clinical context involves potential methodologic weaknesses (see Berkson 1946, Brown 1976). If this is the only sampling method used, it is impossible to know whether addicts seeking treatment are like those who do not seek treatment. Since only a minority of addicts are likely to seek treatment at any one point in time, clinical data alone do not provide information on the number of addicted people in a particular population. Autopsy data can be obtained by testing the blood or other body fluids or tissues for narcotic drugs, but this method assays only a small proportion of narcotic addicts at any one time.* One must also take into account the purpose of a particular study when assessing the sampling method chosen (Edwards 1973).

Addiction rates reported in the literature on Southeast Asia vary widely even when studies have been undertaken in the same population, suggesting that definitional and sampling methods have not been well understood. An anthropologist working in Laos reported that "a number of older (Meo) men and women appear to be addicts" but few younger

---

*Postmortem exams were not done in Laos, but they do have certain advantages when combined with other approaches in the study of addiction (see Luke and Helpern 1968).

people smoke (Halpern 1964a, p. 116). Halpern evidently relied on popular opinion regarding opium addiction—a common error—rather than carefully collecting his own data. Similarly, the anthropologist Bernatzik (1970) working in northwest Thailand wrote that "no Meau was 'addicted' in the true sense of the word" despite his observation that some "rich people . . . smoke every day." It appears that his use of the term addiction "in the true sense of the word" referred to social rather than pharmacological criteria, an error explicated in an earlier chapter. Animal husbandryman Young (1962), with long experience among the Hmong† in Thailand and Laos, has stated that "high numbers of Meo . . . become addicted to opium (about 12%)." Young here indicates that the lifetime prevalence of addiction among the Meo (or Hmong) is about 12 percent, whereas (as we shall consider further on) it is probably well above that. Nonetheless, he did arrive at a figure quite close to the crude prevalence (i.e., rate of addiction in an entire population at one point in time) which I and others have observed in Hmong populations. At the other end of the spectrum, a Thai traveler has written that "most of the Meo" are addicted (Srisavasdi 1963, p. 49). This diversity of opinions among observers suggests either a wide variability of addiction in this group or the gross unreliability of estimates not based on carefully conducted investigations. I believe that studies both in Thailand and Laos indicate that the latter interpretation fits the facts most closely.

METHODS USED IN LAOS

In practice, identification of a case of narcotic addiction in Laos was not as difficult as the various theoretical considerations described above imply. Most chronic daily opium users had initially tried to discontinue or cut down their use of narcotic drugs and had discovered, to their chagrin, that they became ill. After some futile attempts at controlling their usage, most accepted both their condition and the social identity as an addicted person. In Lao this social identity goes by the term *khon tēt dyā fēn* (literally, "person attached to opium"). As described in the previous chapter, addicts ordinarily made this self-identification and assigned this label to themselves before other community members identified them as such.

---

†These three terms, Meo, Meau, and Hmong all refer to the same people. Hmong is the word these people use to identify themselves. Meo, Miao, and Meau are Latinized forms of the Chinese term, meaning "savage" or "barbarian," which the lowland Chinese applied to these people.

There were several other factors favoring the epidemiological study of narcotic addiction in Laos. First was the relative accessibility of the subjects and the data. As indicated above, narcotic addiction did involve some social opprobrium; but it did not possess the same degree of social, moral, and legal stricture as in the United States. Consequently, one might speak with addicts about their opium use in a manner similar to discussing drinking among Americans. In addition, numerous colleagues, coworkers, neighbors, acquaintances, friends, research assistants, and associates from my previous residence, medical practice, public health work, teaching, and research in Laos assisted me with contacting subjects. These people were crucial in providing entrees to villages, neighborhoods, and opium dens. Fortunately, also, by virtue of past assistance to the Ministry of Health, I was able to obtain access to such census data and survey information on addicts as existed. Since over a period of five years I served as consultant to the Ministry of Health in Laos and to the United States Agency for International Development for the establishment of narcotic addiction treatment programs in Laos, I had time and resources to undertake such studies as described here. Lastly, the folk or emic (i.e., intracultural) use of terms like *khon tēt dyā fēn* and *neeng how yeeng* very closely resembled the pharmacomedical or etic (i.e., cross-cultural or scientific) term, "narcotic addiction." This greatly facilitated both communication and the identification of cases.

Certain factors similarly hampered the epidemiological study of addiction in Laos. A major obstacle was the paucity of census data. This impeded the efficient survey of large populations and made it extremely difficult to ascertain age- and sex-specific prevalence rates of addiction. Another problem was the limitation on technical resources and research funds. This prevented special studies such as serum or urine analysis and post-mortem examinations.

I used several means of sampling for the epidemiological study of narcotic addiction in Laos. While it would have been desirable to employ one well-known method, the absence of a widely accepted sampling method in this setting favored the use of several methods in order to assess various research techniques. The methods used consisted of the following:

1. Village network surveys. Sources of information were persons serving as entrees to the village. These included the village chief, village elders, and addicts themselves (who often knew of other addicts when no one else did). All identified addicts were counted and interviewed. Village populations were counted, in a few large

village groups or towns, or estimated on the basis of households and mean number of people per household. This permitted the calculation of crude prevalence rates (i.e., number of addicts in an entire population of men, women, and children) but not age- and sex-specific rates. This method was used in sites 1, 4, 5, and 10 on map 4.

2. House-to-house village surveys. Following initial network surveys in 4 villages (3 Hmong and 1 Khamu), a house-to-house survey was then undertaken in order to discern the validity of the network survey approach. The total population in these 4 villages was 218, with 19 addicts. No new addicts who had not been previously known from the network survey were identified during the house-to-house survey. This method was employed at sites 2 and 3 on map 4.

3. Police registration and census data from Vientiane Prefecture. Data on addicts were obtained from the Ministry of the Interior, after a law was passed in late 1971 that required that all addicts purchasing opium at dens in Vientiane Prefecture be registered with the police. Current registrants during 1971 and 1972 were compared with population data obtained during a census of Vientiane Prefecture done in 1966. This method was used at sites 6, 7, 8, and 9 on map 4.

4. Other studies. No base population data were obtained for two field surveys and two clinical studies. Despite the absence of base population numbers, the composition of these addict groups will be described and compared with the addict groups described above.

COMMUNITY SURVEYS

Six rural areas (see table 1) were surveyed for opium addicts in 1974.* In each location a research assistant well known to the local people assisted in introducing the idea of the study, informing people of its purpose, inviting collaboration, and collecting data. At each location,

*A seventh location, a collection of Akha villages consisting of a few thousand people, was to have been included in this survey. My entree was a village health worker whom I had known in 1965 to 1967. I had participated in his training, and he had welcomed the survey. When I arrived on site, the village chiefs and elders approved the survey, but each made an excuse for not participating in the survey themselves (e.g., "I have to work on my fields," "I must go visit my cousin," and so forth). Presented with this passive resistance, I would not undertake a survey in their villages since (1) this indicated a problem of some kind and (2) I would not have faith in the results of such a survey. In order to save face all around (for them as well as me), I interviewed a number of

TABLE 1   Village Survey

Map number	Ethnicity	Province	Population	Number of addicts	Crude rate per 100 people*
10	Lao (rural *tasseng*)	Xieng Khouang	4,000	72	1.8
2	Lao (circum-town *tasseng*)	Xieng Khouang	1,000	53	5.3
4	Iu Mien (Houei Aw)	Houei Khong	2,740	150	5.5
3	Khamu	Xieng Khouang	43	3	7.0
2	Hmong	Xieng Khouang	175	16	9.1
1	Iu Mien (Nam Kheung Area)	Houei Khong	400	39	9.8

As indicated in the text, age- and sex-specific rates tell us much more than do simple rates. However, accurate census data are needed to achieve these more sophisticated rates. Nonetheless, these crude rates are informative if the reader takes into account the marked difference in sex-specific rates among different ethnic groups.

contact was made with the district or village chief and the village elders. Depending on the village, either a village health worker or a prominent addict (e.g., often a village elder; in one case a village chief) or both assisted in conducting the entire survey. Often the village chief or elders had incomplete information or vague impressions regarding who might be addicted, particularly in larger villages, while health workers and addicts were usually well acquainted with local addicted persons.

Lao Villages

1. Rural area. The first area surveyed was a collection of several rural Lao villages (a *tasseng*). People in these villages had originally come from the northeast area of a plateau, the Plaine de Jarres, in Xieng Khouang province (number 10 on map 4). At the time of the survey, they had relocated to a remote area in the northeast of Vientiane province to avoid the war. In their original location as well as in their refugee location, the people predominantly lived in a collection of agricultural villages. They neither raised opium nor were active in opium commerce. They obtained opium by purchase either from Hmong tribesmen produc-

addicts who knew I was coming and wanted to be interviewed. To this day I am not sure of the problem. It may have been related to the fact that my friend and former student had recently divorced his wife, the daughter of an influential family. Or it may have been because of the traditional stand-offishness among the Akha, who have managed to maintain a political neutrality by avoiding active collaboration with outsiders. Or there may have been other issues outside of my awareness.

ing the opium or from the Lao or Chinese merchants in the provincial capital. As shown in table 1, there were 72 addicts residing among these estimated 4,000 people, a prevalence rate of 1.8 addicts per 100 people. (The estimate of 4,000 population is believed accurate within ±10 percent.) If we assume that about half of the people in such a village would be under the age of 16 and not at risk to addiction, a rate of addiction for the adult population in such a village would be 3.6 addicts per 100 adults. Since about 90 percent of all Lao addicts were male (based on data to be shown subsequently), the rate of addiction among adult men in such a village would be about 6.5 addicts per 100 people, while the rate among women would be approximately 0.7 addicts per 100 adult females, if one assumes a near-equal distribution of adult men and women in the population.

2. Circum-Town Area. The other Lao *tasseng* was once located near the provincial capital of Xieng Khouang province, called Mouang Xieng Khouang or Xieng Khouang-ville (number 5 on map 4). Its population was composed of both farmers and merchants. In its original location, it contained a number of Chinese merchants who were active in the opium commerce between the northern poppy-producing highlands and the consuming regions to the south and east. Among the estimated 1,000 people in this *tasseng*, 53 were addicted, a crude rate of 5.3 addicts per 100 people. Corrected for age, this would be approximately 10.6 addicts per 100 in the adult population. Using the ratio of 9 male addicts to 1 female addict, one would expect about 19.1 addicts per 100 adult males, and 2.1 addicts per 100 adult females (assuming equal numbers of men and women in the general population).

Iu Mien and Hmong Villages

Most opium in Laos was produced by two tribal ethnic groups, the Iu Mien (Yao) in the northwest and the Hmong (also called Meau, Miao, or Meo) in the north and northeast. Both of these groups inhabited mountaintops and mountainous ridges 1,000 meters or more above sea level. Related to one another in race, linguistics, clothing, and custom, there were yet enough differences among them that they inhabited different areas and had relatively little intermarriage. The Iu Mien in Laos, while fewer in number, had a tradition for greater political organization and more literacy (using the Chinese ideographic script).

1. Iu Mien Town (Houei Aw). Iu Mien people at Houei Aw had been forced by war out of their mountain villages further to the north. They lived close to the Mekong River in Houa Kong province (number 4

on map 5). Unable to raise opium at this low altitude, they had turned to opium commerce, buying opium from villages in northern Laos and Burma for sale through Thailand. Here lived 150 addicts among 2,740 people, a crude rate of 5.5 addicts per 100 people. Corrected for age, this would be approximately 11 addicts per 100 adults. The sex ratio of addicts among the Iu Mien is not known, so sex-specific rates cannot be estimated.

2. Iu Mien Village. Iu Mien people in the three small settlements (number 1 on map 5) were somewhat more typical of Iu Mien people in general. That is, they lived within small groups of 75 to 150 people and were involved with opium production. There were 39 addicts among an estimated 400 people, a crude prevalence rate of 9.8 addicts per 100 people. Correcting for age, there were approximately 19.6 addicts per 100 adults.

3. Hmong Village. Three Hmong villages along a mountain ridge in Xieng Khouang province were surveyed (number 2 on map 4). They were of ordinary size (50 to 75 people), remote from roads, and typical in most respects including opium production. Among these 175 people were 16 addicts, a crude prevalence rate of 9.1 addicts per 100 people. Since other data (to be presented later) indicate that the sex ratio of addicts among the Hmong is about two men to one woman, sex-specific rates would be about 24 addicts per 100 adult men and 12 addicts per 100 adult women (assuming a one-to-one ratio of males to females).

Other Ethnic Groups

Khamu people lived in northern Laos at altitudes above the Lao but below the Iu Mien and Hmong (i.e., between 500 and 1,000 meters above sea level). They supported themselves primarily by slash-and-burn agriculture, hunting, and foraging in the forest and also by doing some wage work for the Hmong, Iu Mien, and Lao. Since opium was a medium of exchange in northern Laos, they were often paid with it.

A Khamu village was located about 5 kilometers from the three Hmong villages reported above (number 3 on map 4). Among the 43 people in the village, 3 were addicted (a crude rate of 7 addicts per 100 people).

During the period from 1965 to 1967, I had the opportunity to visit and reside for a few days to a few weeks in numerous rural villages of central and southern Laos (i.e., Sedone and Attopeu provinces) where no addiction existed. These included Lao, Laven, and Nyaheun villages. In contrast, addiction was present in virtually every village of northern

Laos, including not only Lao, Khamu, Iu Mien, and Hmong villages, but also Akha (or Egaw), Lu, Tai Dam, Tai Daeng, and Tai Khow villages. Opium dens and cases of addiction were also encountered in southern riverside towns inhabited by the ethnic Lao, Chinese, and Vietnamese people. These towns included Savannakhet, Thakek, and Pakse.

Interpretation of Findings

These data show that the crude rates of addiction in the villages of Laos ranged from 0 up to about 10 addicts per 100 people. No addiction occurred in the small, remote southern villages well away from areas of opium production and commerce. In the more northern villages close to opium production and commerce (but not actually in such areas), one encountered lower rates of opium addiction, about 2 addicts per 100 people in a sample of Lao villages. Rates increased to about 5 addicts per 100 in Lao and Iu Mien towns (i.e., Mouang Xieng Khouang and Houei Aw) situated along major routes of opium commerce. Data from one small Khamu village suggested that the rate in areas closer to opium production might be slightly higher, although the numbers were too small to be definitive. In the two Hmong and Iu Mien areas where opium was currently being produced, the crude prevalence rate of addiction was the highest: between 9 and 10 addicts per 100 people.

Age-specific rates estimated for adults were about twice that of these crude rates. These approximate adult rates of addiction ranged up to 19 or 20 addicts per 100 people over the age of 15. If only adult males are considered, rates were even higher, ranging up to about 1 addict among every 8 adult females and every 4 adult males in villages where poppy was grown.

These data refer to point-prevalence rates of addiction. That is, only those people in the village who were currently addicts were counted and not those who had been addicts in the past or those who would be in the future. Since it is uncommon for addicts to spontaneously cease addiction, the former group (i.e., those who had been addicted but who were not currently addicted) was small, probably under 5 percent. It can reasonably be assumed, however, that some people would become addicted at some point in their future adult lives but were currently not addicted. This would amount to a rather considerable number of people. What then is the likelihood of an individual's becoming addicted if he or she lives through the age of maximal risk of addiction (say to age 50 or 55 years)? It is, of course, higher than the point-prevalence rates, since some of those currently alive and nonaddicted will subsequently become addicted. The actual lifetime incidence in those with sufficient longevity would be related to several factors: the age distribution of people in the population; the age at which addiction takes place; the differential death rates among both addicts and nonaddicts; and the change rate in the population (i.e., a growing, stable, or declining population). We do not have sufficient information for all of these variables from Laos. But we can conservatively estimate that the lifetime addiction rate for adults would be at least 1.5 to 1.7 times the current point-prevalence rate, given current circumstances.* The lifetime prevalence of addiction could even be as high as twice the point-prevalence rate if one were to take into account the greater mortality among addicts. Thus, the lifetime prevalence of addiction among poppy growers could be as high as 50 per 100 for men and 25 per 100 for women who live up to and through the age of maximum likelihood for addiction (i.e., ages 25 to 50).

CASE REGISTRY

Addiction in Vientiane Prefecture

In 1971 the Royal Lao government passed a law requiring that all addicts and opium dens be registered. Addicts or den proprietors not registered were liable to fine, imprisonment, or both. This law was only applied vigorously in Vientiane Prefecture. This was probably because of several factors: there was an adequate number of police; many of the dens had been established for many years and were reputable commercial enterprises; and much of the population in the commercial center of the city consisted of expatriate Asians who were more readily regulated than indigenous people. Since the law resulted in part from foreign international pressures, its enforcement in Vientiane Prefecture also had the advantage of high political visibility.

Naturally enough, most addicts avoided registration with the police if at all possible. For example, Hmong addicts who smoked opium at home obtained their supply directly from the north. They had no contact with local opium dens and thus saw no advantage to registering. They simply ignored the law, and none ever registered as addicts. This occurred despite the fact that I had interviewed scores of Hmong addicts in the prefecture. Ethnic Lao addicts lived well away from the center of Vien-

---

*This is based on the facts that there was a high death rate after age 40 and that the mean age of onset of addiction was in the late twenties (for the Hmong) and the early thirties (for other groups).

tiane in more isolated areas where dens and opium commerce were not carefully monitored. They also were underrepresented among registered addicts. Certain expatriate Asian groups (such as the Vietnamese, Chinese, and Cambodians), however, lived in the center of town. Here police surveillance was high, and addicts could not purchase opium undetected. These expatriate Asians did not have the covert supply contacts of the indigenous people (in fact, many of them did not even speak Lao). Addicts among these groups did register, if for no other reason than that they had no alternative means for obtaining opium.

These data (see table 2) obtained from the Ministry of Interior apply to addicts registered with the police in Vientiane Prefecture during the ten-month interval between November 1971 and August 1972 (numbers 6 to 9 on map 4). The census data were obtained in 1966 for Vientiane Prefecture by the Ministry of Planning. There was probably some population growth during the five-year interim between 1966 and 1971, so the base population figures may be about 10 to 15 percent low. It can also be safely assumed that the number of registered addicts was lower than the actual number, although the actual proportion is not known.

1. Lao. In absolute numbers ethnic Lao comprised the single largest group of addicts (i.e., 261 out of 933 addicts). In a population of 96,116, their addiction rate was 0.3 per 100 people. Since well in excess of this number subsequently entered treatment in Vientiane Prefecture, this number was far too low.

2. Thai. Thai citizens had the next lowest crude rate, with 0.8 addicts per 100 population (i.e., 112 addicts out of 14,270). Most Thai had come to Laos in order to work in salaried positions as business people, merchants, laborers, teachers, and servants. Like the Lao, they

TABLE 2   Addicts Registered with Police Vientiane Prefecture, 1972

ETHNICITY	Total population[a]	Registered addicts	Crude rate per 100 people
Lao	96,116	261	0.3
Thai	14,270	112	0.8
French	827	11	1.3
Tai Dam	4,955	89	1.8
Vietnamese	9,170	209	2.3
Chinese	5,916	245	4.1
Cambodian	123	6	4.9

[a]1966 census of Vientiane Prefecture.

Map 4. Laos—Research sites.* (From Whitaker, D. P., Barth, H. A., Berman, S. M., et al. Area Handbook for Laos, Washington, D. C. U. S. Govt. Printing Office, 1972.)

*Numbers on map correspond to numbers in Table 1.

were diffusely distributed throughout the prefecture and able to speak the local language. (Thai and Lao are dialects of each other.) Addicted Thai were probably able to obtain their opium in many cases without registering.

3. French. Eleven addicts were reported out of a total 827 French citizens, a crude rate of 1.3 addicts per 100 people. French people generally lived in the center of town with ready access to Chinese opium dens. Older opium addicts who lived permanently in Laos registered, but younger transient addicts did not.

4. Tai Dam. Virtually all of the Tai Dam currently residing in Vientiane had migrated from North Vietnam almost two decades previously following the fall of Dien Bien Phu. Among a population of 4,955 people, there were 89 addicts, a crude rate of 1.8 addicts per 100 people. Their district was close to numerous Chinese-run opium dens. It is likely that some did not register, as they spoke the Lao language and had ties to the poppy-producing north.

5. Vietnamese. Vietnamese had come to Laos in two waves: an early wave of civil servants assisting the French colonialists and a later wave of Vietnamese from the north after the French defeat in 1954. They were not involved in opium production and had few dens in their sector of Vientiane Prefecture (although they lived close to the Chinese sector where there were many dens). Of 9,170 people, 209 were registered addicts (2.3 addicts per 100 people). They did not have ready access to covert supplies of opium.

6. Chinese. Chinese in Laos had primarily been merchants, entrepreneurs, rice brokers, and money lenders. Some were involved in opium commerce. A large proportion of dens in Vientiane Prefecture had Chinese proprietors and were located in the Chinese part of town. Of 5,916 Chinese, 245 were registered addicts (4.1 addicts per 100 people).

7. Cambodians. The small Cambodian community consisted of boatmen, political refugees, students, musicians, and others. Traditionally, Cambodians had engaged in commerce along the Mekong River for decades, if not centuries (see M. Osborne 1975). Opium was a common commodity along this riverine route; and Cambodians in Laos, like the Chinese, had a traditional role in opium commerce. Among their 123 members, 6 were registered as addicts (a crude rate of 4.9 per 100 people).

Interpretation of Findings

Addiction rates obtained from this case registry are certainly underestimates in an absolute sense. Yet other information suggests that they are useful from a relative point of view. For example, ratio of Vietnamese to Chinese addicts seeking treatment at the National Narcotic Detoxification Center in Vientiane was usually about one to one, with a slight predominance of Chinese. As shown in table 2, the proportion of Vietnamese to Chinese registered addicts was also about one to one, with a slight predominance of Chinese. Even as underestimates, the crude rates among the Vietnamese, Chinese, and Cambodians give some indication of the relative prevalence of narcotic addiction among these three city-dwelling ethnic groups.

These data suggest that even in a quasi-metropolitan area such as Vientiane Prefecture, rates of addiction varied with ethnicity. Highest rates occurred among the two ethnic groups who had traditionally been involved in opium commerce, the Chinese and Cambodians. This finding supports the notion from the surveys conducted in rural areas and small towns that exposure to opium greatly affects rates of addiction. In addition, these two urban communities involved in opium commerce (i.e., the Chinese and Cambodians) had crude prevalence rates of 4 or 5 addicts per 100 people, only slightly less than the rates noted in the smaller rural towns of Mouang Xieng Khouang and Houei Aw, which were engaged in opium commerce.

COMPARISON OF HMONG SURVEYS

With my associates, I conducted three surveys of Hmong addicts in Laos between 1967 and 1973. The first of these was done on 32 addicts living in a valley of western Xieng Khouang province (Westermeyer 1971b). The second was done four years later on 28 Hmong addicts in Vientiane province (Westermeyer 1974c). And the third was done among 81 Hmong addicts who voluntarily presented themselves for treatment at the National Narcotic Detoxification Center in Vientiane over a 12-month period in 1972 to 1973 (Westermeyer 1977a).

Sampling Influences on Gender and Age

The number of men to every one woman in the three samples was respectively 1.9, 2.1, and 2.7. If the two field surveys are combined, their ratio of 2.0 men to every 1 woman is somewhat less than the patient ratio of 2.7 men to every 1 woman. Statistical testing (using the Chi Square method), however, did not show a statistically significant difference between the field survey and the patient survey (Westermeyer and Peng 1978; Westermeyer 1981).

The two field surveys did not differ significantly from one another for age distribution. The combined field surveys did differ from the clinical sample, showing a trend toward a somewhat younger mean age in the clinical sample (mean age 39.2 years, standard deviation 9.4) than in the two field survey samples (mean age 43.6 years, standard deviation 10.8), although there was considerable overlap in the two groups. The mean difference in the two samples of 4.3 years was statistically significant at the 0.5 Level using the Student "t" statistical test (Westermeyer 1981).

Age-Specific Rates

Time and resource limitations prevented a census of the populations from which the field surveys were obtained in 1967 and 1971. Fortunately, a Hmong geographer, Yang Dao, conducted a census of representative Hmong families in northern Laos in 1970. He stratified 3,165 Hmong people by age and sex. Using his data, we were able to gain an appreciation of the relative numbers of Hmong addicts in the various age groups.

Table 3 shows the population distribution by age (columns a and b) in the general Hmong population and is based on Yang Dao's survey. Next, the age distribution of Hmong addicts obtained from two field surveys in 1967 and 1971 are presented in column c; and the age distribu-

TABLE 3   Relative Numbers of Addicts by Age

| | | AGE-SPECIFIC RATES OF ADDICTION BASED ON | | | |
| | | COMBINED SURVEY SAMPLE[b] | | CLINICAL SAMPLE[c] | |
a. Age group	b. General population[a]	c. Number of addicts	d. Addicts per 100 people	e. Number of addicts	f. Addicts per 100 people
0–9	1,111	0	0	0	0
10–19	854	3	1.7	2	0.8
20–29	515	12	11.6	6	4.3
30–39	332	14	20.9	33	36.4
40–49	215	16	37.0	26	44.7
50–59	92	11	59.3	11	43.5
60 and up	46	4	43.0	3	23.9
	3165	60		81	

[a] Yang Dao's survey, 1970
[b] Survey sample, 1967 and 1971
[c] Clinical sample, 1972–1973

tion from a 1972–1973 clinical sample is presented in column e. The rates per 100 people in columns d and f are based on an estimated crude rate of 9.4 addicts per 100 Hmong people. Comparison of the 10-to-19 age group and the 20-to-29 age group in the two types of samples shows that the rate of addiction increases about 5 times from the teenage decade to the twenties. From the twenties to the thirties, there is again a large increase, but the factor varies in the two samples from two to several times. From the thirties to the forties the prevalence again increases, but at a slower rate of 1.2 to 1.8 times larger. From the fifties to the sixties there is actually a decrease in both samples, with the rate in the older group being only 55 percent to 73 percent of what it was in the earlier decade.

Interpretation of Findings

In these studies among the Hmong, field survey methods and clinical methods for obtaining addict samples showed fairly similar results. There was a relatively high proportion of female addicts, with about 2.0 to 2.5 men to every one woman if the data in all the samples are combined. Number of addicts per ten-year age group increased dramatically from the teens to the fifties. From life history data in the earlier chapter, one would have expected these increases during the thirties, forties, and fifties, and at least a small increase during the sixties. The precipitous drop in addiction rates from the fifties to subsequent years is actually the reverse of stereotypes about the typical opium addict.

Two possibilities may explain the gradual increase of addiction rates after the thirties and a decrease after age sixty (when a slight increase would be expected). One alternative is that there is a fairly large spontaneous recovery from addiction among addicts during their fifties. Case material and clinical samples do not support this interpretation. Another alternative is that a higher mortality rate exists among addicts after age forty or fifty than in the genearl population. Life histories and clinical experience do indicate that this is the case. After a few decades of addiction, the forty-to-sixty-year-old addict succumbs more readily to illness whereas many nonaddicted people continue into their sixties once they have survived into middle age.

Reasons for the small but significant difference in age rates between the survey and clinical samples are not clear. It could be that very old patients were not making the long sojourn down from the mountains to the treatment facility. Analysis of the data does not support this interpretation, since the major differences in the samples do not occur

119

at the elderly end of the spectrum but rather in the thirty-to-sixty-year range. Another possibility might be that, during the community surveys, we had not identified the younger addicts in the community or that younger addicts were not yet willing to identify themselves publicly. This latter explanation is also not the case, since there are relatively more addicts under age thirty in the survey sample. One would ordinarily have expected those in the clinical sample to be older than those in the survey samples, since people generally do not seek treatment for a problem such as addiction until the disorder has gone on for some years and caused sufficient problems to motivate treatment. In sum, reasons for the age difference produced by the two sampling methods are not clear.

DEMOGRAPHIC CHARACTERISTICS OF ADDICTS

Information in this section was primarily obtained from two sources: lengthy interviews conducted with forty addicts and their families during a survey (Westermeyer 1974c) and questionnaires obtained from 503 addicts at the National Narcotic Detoxification Center (NNDC) in Vientiane (Westermeyer 1977a).

Gender

As indicated earlier, males in all ethnic groups were at greater risk to opium addiction than were women. Proximity to opium production appeared to increase the proportion of female addicts, while distance decreased it. The same finding has been noted around the world with alcohol as well as with narcotic drugs (Dai 1937, Glatt and Hills 1968, Schmidt and DeLint 1969). One explanation has been that depression or neurosis in women may be an equivalent of substance abuse in men. Careful family studies by several researchers strongly support this theory (Kay 1960; Winokur and Clayton 1968; Schukit, Goodwin, and Winokur 1972, Woodruff et al. 1973, Goodwin et al. 1973).

It remains unclear whether these observed gender differences result from biobehavioral factors associated with hormonal differences or from sociocultural role differences that remain constant among all ethnic groups around the world. While the roots of the phenomenon are poorly understood, the phenomenon itself is well described. Perhaps research in animal models will help clarify this issue.

Age

Narcotic addiction in Asia generally begins early in adult life. Of 503 Asian addicts treated at NNDC, 83 percent were first addicted during their twenties, thirties, or forties. Another 7 percent were addicted before the age of twenty, and 10 percent were addicted at age fifty or afterward. It was more typical to become addicted during adolescence (when 7 percent were first addicted) than at age sixty or afterward (when only 2 percent were first addicted). These findings were essentially the same as those outlined in the earlier community survey. In that group, 92 percent first became addicted during their twenties, thirties, or forties. Eight percent were addicted before the age of twenty, and none became addicted at age fifty or afterward.

Illicit narcotic addiction in the Western world over the last few decades usually begins in the teenage years and the twenties, rarely later (Dai 1937, Chien et al. 1964, Vaillant 1973). This was not so when narcotic drugs were more readily available and widely used (Musto 1973). Alcoholism in the Western world similarly tends to begin in the twenties, thirties, and forties, with less frequent onset either before or after these ages. Narcotic addiction in Laos has demographic parallels with addiction as it formerly existed in the West and with alcoholism as it exists today in the West.

Ethnicity

Rather marked differences in addiction rates were noted among various ethnic groups in Laos, and numerous religious backgrounds were encountered among the addicts. Ethnic Lao addicts professed Theravada (Lower Vehicle) Buddhism. Tribal people were predominantly animistic, though a small percentage were Christian. The Chinese and Vietnamese ascribed variously to Upper Vehicle Buddhism, Confucianism, and Taoism. The Thai were mostly Theravada Buddhists, with a few Moslems among them. Indo-Pakistani addicts were Hindu and Moslem. No one religion appeared to either favor or resist addiction. Animist tribal groups in the south had virtually no addiction, while animist groups in the north had the highest rates. Buddhist Lao in the south had little addiction, while Buddhist Lao in the north and expatriate Thai, Vietnamese, and Chinese Buddhists had high rates. These findings indicate that ethnicity and religion per se were not primary determinants in opium addiction in Laos. Rather it was the ethnic or religious group's proximity to opium production and commerce that most influenced addiction rates.

Family and Environmental Influences

Among the 40 opium addicts who were interviewed (most of whom were Hmong), one or both parents were addicted in 23 cases (58 percent of the total). Among these 23 cases, both parents were addicted in 7 cases, the father only in 15 cases, and the mother only in 1 case. Out of a possible 80 parents, 30 of them (or 37.5 percent) were addicted. This rate may not be too much higher than would be anticipated from the lifetime prevalence of addiction in groups with high exposure to opium.

Perhaps a stronger indication of genetic/childhood influence in the genesis of addiction was the prevalence of addiction among siblings. Only 4 of the 17 addicts without an addicted parent had an addicted sibling (i.e., 24 percent). Among the remaining 24 people with an addicted parent, 12 had an addicted sibling (i.e., 52 percent).

Among the seventeen cases in which neither parent was addicted, four of the subjects were women who were introduced to opium smoking by their addicted husbands. Another three were men whose first contact with opium smoking in the family was via their fathers-in-law. These findings implicate the role of environmental family factors during adulthood in the genesis of addiction even when genetic or childhood influences were absent.

Only six addicts out of the forty (i.e., 15 percent) had no nuclear family members or relatives-by-marriage who were as yet not addicted to opium. Among these subjects, other relatives or close friends generally served as entrees or role models for addictive opium use.

Recent Life Change

Over the last decade numerous studies have shown that momentous life change often occurs in the year or two prior to the onset of medical disorders (such as diabetes or heart disease), accidents, major infectious diseases, and psychiatric disorders (Rahe et al. 1964, Holmes and Rahe 1967, Birley and Brown 1970). In order to assess the role of life change in the forty nonpatient subjects, we asked each of them about his or her life in the year previous to the onset of addiction. Their family members and friends also provided information regarding events of the year preceding addiction.

Among the 39 subjects for whom an adequate history could be obtained, all reported major life changes in the year previous to their becoming addicted. Changes included the following: onset of chronic pain, cough, or diarrhea usually associated with some work disability (33 cases); pregnancy (5); refugee movement (3); death of a child and/or husband (2); leg amputation from land mine (2); job promotion, election to *tasseng* office (head of several villages), marriage, and divorce (1 each).

I have neither a group of nonaddicts for comparison nor was a rating scale used to assess life change. Since many of the life change problems reported consisted of pain, diarrhea, or cough, the use of opium as a medication would not be unexpected. Thus, these data do not conclusively prove the argument. Nonetheless, these case histories suggested that life change or stress—rather than hedonistic pursuit of pleasure alone—might play some role in the onset of addiction.

COMMENT

1. Village rates of addiction are proportionate to their access to opium production and commerce (i.e., high access, high addiction rates). Crude rates as high as 10 percent are found in villages that produce opium; 4 to 5 percent in commercial centers where opium is bought, sold, and transshipped; 1 or 2 percent in villages of northern Laos near but without direct access to opium; and 0 percent in remote villages of southern Laos well away from opium production and commerce.

2. Ethnicity apparently affects the rate of addiction through its influence on access to opium, rather than through sociocultural factors per se. For example, a Hmong village and a Yao village, both producing opium, had about the same crude rate of addiction. Similarly, urban Cambodians and Chinese, a Lao *tasseng*, and a small Yao town—all in areas of opium commerce—had similar crude rates of narcotic addiction (about 4 to 5 percent).

VII

Subgroups Among Addicts

WHY STUDY SUBGROUPS?

There are addicts and addicts. To be sure, speaking of the average or typical addict can be useful as a starting point. But not all addicts in Laos were married farmers in their twenties to their fifties who had smoked opium two or three times a day over the last ten or fifteen years. There were also women, children and adolescents, the elderly, light users and heavy users, members of various ethnic groups, those recently and chronically addicted. To understand addiction in Laos, it is as important to know something of these special groups as to know the modal addict.

It has long been said in the alcohol and drug abuse field that substance abusing people are so diverse that it is a waste of time to examine their differences. For those accustomed to studying events that have little variance, such as the social economy of the honeybee or the sex life of the aardvark, there is more than a grain of truth in that statement. But for those who study or provide medical care for people with migraine headaches, coronary artery disease, or skin cancer, addiction is not such a variant phenomenon.

I suggest that we should limit our study neither to the typical or modal addict nor to individual addicts as though each were a universe of one. Rather we should study both. (The last few chapters are an example of the "modal" approach; the case vignettes scattered throughout this book are an example of the latter.) And as an intermediate approach between these two extremes we should study small groups of individuals unlike the typical addict. A combination of approaches will give us some bearings in this complex field, much like examining a tissue specimen under low, medium, and high power magnification.

The subgroups presented here are not exhaustive by any means. Scores of other categories come readily to mind. But these are the first choices made by most epidemiologists and medical scientists approaching a clinical problem.

GENDER

Gender Ratio

Review of the literature on addiction in Asia demonstrates that the sampling method influences the gender ratio. Relatively high rates of women were found among addicts in psychiatric hospitals; and relatively more men were in treatment programs for addicts, case registers, and prisons (Westermeyer 1980). Community surveys produce intermediate ratios, suggesting that they may reflect the most likely situation. So if gender ratios are to be compared among populations, they should be obtained by the same sampling method.

Gender ratios obtained at the Narcotic Treatment Center in Laos were correlated with the community's relationship to opium as follows:

Ethnicity	Role of community	Opium availability	Number of patients		Ratio of men to each woman
			Men	Women	
Hmong	Poppy farmers	High	59	22	2.7
Other tribal people*	Poppy farmers, Opium commerce	High to medium	22	3	7.3
Lao	Opium commerce, Consumers	Inter-mediate to low	302	19	15.9
Expatriate Asians†	Opium commerce, Consumers	Inter-mediate to low	73	3	24.3

*Includes Tai Dam, Khamu, Iu Mien (several people from each group)
†Includes 31 Thai, 23 Vietnamese, 20 Chinese, 1 Indian, and 1 Pakistani.

Field observations suggested that access of women to opium was greater in communities where poppy was grown (Westermeyer and Peng 1978). Women participated in the growing and harvesting of the poppy. Opium was stored in the home and sometimes used in lieu of money for barter. Many women had spouses, friends, or relatives who used opium.

Women had considerably less access to opium in commercial and consuming communities. Opium passed through the hands of middlemen who were rarely women. Exposure among townfolk often occurred first at an opium den, which few nonaddicted women ever visited. Since the crude prevalence in the community at large was lower, women had fewer addicted kith and kin.

Demographic and Drug Use Characteristics

Most addicted women at the Narcotic Detoxification Center were homemakers. There was a trend for slightly more women than men to be divorced ($P < .06$), but the numbers were small. Over 75 percent of both male and female addicts were married and living with nuclear family members.

There were several differences in drug use characteristics between male and female addicts at the Narcotic Detoxification Center. Both Hmong and Lao men tended to use more opium per day than Hmong and Lao women ($P < .05$ for the Hmong; $P < .005$ for the Lao). Rarely was women's consumption of opium worth more than $1.50 per day, whereas about a third of the men spent over this amount. This was probably related to the greater body weight of the men, since other variables (e.g., mode of use, physiological withdrawal as assessed by methadone dose) did not account for it. Men had a somewhat greater tendency to use opium in dens ($P < .07$), and women were more apt to use it within their families ($P < .01$). But there were no differences in duration of use prior to addiction, age at addiction, duration of addiction, previous withdrawal, number of doses per day, mode of use, initial methadone dose for detoxification, or readmission to treatment within one year. Very few women were addicted to heroin as compared to men (this topic is covered more fully in a subsequent chapter).

Women With an Addicted Spouse

As a rule men in Laos first tried opium in the company of other men. Conversely, women were often induced to try opium by a man, usually a husband. While most addicted men did not have an addicted spouse, the opposite was true for most addicted women. Commonly, the wife had opposed her husband's addiction and resisted his insistence that she try it. Frustrated, angry, and depressed at her husband's addiction, she sometimes joined in smoking with him and became addicted.

Of forty-seven women admitted to the National Detoxification Center, forty-six gave their occupation as *mē heuan* or housewife (literally "mother of the house"). One divorced woman employed on a vegetable farm near Vientiane reported her occupation as farming. Most were rural women, although several came from larger Mekong River towns. None was a bar girl or prostitute. All the women had been or were still married, whereas 6 percent of the male addicts in the sample were single.

Among the hundreds of female addicts I encountered in Laos over a decade, I never met one who was single. In questioning informants about single female addicts, I did obtain a secondhand report of one case. Both her parents were addicted, and she became addicted early in her teenage years. She remained single into her adult years. "No one would marry an addicted woman," my informants told me. Nonetheless I interviewed a few divorced or widowed female addicts who did subsequently remarry—but always to addicted men.

An addicted husband could obstruct treatment for the addicted wife in several ways. He might refuse to go for treatment himself or threaten to leave his wife if she left for treatment. During a follow-up study, we found that recovering female addicts were often seduced into readdiction by their addicted husbands, who would smoke in their presence and offer them the pipe.

Addiction, Marriage, and Divorce. Most addicted women had an addicted husband. The case of Nee Fua, a fifty-year-old Hmong woman, was typical. The wife of a village chief, she had had a total of twelve children, nine of whom were still living. Her husband had been addicted for many years, and her father and older brother were also opium addicts. While pregnant with her last child, she came down with severe abdominal pain and bloody diarrhea. Healing rituals and herbal medication did not stop the pain and diarrhea, and her weight and strength began ebbing away. It appeared she might die. As a last resort, with the approval of her family, she began to smoke opium twice a day. She recovered from the diarrhea and went on to have the baby. Despite her recovery, she continued to use opium daily with her husband over the ensuing eight years before seeking treatment at the Narcotic Detoxification Center.

Few women ever became addicted if their husbands did not smoke opium. In cases where the husband was not addicted, the outcome was generally like that of Vang Nia, a fifty-five-year-old Hmong woman separated from her husband. Her father had been an opium addict, but her husband was not. Her addiction had begun at the age of thirty, soon after the death of her last-born infant. Around that time she began to have chronic lower abdominal pain. Six traditional healers treated her at great expense to the family but without success. In order to obtain relief from her pain, she began to smoke opium, first once and then twice a day. Her husband tolerated her addiction for several years, but then he took a second and younger wife. While her husband never forced her out of the home, she and her husband became increasingly estranged from one another. Eventually Vang Nia left home and spent her time moving around and living with her several grown children during different times in the year.

A few women became addicted following divorce, as in the case of Yua Na, a Hmong woman. Like Vang Nia, her father had been an addict. She had been married to a farmer who was not addicted. Together they had four children. Marital dissension had led to their getting divorced when she was thirty-three. After this time she recalls becoming sick, although the symptoms were quite vague and more suggestive of depression or psychophysiologic disorder than of infectious disease. Approximately a year following her divorce, some relatives with whom she was celebrating the New Year invited her to join them in smoking opium. She was soon addicted, and remained addicted over the subsequent twenty-one years.

AGE

Childhood and Teenage Onset of Addiction

While I never encountered a child addict in Laos, I interviewed or treated several addicts who had started using opium or had been addicted during childhood. All had at least one addicted parent, and both parents were usually addicted. Most stole opium from their parents or from poppy fields, but a few were given opium or were allowed to take it on their own. One twelve-year-old Hmong addict was treated at the National Detoxification Center in 1973.

Occasionally a teenaged addict was encountered during a survey, in the general hospital setting, or in treatment for addiction. This was not common however. Among a sample of 559 addicts seeking treatment at the Narcotic Detoxification Center, only five were aged fifteen to eighteen. As with childhood-onset addicts, they usually had addicted parents.

The relatively small number of adolescent addicts is of interest, given the relatively high number of young substance abusers in some other societies. It may relate in part to the fact that traditionally adolescence was not a distinct lifetime experience in Laos. Villagers went rapidly from childhood to adulthood, with little time in between. This situation had begun to change rapidly during the early 1970s with increasing education, especially in Vientiane where there were many schools. Young literate men and, infrequently, young women began to abuse beer, whiskey, cannabis, and heroin. It is of interest to note that they avoided the traditional rice wine (*lao hai*) and opium. Addiction among children remained a rare event, however.

Younger Versus Older Addicts

Forty-six addicts in their thirties or younger were matched with 46 addicts in their fifties or older. All were patients at the Narcotic Detoxification Center. They were matched for sex (41 male pairs, 5 female pairs), ethnicity (29 Lao, 9 Hmong, 8 other), and type of drug (44 pairs on opium, 2 on heroin).

On the average the older people had been addicted 10.2 years longer than had the younger ones (14.5 vs. 4.3 years, $P < .000$). There were more youthful soldiers and more older farmers. No significant differences were found regarding doses per day, amount spent per day on drugs, duration of preaddictive use, mode of use, detoxification dose of methadone, readmission, marital status, or employment status.

Longevity, Duration, and Dose

Younger addicts tended to have relatively recent addiction, while older addicts tended to have been addicted for a long time. There was some overlap in both directions, with some addicts in their twenties having been addicted for over a decade and a few addicts over the age of sixty having been addicted for less than five years. These few exceptions went against the general rule, however.

It was unusual even for elderly addicts to have been addicted for more than three decades. Only 6 percent of those admitted to the Narcotic Detoxification Center had been addicted for over thirty years, regardless of age. These data suggest that opium addicts in Asia are not likely to survive beyond thirty years of addiction even if they have an early onset of addiction.

The number of doses taken per day tended to change with age. There was a particularly notable increase from the teens up to the thirties, a subsequent slight decrease and leveling off during the forties and fifties, and a further decrease into the sixties, seventies, and eighties. Cost per day of narcotic drugs showed a similar trend, with the greatest amounts being spent by younger addicts in their twenties and thirties and gradually decreasing amounts being spent into the older ages. Opium smoking was most prevalent earlier during addiction, with opium eating becoming progressively more common in later years. Beyond the age of sixty, opium eating was more prevalent than opium smoking. As noted in an earlier chapter, there was a trend for prevalence rates of addiction to increase rapidly from the teens to thirties, to level off during the thirties to fifties, and to decrease during the sixties.

ETHNICITY

Land of Opportunity

Hughes and Crawford (1974) have pointed out the advantage of studying opiate epidemiology in high-use communities. Laos presented additional riches in the cultural realm. Scores of tribal groups inhabited the uplands, such as those mentioned in previous chapters (e.g., Lu, Tai Dam, Khamu, Dya Heun, Laven). Larger groups of Chinese, Vietnamese, and Thai together with smaller numbers of Cambodians, Burmese, Indians, and Pakistanis lived in towns. Caucasians from Europe, North America, and Australia came to Laos as volunteers, government employees, entrepreneurs, and tourists.

Ecologic setting vis-à-vis opium production and use also varied widely. As mentioned previously, some ethnic groups produced opium, some conducted opium commerce, some did neither but had access to opium for consumption, others did not even have ready access to it. And at times different communities among a specific ethnic group might occupy more than one of these ecological niches in relation to opium.

Culture and Addiction

There were amazingly few differences among addicts from different cultures. One difference mentioned above, gender ratio, appeared more related to opium availability than to culture per se. Another characteristic, age at onset of addiction, was probably related to different access among various ethnic groups rather than to culture per se. Opium producers such as the Hmong tended to become addicted several years earlier on the average than did people from commercial or consuming communities (Westermeyer 1977a). There was also a strong tendency for the opium-producing Hmong to become addicted more rapidly after beginning opium use as compared to other peoples. Neither of these latter two characteristics varied among several other nonproducing ethnic groups, however. It seems likely that ready access to opium rather than ethnic factors accounted for these observations.

Daily expenditures on opium differed considerably among various ethnic groups. Expatriate Asians and Caucasians spent the most, the Hmong were intermediate, and the Lao spent the least on their daily opium supply. The Lao were similarly more apt to consume their opium by eating, unlike the former groups, who generally smoked their opium. These differences were probably due to economic factors. Lao people had the smallest incomes and had to purchase their opium at retail prices, usually from the Hmong. The Hmong themselves obtained their opium at wholesale prices, either by raising it themselves or purchasing it close to its source from a relative or neighbor. Expatriate Asians, such as merchants, artisans, and teachers, had the highest incomes and paid retail prices for opium. These differences, then, were tied to economics and to mode of administration rather than to cultural values or attitudes.

Similarities in addiction among these different cultures, despite their disparate geographic and economic milieu, were numerous. These included the number of times opium was used per day, duration of addiction before seeking treatment, detoxification dose of methadone, and readmission for readdiction (Westermeyer 1977a and 1978a).

SOCIOECONOMIC STATUS

Most addicts encountered in Laos were rural farmers or middle class town people (e.g., soldiers, civil servants, merchants, artisans). This was true no matter how the subjects were contacted (through a house-to-house survey or an addict-network survey) or where they were contacted (general hospital, addiction treatment facility, or opium den).

There were some lower class addicts, if we define lower class as beggars and unskilled day laborers without stable employment, but these comprised less than 1 percent in most samples. They were most apt to be found in opium dens: three out of thirty-five addicts in a den survey were assigned to this category (Westermeyer 1974b). Of these three, one

Lao man had been a beggar during all of his adult years (he was mentally ill). The other two had gradually alienated their families in association with their chronic addiction.

Politically elite and wealthy people also became addicted. One person interviewed during a neighborhood survey was a sister and household member of a former prime minister. Among the first 1,000 people treated at the National Narcotic Center were several people from families in which members were governmental, commercial, or professional leaders. A prominent member of the king's household was a publicly known addict.

GEOGRAPHIC CORRELATES

The Western world conceives of addiction as an urban phenomenon. Not so in Laos. As shown earlier, the highest prevalence, most rapid onset of addiction, earliest age at addiction, and highest percentage of female addicts occurred among rural peoples who raised opium. At the other end of the spectrum, rural populations in southern Laos had sometimes not even heard of opium. Other rural groups, such as Lao villages in the north, had relatively low rates of addiction even though they could see the poppy-strewn mountains on a clear day.

In towns ethnic boundaries sometimes served the same function as geographic distance. Most Vietnamese in Vientiane lived within a kilometer of a Chinese opium den; that is, no farther than a fifteen-minute stroll over to the morning market where food and clothing were purchased. But Vietnamese people did not ordinarily frequent Chinese opium dens any more than they went to Chinese movie theaters or restaurants. Similarly, the Chinese did not repair to Vietnamese night clubs or bars. In this sense, ethnic affiliation really did influence addiction rates, as was shown in the chapter on epidemiology—but here again, it was by influencing access to drugs rather than by cultural factors per se. (Recall from the previous chapter that crude addiction prevalence was 4.1 percent among the Chinese and 2.3 percent among the Vietnamese in Vientiane. Soon after assuming control of South Vietnam, the Vietnamese government estimated that the crude prevalence of addiction in Saigon was 5 percent, suggesting that Vietnamese rates also increase when their communities become involved with opium commerce.)

Sterile quantitative data showed few differences in the course of opiate addiction among countryside and urban dwellers. The differences became much more apparent, however, if one had the opportunity to provide medical care for addicts from both regions or could talk with those medical workers who did so. By comparison, countryside addicts tended to be relatively more flexible, pleasant, stoic, appreciative, and cooperative with each other and with staff members. Those from Vientiane and the larger towns were relatively more demanding, complaining, manipulative, individualistic, negativistic, rigid, and noncompliant. To be sure, there were always exceptions, but they were notable by their scarcity.

COMMENT

1. The ratio of male to female addicts in Laos varied widely in different groups, from as low as 2 to 1, to as high as 20 or 25 to 1. Poppy growers had relatively more female addicts.

2. In most respects male and female addicts in Laos resembled each other with regard to their narcotic use and the course of their addiction. Women were more apt to have been married, to have an addicted spouse, to use less opium per day, and to use opiates at home rather than at a den. Pharmacological factors and the addictive course predominated among the similarities, whereas gender-related biological and social factors (e.g., size, occupation) probably accounted for the differences.

3. As elsewhere in the world, substance abuse in Laos occurred predominantly among young and middle-aged adults. Addicted children and adolescents usually came from families with one or both parents addicted. The young and the old tended to use less of the drug; young adults used the most. Opium eating increased past middle age.

4. Most features of opium addiction were remarkably constant across ethnic groups. One notable difference was the amount of money spent per day on drugs. Those with the lowest income spent the least on drugs; opium eating prevailed among them. Those with the highest incomes spent the most for drugs; they preferred opium smoking.

5. Ethnic boundaries sometimes served the same function as geographic distance in reducing opiate addiction. Despite their proximity to Chinese opium dens in Vientiane, the Vietnamese maintained a considerably lower prevalence of addiction.

VIII

Opium Dens: Evil or Asset?

A Vientiane Den. In Vientiane, the hot, sleepy capitol of Laos, there are more than sixty licensed opium dens, and many more unlicensed back rooms where the drug can be used. The streets of the city are patrolled jointly by soldiers of the Pathet Lao and the Royal Lao Government, part of the agreements of the 1973 Paris Peace Accords. Neither side makes any serious effort to interfere with the longstanding acceptance of opium use in the culture.

In a little wooden house, on a side street two blocks from the center of town, and only a little farther from the American Embassy, is one of these dens. The house is set back twenty feet from the road, and banana trees grow in a circle around a well in the front yard.

The front door is open so that passersby can easily see the opium smokers through the blue haze exuding from the interior. Inside are a dozen or so people sitting or lying on long wooden pallets that run along both sides of the 12 x 15 foot room. The ceiling is low, and the room is dark, even in the middle of the day.

Although the patrons are almost all Laotian, these dens are occasionally frequented by Caucasians, particularly "world travelers" from the European counterculture; so there is an acceptance of outsiders.

The opium pipes are ornate and valuable. They are owned by the house and rented for the duration of a person's stay. They consist of a long thin tube, about two feet long and an inch thick; and they may be made of bamboo, wood, or even carved ivory. A few inches from one end there is a hollow, closed clay bowl with a small hole in the top.

OPIUM DENS: EVIL OR ASSET?

Opium, black and sticky like tar, is bought in small portions known as *kham* or *ngoi*. They resemble small black peas. The cost is low: at the present highly favorable exchange rate about 20¢ per *kham*.

Choosing a place on the pallet among the other smokers, one lies full length on one's side, resting one's head on a small movable wooden pillow. One of the attendants then begins to prepare the opium for use.

The attendant heats the clay bowl over a flame from a little spirit lamp and uses a small wire to scrape away the accumulated debris left from previously smoked opium, making sure that the small hole in the top of the bowl is open. With the same instrument, the attendant breaks off a small piece of opium and transfers it so that it is adjacent to but not occluding the hole at the top. Passing the end of the pipe to the smoker, he turns the pipe so that the bowl faces down. The flame plays directly on the opium causing it to soften and bubble in the heat.

Meanwhile, the smoker is inhaling deeply, drawing in the smoke of the boiling opium. The smoke is strong and acrid and can cause the unaccustomed smoker to cough if he inhales. After a few puffs, the opium turns to a dry crust and the attendant must break off another small piece from the deposit on the side of the bowl.

It takes about twenty minutes to use up the entire *ngoi*. During this time the smoker has rested and relaxed, having done nothing but draw in the smoke. Having a second person prepare the pipe is considered essential, so that the smoker can devote his total attention to the pleasure of the drug without becoming distracted by the mechanics of handling the pipe.

Between pipes, many smokers will drink hot tea served in an old glass. The reason for drinking the tea is not clear. Some argue that it potentiates the effect of the opium, adding to the mellow sensation of the drug. Others claim that its main effect is in settling the stomach and eliminating the nausea that opium often causes, particularly for the uninitiated.

Peter Bourne, M.D., M.A.
Drugs and Drug Abuse Education Newsletter
6 (4) :5–7, 1975

Peter Bourne and I together visited the den he described above. Owned by an ethnic Chinese man, it was one of the oldest, largest, and best-run dens in Vientiane. A picture from the outside, with the well in front described by Dr. Bourne, is shown in plate 4. Chinese, Lao, and Hmong frequented it.

Yi Fu's Den. On entering Yi Fu's den, I was always given a comfortable seat in an auspicious place in the room. After an exchange of the usual pleasantries, tea was brought out and served respectfully. On the first visit, Yi Fu began slowly and gently discussing my past work in Laos, our mutual acquaintances, and—eventually—my reasons for wanting to learn about opium addiction and dens. Other attendants in the den gradually began to intersperse questions and then comments. They conducted a sensitive yet searching interview, virtually an investigation of me and my purposes.

After a time it became evident that Yi Fu and his clientele were ready for my questions. These were answered with considerable thought and attention to accuracy, often with lovely prose and creative analogies. My addict-teachers verbally supported each other at times, at other times disagreeing and offering their own footnotes to one another's viewpoints. The den habitués took considerable pleasure in instructing me, making sure that I understood precisely and completely.

Once, early in this work, one of my nonaddict entrees made a critical statement about addicts. Based on his own stereotypes, he disparaged their honesty. Silence fell like a guillotine for some moments. Only after I quietly demurred from my companion's gauche remark, in a stage whisper loud enough for all in the room to hear, did the discussion continue actively.

Yi Fu, a forty-eight-year-old man, had emigrated from southern China in his youth. This den was home for Yi Fu, his Lao wife, and their eight children. All of the children attended school and were always nicely dressed and well behaved. The neatly kept home consisted of three rooms with a cement floor. (The latter was a status symbol in this district, most homes having tamped earthen floors.) Customers consumed their opium—and noodle soup, if they wished to purchase it—in the front room. Smoking apparatus and opium were kept in the middle room, the family's common sleeping room. A kitchen in back comprised the third room. Compared to other homes in the vicinity, their residence was above average in space, housekeeping, and accouterments.

This den was frequented by a regular group of middle-class people, mostly Lao government workers and Chinese merchants. All of them male, they came to the den only at midday and in the late afternoon. Customers were not found there at other times.

Formerly, Yi Fu had been a merchant. Twenty-one years ago he had become addicted during a severe respiratory illness. Progression of his illness (diagnosed at a medical facility as tuberculosis) led relentlessly to increasing weight loss, weakness, and disability. Eventually Yi Fu became housebound. At that point he established a den in his home. Sale of opium and noodle soup (prepared by his wife) had supported the family in reasonable style over the past several years.

GAINING AN ENTREE

Make no mistake: opium dens had a bad reputation in Laos. Not only Westerners but Asians, also, did not think well of opium dens. Even many opium addicts in Laos would not visit a den. Some might go to a den to purchase opium but would not stay to smoke there.

My first visits to an opium den occurred in 1966 at a town in northern Laos. At first these were made out of curiosity, since some of my addicted patients visited there. Later, in the period from 1971 to 1975, I made visits to several opium dens located in Vientiane. Initial curiosity was replaced by a specific intent: to learn who frequented dens and for what apparent reasons and to observe the usual behavior and interactions that transpired there. There was never pressure for me to use or purchase opium in any of the dens.

It was necessary to approach a den with the same degree of circumspection, consideration, and respect with which one approached an addict. First, the den proprietor must be contacted through a go-between. The proprietor wanted to know the identity of the stranger wishing admission, the person's background, the reasons for wanting to visit the den, and what the individual planned to do there. Just as the addict was host to the interviewer during an interview, the proprietor was host to the visitor during a den visit. Barging into an opium den uninvited would be rude. Dens were seldom public places. They were usually private homes where opium smokers gathered to purchase opium, smoke and converse together. A fairly constant clientele—each person known to the others—tended to use any given den.

Might not one run the risk of opium addiction by frequenting a den and using opium? No doubt about it. I have known a journalist, a social scientist, a former Peace Corps worker, and a refugee worker, all of whom became addicted following "curiosity visits" to the dens of Malaysia, Thailand, and Laos. By contrast, of the hundreds of Laotian addicts whom I have encountered, not one was first introduced to opium in a den.

COMMUNITY SIZE

In the villages and towns of Laos presence of opium dens could be readily ascertained, since their existence was common knowledge. After the passage of an antiopium law in 1971, it was even possible to obtain information on registered dens from the police in Vientiane.

During seven visits to Laos from 1965 to 1975, I became acquainted with 28 different rural villages and small towns with under 2,000 people. The smallest of these was a Khamu village containing 45 people. The largest was a Lao district composed of 4 separate subvillages and containing approximately 4000 people. The 28 sites included the following communities (village groups or small towns): 8 Lao, 8 Lao Theung (with ethnic Nya Heun, Khamu, Lu, Laven, and Tai Dam), 7 Hmong, 4 Iu Mien, and 1 Akha. In none of these locations was there an opium den. A conservative estimate of the population in these 28 locations would be approximately 20,000 people.

For several months during 1965 to 1967, I worked in Sam Thong, a small town in southern Xieng Khouang province. During that time Sam Thong burgeoned from an oversized Hmong village of several hundred people to a small town of some 4,000 people as refugees from northeastern Laos fled the war. When Sam Thong reached about 4,000 people, a single opium den was established. (Perhaps symbolically, the den was about halfway between the hospital and the center of the market, a total distance of some 500 yards.) A town similar to Sam Thong, called Ban Son, later underwent a similar, remarkable growth, several years after Sam Thong. Located in northern Vientiane province, it was also a multiethnic town containing approximately 10,000 people. Within its extensive boundaries were three dens.

In 1974, three years after the antiopium law of 1971, the police in Vientiane reported that the number of registered opium dens was remaining fairly stable at eighty. (Each year a few dens would close, while a few new ones would register.) The police also estimated that there were another 115 dens, mostly small or recently established, that were not registered. A 1967 census of Vientiane revealed a population of about

PLATE 1.   A Hmong village, San Thong, Xieng Khouang province, 1965.

PLATE 2

PLATE 3

PLATE 4

PLATE 2.   Author in a poppy field, early dry season, Thailand, 1979.

PLATE 3.   Opium smoking equipment, Vientiane opium den, 1973.

PLATE 4.   Opium den described by Peter Bourne in opium den chapter, 1975.
(Photo by Edward Kaufman, M.D.)

PLATE 5

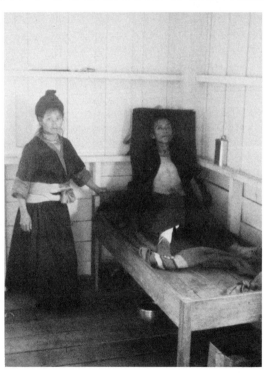

PLATE 6

PLATE 7

PLATE 5. Sam Thong Hospital, 1965.

PLATE 6. Hospitalized Hmong addict and wife—my patient Sam Thong Hospital, 1966.

PLATE 7. Author and Dr. Charles (Jigs) Weldon, Bangkok, 1982.

PLATE 8

PLATE 8. Recovering addict working in garden, National Narcotic Detox-ification Center, Vientiane, 1974.

PLATE 9. Dr. Soudaly, auto mechanic, and recovering addicts, 1973.

PLATE 10. Dr. Soudaly, machinist, and recovering addict, 1973.

PLATE 9

PLATE 10

PLATE 11. Nya-Heun girl—the tobacco growers, Laos, 1966.

PLATE 12. Nya-Heun man—the tobacco farmers, Laos, 1966.

128,000. Thus the concentration of dens was approximately one den for every 600 to 700 persons.

If one were to use the standard of one den per each 600 persons, many of the larger villages and small towns would theoretically have at least one den. Towns such as Sam Thong would have several. Ban Son and Long Cheng would have a score. Conversely, if towns and cities functioned as did the villages, there would be no dens. But dens existed in any town of 4,000 or 5,000 in Laos. Almost every square kilometer of Na Hai Deo, Nai Mouang, and Phonsaat districts of Vientiane Prefecture had a den or two. Smaller operations might sell to only ten or twelve addicts, while registered dens sold to as many as forty or fifty addicts in a day.

Lee Ching's Den. A fifty-one-year-old Chinese immigrant from Yunnan province, Lee Ching had been a baker and a merchant prior to becoming an addict. His den consisted of a single large room with eight cot-like beds. Off to one side was a fire used for preparing meals. Like most ground-level homes in the area, the floor consisted of tamped dirt. Its wooden walls contained no windows, so the dim light combined with the lack of housekeeping lent a dingy aspect to the place.

Customers at Lee Ching's had marginal economic resources. For example, one Chinese addict begged and worked at odd jobs; a tribal Hmong veteran missing a leg lived on a government pension; the few Lao using the facility were common laborers. Four addicted women, all Hmong, regularly visited the den. Of the four, three were widowed and one was divorced. One of the women was living in a common-law relationship with an addicted Lao carpenter.

Lee Ching's place was crowded with regular clients in the latter half of the day as single, divorced, or widowed workers drifted in from the day's labors. Among the two or three men deep in opium slumber was usually Lee Ching. Most of his profits disappeared in the smoke of his pipe.

DEN CLIENTELE

Forty addicts were surveyed regarding their den usage. Ten were contacted in opium dens; the remainder were contacted elsewhere (i.e., twenty in their homes and ten in other public places). Three of the forty addicts were excluded from the data because they were den proprietors. They smoked in what was simultaneously their home and a den. Two other addicts were excluded because they did not provide sufficient information about the locus of their opium consumption to allow a categorization. This left thirty-five addicts.

This method for obtaining the data was biased, since twenty addicts were contacted at home and seven were contacted in dens. Still, the results were interesting. Five addicts used opium only in the den, while twenty-three took opium only at home. Seven addicts consumed opium both in dens and at home.

The five "den-only" users were unskilled workers or peasants who were single or divorced. They included a Lao beggar, a young amputee Hmong veteran, a Chinese beggar, and a divorced Hmong woman whose children were in a local orphanage. The one man in this group with a stable heterosexual relationship was the Lao carpenter, a refugee from northern Laos who was mentioned earlier. The den played a primary role in the lives of these people. They took meals there, had their social affiliations there, and sometimes even stayed there at night.

The twenty-three "home-only" users all had families, jobs, and homes of their own. They were mostly farmers.

The 7 addicts using "den and home" included artisans, peasants, and civil service employees. More than half of this small group had no spouse (three women and one man were widowed). For them the den was a social or recreational place, but they slept and took most of their meals at home. They also had other affiliations at home, unlike the "den-only" addicts.

In some instances the addict's locus of opium usage had previously been different. Two of the five "den-only" users had smoked opium mostly at home earlier in their opium-using careers. As young men, several of the "home-only" users had frequented dens at one time or another.

Bluey Mua's Den. Least impressive of the dens in Na Hai Deo district, Bluey Mua's den consisted of a large shed appended to a small Hmong-type wooden home. Bamboo matting served as walls, a tin roof provided shelter from rain and sun, and the floor was tamped earth. Three beds and two double bunks comprised the meager furnishings of the room. Mobile vendors sold food just outside the den at various times in the day.

All the clientele here were tribal Hmong, as was Bluey Mua himself. Since the shed also served as an inn for traveling Hmong at night, women and children were usually lounging inside and about the premises. Addicts using this den were mostly Hmong men who were making a brief visit to the city. At times (especially on holidays and weekends), the den filled with nonaddicted Hmong men coming to share an opium smoke with relatives and friends.

The only two regular addicts at this facility were both amputee veterans who lived in the capital city to ensure reception of their regular pension. One was Bluey Mua himself, married and forty years of age. The other was a Hmong man, twenty-seven years old and single.

DEN ATTENDANCE AMONG ADDICT-PATIENTS

At the National Narcotic Detoxification Center, 353 addicts were asked about their den attendance. Many went to dens infrequently or only to buy their opium so they could subsequently use it at home. Regardless of frequency of visits, any addict who had ever gone to a den was classified as a "den user." These data are shown in table 4.

Den users were more apt to be male. This was as expected, since single or married women did not ordinarily visit dens. More of them were expatriate Asians, since this group of people more often lived in towns where dens were located. As suggested by our field survey, a greater percentage of them were divorced and not living with family. Relatively more den users were unemployed—again a status reserved primarily for town dwellers rather than rural people. Relatively more heroin addicts visited dens. And as we shall see in a subsequent chapter, all of the heroin addicts in Laos at this time came from a specific urban area.

Wen Yu's Den. Wen Yu was born in 1924 in Yunnan province, south China. A younger son of peasant parents, he decided he would have to strike out for new territory if his ambitions were to be realized. So he headed for Hmong hill country where he could use his six years of education to good advantage. Among the illiterate Hmong he could write and decipher letters, act as go-between in dealings with Chinese merchants, and tutor a few children of the wealthier villagers in Chinese glyphics.

TABLE 4   Characteristics of Den Users

CHARACTERISTIC	NUMBER OF DEN USERS	NUMBER OF OTHERS	STATISTICAL SIGNIFICANCE[a]
Sex			
male	105	209	$X_1^2 = 4.4920$
female	6	33	$P < .05$
	111	242	
Ethnicity			
expatriate Asians[b]	32	28	$X_1^2 = 14.7768$
indigenous peoples[c]	79	214	$P < .005$
	111	242	
Marital status			
divorced	12	6	$X_1^2 = 9.5162$
single, married, widowed	96	234	$P < .005$
unknown	3	2	
	111	242	
Residence			
with family, relatives	97	224	$X_1^2 = 6.4812$
with friends, alone	13	9	$P < .02$
unknown	1	9	
	111	242	
Employment			
employed	96	233	$X_1^2 = 5.9265$
unemployed	12	9	$P < .02$
unknown	3	0	
	111	242	
Type of drug			
opium only	87	223	$X_1^2 = 12.2401$
heroin, with or without opium	24	19	$P < .005$
	111	242	

[a]Unknown data are excluded from statistical analysis.

[b]Chinese, Vietnamese, Thai, Indo-Pakistani.

[c]Lao, Hmong, Yao, Tai Dam, Khamu.

He did well. Accustomed to hard work, with a core of peasant honesty, he served the Hmong diligently and reaped rewards for his efforts. In addition to his documentary work and teaching, he increasingly engaged in business and money lending.

His good fortune was not boundless, however. Over a period of months he began to lose weight and develop a dry cough. One day

during a fit of coughing he suddenly produced a tablespoon of blood
—an ominous sign in a country where tuberculosis, lung flukes, and
other chronic lung ailments claimed a large number of victims.

Wen Yu consulted a *maw dya,* a herb doctor. Despite a variety
of nostrums, he continued to be racked with coughing spells. He tried
another herb doctor, with the same results. A few of the Hmong villagers told him to try opium for a month or two.

Try it he did, and it worked! Not only was his cough less severe
but he gained the strength to resume much of the work he had been
neglecting. For another year he continued in the same way—hard
work every day and opium every night.

By now he had a decent fortune by local standards, and he was
only about thirty. "What was it all for?" he asked himself. "For nothing,
unless I have children," he decided. But who would marry an opium
smoker, and a Haw Chinese* at that, without any relatives for hundreds
of miles? He would have to quit opium. Abstinence and his wealth—
they would gain him a good wife.

They did. One of his Hmong business contacts betrothed his
daughter to him. She was a good woman: quiet, purposeful, industrious. Toward the end of their first year of marriage she bore him the
first of their children.

Before that first child was a year old, Wen Yu's cough returned,
again with occasional bloody sputum. Much to his own disappoint-
ment, and his wife's as well, he went back on the opium. As the years
slid by, he worked, and worked hard, but his lung condition was taking
its toll. By the time he had been married several years, Wen Yu could
no longer travel with his mules into the hills to barter and sell. Without
that income his family couldn't survive.

His wife Jee had an idea. Many northern Lao and Hmong people
were going to Vientiane, the capital city of Laos. Some worked for the
government, others were refugees who took whatever work they could
get. Whatever their reason for going, there would be opium smokers
among them. It would be a good time to start an opium-smoking place.

It was indeed a good time for such a venture. In Vientiane, they
soon built a reliable trade of government functionaries and skilled
workmen. As salaried men, their clients also had money to buy a bowl
of soup and cup of tea when they came to smoke opium. Jee could
just put on more food while she was cooking for her brood. And Wen

*The Haw Chinese had emigrated directly from south China into Southeast Asia. Vir-
tually all were men who intermarried with local women. The Cantonese and Fukinese
Chinese from Thailand and Vietnam, with greater education and their own Chinese
women, generally disdained the Haw.

Yu met his opium needs from the supply that flowed through his hands.

When I knew him, Wen Yu was sorely wasted and could not walk from one room to another without panting. But his home, while small, was one of the sturdiest and cleanest in the district. All his children were literate, and most were still in school. His seventeen-year-old would be the man of the house soon. Wen Yu disdained opium and his addiction to it. But it had enabled him to persist in his labors even while ill in his younger years, and now its sale brought a good living to his family. "I owe my life to opium!" he told me.

SOCIAL FUNCTIONS

Dens served a stable clientele of addicts (varying from about a dozen up to about thirty addicts). The same addicts frequented a given den, with little apparent transience among dens. (I encountered only one addict, a young, single Hmong man, at two different dens.) A few dens did have a turnover in customers, especially those catering to traveling addicts.

Diverse needs of the regular clientele were met in most dens. Meals might be taken at them. Some served as a hotel or as a rooming house. These services were provided for a group of people, many of whom had no spouse and who—because of emigration from another province or country, refugee movements, psychological deviance, or disabled veteran status—were receiving no support from their kinship groups.

Dens also served the recreational and interpersonal needs of the addicts. The clients knew and depended on one another. Their conversation centered on topics of mutual interest: the price and supply of opium, what treatments they had tried, news of friends or relatives. They offered advice to one another and, where possible, they helped each other in small ways. Word of jobs was passed around at the den. One energetic old crone, a superb businesswoman, sold the tribal handicrafts of several fellow-addicts in the streets of Vientiane.

During many of our discussions in the dens, an atmosphere of warmth and mutual support was evident. When an addict gave information with which the others disagreed, a good-natured teasing gentled the speaker back to more realistic reporting. On the topic of addiction, an in-group solidarity was especially apparent. They sang the praises of good opium and admired one another's analogies in describing opium intoxication. And they bemoaned the high price, both in economic and personal terms, that opium had exacted from them over the years. Much of this affable atmosphere occurred among people of varied ethnic groups, who in other settings might barely speak to one another in a civil manner.

The economy in Laos was primarily a subsistence one: small kinship groups provided themselves with virtually everything needed to survive. In such an economy, food production and preparation, the maintenance of a dwelling, and production of clothes and utensils required intensive day-long labor at certain times of the year. As a result, division of labor by age and sex was necessary. A solitary individual, unless he was wealthy and could hire family substitutes (that is, servants) simply could not survive. Solitary persons had to find a family to which they could attach themselves. Usually this posed no insurmountable problem. One could marry, live with relatives, become a family's "handyman," or work as a servant. If one were an addict, however, this was not easily accomplished. While families might accept their own addicted relatives, they did not readily integrate a nonrelated addict into their ranks. Solitary addicts faced a major dilemma especially in larger towns where distant kinship or old family ties carried less weight. In need of a substitute family, the solo addict found that an opium den could meet this need eminently well.

While the "den as social resource" may seem unlikely, the "tavern as social resource" has been well described. Dumont (1967), a community psychiatrist, noted the importance of taverns to homeless men in Chicago. In Dumont's words:

> The barroom hangout of homeless men does not exist only to exploit and aggravate social pathology. It performs a life-sustaining function for men who have literally nothing else. It may provide their only opportunity for a tolerant and supportive environment, for socialization, for rest and warmth.

Dumont's tavern dwellers bore other resemblances to the den habitués in Laos. They were alienated from their families, worked only irregularly, and spent several hours each day at the tavern. A certain stability of intoxicant usage was maintained by the regular adherents to the group. For these regular members, the tavern group became their main, or only, reference group. Each of these characteristics applied to the den-using addicts in Laos.

All of the den-using addicts in Laos had deviant social features besides their opium addiction, much like the tavern devotees in Chicago. As an extreme example, three mentally ill people were noted among Dumont's tavern members, and one mentally ill person was found in the survey of den-using addicts in Laos. Sociologist S. E. G. Cavan (1965), in a study of 100 bars in San Francisco, has made the point that a broader range of behavior is tolerated in bars. Perhaps deviants can tolerate the deviancy of others better than can society at large.

The den may allow addicts to form the kind of interpersonal relations that they have been unable to form outside. As phrased by Sutter (1969), based on interviews with heroin addicts in San Francisco, "the addict culture generates forces which make it relatively easy for people to form intense interpersonal relations." It could be argued that den users were virtually as dependent on the den milieu for their social needs as they were dependent on opium. Especially in towns, some addicts were not only drawn to but were probably also pushed by others toward the den setting.

An Unregistered Den. Changsup and Chanthavy ran a small den in Vientiane. They occupied a single room, about eight by ten feet, with a fire in one corner, a sleeping platform in another, and smoking apparatus in a third. A charming ethnic Lao couple in their sixties, always trying to be pleasing as host and hostess, they had established their den only in the last year. Their only son had been killed in the war, and they were getting too old to farm. In the last few years Changsup had himself become addicted while trying to stifle his arthritic pains while farming.

Only a few close neighbors and friends smoked at their home. Most people dropped by to purchase opium for smoking at home. In recent months they had been selling to an occasional Caucasian sent to them by a friendly restaurant owner down the street. They were quite pleased with their decision to open a den and were looking forward to comfortable years of semiretirement. Steeped in traditional courtesies from their rural upbringing and honest in their dealings, they had attracted a regular clientele in a relatively short time.

COMMENT

1. Opium dens did live up to their image to a certain extent, for their habitués tended to be more marginal in society as compared to other addicts. They were more apt to be divorced, expatriates, unemployed from time to time, and heroin users.

2. Dens served important social functions for addicts in towns. The larger the town, the more dens there were. Dens may tell us as much about our urban societies as they tell us about addicts or addiction. Like opiate addiction, dens can be a window, a vantage point from which to study ourselves as humans: our psychology, our families, our societies.

IX

Appearance of Heroin Use

Starting Out on Heroin. Van Tuong was a twenty-year-old Vietnamese man from Vientiane. Born in Hanoi, he had come to Laos with his family in 1954. His father was a teacher who owned and operated one of the several private elementary schools that served the Vietnamese community in Vientiane. This enterprise provided a comfortable though not affluent living for the family.

The eldest son of a successful teacher, Van Tuong felt considerable pressure to succeed academically. Unfortunately, he had neither the interest nor the aptitude. He preferred his play and found that whatever he pushed painfully into his memory tended only to fall out in rather short order. For a time at the French *lycée* (secondary school), he did pursue his studies diligently. But his academic performance was mediocre at best, and he flunked the *bachot* exams that would have allowed him to continue.

The family had a number of meetings about the matter, considering a variety of alternative vocations for Van Tuong. It was decided he should become a tailor, with the hope that some day he might manage his own shop. Van Tuong concurred in the decision and launched into his new career, albeit somewhat diffidently. While he was clearly more successful at tailoring than at academics, his eventual boredom with the repetitive work and his family's indifferent response to his new career discouraged him.

There was one advantage to his new lifestyle: he had his evenings and Sundays free, with no need to do homework. He began chumming with a few young men like himself: refugees from academe searching for a niche. When their finances permitted, they frequented the Vietnamese-owned bars and nightclubs around town. Mostly they met in the evenings along the Mekong River to talk and smoke cigarettes and *sā daeng* ("red tea," a type of marijuana).

At their ritual evening meeting, one of Van Tuong's friends brought a packet of white powder, heroin, in which to dip their cigarettes. While the heroin made him nauseated and caused some abdominal discomfort, it still was an experience like none he had had before. Ennui, worry, and dejection floated away, replaced by a feeling of serene calm and distance from his cares. It was a sensation worth living for.

By the next week he thought about virtually nothing else all day long except his evening heroin highs. Another few weeks and he had to smoke in the morning to relieve his runny nose. The following week he had to have a few smokes at noon to relieve his inner tension and shaky hand. Over the subsequent four months Van Tuong spent every cent he made on heroin. He began missing supper at home, partly in preference for his evening heroin highs and partly to avoid discovery of his addiction by the family.

Despite Tuong's efforts at hiding his addiction, the family found out about it. Suspicious about his absences and dramatic weight loss, they had spoken with the master tailor to whom he was apprenticed. He too had grown alarmed at Tuong's diminished productivity, social withdrawal, and gaunt appearance. It was an easy matter to confirm that his nightly forays involved heroin and that he was indeed addicted. They confronted him and threatened to cast him out from home and employment if he did not seek treatment.

Van Tuong entered the National Narcotic Treatment Program in Vientiane. Although he cooperated with the treatment staff and persisted with follow-up visits, his craving for heroin seemed to mount by the day. Within a few months he was back to using heroin again. Following a second round of detoxification, his craving again resumed a few weeks after discharge. When I last saw him, Tuong was coming to the Center daily for a long-term, outpatient detoxification on methadone. This greatly relieved his craving but left him with his ennui, continuing disapproval from his family, and no friends. He was three steps behind where he had been a year earlier and uncertain regarding what his future might bring.

PHARMACOLOGY OF HEROIN

Like opium, heroin could be smoked. Some addicts simply dipped their cigarettes into heroin before lighting them. This was called the "ack-ack" method because of its resemblance to the small puffs from antiaircraft guns in World War II. This had the advantage of enabling one to consume heroin publicly while on the job, with no one being the wiser. Heroin could also be volatilized on a piece of tinfoil, with the fumes then inhaled through a straw (the "chasing the dragon" method) or through a match box cover (the "mouth organ" method). While the latter methods were more efficient, they obviously marked the smoker as a heroin user. They also required more skill.

If conservation of the drug became important (whether because of decreased supply or increased cost), heroin could not be effectively ingested as could opium and morphine. But it could be injected under the skin or into the vein. Parenteral injection in Laos occurred mostly among Caucasian addicts. While this route of administration was more economical, it also exposed the user to the risk of infection and other maladies.

Heroin is excreted more rapidly from the body than are the various subfractions of opium. In practical terms, this means that, to stave off withdrawal, the heroin addict needs another dose of heroin in four to eight hours, while the opium addict needs a dose only every eight to twelve hours. Heroin addicts thus have more episodes in the day when they are intoxicated (right after their doses) and when they feel uncomfortable or ill (as withdrawal begins). Consequently, compared with opium addicts, they have a shorter time during the day when they can function normally.

The period of withdrawal from heroin is shorter although often stormier when compared to opium withdrawal. Heroin addicts complete their withdrawal within several days or less, while opium addicts are often ill for one or two weeks. Severity of the addiction also affects the duration and morbidity of the withdrawal.

AN ANTIOPIUM CAMPAIGN

Effects of War

During my early stay in Laos, from 1965 to 1967, opium addiction was often a personal and a family problem but not a great social or political problem. Addicts did not rob or steal, and few were identified as being among a criminal or deviant element in society. Opium addiction involved a certain cost for political units, from the village up to the nation, in lost labor and early incapacity or death of workers. But it also brought cash into the country, thereby providing a means for the import of iron, precious metals, and a limited variety of manufactured goods (e.g., soap, cloth, shoes, medicines). By the time of my second visit to Laos in 1971, this had begun to change. Incursions by Vietnamese into Hmong and Iu Mien lands had forced many farmers down from the mountains into the valleys and onto the northern Vientiane plain. Some opium continued to be raised, especially in the provinces adjoining Thailand and Burma (i.e., Sayaboury, Houa Kong). It is a moot point whether this limited production was sufficient to meet local needs or whether Laos became at that point an opium importing, rather than exporting, country.

In any event, addicts in virtually all of Laos outside Sayaboury and Houa Kong provinces had to purchase their opium. Addicted poppy farmers, now refugees away from their source of income, had neither their own poppy production nor the means to purchase opium. Many northern Lao and Lao Theung tribespeople, among whom addiction was more prevalent than among southerners, also no longer raised rice or produced other goods with which they might finance their opium purchases. To further complicate matters, the price of opium began to increase at an alarming rate (except in Houa Kong province, close to Thailand and Burma). Whereas previously large habits had cost $10 to $15 per month, by 1971 even moderate habits cost $30 to $60 per month (but only $12 to $20 in Houa Kong).

Consequences for Addicts

Of forty addicts interviewed in 1971, all had cut down on their opium doses. Most reported daily doses of one-half to one-quarter of their previous amounts. This was also reflected in the amounts of narcotic needed for withdrawal treatment. Whereas previously a daily dose of narcotic equivalent to thirty to forty milligrams of methadone was standard, fifteen to thirty milligrams had become sufficient in most cases.

Another result was a decrease in frequency of daily dose. Whereas thrice-daily doses had been common in 1965 to 1967, most of the forty opium addicts interviewed in 1971 had cut down to twice-daily doses. Three of the forty would occasionally use only one dose a day in order to stretch their supply.

A third ploy was to change the route of administration. Whereas smoking was the preferred method of use for all forty opium addicts, only five well-to-do addicts could afford to take opium entirely by smoking. The remainder consumed at least some of their opium by eating it. Most ate opium in the morning to stave off withdrawal and then smoked for relaxation or intoxication in the evening. (Some addicts preferred the latter strategy, i.e., morning eating/evening smoking, even when opium was plentiful; but the relative number had increased by 1971.)

Fourth, many addicts sought sources of income besides their traditional ones. This is considered in greater detail below.

Effects on Family and Society

Addiction in a family member was often an economic burden even under the best of circumstances (as has been shown earlier). Refugee moves taking people away from their sources of income further exacerbated the economic problems for most addicts' families. Scarce savings and resources that were needed for food supplements and clothing were instead used to purchase opium. In particular, children, the aged, and women were often deprived of adequate nutrition. In some instances even basic refugee supplies (i.e., rice, blankets, a cooking pot) were sold to purchase opium.

Another widespread problem was theft. Increasingly, addicts in refugee camps stole from their families, clan members, and fellow villagers—a phenomenon that had not been known in Laos in recent decades. The usual Laotian stereotype of the addict included no connotations of theft. But by 1970, local refugee leaders, government officials concerned with refugee resettlement, and even local philanthropic groups (such as the Buddhist Women's Association) had grown alarmed over the situation.

An Antiopium Law

Local concern within Laos about opium-related crime joined with international pressures, especially from the United States. The rate of addiction among American soldiers in Vietnam was growing at an alarming rate. Laotian heroin was implicated as the main supply source, no doubt erroneously, as indicated above. Sentiment against the war in Vietnam was linked with the American presence and opium commerce, admixed with considerable sensationalism and faulty logic. Several American writers made brief visits to a Mekong River town, obtained second- and third-hand reports, and "proved" that the real evil in Southeast Asia was the American governmental support of opium production and trade.* While these simplistic interpretations of scattered effects appeared ludicrous from the local Laotian perspective, they were widely published and believed in the United States. This led to great pressures by the American government against the Royal Laotian Government (RLG) to abandon its laissez-faire policy regarding opium production, commerce, and use. At the time it was difficult for the RLG to ignore these demands, since the United States was the primary financial guarantor of the government's annual budget.

International factors augmented American and local Laotian pressures to do something about opium in Laos. Opiate addiction was increasing in parts of Europe and Africa. The United Nations and the Narcotics Control Commission had long pressured for effective government control over opium production and commerce in Laos. Lauditory as this may be from an international perspective, the notion of effectively suppressing opium in a country at war with both a powerful neighbor and certain elements of its own citizenry is not a sound one. Yet, these international agencies colluded with Laos in the development of its law against opium.

Faced with these pressures, the RLG passed a law against certain aspects of opium production and commerce while allowing other aspects of opium production, commerce, and use to continue. According to this law, poppy farmers could continue to produce enough opium for their own consumption but not for sale to anyone else, not even an addicted fellow villager or relative. Second, all opium dens and all opium addicts had to register with the Ministry of Interior. Registered addicts could continue to consume opium, and registered dens could sell it. Third, the law provided for penalties against those caught in the commerce of opium. And fourth, government organs were established to halt the commerce in opium. Note a particular contradiction in these laws: registered dens and addicts could sell and purchase opium, but there were no legal means to produce or transport opium. This rather confusing piece of legislation (not atypical of others passed by the RLG during its brief twenty years of existence) was the cause for considerable mischief, as we will consider later. (See Appendix 1 for an approved translation of this law.)

The RLG was not alone in pursuing this contradiction, however. The American government contributed manpower, supplies, and money

---

*A few of these were American academics without any training in field research or experience in Laos. Their writings include a scattering of facts, a good deal of false information, considerable innuendo, and some very faulty logic. That their works were so popular is a sign of those times. Careful and innovative work coming out of Southeast Asia by reputable researchers (several of whom are referenced in this text) was at the same

to block the transportation of opium within Laos. A senior American narcotics agent was brought from Marseilles to head the effort. A few dozen American narcotics agents were billeted to towns along the Mekong, to Laotian airports, and to other commercial points. American narcotics agent advisors were assigned to the new Laotian police division concerned with suppression of opium commerce. The American government contributed guns, boats, jeeps, aircraft, and photo reconnaissance missions to this effort.

The results lead to one of the sorrier chapters of the American presence in Laos. Whereas previously the American presence in Laos tended to be relatively low key (at least compared with American presence elsewhere in Indochina), now any visitor to Laos was greeted by a Lao-American pair searching for narcotics. The boss in this duo was usually a pushy American, often angry looking and apparently suspicious of his shadow. On a few occasions I visited a northern town, Ban Houei Sai, where the American narcotics agents presented a particularly nasty image. By day they cruised the river, submachine guns at the ready, stopping the occasional boatmen bringing vegetables to market. By evening, they caroused and drank. Their evident bravado, driving the few dusty streets in a jeep with guns sticking out in all directions, contrasted with their even more evident discomfort in the presence of local inhabitants, whether Lao, expatriate Asian, or expatriate Caucasian. Not unexpectedly, one agent developed delirium tremens from alcoholism and a few others were also sent home for various misbehaviors.

Despite the Keystone Kops appearance of this American contingent, the antiopium law did have certain consequences. As one might expect, it did not influence local poppy production (as gauged by photo reconnaissance).* It did lead to registration of addicts and dens in Vientiane Prefecture, a metropolitan area of some 130,000 people served by a relatively efficient police force. And it did stop the importation of raw opium supplies into Vientiane Prefecture.

Results of the Antiopium Law

The successful halting of opium supply into Vientiane Prefecture had two results. The first of these was corruption of the police. (One

---

time denounced as mere effluvia by the Central Intelligence Agency. It was a time when trash was glorified as enlightenment and excellent work having humanitarian import was denounced as treason.

*These photos were taken by American planes and interpreted by an expert from Singapore. In my role as a consultant, both American and Laotian officials oriented me to these data and demonstrated the photo reconnaissance method used for the study.

could say further corruption of the police, but by Southeast Asian standards at the time the Laotian police were paragons of virtue, almost on a level with those of Malaysia and Singapore.) Whereas previously the police had no particular interest in narcotic drugs, they could suddenly collect large sums of money for ignoring opium commerce and use. Many of them had no personal and social objection to its use, so collecting money for allowing that which they did not oppose involved no conflict of conscience. Opium smoking and addiction were not rare within the police force, so this provided an easy entree of suppliers to the police. In the *pas de deux* that ensued between the righteous and the corrupted, a senior police official was arrested by narcotics police at his home with more than two tons of opium in his bedroom. On a more mundane level, scores of police officers were satisfied with monthly supplements to their salary for merely ignoring opium commerce.

While the neighborhood police might accept a bribe for local sale, this was not so easily arranged with the pairs of American and Laotian narcotics agents surveying the supply routes into Vientiane Prefecture. Opium was easy to detect: bulky, heavy, and with a distinctive odor. Consequently, large-scale shipments became difficult to deliver. Small entrepreneurs, carrying a kilogram or two of opium, did not want to risk arrest for such moderate profits, especially if they traveled by boat, bus, or airplane into the city. The situation was ripe for heroin introduction.

Heroin had several advantages over opium in a context of illicit commerce. As a powder, it was more easily packaged into various sizes and shapes than the resinous opium tar. It emitted virtually no odor compared to the pungent opium scent. In preparing heroin from opium, over 90 percent of the inactive and less active substances within opium were removed, thereby greatly increasing the value per unit weight. And heroin, with its two acetyl groups, produced a more desirable effect than morphine with its single acetyl group. By contrast to opium, heroin was a smuggler's dream.

Heroin brought certain socioeconomic complications, however. Opium could be raised, processed, transported, and sold as a cottage industry. No one involved in the process needed to be literate, rich, powerful, highly organized, or have access to materials not indigenous to Laos. None of this was true for heroin. Heroin required fairly sophisticated chemists and chemical apparatus, access to large volumes of industrial grade acetyl anhydride, a means of collection from many opium producers, the purchase of large volumes of opium and the sale of large amounts of heroin in order to pay for the processing, payments for security (either a private security force or corruption of the police), leadership and integration of a complex organization, a means of distribution, and large amounts of risk capital. This was no cottage industry; it was a large industrial complex requiring the orchestration of thousands, even tens of thousands of individuals. For a few at the top of the complex, it brought great financial rewards. For some in the middle—the chemists, police, and traffickers—it provided a somewhat more comfortable existence. And it increased the economic burden of addiction, for it was ultimately the addict, the addict's family, and the addict's society that paid for the greater cost of the heroin industrial complex as compared with the lower cost of the opium cottage industry.

The Pedicab Driver. "I am Vongsa, the *samlor* [pedicab] driver. Forty-eight years ago I was born in this province, in a village within a day's walk from Vientiane. Almost twenty years ago I brought my young wife and children here to Vientiane city. We were a new nation, the town was beginning to grow, and I knew they would need samlor drivers here. My children could attend school and my wife would not have to labor so hard as in the village.

"At the time my decision was a wise one. My wages were good, and my children all completed elementary school. But my fortune did not stay good. Cars replaced samlors, so that now it is the taxi drivers who make good money. I cannot read or write, so I cannot obtain a license. Each year it is more and more difficult for me to peddle the samlor. People choose the young men who can peddle faster and take larger loads.

"Five years ago, in 1967, my luck was very bad. My eldest son, upon whom I relied to help me support the family, was killed as a soldier in the war. My daughter had a disagreement with her husband, so she returned with her two children to live with us. So then we had to take care of them also. I was wracked by headache and worry. Each day it was harder and harder for me to peddle the samlor. A good friend, a samlor driver and an opium user, told me that I should use opium. He said if I used only a little bit, just in the morning and once in the middle of the day, it would be all right. In 1968 I took his advice and found that he was correct: I could work longer and harder without fatigue. But I did not stay with small doses. Each month they grew a little bigger. Than I would take a little at night to sleep. A year later I was addicted.

"For three years I used only opium, usually eating it but sometimes relaxing or celebrating with a few pipes. Then in 1971, after the law, it was sometimes difficult to obtain opium, but it was possible to buy this new thing, heroin. At first they were almost the same price, but it was necessary to use the heroin more often to prevent the [withdrawal] illness. I could not eat the heroin during the day as I ate opium, but I could smoke the heroin in a cigarette between jobs so no one would know.

"I like the heroin. It is convenient, and it brings a good feeling. But I don't like the price. I must pay 1,500 kip a day for my heroin. The opium only cost me 500 kip a day. Now I must work even harder to pay for it. My wife argues with me about it every day. It is like a circular road which has brought me back to where I was five years ago: older, weaker, and worried about my future."

A HEROIN "EPIDEMIC"

Chronology of Heroin Use in Laos

Heroin "epidemics" have been reported in several cities in the United States for more than a century (Musto 1973). Sudden, widespread use of heroin among the American military forces in Southeast Asia has also been reported (Robins, Davis, and Goodwin 1974). Rapid spread of heroin addiction similarly occurred in Laos during the period 1971 to 1975.

I encountered no reports of heroin addiction in Laos during the period from 1965 to late 1971. In March of 1972 (five months after passage of an antiopium law), however, several opium addicts told me that they had heard of heroin use in Vientiane. One opium addict stated that a few of his addicted friends had begun using heroin in lieu of opium and that he had visited a den where heroin was sold in Vientiane. (He himself was adverse to using heroin, since he stated heroin users got "too intoxicated," had to use heroin again too soon in order to relieve their withdrawal symptoms, and spent entirely too much money on the drug.)

By late 1972, heroin had become more widely available. From the opening of the National Narcotic Detoxification Center (NNDC) in September of 1972, about 10 to 15 percent of all admitted addicts were using heroin part or all the time. Most of these early heroin addicts had previously been addicted to opium. Initially they continued using opium for a time, supplementing it with heroin. Eventually most switched completely to heroin. Some financially destitute addicts would use opium to stave off a withdrawal until they could resume heroin.

Geographic Spread

Of sixty-five Asian heroin addicts admitted to NNDC, sixty-two were currently living in Vientiane Prefecture. This early group initially came from two districts in Vientiane, Sikhay and Mixay. Many boatmen lived in these districts, which were west of the center of town. The three addicts not from Vientiane came from Tha Deua, a town twenty miles east of Vientiane. Sikhay, Mixay, and Tha Deua are all located along the Mekong River across from Thailand. Since the Mekong is navigable much of the year at Tha Deua but not at Vientiane, most heavy transport between Laos and Thailand took place there. Several Thai addicts who sought treatment at NNDC came from Nong Khai, a Thai town across from Tha Deua. Nong Khai is a major town with a railroad head and an arterial highway, both going all the way to Bangkok. It also has an airport with regular commercial air service. Legal import and export, transport of people, and smuggling between Laos and Thailand took place primarily at the Tha Deua-Nong Khai crossing.

None of the several thousand addicted patients at the NNDC and Wat Tan Kha Bok coming from the rest of Laos (i.e., outside Vientiane Prefecture and Tha Deua) reported any use of heroin during the period from 1972 to 1975. At times during 1965 to 1975, heroin factories had been reported in the provinces of Houa Kong, Sayaboury, and Luang Prabang. Yet none of the scores of addicts coming from these three areas reported any use of heroin, either currently or in the past. If there were factories in those areas, they were not flooding the local market with heroin.

Most of fifty-six Caucasian addicts studied at NNDC were currently residing in Vientiane when they came for treatment. Ten of them, mostly long-term employed residents of Laos, were using opium obtained through essentially the same channels as an indigenous Asian might use. Among the forty-six others, thirty-nine were using heroin exclusively and seven were using both heroin and opium. These Caucasian heroin addicts primarily obtained their drugs in the center of town, either at a few dens that had heroin available or through Caucasian addicts who were supporting themselves by buying and selling heroin. These "world-traveler" addicts could obtain heroin in or near four low-rent hotels near the center of town.* Longer-term Caucasian residents addicted to heroin lived in several different districts (i.e., Wattay, Phone Keng, Dong Phalane, Nai Moung, and Mixay) but obtained heroin during regu-

*These included the old Lido Hotel and the more recently established Bungalow, Saylom Villa, and Vieng Vilay.

lar forays to the downtown district for work, meals, mail, newspapers, or social contacts. Of the forty-six Caucasian heroin addicts, only six of them were first addicted to heroin in Laos; all of these six had been introduced to heroin between 1972 and 1974. A seventh person, an Englishman, had become addicted to opium three years previously in another Laotian town (Luang Prabang) but subsequently began using both opium and heroin when he moved to Vientiane. The other thirty-nine Caucasian heroin addicts had originally started using this drug in other countries besides Laos and then resumed their heroin use when they arrived in Laos after 1971. This group will be described more fully in a subsequent chapter.

World Travelers

Did world travelers from Europe, Australia, and America introduce heroin into Laos? Several facts suggest an association between the two. First of all, more than 80 percent of the Caucasian addicts admitted to NNDC were using heroin while less than 15 percent of indigenous Asians at NNDC were using it. Also, a drug-using Caucasian group—many dressed in "hippie" garb—first appeared in late 1972 and increased tremendously from early 1974 through early 1975.

Careful analysis of the evidence suggests that Caucasian world travelers were not responsible for the massive introduction of heroin into Laos, however. Prior to the 1973 peace accords in Laos, few tourists came to Laos because of security restrictions, difficulty in travel, and the high mortality among travelers who chose to disregard the military realities and to wander about the country. Data from Caucasian addicts, both those who were patients at NNDC and those who were not, indicate that Caucasians becoming addicted in Laos up to 1972 were using opium. The huge influx of young Caucasian tourists into Laos by the thousands did not occur until 1974, long after the introduction of heroin.

Data from the National Narcotic Detoxification Center also demonstrated the arrival of many addicted travelers in Laos. During the 16 months between September of 1972 and December of 1973, only 13 Caucasian addicts were admitted to treatment (i.e., 0.8 addicts per month). During the subsequent 12 months of 1974, 47 Caucasians were admitted (i.e., 3.67 addicts per month), a rate increase of 490 percent. This rate was still rising in early 1975.

In addition, the number of Asian heroin addicts seeking treatment at the Detoxification Center was consistently larger than the number of Caucasian heroin addicts. For example, the number of Asian heroin addicts being admitted each month during 1972 and 1973 was 5.4 as compared to 0.75 Caucasian heroin addicts. This was a ratio of 7.2 Asian heroin addicts for every one Caucasian heroin addict.

COMPARISON OF OPIUM AND HEROIN ADDICTS

Regular opium use, even opium addiction, has often been depicted as a rather benign habit among Asians, more a social tradition than a problem-producing behavior. On the contrary, heroin addiction has been generally viewed as more debilitating, a true addiction or disease that produces social, psychological, and biomedical deterioration. Study of opium and heroin addicts at the treatment facility in Laos provided an opportunity to test these hypotheses.

Of 503 patient-addicts admitted to NNDC, 438 were using only opium and fifty-one were using only heroin at the time of admission to treatment. Fourteen people who were currently using both opium and heroin were excluded from the study. On most demographic and clinical variables, these fourteen addicts resembled the heroin addicts. It was thought, however, that their exclusion would provide an unambiguous contrast between the two groups.

Social Characteristics

Among the 438 opium addicts, 46 of them (11 percent) were women. Only one of the 51 heroin addicts (2 percent) was female, a twenty-six-year-old Vietnamese women whose husband was also a heroin addict. Despite the trend for fewer women among the heroin addicts, the difference was not statistically significant.

Opium addicts were a considerably older group. Their age ranged from 15 to 88 with a mean of 50.0 years (standard deviation 12.1). By contrast, the heroin addicts varied in age from 18 to 60 with a mean of 35.1 years (standard deviation 8.8). This difference was significant at the .001 level (Student "t" = 8.4715, 489 degrees of freedom, two tailed). Similar proportions of both groups were ethnic Lao: 64 percent of the opium addicts and 65 percent of the heroin addicts. Addicted to opium were all of the rural tribespeople, including Hmong, Tai Dam, Iu Mien, and Khamu. A majority of the expatriate Asians were opium addicts; but, compared to other ethnic groups, a relatively greater proportion of them were heroin addicts. As merchants, artisans, laborers, and truck farmers, many of them lived in and around Vientiane where heroin use occurred.

Relatively more heroin addicts were single in comparison to the opium addicts (27 percent versus 3 percent). The percentage of divorced or separated persons was the same in both groups (5 percent). The difference between the two groups showed only borderline probability of .08 (using Chi Square) for marital status.

Occupation reflected the urban residency of heroin addicts. They were predominantly merchants, artisans, laborers, and civil service workers. The opium group consisted primarily of farmers and rural housewives. The difference in occupation between opium and heroin addicts was highly significant at the .005 level on Chi Square testing.

Past Narcotic History

There was considerable overlap in the age at which the two groups first began narcotic use, with most beginning in their twenties, thirties, or forties. The mean age at initial use was lower for heroin addicts (30.6 years) as compared to opium addicts (34.4 years), however. The difference was statistically significant at the .01 level. The mean age of first becoming addicted was 4.3 years older for the opium addicts as compared to the heroin addicts. This difference was statistically significant at the .01 level. This is not surprising in view of the younger age among the heroin addicts.

Heroin users tended to maintain nonaddictive use for a shorter period of time (0.7 years) as compared to opium users (1.3 years). Despite this trend, statistical testing did not show a significant difference.

Time delay between first becoming addicted and seeking treatment at NNDC was 14.3 years among the opium users. Mean duration among the heroin users was only 3.8 years, more than a decade less on the average than among the opium users. The difference was highly significant at the .001 level of probability. This was probably influenced in part by the younger age of heroin addicts and the more recent introduction of heroin. At the same time, a number of these heroin addicts had previously been on opium. Thus, these data suggest but do not prove that heroin may hasten the onset of problems that prompt the addict to seek treatment. (The matched-pair study later in this chapter was undertaken to further clarify these issues.)

Current Narcotic Use

Opium addicts were eating or smoking opium an average of 2.4 times a day (standard deviation 0.6). Heroin addicts were taking an average of 3.3 doses per day (standard deviation 1.3). This marked difference (significant at the .001 level) was in the expected direction. The one chemical compound of heroin (diacetylmorphine) is metabolized and excreted by the body more rapidly than are the numerous active and inactive compounds of opium (i.e., morphine, codeine, narcotine, narceine, thebaine, papaverine, etc.). Consequently the intoxicant effects of heroin are more short lived, withdrawal symptoms begin to appear sooner, and the addicted person takes more frequent doses.

Opium addicts spent an average of $1.58 per day on their drug. Heroin addicts were spending an average of $4.13 per day, $2.55 more than the average amount spent by opium addicts. This was also in the expected direction, since heroin manufacture required high capital expenditure, modern equipment, trained people, bribery, and a large profit return to balance the high risk. On the average, heroin smokers were spending 2.6 times more per day on their drug than were opium addicts.

Among the medical staff at NNDC, it was believed that heroin addicts required greater initial doses of methadone to alleviate withdrawal but could be withdrawn more rapidly over one to three weeks, whereas opium addicts seemed to require smaller initial doses but longer withdrawal regimens of three weeks or more. Average initial 24-hour methadone detoxification dosage among opium addicts was 27.9 milligrams; among heroin addicts it was 33.9 milligrams. This difference was significant at the .001 level, supporting the clinical wisdom among the staff.

A MATCHED-PAIR STUDY

Each of fifty-one Asian heroin addicts from NNDC were matched with an Asian opium addict for sex, ethnicity, and age. The pairs were identical for sex and ethnicity, and there was no statistically significant difference for age. Where more than one opium user was eligible for the match, the choice was made randomly (see Westermeyer and Peng 1977b). This allowed comparisons between opium and heroin addicts that were not biased by sex, ethnicity, or age.*

Social Characteristics

The two samples did not differ statistically on marital status. Most addicts in both groups were married and living with their spouses. About 90 percent of both groups were living either with family or relatives.

*Statistician Grace Peng labored over this match to make the two groups as similar as possible on these three variables.

There was the expected difference in occupation. Opium addicts were more likely to be farmers, while heroin addicts were more likely to be merchants, artisans, and laborers (significant at the .005 level). There was also a slightly greater rate of unemployment among the heroin addicts, significant at the .02 level. These differences were due to the predominantly rural residence of opium addicts and the urban residence of heroin addicts.

Narcotic History

Heroin and opium addicts in the matched-pair study had similar durations of narcotic use prior to addiction: 0.7 years on the average in both groups. Heroin patients were addicted for a mean of 3.8 years before seeking admission to NNDC (indicating that many of them had previously been addicted to opium since heroin had not been available in Laos for that long). They sought assistance 4.6 years sooner than did the opium patients, whose mean duration of addiction was 8.4 years.

Heroin addicts in this sample became addicted at an older age than did the opium addicts, a finding opposite to that of the previous study in which heroin addicts were shown to become addicted at an earlier age than opium addicts. There was also a later age of onset for addiction among heroin addicts, again contrary to the findings of the earlier comparison. Both of these differences between the two findings were related to the method (i.e., making the matched-pair comparison) and also to the shorter time period between onset of addiction and seeking treatment among the heroin addicts as compared to the opium addicts.

Current Narcotic Use

These heroin addicts were taking significantly more doses per day (3.3 on the average) as compared to opium addicts (2.4 on the average). Of interest, the mean and standard deviation of doses among these 51 matched opium addicts were identical to those of the original 483 opium addicts. Similarly, the 51 matched opium addicts were spending about the same amount on narcotics per day ($1.78) as were the original 438 addicts ($1.58). This was significantly less than the $4.13 being spent per day by the heroin addicts. Differences between heroin and opium addicts for doses and daily cost were both statistically significant at .001.

The first twenty-four hour methadone detoxification dose was significantly higher among the heroin addicts. Although there was some overlap in the lower and intermediate doses between the two groups, only heroin addicts received methadone doses between forty-six and eighty milligrams. Thirteen heroin users received dosages in this high range. This difference between the two groups was significant at the .005 level.

Readmission rates to treatment within 365 days of discharge were also assessed for the two groups. They did not differ on this variable.

COMMENT

1. Although the technology for producing heroin has been available for almost a century, widespread heroin use did not appear in Laos until 1972.

2. Heroin use began in the capital city of Vientiane within months after passage of the antiopium law. Police power was strongest in the capital city, and police officers (goaded by American narcotics agents) vigorously enforced the law. This soon led to a decrease in the metropolitan opium supply, since it was difficult to bring this bulky and odoriferous drug along the roads and airways supplying Vientiane without being arrested and having the opium confiscated.

3. Geographic distribution of heroin addicts in Laos suggests that heroin was brought from Thailand into Laos through the Thai town of Nong Khai in early 1972. Heroin was first distributed among Asian addicts in the Sikhay and Mixay districts of Vientiane and across from Nong Khai in the Lao town of Tha Deua.

4. Once introduced into Vientiane, heroin use spread rapidly among the Lao, expatriate Asian, and Caucasian addicts.

5. Certain aspects of drug use and clinical effects appeared related to the differing pharmaceutical and pharmacologic characteristics of opium and heroin. Heroin addicts spent more per day for their drug than opium addicts, and heroin addicts took more doses per day. Initial doses of methadone for detoxification were greater for heroin addicts.

X

Caucasian Addicts

The Australian Couple. Margaret was 25, a school teacher. Jack was 27, an engineer. They had lived together in Melbourne for a few years and had decided it was about time to get married. But before settling down, they agreed to combine their savings and travel for a year in Asia. When we met at my favorite Vientiane restaurant they were about halfway through their trip, having begun in the Philippines and worked their way up the Malay Archipelago into Southeast Asia. Though not preocuupied with using drugs, they had tried cannabis in many places along the way. Meeting other young world travelers provided them a ready, almost automatic access to drugs throughout Asia in the early 1970s. They had not run into heroin in the Philippines or Indonesia, but they did meet fellow tourists in Malaysia who had some heroin. Both of them tried a heroin cigarette there for the first time. Jack experienced quite a jolt from it and spent the entire evening nauseated and vomiting. Margaret had a cold and could not keep the fumes down without coughing. She did not feel any effects. Still curious, she took advantage of a subsequent opportunity in Thailand. (By that time Jack had no interest in repeating the ordeal.) Forewarned by Jack's experience, she spaced her inhalations so as not to take too much drug. Although she didn't vomit,. she did become nauseated and drowsy. For her there were no unbounded pleasures or heavenly dreams. "I'd rather stick with this," she said pointing to the Algerian red table wine that the waiter had just brought to our table. Surrounded by inexpensive opium and heroin in Vientiane, they had no interest in further pursuit of the Big Smoke.

SAMPLING AND DATA COLLECTION

Depending on where one collected data and what data were collected, one might conclude that (1) opium smoking is an entirely benign pastime, (2) opium smoking is potentially dangerous for some but not for others, or (3) opium smoking has the potential for wrecking the lives of almost anyone who tries it. As we have seen and will see, all of these statements are true at times and false at times. The individual, the drug, the timing, the social context all play a role. If we examine opiate use through only one method, we see only one facet of the phenomenon. Actually it is intellectually simpler that way because using another approach may reveal a facet diametrically opposed to the first. That complicates matters. In place of gratification one discovers discomfiture and awe, a quest rather than a destination.

The study of Caucasian addicts in Asia exemplies this complexity. As we shall see, this group is different from Asian addicts; but it is also different from Caucasian addicts who remain at home.

Visiting Opium Dens

During six visits to Laos from 1971 to 1975, I repeatedly visited several opium dens. My purpose was to describe the physical characteristics of the den, the social characteristics of the den owner and habitués, and the behaviors that transpired in the den. Some of these observations appear elsewhere in this book and in a published report (Westermeyer 1974b).

In the course of these sundry visits, a score of people accompanied me to the dens at various times: eight Caucasians and approximately a dozen local Lao and Hmong people. None of the latter ever tried opium smoking in my company, even though invited upon occasion by the den proprietors to do so. Of my eight Caucasian fellow visitors, six did try smoking opium. None had ever used opium before, and to the best of my knowledge none has ever used it again. They inhaled relatively small doses, apparently more from curiosity and to say "I smoked opium" than from any fervent wish to make this ritual part of their regular lives. All were married, in their thirties, employed, getting along well in their lives, and mostly in professional fields; and they did not live where they had ready access to opium or opium dens. They resembled my dozen Laotian confreres in all but the latter characteristic: these local Hmong and Lao people did have ongoing exposure and access to opium. Any curiosity was more than outweighed by their fear of addiction. For them there was no value in saying "I tried it," as there was for my Caucasian colleagues back home at their seminars and cocktail parties.

Among my adventuresome friends and acquaintances, a few non-smokers could not inhale the smoke deeply into their lungs and keep it there. A few others felt nothing after one or two inhalations. And a few more experienced some nausea and lethargy after finishing a pipe or two. None of them reported anything resembling pleasure or euphoria. One man having a bout of diarrhea at the time found that two pipefuls greatly relieved this condition (much as one would expect from a dose of the old nostrum, tincture of opium).

I have followed the lives of these eight people (seven men and one woman) over a six-to-ten-year period since their smoking opium in one or another Laotian den. None has become an opium addict or, for that matter, an abuser of any other substance. I did not expect that they would. Had any of them done so, I would have been greatly remorseful. Was the risk, while small in my opinion, worth our small adventure? That is difficult to answer directly. We were all explorers of a kind or we would not have been in Laos—and in an opium den at that. I might beg the question by saying we were all several years younger then and more bent on riskful adventure than cautious conservatism. Such ventures together also cemented the bonds between us. But there is a risk to curiosity about opium as we will see further on, especially if it remains readily available to the experimenter and if the experimenter has an ongoing problem, such as chronic pain, loneliness, or fear.

Interviews in the Community

In the course of living and working in Laos over a decade, I met and talked with many Caucasian people who had used opium and some who were or had been addicted. No doubt my identity as someone doing research on opium use, as a physician who treated addicts, and as a consultant to the local treatment program for addicts favored more open communication on the topic than might otherwise have been likely. Experience in interviewing a few thousand addicts and alcoholics, my interest in the topic, and a familiarity with users' and addicts' common life experiences and perceptions probably contributed to our mutual entertainment from such conversations.

We met in a variety of settings. A few of the people reported in the vignettes accompanying this chapter told me about themselves over dinner. My favorite restaurant for this preoccupation was run by a Vietnamese family who bought fresh Lao food at the local market and cooked it French style. The resulting cuisine was both superb and inexpensive, and I count my times collecting data there among my favorite "field study" memories. Since the place was generally crowded and people had to share long rows of tables, it provided an excellent means for meeting expatriate visitors to Laos. In other settings I met Caucasian addicts through mutual friends in Laos. One man who had been addicted sought me out at an international meeting in the United States. A meandering student doing research in Laos on addiction turned out to be an addict herself. Unknown to me at the time, one Caucasian addict was a coworker with whom I shared meals, sleeping quarters, and (during an attack on a refugee camp by the North Vietnamese) a foxhole and a hairy-scary helicopter escape under cover of darkness.

For any social scientist but especially for a clinician, interviewing addicts outside the clinical setting is a crucial experience. It lends some logic (albeit imperfectly) to what, from the purely clinical vantage point, often appears absolutely crazy or suicidal behavior. It removes the doctor-patient relationship, with its various transactional gambits and biases. Yet, such nonclinical interviewing has its limitations, for the interaction generally occurs over a relatively brief time and often excludes references to familial, financial, health, sexual, and other problems associated with addiction, since addicts not in crisis generally minimize the problematic aspects of their opiate devotions. After several conversations with addicts in social settings and then several more with addicts and their families in clinical settings, one can appreciate the wide perceptual gap that often separates social scientists and clinicians who are studying the same problem (whether it be diabetes, schizophrenia, or addiction).

Research in the Clinical Context

During the period from October of 1972 to May of 1975 (three years and eight months), 130 Caucasian addicts sought treatment at the National Narcotic Detoxification Center. When compared to treatment programs elsewhere in Asia, this was an extraordinary occurrence, since the number of Caucasian addicts in treatment is nil (or at least under 1 percent of patients). Acceptance of Caucasian addicts at the Treatment Center was probably due to several factors, among them being (1) the tolerance of many Laotian citizens for people of other backgrounds (critical in a country with scores of ethnic minorities), (2) absence of police pressure as a result of seeking treatment, and (3) staff facility in French (i.e., the director, Dr. Chomchan Soudaly) and English (i.e., an American administrative liaison, Larry Berger).

This ready acceptance of the Center by expatriate addicts provided a unique entree to a group about whom little was known. Demographic and clinical data were obtained on these Caucasian addicts, just as from indigenous addicts. In addition, the author had the opportunity to interview several of them at length during their treatment and follow-up visits. They were a pleasant group, most of whom were quite willing to educate me to their experiences and points of view.

The Peace Corps Teacher. Life had always presented Bob with struggles. A loner, he felt intensely uncomfortable in almost any social setting. A neurological disorder from childhood had left him crippled and dependent on orthopedic devices. Halfway through his teens, in association with his neurological problems, he developed the kind of degenerative arthritis that most people do not experience until their sixties or seventies. Anxious to transcend his psychological and physical disabilities, he had achieved a graduate degree in his field. He then joined the Peace Corps in the hope of finding a better social fit for himself in another society. Predictably, his chronic pain, isolation, and ennui followed him to his teaching position in the Malay Archipelago. After several months in Asia, a Chinese colleague—trying to show him a bit of local color—took him to a local opium den for a few pipes. Somewhat to Bob's surprise, he thoroughly enjoyed the experience: the feeling of relaxation and pleasure from the opium, the adumbrated camaraderie of the other smokers, and the absence of familiar (and painful) reminders of his lamentable past. There in the den he was not the wallflower at the high school dance, the bystander at physical education, the stoical enigma among his grad school classmates. The Chinese habitués enjoyed having the foreign devil in their presence, and he appreciated their easy acceptance. The next weekend he repeated his visit, and soon he was returning midweek to smoke. Within a few months he was addicted.

At the end of his tour, he included a few kilograms of opium in his personal gear to meet his needs during a visit home. As his supply dwindled, he began urgently seeking a position back in Asia. He took a job in Laos as an office worker. There he met and married an attractive and energetic Lao widow, the mother of four children, whose husband had been killed in the war. Aware of his opium use, she at first accepted it as a bad habit from which she expected to wean him. Soon after their marriage she found that he spent most evenings and virtually the entire weekend sotted on opium. She began to confront him about the poor example he set for the children and the financial drain from his ever-increasing addiction. Finally, her threat to leave him provided the occasion for Bob and me to meet. He sought treatment at the Narcotic Treatment Center. When I last saw him one year following treatment, he was still abstinent from opium. His self-confidence had grown through his role as husband and father, although his physical disabilities were as bothersome as ever.

INTRODUCTION TO USING OPIATES

Where?

Fifty-six Caucasian patients at the Narcotic Treatment Center were asked where they first used narcotic drugs. Only 11 of them (20 percent) first used these drugs in their country of origin: 6 in Australia, 2 in the United States, 2 in France, and 1 in Germany. Three others first became addicted in places outside Asia (i.e., 2 Frenchmen in Holland and 1 Frenchman in the United States). Thirty-nine of them (70 percent) were first addicted in Asia. The remaining 3 addicts either were not certain where they first used opiates or preferred not to say. This trend for travelers to become addicted away from home is not so extraordinary in view of the fact that the United States and some other countries do not allow convicted felons or those on probation to obtain a visa without a rather thorough investigation.

Of the thirty-nine people who first used opiates in Asia, 23 of them began use in countries besides Laos. These included the countries of south Asia (India, Afghanistan, Pakistan), Southeast Asia (Thailand, Vietnam), and the Malay Archipelago (Malaysia, Indonesia).

Sixteen addicts, 13 of them French, first began opiate use in Laos. Most were currently employed and living in Laos, including 10 who were French and 1 who was British. People in this latter group had generally been addicted from several years to a few decades. The remaining 5 addicts—3 French, 1 British, and 1 Dutch—were unemployed travelers who had become addicted in Laos relatively recently.

Countries of initial narcotic use and number of addicts for each location were as follows:

Asia (n = 39)

Laos	16	(29%)
Thailand	8	(14%)
Vietnam	4	(7%)
India	3	(5%)
Malaysia	3	(5%)
Indonesia	2	(4%)
Afghanistan	2	(4%)
Pakistan	1	(2%)

Europe (n = 5)

Holland	2	(4%)
France	2	(4%)
Germany	1	(2%)
Australia	6	(11%)
United States	3	(5%)
Unknown	3	(5%)
	56	(101%)*

*Because of rounding off of percentages, the sum is more than 100%.

In most instances people became addicted in the same country where they began to take opiates.

How common is it for addicts in the United States to begin opiate use in Asia? Quite infrequent it would appear. Of 100 addicts from Minneapolis studied by Berger and me (1977), only one man had become addicted outside the United States. A graduate student, he had begun injecting heroin while traveling in Nepal.

Why?

One of the more labile bits of data obtained from addicts concerns their reasons for first trying opiate drugs. One can obtain one response from an addict in the morning and an entirely different response from the same person that evening. Nowhere are the whim of the moment and the biases of the investigator more apt to hold sway than on this variable. People seem willing to provide whatever rationalizations the questioner wants.

With these caveats in mind, let us look at responses of NNDC Caucasian and Asian addicts in 1973 and 1974 to the question, "Why did you first use opiates?" No categories were provided from which the patients might select. Instead, their responses were tabulated and categorized after the fact. Their responses were as follows:

Reason	Number of addicts (percentage)	
	Caucasians	Asians
Curiosity, voluntary	10 (18)	260 (52)
Medical problems	0 (0)	143 (29)
Friends, peer pressure	33 (59)	61 (12)
Relatives, family	0 (0)	13 (3)
Unknown, other responses	13 (23)	21 (4)
	56 (100)	498 (100)

From a statistical perspective, these two groups were very different ($X^2_4 = 115.5493$, $P < .001$). It appears that the Caucasian addicts were much more influenced by friends and peers—not a surprising finding since they were mostly living or traveling in the company of nonkin. Both curiosity and medical problems were considerably more common reasons among Asian addicts.

Prior military service in Indochina was not common among these Caucasian addicts. Only one American had been on active duty in Vietnam. He had used narcotic drugs there but had also used drugs heavily prior to entering the service.

The French Drug Dealer. Jacques's father had been a colonel with the French army in Indochina during the 1940s and 1950s. After Jacques had dropped out of the *lycée*, impregnated the daughter of a prominent family, and proven unable to hold any of several jobs, his father suggested that he might seek his fortune in Indochina. Besides giving Jacques a one-way airline ticket, his father promised to send a small monthly stipend from his service pension. (It seems likely that his father sent him with the expectation that Indochina would make a gentleman or a corpse of his wayward son.)

Jacques soon met two other countrymen like himself, both selling heroin to world travelers and using it themselves. Within a month of arriving in Vientiane, he was addicted. During the subsequent two years he fared better than he had in France. He made reasonably good profits with relatively little effort, lived in the Bungalow (one of the better class B hotels in town), and had girlfriends from time to time.

Jacques and I sometimes shared adjacent tables at a downtown restaurant in 1975. He told of getting strung out on too much heroin some five months earlier. At that time he was treated at the Narcotic Detoxification Center. He remained abstinent for several weeks, then began chipping,* and was currently using daily again—but taking care to limit his dosage. As I repeatedly encountered Jacques and his two friends around Vientiane, the steadfastness of their three-sided partnership became evident. All three comprised an armed, mobile heroin business. They carried concealed small handguns and volumes of heroin and could make change in several currencies on the spot. Yet they were known to be fair to their clientele and generous in their charitable contributions to the local police. Perhaps in his own way, Jacques was on his way to growing up. Pity I was not able to see over time whether the colonel ever got back a gentleman or a corpse.

DEMOGRAPHIC CHARACTERISTICS

Age and Sex

These 56 Caucasian people studied at NNDC ranged in age from 18 to 52 years, with a mean of 27.1 years (standard deviation of 6.3). They were predominantly young adults, with 82 percent under the age of 30. Age distribution by decade was as follows:

under 20 years	1	(2%)
20–29 years	45	(80%)
30–39 years	7	(13%)
40–49 years	2	(4%)
50–59 years	1	(2%)
	56	(101%)

Of the 56 Caucasians, 45 were men and 11 were women, a sex ratio of 4 to 1.

---

*This refers to episodic, nonaddictive opiate use.

172

Nationality

National origins for the 56 addicts were as follows:

France	25	(45%)
United States	11	(20%)
England	7	(13%)
Australia	7	(13%)
Italy	3	(5%)
Canada	1	(2%)
Germany	1	(2%)
Holland	1	(2%)
	56	(102%)

It is not surprising that French people comprised the largest group. Laos had once been a French colony, and numerous French citizens had lived in Laos for decades. Laos remained a favorite of French tourists, since French was the second most widely spoken language in the country. An extensive French literature on the history, anthropology, architecture, religion, art, and medicine of Indochina also drew French scholars as well as tourists.

Several Caucasian addicts had been born into families who had worked abroad for the diplomatic corps, in the military, or for business interests. For example, two out of the twenty-five French addicts in this sample were born in Saigon, and a third Frenchman was born in Algeria. Prior to their current Asian sojourn, several other addicts had journeyed to foreign countries with the military, as civilian employees of private enterprises or their governments, as students, or as tourists.

Marital Status and Residence

Marital status among the 56 Caucasian patients was as follows:

Single	39	(70%)
Married	11	(20%)
Divorced	5	(9%)
Unknown	1	(2%)
	56	(101%)

Unlike the Asian addicts, most in this group were single. Among those married, two addicts were married to each other, eight were still living with nonaddicted wives, and one man's wife had recently gone to live with her parents. The "unknown" case was not sure if he was still married or whether his wife had permanently separated from him.

Current residence was as follows:

Alone	33	(59%)
With friends	11	(20%)
With family	10	(18%)
With relatives	1	(2%)
Unknown	1	(2%)
	56	(101%)

Again unlike the Asian addicts, most of this group were currently living alone. These solitary addicts were world travelers who were in Laos only temporarily. Their peripatetic habits were largely the result of visa restrictions in most Asian countries that readily permitted brief visits and repeated reentries but stringently prohibited prolonged stays. Only the French nationals could readily attain lengthy residence because of the absence of a visa requirement for anyone with a French passport. Many nationals from other countries participated in continuous transmigrations from one country to another. Some would prepare for this by gradually reducing their dosage in anticipation of missed doses. Other itinerants knew that they could take their morning dose in country A, make it through emigration customs, travel, and clear immigration customs in time to obtain heroin or opium from their usual dealer in country B by noon.

Most of those with stable employment in Laos lived with family or friends. One young Frenchman lived with his relatives. This group was comprised primarily of French people, although there were a few other Europeans and North Americans in the group.

Occupation and Employment

Prior to beginning their peregrinations, many of those in their mid-twenties and older had worked at skilled occupations. These included shoe repair person, business person, barber, secretary, chef, teacher, reporter, surveyor, musician, artist, and welder. About half had a college education in such fields as education, journalism, chemistry, engineering, and statistics. One man held a master's degree in his field. Six younger addicts had been students prior to leaving home; they had never been regularly employed.

Of the 56 addicts, 37 of them (66 percent) were currently unemployed. Seventeen were employed (i.e., 30 percent), and 2 people were not sure if they would be allowed to resume their positions (i.e., 4 percent). The largest current occupation was teaching (10 subjects); the people were temporary language tutors and young French volunteers working for a year or two in Laotian schools. Other current occupations included two journalists, two office workers, an engineer, a businessman, and a security officer.

All five people addicted for three years or longer had settled in Laos more or less permanently, and they were employed in stable positions. Most of those with shorter addictions were on an extended tour of Asia, supported either by their savings or family money. A few addicts had exhausted their funds and/or their family's patience, and were working at parttime or temporary jobs as they journeyed.

My Foxhole Friend. Tom was well on his way to becoming an old Asian hand. Following college, he had spent two years in Thailand with the United States Peace Corps. After working there on a rural development project, he decided to remain in Southeast Asia. His next position was with the International Voluntary Service (I.V.S.) in Laos, again working in rural areas. Sociable, pleasant, and hard working, he was soon asked to join an Agency for International Development refugee relief program working in northern Laos. It was in that context that we came to know each other in 1966. Tom's refugee aid group had an office and warehouse a few mintues' walk from the hospital where I often worked.

On a few occasions we worked together among refugee groups in remote areas, Tom looking after their need for food and blankets, while I attended to acute infectious disorders, minor epidemics, and wounds. On one occasion we were together in a small valley town when it was attacked with mortars and machine-gun fire. We spent some hours in ditches together trying to blend with the earth, eventually making our way to a field from which we were happily rescued. That first baptism of fire for us both lent a special camaraderie to our friendship.

It came as no small surprise to me, then, when Tom was suddenly discharged from his job one day. He had tried opium initially out of curiosity, as had many of his peers. Unlike them, he had become addicted. Perhaps it was the timing. Recently two other volunteers with I.V.S. had been killed by communists while engaged in rural development work. Mass refugee moves demanded that he work long hours, seven days a week, for weeks at a time. The locale where he worked was considerably more proximate to danger than were the locales of his two dead comrades. A third refugee worker had recently been killed in an attack on another valley town. Within a few months of trying opium, Tom was addicted. He successfully hid it from his American colleagues. Though I saw him frequently during this time I had no inkling that he was even using opium, much less that he was addicted.

Word of his addiction readily spread among the Hmong, who knew he was frequenting an opium den on a regular basis. Tom's position was an important link in the refugee relief work among the Hmong and other peoples of northern Laos. They could not accept the risk of having an addict in this key position on which so many lives depended. A deputation of Hmong leaders went to Tom's supervisor about the matter. To a man, they spoke of his industry and their personal affection for him, feelings shared by his supervisor and other Americans who knew him. Despite everyone's affection for him, there was only one resolution to the problem. On the same day, Tom was on his way back to the United States.

PATTERNS OF USAGE

Preaddictive Narcotic Use

These 56 Caucasian addicts began using narcotic drugs at the average age of 24.1 years (standard deviation 5.1). This was about one decade younger than the average age of Asian addicts in Laos at initial use. The average duration of preaddictive use among these Caucasians was 0.5 years (standard deviation 1.2), shorter than the mean values for both Asian heroin addicts (0.7 years) and Asian opium addicts (1.3 years). A few Caucasians became addicted within a month, while at the other end of the spectrum one man used heroin off and on for 6 years before experiencing physiological addiction. Most became addicted after taking narcotic drugs for some months, as indicated here:

under 12 months	44	(79%)
12–23 months	5	(9%)
24–35 months	2	(4%)
36–47 months	3	(5%)
48 months or over	2	(4%)
	56	(101%)

One of the fifty-six was initiated into opiate use by a spouse, and another by a relative. All of the remainder received their introduction from acquaintances. Opium den owners and other narcotic salesmen did not force or pressure any of them to try opiates.

Addictive Course

Distribution of age at addiction was as follows:

under 20 years	8	(14%)
20–29 years	41	(73%)
30–39 years	6	(11%)
40–49 years	1	(2%)
	56	(100%)

Mean age at addiction was 24.6 years (standard deviation 4.9).

Subsequently, these 56 addicts sought treatment for addiction in Laos after having been addicted for an average of 2.5 years (standard deviation 4.3). The briefest duration of addiction prior to treatment was 3 months, and the longest was 19 years. Duration of addiction prior to treatment was as follows:

under 1 year–21 ⎫ 1–5 years –31 ⎬	52*	(93%)
6–10 years	2	(4%)
over 10 years	2	(4%)
	56	(101%)

*The number of addicts in the first 5-year period has been separated into those addicted for less than one year (i.e., 21) and those addicted from 1 to 5 years (i.e., 31, or a mean of about 8 per year). This has been done to demonstrate the relatively large number of

Out of the entire group, forty-four people (79 percent) had previously undergone narcotic withdrawal; some of them numerous times as they traveled from country to country. In order to avoid carrying drugs through customs, they either gradually discontinued their dosage, went through "cold turkey" withdrawal (i.e., abrupt cessation of drugs), or counted on making a connection (i.e., buying drugs) in the next country before withdrawal became severe. Examples of withdrawal episodes and countries were as follows:

23-year-old French female—4 withdrawal episodes (Australia, Malaysia, Thailand, Laos);

25-year-old French male—4 withdrawal episodes (Holland, Malaysia, Thailand, Laos);

26-year-old French male—3 withdrawal episodes (France, India, Laos);

28-year-old American male—3 withdrawal episodes (Malaysia, Africa, Laos);

31-year-old American male—5 withdrawal episodes (United States, India, Afghanistan, Thailand, Laos).

Several people who first became addicted in Laos, either in recent months or years ago, had never gone through withdrawal.

Type of Drug and Mode of Administration

The number of Caucasian addicts currently using various opiate drug combinations was as follows:

heroin only	39	(70%)
opium only	10	(18%)
opium and heroin	7	(13%)
	56	(101%)

In general, opium users were employed and residing in Laos and heroin users were world travelers. There were exceptions in both directions, with a few travelers using opium at times and a few Vientiane residents using heroin.

---

addicts in this group coming early to treatment, unlike indigenous addicts who tend to come for treatment much later on.

Mode of administration occurred as follows:

injecting	27	(48%)
smoking	19	(34%)
snuffing	8	(14%)
smoking-and-eating	2	(4%)
	56	(100%)

All of the snuffers and injectors were using heroin. The two who combined smoking and eating were on opium. Smokers included both opium and heroin users.

The predominance of heroin use, injecting, and snuffing among the Caucasians was in marked contrast to indigenous practice (i.e., mostly opium eating or smoking, with some heroin smoking). This points up the separate realms of some Asian and Caucasian opiate consumption in Laos, with some influence of Asian practice on certain Caucasians. Only infrequently did Caucasians and Asians join one another in opiate use. (The case of the Peace Corps worker in Malaysia described earlier is an exception to this general statement.)

Doses Per Day and Daily Cost

A dose is defined here as a specific time during which the drug is taken. For example, 5 opium pipes taken 3 times a day would comprise 3 doses. Twenty heroin cigarettes taken at 20 intervals during the day would be 20 doses.

There was a bimodal distribution of daily doses as follows:

once daily	2	(4%)
twice daily	6	(11%)
three times	15	(27%)
four times	4	(7%)
five or more times	27	(48%)
variable	2	(4%)
	56	(101%)

This bimodal distribution was largely due to opium addicts taking 1 to 3 doses per day and heroin addicts taking 3 or more doses daily. Heroin injectors took between 3 and 7 doses per day. Those smoking or snuffing heroin took 3 to 20 doses per day.

The daily cost also showed a bimodal distribution:

under $2.00	3	(5%)
$2.01–$4.00	13	(23%)
$4.01–$6.00	4	(7%)
$6.01–$8.00	10	(18%)
over $8.00	10	(18%)
unknown, variable	16	(29%)
	56	(100%)

Opium addicts were all spending less than $3.00 per day. Heroin addicts were spending between $2.50 and $12.00 per day. Many recently arrived addicts could not describe their usual daily cost, either because of the great variability in price, lack of familiarity with local exchange, or both.

During 1973 one gram of fifty-to-eighty-percent-pure heroin sold for $5.00 to $10.00 in Vientiane, at least for the experienced person able to obtain a reasonable price. Despite these relatively low prices for opiates, drugs still comprised the major daily expenditure for most Caucasian addicts. At the time of the study most world travelers paid between $0.50 to $0.75 for lodging at one of the four small hotels that catered to them. They could purchase adequate food at soup shops and fruit stands for $1.00 to $1.50 per day.

Context of Opiate Use

The most usual social context of opiate use among these Caucasian addicts was as follows:

alone	30	(54%)
with peers	21	(38%)
with family	5	(9%)
	56	(101%)

This current context differed considerably from their original use, which took place in a social context rather than alone.

About a third of these addicts (31 percent) had never been to an opium den. Several others had purchased narcotic drugs at a den but had never consumed them there. The remainder had used drugs in a den at some time, but none was currently consuming drugs regularly in a den setting.

The European Social Scientist. Eric and I met at an international meeting, where our common interest in Asian mountaineers brought us together. He told me of his first becoming addicted a decade earlier, while he was in his twenties, at the time he was undertaking his first field research. There were the usual anxieties of undertaking field work. (Will they accept me here? Will I succeed?) Added to this were the unfamiliarity of the food and the surroundings, the early difficulty with the language, the isolation from fellow expatriates, and (from his perspective) the repetitive, unexciting weeks as they flowed into months.

Initially he was curious about observing opium smoking as he was about many facets of mountain life. Sensitive and almost pain-fully shy, he was reluctant to ask if he might join in the experience although he wished to do so. Eventually one of his main informants asked him to share a pipe. Despite the initial nausea, he enjoyed the relaxation and high spirits that the substance engendered in him. Soon he was smoking every evening with his host during their research interviews, and after a few more weeks he was taking morning doses to stave off his withdrawal. For the remaining several months of his research project Eric remained addicted. During his last few months in the country's capital city, he withdrew himself "cold turkey." Severe bodily aching and gastrointestinal symptoms persisted during this time; and myalgia, dysphoria, and insomnia lasted several weeks more after his arrival in his home country. During an interim of several years in Europe he did not crave or attempt to seek narcotic drugs, and he did not abuse alcohol or other drugs.

Upon returning to Southeast Asia after several years to resume field research, he became readdicted within several days of arriving. Again, he remained addicted throughout his stay and then suddenly withdrew himself a few weeks before returning home. When I met him a few years later, he still neither craved opium nor abused other drugs. Nonetheless, he stated quite affirmatively that he expected to resume addictive opium use if and when he returned to Southeast Asia. Parenthetically, his research work was substantive though not prolific. In his late thirties, he remained unmarried and continued to manifest considerable shyness. For those with the persistence to breach his timidity, Eric was a pleasant, bright, and articulate colleague.

CLINICAL OBSERVATIONS

Presenting Problems

These fifty-six Caucasian addicts came for treatment with problems similar to those of addicts seeking help elsewhere. Typical chief complaints included:

"My life is caving in on me."

"I feel sick most of the time."

"I have no work or money, and I want to get my wife and child back."

"I cut my brother's neck because he wouldn't give me money for heroin" (from an eighteen-year-old American in a Laotian jail for attempted murder).

Several addicts were brought to treatment by friends or acquaintances who were not addicted or who, if using narcotic drugs, still used them episodically or in a controlled fashion. In some cases these same comrades helped the addicts regain their health and continue their travels or return home. A few more were pressured into seeking help by wives tired of the financial drain and other consequences of addiction.

As was true of addicts anywhere, it was difficult to assess motivation for treatment. To be sure, all wanted help—but not necessarily the kind of help that the staff thought it was providing. Some wanted to get off heroin temporarily so they could travel to another country and resume narcotic use there. Others primarily wanted to regain health, self-esteem, employment, or family affiliation in order to continue narcotic use without the associated problems. A few wanted to get off drugs for good.

I followed the posttreatment course of several Caucasian addicts in Laos for a year or more. A few did remain abstinent, a few more resumed narcotic use in a more controlled fashion, and a few others returned to heavy use. Those few who remained abstinent were married and employed. Several other addicts left treatment with plans to return directly to their home country.

Initial Methadone Dose

Each patient's chart was reviewed to assess the total withdrawal dose of methadone given during the first twenty-four hours. An initial dose was given based on the history of recent narcotic use and the patient's physical evidence of withdrawal signs. Initial twenty-four-hour methadone doses given to this group were as follows:

5 mg.	1	(2%)
20 mg.	2	(4%)
30 mg.	5	(9%)
40 mg.	16	(29%)
50 mg.	17	(30%)
60 mg.	7	(13%)
70 mg.	1	(2%)
80 mg.	5	(9%)
90 mg.	2	(4%)
	56	(102%)

The patient who received only five milligrams of methadone, a twenty-seven-year-old Dutch woman, was probably not physiologically addicted at the time of treatment. She had been smoking opium for a year and had tried two times to decrease her dosage gradually and withdraw herself. Each time she became panic-stricken at the thought of going without opium and increased her dosage again to addictive levels. Minimal amounts of methadone for a few days, followed by placebos and a few weeks of daily supportive outpatient visits enabled her to discontinue narcotic drugs and to return home to Holland.

Except for this one woman, all of the Caucasian patients showed physiologic signs of addiction. Those using opium required smaller amounts of methadone initially (20 to 50 milligrams) but had to continue it over a longer period (2 to 4 weeks). Heroin addicts needed larger initial doses (usually 40 to 90 milligrams) but could be withdrawn more rapidly (1 to 3 weeks). Most patients were followed in the outpatient department for a month or two.

Readmission

All charts were surveyed 365 days following discharge. During this period only one person was readmitted, an eighteen-year-old American who had been injecting heroin for less than a year. On the first admission he quit treatment after one week. Two-and-a-half months later he returned for treatment after having twice attempted to withdraw himself. On the second admission he completed withdrawal treatment.

In Search of a Stern Parent. Hans was one of the more skillfully obnoxious people it has been my fortune to meet. The youngest son of a wealthy German industrialist, he was a past master at the art of alienation and social masochism. Within five or ten minutes he could antagonize the most phlegmatic government functionary at the Narcotic Detoxification Center. It seemed to be the only skill he had acquired in his twenty years, at least besides linguistic proficiency in several European languages. He had no difficulty conversing with the Lao staff in fluent French. With me he spoke a flawless, clipped, London version of English, without a hint of Germanic overtones (except perhaps in his haughty mien). His appearance was as initially intriguing as his surface sophistication. Delicate, with finely chiseled features, he wore an expensive, embroidered black silk Chinese tunic over a pair of rough canvas pants cut high above his Asian thongs.

Hans had developed his brief social exchanges to a high art. They began with his smoothly attracting someone, anyone, into conversation. There followed in short order some outrageous demand: a wish to be served breakfast at a restaurant in the afternoon, a request for a watch on credit in a jewelry store, approval from the medical staff at the Center that he receive morning doses of methadone to stave off his withdrawal so he could have glorious heroin trips in the evening. When refused, Hans would launch into a cool, scathing string of insults and diatribes against the individual whom he had so recently engaged —and who in many cases then became (ambivalently) his persecutor, tossing him out of shop, clinic, or restaurant on his ear.

In several brief snatches, Hans allowed me some glimpses into his past life. He had been raised by a series of French *au pair* girls and English matrons, none of whom could apparently tolerate him (or possibly his parents) for more than several months. When old enough to attend school, he matriculated transiently through a series of Swiss and English private schools. At eighteen, when he came into a small annual inheritance, he promptly dropped out of school and began his world travels. Two years later found him in Laos on heroin, again replicating the isolated and alienating lifestyle that he had learned many years earlier.

COMPARISON WITH AMERICAN "AT-HOME" ADDICTS

Ideally, this group of fifty-six Caucasian addicts should be compared with addicts in their home countries who had the same characteristics, but that was not feasible. They could readily be compared with addicts from the United States, however, and this was undertaken by Berger and me (1977) using 100 addicts from a Minneapolis methadone program. The Minneapolis addicts were admitted for treatment at the same time as the fifty-six Caucasian addicts in Laos (late 1973 to early 1975). In addition, the American group was selected to resemble the Caucasian group in Laos by age and sex distribution.

Demographic Characteristics

As compared to the American addicts, more of the Caucasian addicts in Laos had never been married (30 percent versus 58 percent). More of the Vientiane group were also living alone (59 percent versus 11 percent). Approximately two-thirds of both groups were currently unemployed.

The occupational and educational levels of the two groups were considerably different. Most of the Vientiane addicts had training for specific job skills or had attended college, and they had previously been employed in their countries-of-origin. By contrast, the Minneapolis group included sizeable percentages of high school dropouts, ex-convicts, prostitutes, and people who had never been regularly employed. There was some minimal overlap between the two groups, with one graduate student in the Minneapolis group and several youths without training or job experience among the Caucasians in Laos.

Narcotic Use

The Vientiane group started using narcotic drugs at a mean age of 24.1 years, as compared to a mean of 20.0 years for the Minneapolis group. The world travelers used opiates for an average of 0.5 years prior to becoming addicted, as compared to 1.5 years for the Minneapolis group. The travelers were also addicted for a shorter average time before seeking treatment: 2.5 years as compared to 6.0 years among the Minneapolis group. Despite their shorter period of addiction, slightly more of the Vientiane group had gone through withdrawal previously as compared to the Minneapolis group (84 percent vs. 79 percent).

Daily cost of opiate drugs was compared for 40 Vientiane and 40 Minneapolis addicts. Expenditures in Laos ranged from $2.00 to $12.00 per day, with a median of $6.00 and a mean of $5.80. Daily expenditures in Minneapolis varied from $30.00 to $250.00, with a median of $85.00 and a mean of $94.00.

A College Without Walls. Ruth had left messages in several places around Vientiane that she wanted to interview me about opium addicts for a college course. She had heard through the American grapevine that I was back in Laos to do a follow-up study of treated addicts. Helping someone write a term paper was not my idea of how best to enjoy a few leisure hours while in Vientiane on a tight work schedule, so I ignored her messages. Finally Ruth trapped me in a tea-and-soup shop on the small main thoroughfare as I was trying to catch up on the week's world news in the Sunday *Bangkok Post.* Unable to tactfully extricate myself, I helped her with those questions that she hadn't been able to answer on her own.

While we talked, two things struck me about Ruth. First, she was wearing a long-sleeved blouse in late March—a scorching time of year. And second, she was sweating buckets, much more than either the temperature or the warm soup could account for. Her interview over, I asked if I could interview her. "Sure," she said. "Are you on heroin?" I asked. "Sure," she said. "Would you mind telling me about it?" I asked. "Be glad to," she said.

Ruth first used heroin while she was attending a private boarding high school in Connecticut. From time to time, her roommate from Manhattan took her home for visits, and they both shot up during these occasional weekends. Following graduation, Ruth decided on a Manhattan college. While there, she began using heroin more frequently. During her holiday visits to her parents' home in eastern Africa, she found she could obtain heroin there. Before long she was addicted.

College and heroin didn't mix well. Failing grades forced her out of school, precipitating the threat that her parents' support of her education might cease. So Ruth enrolled in a "college without walls," in which physical attendance in classes and at lectures was not required. This led to her current world travels. Although she was off narcotics for the early part of her trip (following treatment), she became readdicted in Malaysia. This had cut deeply into her educational plans. For a year she had supported herself and her habit as a taxi dancer, living intermittently with a few men. She had journeyed to Laos with an American boyfriend, also addicted.

A few Sunday afternoons later at my favorite reading-and-tea shop, I was again cornered by Ruth, who had a fever of 103° and a swollen left arm. On examination, she had a severe thrombophlebitis of her left forearm (from injecting heroin) with several enlarged and tender nodes in her armpit. She wanted to know what to do. "Antibiotics, warm packs to the arm, bed rest, and plenty fluids," said I. "Okay, except for the antibiotics," said she with no hint of irony; "I don't like to put anything unnatural in my body."* "You may not have a body soon if you don't," I responded. We ambled down the block to a pharmacy for her medicine, and I gave her the directions to the Narcotic Detoxification Center in case she wasn't well in a day or two. And I suggested she might consider treatment for her addiction there. My Lao colleague at NNDC said she never showed up.

COMMENT

1. For some Caucasian addicts in Asia, narcotic drugs served as a social ticket into certain groups and activities, much as alcohol often plays a similar role (Lurie 1970, Westermeyer 1972c).

2. Travel removed the constraining influences of family, society, and day-to-day responsibilities from many of these subjects. With this new social anonymity, they were at greater liberty to take risks and experiment with behaviors in which they had not generally engaged at home. Travel replaced the usual social influences with increased peer influence from fellow world travelers. In this context, these Caucasians accepted a socially forbidden behavior that most of them had not sought previously.

3. Most Caucasian addicts in Laos (with a few older French people as exceptions) did not participate in the indigenous culture. They were isolated by language, cultural distance, and lack of affiliation. As indicated

---

*This is not an unusual response among some of today's more youthful substance abusers. Several abusers of alcohol, heroin, PCP, and other drugs have refused therapy with disulfiram, methadone, antibiotics, and other medications because they are "unnatural." Such ludicrous inconsistency does lighten the practice of medicine by providing opportunities for belly laughs in the clinical situation.

by an extensive literature on this topic, such isolation can result in a variety of social and psychological disorders (Odegaard 1932; Frost 1938; Roberts and Myers 1954; Hes 1958 and 1970; Mezey 1959; Prange 1959; Astrup and Odegaard 1959–1960; Ward 1961; Malzberg 1964; Gordon 1965; Wintrob 1967; Arnold 1967; Krupinski 1967; Copeland 1968; German and Arya 1969; Parker, Keliner, and Needelman 1969; Fong and Peskin 1969; Bagley and Binitie 1970; Seelye and Brewer 1970; Nicol 1971; Stephan and Stephan 1971; Bourne 1975).

4. The Asian countries to which they journeyed provided these predominantly middle-class travelers with ready access to inexpensive narcotic drugs. High availability of inexpensive drugs has been shown to play an important role among American soldier-addicts in South Vietnam (Robbins, Davis, Goodwin 1974) and in heroin "epidemics" within the United States (Greene 1974). This access to narcotic drugs probably affected the form that psychosocial disability took among these travelers, who tended to experience drug-related problems rather than depression. Narcotic addiction may also have motivated some travelers to remain in Asia close to the supply of drugs, while depressive homesickness or psychosomatic disorder might have motivated them to return home.

5. An admittedly incomplete comparison with American addicts in Minneapolis indicates that traveler addicts tended to be older, single, and better trained or educated and to have a better employment history. The expatriate Caucasians became addicted at a later age, used for a shorter time before becoming addicted, and sought treatment sooner as compared to the Americans. Routes of opium and heroin administration among Caucasians indicate that Asian traditions did influence a segment of this group, but most addicts employed European and American modes of heroin administration (i.e., injection, snuffing).

XI

Treatment Modalities

FOLK TREATMENTS

The Decision

As indicated earlier, opium addiction eventually exacted a high price from most addicts and their families. Their labor and wealth gradually disappeared like the haze from their pipes.

Out of such circumstances evolved pressures against continued addiction—or at least wishes that opiate use could be associated with fewer problems. Pressure usually came first from family members, whose nagging difficulties expanded into full-blown tragedies, until they could no longer abide their family member's addiction. In time most addicts gradually became aware that the source of their enjoyment had become a tyrant, ruling over their thoughts and behavior in myriad small and large ways. Slowly it dawned on them that they had given up considerable control over their lives to opium. The drug had come to dominate them, determining what they could and could not do, should and should not decide. Some blamed the opium itself for their discontent. "This opium today isn't as good as it was ten years ago," said one. "Opium, which was like a beautiful woman in my youth, has became an old hag with the years," opined another.*

Forty addicts (the field survey sample described earlier) were asked if they had ever tried to stop their addiction on their own or had ever

---

*In describing their experiences with opium, male addicts (especially among the Hmong) often wove analogies about women, their attractiveness, and the love-bond between a man and woman.

sought treatment. Twenty-nine of them reported having done so. These 29 had been addicted for a longer time (i.e., mean duration of 18 years) as compared to the 11 who had not made major efforts to stop using opium (i.e., mean duration of 8 years). Some had made efforts at self-treatment or had received assistance from their families. Others had gone to healers or traditional institutions to receive help, some of which provided treatment for opium addiction.

Decreasing Dosage

Considerable variability occurred in the extent of control exerted by addicts over their addiction. Some had maintained quite stable dosages over decades ("titer" addicts), while others used virtually all the drug that they could afford ("binge" addicts). Like alcoholics who have learned to drink themselves off of a binge by gradually reducing their intake, both "titer" and "binge" opium smokers knew that they could increase or decrease dosage with predictable effects. Increasing dosage suddenly would cause them to become intoxicated (*mow* in Lao). Decreasing dosage in small increments allowed them to titrate their withdrawal effects. For example, a 5 or 10 percent daily decrease in dosage might produce some malaise, insomnia, and loss of appetite but would not produce the days of agony, diarrhea, and vomiting produced by sudden "cold turkey" withdrawal. Relatively few addicts ever decreased their dosage gradually to nothing.*

More commonly addicts reduced their dosage for practical reasons, without any intent to totally discontinue addiction. Such reasons included planting time, harvest time, or a long trip. During the decade from 1965 to 1975, refugee movements and a decreased opium supply stimulated reduced doses among many addicts in Laos. For example, all of the forty addicts interviewed during 1971 and 1972 were using less opium than they had previously. Most of them were refugee farmers who could raise only small poppy crops on poor soil in refugee relocation areas. Others who purchased their opium, such as the Lao and Chinese, found that the increasing cost prevented their purchasing the large amounts to which they had become accustomed.

---

*Knowledge of this reality (i.e., that they could withdraw themselves) and the ability to implement it were two different things. As addicts reduced their doses to minimal levels, they often experienced fears of death, panic attacks, and overwhelming dysphoria.

A Resolute Man. Ah Kuh was a quiet man, aloof and somewhat uncomfortable in the company of his neighbors and clan members. He preferred to work and hunt by himself rather than join in the small mutual-
help groups favored by other Hmong. What he lacked in sociability,
however, he made up for in his industry. He enjoyed working hard and
keeping busy. As a young man in his twenties his labor brought considerable wealth to his family. His wife had so much silver around her
neck that she complained about the weight of it. Not satisfied with just
his own cash crop profits, he also began to trade and sell (during the
dry season) when he was around thirty.

 Although he had raised poppy for over half his life, he had never
smoked it. But as he began to travel and trade among the Hmong,
he tasted and smoked small quantities of opium to assess its quality
and value. Over time he observed that this ritual had an additional
benefit: it alleviated his feeling ill at ease during the inevitable bargaining and social rituals that attended his business. Still, for some years
he only smoked opium on his trading trips. Back at his solitary farming
and hunting activities during the rest of the year, he felt no need for
opium.

 During his fourth year of trading, however, Ah Kuh began to
smoke every evening. When he returned from that trip, he felt the
opium sickness when he tried to stop it. Since his opium habit had
caused him no harm and since he was a relatively wealthy man, he
saw no reason to give it up.

 Yet gradually over the subsequent sixteen years, his opium habit
began to wear upon him. He found that his ambitions had become
dulled and most of his profits were being consumed by opium smoking. Along with this, his family fortunes had waned. His wife wore old
patched clothes and no silver ornamentation. His children were virtually
illiterate and not particularly outstanding in their achievements. One
day he decided to reverse this so that he could become more committed to his work, increase his wealth, and become a model to his
children.

 Characteristically for him, Ah Kuh attacked his problem in the
same fashion by which he farmed, hunted, and traded: by himself.
With only enough opium to wean himself gradually from addiction, he
went off in the forest to live alone for two weeks. Asked his reason
for doing so, he responded that he had isolated himself in order to
remove the temptation to smoke that always affected him in familiar
surroundings. He did indeed successfully withdraw himself and re-

turned to his village a few weeks later. He remained abstinent and began to work more diligently.

After two months of abstinence, he developed a bout of diarrhea (a common malady in the area). For a few days he tolerated it, but then he decided that certainly a small amount of opium might help him and not lead to readdiction. After all, he reasoned, hadn't he managed to remain abstinent for two months? Certainly a little opium could not shake such resolve. From the first draught of opium from the pipe, the dosage and frequency with which he took the drug inexorably increased so that within a few weeks he was as addicted as ever.

A Group Plan. An assault on a Hmong village by Vietnamese forces had forced the villagers to move southwest out of Sam Neua province. It was several months before they were able to find a secure area large enough to accommodate them and to reestablish themselves. During this time the twelve addicts in the village developed a self-help group.

Two weeks after leaving their village, a few of the addicts began to go into withdrawal. This jeopardized the entire village group. Remaining in one place was impossible, since the villagers relied on foraging through the forest to obtain food. This rapidly depleted the nearby area of roots, berries, edible leaves, and small animals, and the group had to keep going in order to provide itself with food. In addition, they were still well within the area controlled by the North Vietnamese, and they were fearful of a repeat attack. Both the very old and the very young were beginning to weaken from the trek and the lack of shelter from the sun, the cold, and the rain; everyone wanted to move on rapidly to a place where shelter could be safely constructed. But moving on could mean death to the withdrawing addicts, since they were too weak either to move with the group or to look after their own needs if abandoned.

An older man, himself an addict, called a meeting of all of the addicts in the village. He explained that they should surrender all of the opium that they had with them into one common supply. Then if they all gradually decreased their opium dosage a small amount each day, they could stop using opium within a few weeks and have no fear of sickness or death. The common opium supply would be attended by the village leaders. All of the addicts agreed that they would carry out this plan together using what remained of their opium supply.

The plan worked well, and the villagers were able to resume their flight and reach a secure place some months later.

From Smoking to Eating Opium

Opium smoking provided a rapid onset of narcotic effects. Most addicts greatly preferred smoking opium over ingesting it, but the former method required a greater quantity of opium since much was wasted as smoke lost to the atmosphere. Consequently it was a more expensive means of narcotic administration. In contrast, opium eating was considerably less expensive than smoking, since most of the ingested drug was absorbed. This route of administration gave maximum pharmacological effect per unit of drug. It also lent itself more readily to work and travel, since the gradual onset of action was not so apt to be intoxicating. Ingestion of opium appeared less desirable to many addicts since, in comparison to smoking, it took a longer time to relieve withdrawal effects and did not produce the "rush" of sudden intoxication highly sought after by many addicts.

In the mid-1960s, when abundant opium was produced in northern Laos and the price was stable, most addicts took at least some of their opium by smoking. Some addicts might eat opium early in the day when they were working in order to stave off withdrawal (in their words, to provide strength) and then smoke opium to the point of intoxication in the evening before going to bed. Most addicts eating all of their opium in place of smoking it were financially destitute. As a temporary measure, addicts would use this route of administration during a period of planting, harvest, or travel.

By the early 1970s the situation had changed dramatically as poppy farmers from northern Laos became refugees because of the war in the north. Opium had to be brought from Thailand and Burma, and its price rose precipitously. Addicts responded to this dilemma by eating opium rather than smoking it, especially those who had to purchase their opium. For example, among 321 Lao patient-addicts treated at the National Narcotic Detoxification Center (NNDC) in 1972 and 1973, 40 percent were eating their opium and another 17 percent were combining the smoking and eating methods. By contrast, 20 percent of 81 Hmong (some of whom continued to grow some opium) were eating their opium and 6 percent were using the combined smoking-eating method. Chinese and Vietnamese addicts, who as merchants and artisans had larger incomes than Lao farmers, could afford the higher prices. Only 2 percent of these latter 43 addicts were eating their opium, while 12 percent were using the combined smoking and eating method.

Change from Opium to Other Drugs

Occasionally addicts gave up opium, only to replace it with large amounts of alcohol. When heroin first appeared in Laos, a few addicts took it as a cure for opium addiction, much as did opium addicts in the Western world over a century ago. Among Indochinese refugees in the United States who had formerly been addicts, a few have abused analgesic and sedative medications.

The War Widow. Chee Yua's father had been an addict. Having seen and experienced the trials that her addict-father imposed on his family, she resolved to marry a man whose kinship included no addicts. She achieved this goal in her marriage with Tou Sa Yang by whom she bore four children, three of whom survived infancy. Chee Yua was pleased with her life and made daily offerings to the ancestor spirits for having sent her better fortune than her mother's.

Chee and Tou Sa lived only a few valleys away from Dien Bien Phu. As war clouds gathered over Indochina again in the early 1960s, they were among the first Hmong affected by it. When other men of his village joined the militia on the side of the Royal Lao Government, Tou Sa joined with them. For a few years they harassed Vietnamese forces with small ambushes and hit-and-run tactics. Finally the Vietnamese moved against their village, attacking at night in their usual fashion. While Chee Yua, the other women, and their children all made it safely away from the village, about half of the young men died in the assault. Among the dead was Tou Sa. Chee and her children reached a refugee camp after trekking southeast for some months. During this time her youngest child died of malnutrition.

Tuberculosis was not particularly prevalent among the Hmong in their sparsely settled mountains, but it spread rapidly in the crowded refugee settlements. After about a year in the camp Chee developed a chronic cough. When herbal and spirit healers were unable to cure her, she began taking opium. She discovered that the drug not only alleviated her cough but also provided respite from the constant sadness and hopelessness that she had felt since her husband's death. A few years later her family brought her to a hospital that had recently been established in the mountains. There she was told to seek care for her illness in Vientiane, the capital city.

Opium was expensive in Vientiane, Chee discovered. The medicine that she received in Vientiane for her cough and weakness had helped, so she no longer needed the opium for that problem. She decided to try to do without it. On two occasions she successfully withdrew herself from opium using a Lao folk remedy consisting of herbal medications and rice whiskey. Each time after discontinuing the herbal whiskey, her old sadness and hopelessness returned (although her husband had been dead for several years). She would spend much of the day sitting, crying for no reason, unable to continue her wagework as a maid or care for her children. She found that drinking four tumbler-sized glasses of the rice whiskey each day helped, even without the herbs; but so much whiskey a day irritated her stomach and gave her headaches. Between the whiskey and the opium, Chee clearly preferred the opium. So each time she eventually returned to opium. At the time that I met her in 1971, Chee affirmed her urgent wish to stop her dependence on both substances, since as a poor widow she could afford neither. Yet without either of them, she found her existence unbearable.

Herbal Medication

This popular method of treatment was known to many addicts and their families. Herbal medicines for addiction sometimes contained some opium or alcohol mixed with a variety of other indigenous nostrums. Surprisingly, many addicts even used the herbal nostrums of other ethnic groups in an effort to effect a cure. Opium-containing spherules prepared and sold by Chinese herbalists were well known in Lao towns for relieving the withdrawal illness.

Physical Methods

Massage was used by the people of Laos for a wide variety of ailments. One form consisted of merely rubbing the skin in a fairly superficial manner, and another consisted of deep kneading and pinching of the flesh and muscles under the skin. Placing coals under a cotlike arrangement of boards, so that the hot air and steam rose through the planks, was used for sweat baths. A blanket might be put over the person to further capture body heat or to capture the steam. This had the benefit of relaxing the person but further accentuated fluid loss by perspiration. A third procedure was cupping or moxybustion. Small warmed glasses (or shells from a squash) were placed over the skin. When the warm air within the glass cooled, it produced a partial vacuum. The cup was then left there for some time until it produced a superficial bruising of the skin. At times this small ecchymosis was pierced in the middle with a pin or knife to induce bleeding, the theory being that this removed the bad blood in which the illness resided.

These remedies were used during the acute, toxic phases of withdrawal. At times they were applied by family members and at times by traditional healers or Buddhist monks. As familiar modes of therapy, they provided at least some placebo benefit (much as over-the-counter compounds or massage in our own society). Humoral theories of disease provided the rationales for these therapies, which were used by tribal groups, Lao, and expatriate Asians.

"Cold Turkey" Withdrawal

Abrupt cessation of opium was not voluntarily taken by most individuals after their addiction was well established. Addicts had a strong aversion to this approach, often stating that they felt certain death would ensue if they tried it. Despite this, about 3,000 Laotian addicts accepted this form of treatment when it was undertaken within a group setting at a Buddhist monastery in Thailand. This monastery, called Wat Tan Kha Bok, was known in Thailand for its treatment of opium addiction. Large numbers of Laotian addicts went there voluntarily despite their knowledge beforehand that painful "cold turkey" withdrawal awaited them. Since entire groups of addicts from whole villages went there together, an *esprit de corps* reinforced their commitment, permitting them to do that which they were not likely to do as individuals. (This facility is described in greater detail later.)

Indigenous Sanitariums

Various chronic ailments of psyche and soma were treated by some traditional healers in their homes. These healers tended to be older men who had studied in Buddhist monasteries during adolescence and early adulthood. Most came from rural peasant backgrounds and had practical approaches to chronic physical and emotional disability among people from similar backgrounds.

One of these men, a Lao who had previously lived for a time as a Buddhist monk, treated addicts as well as patients suffering from hypochondriasis, depression, and other forms of chronic neurosis or borderline psychosis. He used what might be called a multimodality approach. First, he assessed individually each person coming to him, listening carefully to what the problem was and asking questions to clarify certain issues. If he decided to accept the person into his home (which had been enlarged to accommodate his clients), negotiations were made regarding length of time for treatment and the fee to be paid. At any one time he had between eight and twelve residents, all of whom slept in a large room and took their meals with him and his wife. The client's day while at the facility was a busy one, beginning with light housekeeping chores such as folding the bed clothes, cleaning the large room, and doing any necessary laundry. Morning was largely spent in receiving exhortations and instruction from the *achan* (honorable teacher, professor). His homey precepts included many concepts from modern ego psychology and Freudian psychology, along with the proper modes of conducting one's life according to Buddhist, Hindu, and traditional Lao precepts. During the afternoons there were individual sessions with the *achan*, some consisting of healing rituals and others consisting of individualized counseling sessions. During this time people might rest, volunteer for household tasks to be performed (e.g., carrying water, doing house repairs, or attending the garden, chickens, or pigs). In the evenings there were religious rituals and time for meditation. People stayed with the *achan* for several weeks to several months. After discharge from the sanitarium, clients continued for a time to make regular weekly visits to the *achan*. At these weekly visits they received ritual blessings as well as education and exhortations regarding the proper life.

During my visits to the *achan*, I found him to be an open, optimistic, and dynamic man around fifty years old. He spent hours telling me about his theories, treatment approaches, and education program. The latter was an amalgam of old Buddhist lore from Sanskritic scrolls handwritten in Pali and modern psychology out of Thai texts printed in Bangkok.*

A Disabled Devotee. Lee Pah was a Hmong veteran who had stepped on a landmine in 1966. By comparing times and details, we decided that I had performed his below-knee amputation at Sam Thong Hospital

*Thai and Lao are dialects of each other. While there were several differences in the written scripts of each language, many literate Lao eventually learned to read Thai since the range of Lao printed materials was quite limited and there were thousands of Thai books available.

in Xieng Khouang province. Following his amputation he was fitted with a prosthesis at the Orthopedic Center in Vientiane. Although quite pleased with his artificial leg, he experienced several problems when he returned home to his village. First, he could traverse neither the steep terrain nor even the more gentle slopes when rain made the red laterite soil slippery. Second, he found virtually impossible most male responsibilities, such as clearing land for slash-and-burn agriculture, hunting, and building a house. And third, although he had saved bride price from his years as a soldier, no woman would marry him because of his inability to work productively.

After a few years he came down to Vientiane with a purpose in mind. He could receive and live on a disabled veteran's pension while he learned a trade, such as clothes- or shoe-making. Lee Pah had not anticipated the loneliness and isolation that he experienced there, however. In order to be among other Hmong, he stayed at a place that was a Hmong opium den during the day and a hostel or inn at night. Before long he was smoking opium and soon he was addicted. His training plans were abandoned; and to buy opium he began begging to supplement his small pension. We met again several times at that phase in his life, usually while I was interviewing addicts at his habitual den. A few times I stopped to chat with him while he was begging. He had become disgusted with himself and his aimless existence, but several attempts at ending his addiction had been failures.

After having been away from Laos for a year, I had just returned and was walking along a street in Nao Hai Deo district. From behind me I heard someone yelling excitedly "*Than-maw, than-maw* (Doctor, doctor.)" Scanning the faces of the midday crowd, I saw a young Hmong man gesticulating wildly and dodging through the traffic with the hop-skip-run of an amputee. "*Than-maw,* I have found someone who can cure the addiction. He is Achan Salee. Come, come, you must meet my *achan.*" On the advice of friends Lee Pah had sought out Achan Salee and remained with him for two months in exchange for giving the *achan* his pension during that time. When we met several months after the treatment, Lee Pah still remained abstinent. He continued to meet with the *achan* weekly, at which time he attended an evening ritual.*

Treatment Combinations and Alternatives

From the vignettes above it should be evident that treatment approaches were often combined rather than applied separately. For ex-

---

*The details of this program are presented above in the section on Indigenous Sanitariums.

ample, one addict who isolated himself from other addicts in a forest used the method of gradually decreasing his doses. At the Buddhist monastery where "cold turkey" withdrawal was used, clients also received an emetic herbal medication, induced sweating, and religious exhortation—all in a group setting with their fellow villagers. The man receiving residential care, moral exhortation, and education by the *achan* at the sanitarium initially received a combination of herbal medication with opium for several days.

Folk treatment strategies were chosen by addicts depending on their particular goals or expectations from treatment. Some only wanted to decrease their dosage rather than to discontinue the drug. Others wanted temporary abstinence from opium and intended to resume its use later. Temporary abstinence not only provided addicts with an opportunity to get their lives organized for a time but it was also associated with enhanced pleasure from the drug when it was resumed. At times addicts wanted to make an attempt at discontinuing the drug altogether. Certain modalities lent themselves to abstinence, such as the "cold turkey" withdrawal. Other modalities served mainly to decrease the dosage rather than to discontinue use entirely, such as eating opium in lieu of smoking it. Most modalities lent themselves to either alternative, such as the decreasing-dosage strategy.

TREATMENT AT A BUDDHIST MONASTERY

Tan Kha Bok* is a town in Thailand located near Saraburi in west-central Thailand. Under the charismatic leadership of its abbot, Phra Archarn Chamroom Parnchan, the Buddhist monks at the Tan Kha Bok temple have treated thousands of drug addicts over a decade and a half. Articles have appeared in the world's press about the abbot and the temple (see Rolnick 1974, Ho 1977, Yogachandra 1978).

Background

A woman of Thai-Lao ancestry was responsible for first sending addicts from Laos to the Tan Kha Bok temple. A resident of Vientiane, the capital of Laos, she occasionally returned to her home in Thailand. During a visit, she learned of a relative who had been cured of his addiction at a Buddhist monastery. She went to visit the monastery herself and learned firsthand of the monks' efforts there. Impressed by what

*Pronounced Tan Kra Borg in Thai, but Tan Kha Bok or Than Kha Bok in Lao dialect. *Wat* refers to a temple.

she saw, she returned to Laos with a mission. As a result of her efforts, about 3,000 addicts from Laos went to Wat Tan Kha Bok over the subsequent five years.

At that time (the late 1960s) the Ministry of Social Welfare in Laos had a pressing concern. Increasing numbers of addicts were causing problems in refugee areas. In their own villages to the north, they either raised their own opium or produced enough goods to barter for it; but the refugee relocation areas were located in areas where the land was insufficient or unsuitable for raising opium. Addicts began to sell whatever they had to obtain drugs—a gold tooth, a treasured transistor radio, an only pair of shoes, a blanket. Then they began to sell goods that belonged to the family in general—cooking utensils, sleeping mats, farm implements. Money that should have been spent for children's education or for food was instead used to purchase opium. When resources within the nuclear family were exhausted, addicts went around to extended family members and friends from the past, begging from them or pressuring them to meet old obligations by providing money or opium. Addicts who had always provided for themselves began begging door to door and along roadways. Widespread theft began to be reported, an event virtually absent in the north during previous times. Some addicts were maimed and even killed in the act of thievery to obtain money for drugs.

Aware of these social problems with refugee addicts in the north, the Thai-Lao woman contacted her women's Buddhist auxiliary, which agreed to help. Then she went to the Ministry of Social Welfare and told them of her plan. Ministry officials agreed to facilitate the treatment of the refugee addicts at the Thai temple. She also contacted a Christian philanthropic group, which made a donation.

The first addicts were sent to the monastery in 1970, mostly with privately donated funds. During 1971 and 1972, the Ministry of Social Welfare, impressed by the results of treatment at the monastery, provided further supplementary funds. During 1972 to 1974, the United States Agency for International Development made additional funds available for the treatment of 1,700 addicts. Other groups, such as the Asia Foundation, made contributions as well.

Treatment Process

Addicts first had to get themselves to a central collecting point located in their district or province. Depending on their residence, this could be difficult or relatively easy. Once they were at the collecting station, responsibility for their food, transportation, and board was borne by the Ministry of Social Welfare. People were transported down into Thailand by large truck in groups of about fifty. This was not at all pleasurable, since roads were mostly stone and dirt. The trip over hundreds of kilometers was dusty, bumpy, and long. A representative from the Ministry of Social Welfare accompanied each group. Later in the program a male nurse also accompanied each group. Cost to the Ministry of Social Welfare was slightly over $50 per person in 1973.

Each addict was asked upon admission at the monastery if he (or she) had the sincere desire to get rid of his addiction forever. If there was a serious hesitation, if the person said that he had been pressured to come or that he wanted to abandon addiction only temporarily, he was sent away. Only if he genuinely and voluntarily wanted to remain (at least by verbal report) was he accepted for treatment. If accepted, addicts had to commit themselves to remain throughout the course of treatment. There was no individual assessment of medical condition, addiction history, or social resources. No records were kept.

The next step was confiscation of all clothes and belongings. This was done because many addicts had sewn opium spherules into the folds of their clothing or had stashed opium in food or other personal effects as a hedge against unbearable suffering. Once they surrendered all of their belongings to the monks, they were given a sarong (for women) or pajamas (for men) to wear. All addicts wore the same clothing.

Then they were given a pungent herbal medication that induced vomiting. Alternating sweat baths and cold showers were provided (a traditional treatment). At night they slept among some fifty or sixty people in a large dormitory, men and women, old and young together.

By the second day narcotic withdrawal had appeared, with abdominal cramps and body aching. On the third day many addicts experienced vomiting, diarrhea, and weakness. Heroin addicts had a stormy onset of withdrawal but began feeling well by the fifth day. Opium addicts had a more gradual onset but were still recovering after several days.

Throughout this time the monks constantly attended the withdrawing addicts. They brought them water and a thin rice gruel, exhorted them, reassured them, helped them from the sauna to the shower and back again, massaged their aching and painful muscles.

The Abbot

An integral part of the treatment experience was Abbot Chamroon himself. After spending a day with this exceptional man, I was impressed and thoroughly charmed by him. Following a similar visit to the abbot, Dr. Charles Weldon wrote the following in 1971:

> The room we entered was immaculate and bare except for a small Buddhist altar in one corner . . . after a few minutes, a saffron robed monk entered the room. He appeared to be in his middle thirties (actually he is 47). He was above average height for a Thai and physically rugged and dynamic. . . . the monk of Than Kha Bok was born at Loburi 47 years ago of undistinguished parents. He went to the local schools, as a young man became an officer in the National Police, married, had two children and though of low rank in the police was an important figure in setting up a national intelligence service. At the age of 27 he abandoned his family and entered the wat. He has that undefinable charisma that one occasionally sees particularly in the Orient that attracts, leads, controls and inspires devotion and dedication. He is highly intelligent, poorly educated, empathetic and a master of applied psychology. He is humble, unassuming but has complete confidence in his power to influence people for good. By his own statement this power has come to him by rigid self-discipline and adherence to the middle way. He only walks and will not enter a vehicle of any sort, eats sparingly once daily, works about 20 hours a day, sleeps four hours or less and devotes himself completely to helping troubled people who come to him regardless of what their troubles may be.

As evidence of Abbot Chamroon's prominence in Southeast Asia, he received the Magsaysay Award in 1975. This prestigious honor is conferred to only one person each year and includes a prize of $10,000. The abbot refused to go to the Philippines to accept it personally since this would break his vow, as well as a monk's disciplines. The award money was used to underwrite the treatment at the temple.

Some addicts stayed on as monks to care for other addicts. Donations were accepted, but the abbot took anybody coming for help so long as the monastery had sufficient funds to provide for them. Many human problems were treated at the monastery, of which addiction was only one type (other examples were impotence and emotional disturbances).

Laotian Addicts

By mid-1971, the Laotian Ministry of Social Welfare was sending refugee addicts to Tan Kha Bok in groups of forty to sixty. Between one and three groups were being sent every month. People from the same village tended to go in groups, so that anywhere from five to twenty addicts from the same village or *tasseng* (i.e., several villages in the same district) were traveling together. Especially from the larger villages or *tasseng,* groups of addicts often came sequentially. In 1971 for example, from Veunkham, twenty-seven addicts went for treatment on July 23; eleven more went on October 14; and finally three more went on December 13. When ex-addicts returned praising the care that they received and looking healthier than before, others were induced to go.

Most of the refugee addicts going to Tan Kha Bok initially were ethnic Lao. They had come from northern provinces (i.e., Xieng Khouang, Luang Prabang, and Sam Neua) but were currently living in refugee relocation areas in Vientiane province. A high proportion of these refugees were addicted. For example, of 30,000 Lao refugees coming off the Plaine de Jarres in Xieng Khouang, the Ministry of Social Welfare estimated that over 1,000 of them were willing to go for treatment for addiction, more than 3 percent of the total population.

By the middle of 1972, over 2,000 addicts from Vientiane province had gone voluntarily for treatment at Wat Tan Kha Bok. Around this time the number of addicts in Vientiane province seeking treatment at the *wat* began to dwindle. Refugee relief workers in Houa Kong province in the northwest of Laos began to send refugee addicts down to Thailand. Most of these refugees were from tribal groups, including the Iu Mien, Hmong, and Akha. Approximately 1,000 of these addicts also went to Wat Tan Kha Bok.

THE NATIONAL NARCOTIC DETOXIFICATION CENTER

Through 1971 the Ministry of Social Welfare and private religious groups had shown the most interest in assisting addicted persons in Laos. By early 1972 the Ministry of Public Health had also begun to examine alternatives for an addiction treatment program. Initially there were more questions than answers regarding the treatment of addicts in a medical setting. Would addicts come for treatment? Where would they come from? What problems would be encountered in their treatment and rehabilitation? Would the high rates of readdiction, well known at Thanyarak Hospital for Addiction in Thailand and the early programs in Hong Kong, make the effort and financial investment worthwhile?

The Ministry of Health sought the guidance of Dr. Charles Weldon, chief of the Public Health Division/United States Agency for International Development in Laos (USAID). He in turn suggested a consultation by me, which led to my collaboration with the Ministry of Health over the subsequent four years. Elements of this consultation have been described elsewhere (Westermeyer and Hausman 1974a and b). Briefly,

I first consulted with the Ministries of Health and Social Welfare and USAID in November 1971. At that time about a score of alternative programs were suggested. Of these, two were accepted: (1) continued support and expansion of the Wat Tan Kha Bok program and (2) establishment of a medical treatment facility in Vientiane. In 1972, I returned to advise regarding staff, physical plant, logistics, treatment schedules, and policies. During that same year I arranged for several weeks of intensive training in the United States for the designated director of the program (Dr. Chomchan Soudaly), the USAID public health officer working with the project (Dr. Frank Becker), and USAID liaison-advisor Larry Berger).* In 1973 I returned a few months after the treatment program had started in order to assist in resolving the initial difficulties that any such program encounters. During the subsequent year, a colleague in Thailand, Dr. Aroon Showanasai, and a colleague in Hong Kong, Dr. James Ch'ien, graciously provided training for medical, nursing, and administrative staff. Finally, in 1974 I returned to Laos for several weeks in order to conduct an evaluation of the various programs that had been undertaken. This program has been described in the scientific and popular press (see Foisie 1973; Porter 1974; Westermeyer, Soudaly, and Kaufman 1978).

Resources

The treatment center was located in two large, adjacent villas that had once been embassies. Although barely two kilometers from the center of Vientiane, the site could also be considered on the outskirts of the town. Gardens and paddy rice fields were within stone's throw in all directions, and water buffalo regularly lumbered past the center. A garden soon replaced expansive lawns around the villas, and fowl were raised—both for food and as a way to involve the recovering addicts in traditional occupations.

The offices, medical records area, pharmacy, a conference room, and a carpentry shop were located in one of the two buildings. There was also a waiting area for new patients and an examination room/ treatment room where newly admitted patients were examined and medical treatments undertaken. In the adjacent building were the twenty-seven inpatient beds, a dayroom area, treatment room, nurses' station, patient activity area, kitchen, laundry, and dining area.

*Soudaly was from the northern province of Houa Kong and had observed opium use since his childhood. Becker had worked in Laos for several years and was familiar with the indigenous peoples and local medical politics. Berger had worked with the Peace Corps in Thailand and then with the refugee program in Laos.

Staff for the center consisted of approximately thirty people. These included two physicians (a director and deputy director), a nurse supervisor and twelve nurses, a pharmacist and pharmacist assistant, a chief administrator/medical records officer, and three secretarial assistants. Support staff included three cooks, four maintenance people, a chauffeur, and a carpenter. There was also an administrative liaison officer from USAID, who assisted with supply and logistics and served as an administrative consultant.

All of the professional staff members were ethnic Lao. A few of them had come from the north (including the director) and were well acquainted with narcotic addiction. The father of one senior staff member had once been an opium trader in northern Laos. Several Tai Dam tribespeople worked as maintenance staff. One of the secretarial staff was half Chinese and half Lao. The American liaison officer had previously worked for two years with Thai-Lao people in Thailand and for two years with Hmong and Khamu refugees in the north; he spoke fluent Lao. Besides this ethnic diversity, there was also political diversity. The director had long been loyal to the centrist and rightist elements of the Royal Lao Government, although his father had been executed by the French during colonial times for political reasons and certain close relatives had been active in communist party associations. The deputy director during 1973 to 1975 had received his medical degree at the University of Moscow in the Soviet Union and was associated with the Pathet Lao party.

Support for the treatment program came largely from the Ministry of Health, which provided all of the professional staff, administrative support and leadership, and some office and pharmaceutical supplies. During the first two-and-a-half years of the Center's operation, USAID also assisted by providing salaries for some support staff, some pharmaceutical supplies, an American liaison officer, a consultant (myself), and a vehicle. Gradually other philanthropic organizations and international agencies began to provide support (e.g., World Health Organization, various auxiliaries).

Patient Population

Lao officials had anticipated that most addicts would be ethnic Chinese and Hmong. Surprisingly, the predominant ethnic group seeking treatment month after month was Lao. During the Center's two-and-a-half years of operation, from late 1972 to early 1975, ethnic Lao people comprised 64 percent of the patient population. These Lao people were not just from Vientiane; they came from every province in Laos. Those coming from southern provinces lived in or adjacent to larger towns along the Mekong River (i.e., Pakse, Thakek, Savannakhet). Those coming from the north were from villages as well as towns.

The location of the treatment facility in an ethnic Lao area and the predominance of ethnic Lao among the professional staff might have discouraged use of the facility by other ethnic groups. On the contrary, several ethnic groups appeared in the patient population with even greater frequency, relative to their numbers in the population, than ethnic Lao themselves. For example, expatriate Asians appeared as patients three times more often than one would expect on the basis of their proportion in the general population. Northern tribal groups appeared about twice as frequently among the patients as one would expect based on population. Underrepresented were the tribal groups of southern Laos, among whom addiction was virtually nil.*

People heard about the treatment program by radio and by word of mouth throughout the entire country. Every province was represented, from Phong Saly in the north, Houa Kong in the east, and Champassak and Attopeu in the south and east. Patients came by pirogue down streams, by river boats on the Mekong, by elephants and mountain ponies, by trucks and airplanes, and by foot. A few reached the facility after a short fifteen-minute saunter, others traveled for days out of remote mountainous areas using several modes of travel. All came at their own expense, although there was no charge for treatment at the facility.

There was also a distinct international flavor to the patient population. Thai addicts with relatives in Laos gradually heard about the program and came for treatment. Over two years, several dozen Thai addicts, mostly peasant farmers from across the river, and a few hundred Caucasians came for treatment. One group of three Thai farmers came from Ubon, a Thai town 400 kilometers away. One young ethnic Chinese addict came from Bangkok. An American addict read about the program in a newspaper while in Bangkok and came for treatment. Over a score of nations and four continents were represented among the patients at various times.

Treatment Program

Addict-patients from village areas often came as a group, were admitted together, assigned to the same sleeping area, and discharged

*This statement is based on visits to three Laven and two Nyaheun villages on the Plateau de Bolovens and interviews conducted with members of several other tribes in Saravan and Attopeu.

together. Those from towns generally came individually. Inpatients were required to surrender their clothes and personal effects, which were then stored until discharge (due to the same problem at Wat Tan Kha Bok— hidden narcotics). Family and friends were not allowed to visit except at certain times and in a prescribed area. This was unlike most medical facilities in Laos, where family essentially lived in the same room as the patient much of the time. This traditional method was countermanded in order that drugs not pass through family and friends to the addict-patients.

One of the physician staff interviewed and examined each newly admitted patient. Limited laboratory evaluation was also performed. A questionnaire regarding his or her past narcotic history and current narcotic use was completed at the same time.

Detoxification consisted of gradually decreasing doses of methadone. Initial dosage was based on evidence of withdrawal symptoms, history of recent narcotic use (i.e., dose and frequency of use), weight, age, and associated clinical condition. Generally patients received an immediate dose of 20 to 30 milligrams of methadone. Medical and nursing staff reevaluated the response to this initial dose at 8 to 12 hours, so that repeated dosages might be given once or twice more within the first 24 hours. Most opium addicts required 20 to 40 milligrams of methadone in the first 24 hours to stave off withdrawal. Heroin addicts generally required 30 to 60 milligrams. Occasionally heroin addicts might receive up to 90 milligrams of methadone in the first 24 hours to alleviate their withdrawal. Out of the first 800 patients, 4 were given either no methadone or homeopathic doses (i.e., 5 milligrams of methadone) because they had reduced their dose of opium to such small amounts that they could be withdrawn readily. In the latter cases the patients were more psychologically dependent on the drug than physically addicted, so they only required support and the ritual aspects of medical treatment to reassure them that they would not die if opium were discontinued.

Several factors influenced the duration of withdrawal. Heroin addicts could be withdrawn more rapidly, so the dose was reduced by 10 to 15 percent each day. Opium addicts required a longer withdrawal period, with daily reductions of about 5 to 10 percent. Addicts over fifty-five or sixty years of age were withdrawn more slowly, since sudden death during withdrawal was most apt to occur in this age group. Patients with a long duration of addiction needed more gradual withdrawal, especially if chronic lung disease was present, since they were likely to develop an asthmalike condition with rapid detoxification. Patients ill with malaria or other acute conditions also did better with a prolonged withdrawal. Conversely, detoxification might only take a few days for addicts still psychologically dependent on very small doses of narcotic drugs.

All methadone was given in a solution of Tang, an orange-tasting liquid. Dosage was under the direction of the medical staff, and the patients were not informed regarding their current dose of methadone. The last few doses contained no methadone. When these last, drug-free doses were finally stopped, addicts tended to be surprised that they no longer required an active compound since they had anticipated withdrawal symptoms when the Tang solution was discontinued.

A variety of medical conditions prevailed in this patient population. These included various gastrointestinal parasites, vitamin deficiencies, chronic lower respiratory tract infections, urinary tract infections, and malaria. Medical and nursing staff attended to these various ills. Most patients received parenteral fluids and vitamins at some time during the first day or two when their discomfort, nausea, anorexia, and weakness were at their peak.

Since many addicts had fallen into a lifestyle relatively devoid of schedule (other than regular opium doses), a daily routine of activities was planned. Everyone was awakened at 6:00 A.M. Light housekeeping, laundry, personal grooming, and toilet were attended to in the first hour, followed by a light morning meal. Between 8:00 A.M. and 10:00 A.M., patients were available for medical rounds by a physician and the nurse supervisor. Work chores in the late morning consisted of tending the garden, assisting the carpenter, or doing other light work. During a two-hour period at midday there was a second meal followed by a rest. Afternoon group meetings then took place. These varied among educational sessions conducted by a physician regarding the biomedical aspects of addiction, a group meeting led by one of the nursing staff to discuss addiction and plans for maintaining abstinence at home, a combined meeting of patients and staff, and religious exhortations and rituals conducted by Buddhist monks. One group of addicts suggested that sweat baths (similar to a sauna) be arranged for those wishing them. This traditional modality was subsequently added to the therapeutic regimen. After the evening meal, time was available for a variety of activities. These included informal discussions among the addicts themselves, talks between nursing staff on evening call and the addicts, repair of personal effects, and the manufacture of new articles (since many had arrived at the center with clothes, thongs, and other personal effects in poor repair).

An important aspect of the overall regimen was adequate amounts of food. By the third or fourth day most addicts became ravenous for food and ate huge amounts of it. Most were thin or even cachectic upon arrival but left with good nutritional status. On the average, each person gained two to three kilograms over a two-to-four-week period; many gained twice that. Since most addicts initially weighed around forty-five to fifty kilograms on admission, these were appreciable weight gains.

Over the fifteen to thirty days that most addicts remained at the Center, three general phases could be observed. During the first five to ten days their cognitive focus was mainly on themselves and their bodies. They had numerous somatic complaints, generally referable to mild withdrawal, such as insomnia or malaise. Other complaints had little apparent physiologic basis and appeared to be primarily requests for help or support. During the next five to ten days, the complaints and negativism continued; but the focus switched from their body and its functions to the Center's location and social milieu. They complained of too much dust in the air during the dry season and too much water on the grounds during the wet season, that nurses and medical staff came around too often or they were not nearly as available as they might be, that there was too much of one kind of food and too little of another (and the complaints would change the next week in the opposite direction, though the food quantities remained the same), that there was too much to do and inadequate time for rest or too little to do and boredom. During the last five to ten days, most patients became a treatment resource for the other addicts. Rather than complaining, they became optimistic about their treatment and praised their care to newly admitted addicts. They began focusing on the future, on their plans when they returned home. Prior to leaving, many formally expressed gratitude to the staff at the Center (not an established tradition in the medical and social facilities in Laos).

At the time of discharge a meeting was held between the patient and one or more of the staff members. If the addict's family was available, they would be requested to attend this meeting. Those patients coming in a group from a village attended the meeting in a group. This meeting emphasized the need for beginning a new life, avoiding any use of narcotic drugs, and mutual support.

Average length of stay at the Center remained consistently at 17 to 18 days. Average cost per inpatient day for all expenses, including both local and international contributions, was $8.60 in 1973. Using 17.5 days as an average length of stay, cost per addict treated was $150.50.

The occupancy rate for the twenty-seven beds over the entire year was 94 percent (high for most medical facilities). During planting, harvest, and certain national holidays, occupancy dropped slightly. At most other times, it was 100 percent, with demand for admission greatly exceeding available beds.

SUPPLEMENTAL AND FOLLOW-UP PROGRAMS

Several rehabilitation programs supplemented the Buddhist temple and medical programs described above. These were begun after 1972 to meet the special needs of certain addicts. The focus of these programs was to provide supportive services during the follow-up period.

Outpatient Care

Patients previously treated at the Thai monastery or the medical facility in Vientiane were invited to return to the outpatient service at the Detoxification Center. Scores of patients in the greater Vientiane metropolitan area took advantage of this program. They returned to outpatient care for several months to a few years following discharge, often with a variety of neurotic and psychophysiologic complaints (e.g., depression, insomnia, sexual impotence, vague somatic and bowel complaints). The program consisted of medical evaluation, reassurance, supportive psychotherapy, and symptomatic medication.

Outpatient detoxification was tried for about fifty selected addicts. One group consisted of salaried or self-employed people in Vientiane who were felt to be optimal treatment candidates. This was undertaken so that they could continue to work during treatment (some addicts would not leave work for residential treatment). Another group consisted of Caucasian addicts, most of whom could not speak or understand Lao, the language used at the treatment facility. These patients tended to feel isolated from other patients and most of the staff.

These patients receiving outpatient detoxification had to come to the Center twice a day, once in the morning and once in the late afternoon, to obtain their detoxification dose of methadone. They were seen each day by a staff member. No methadone was given to them to take home; all of it had to be consumed in the presence of the pharmacist or pharmicist's assistant. Failure to religiously show up for appointments meant automatic discharge from this program. (There had been an attempt to administer take-home methadone during detoxification, but this was not successful.)

A Halfway House

A modest Lao house about four kilometers from the Center in Vientiane served as a halfway house. One of the nursing staff and his family received free room at this facility for serving as houseparents. This facility met the needs of three patient groups. First, some addicts who had completed the early phases of their medical evaluation and withdrawal treatment at the NNDC stayed here, especially when beds were needed for newly arriving addicts. Second, some NNDC patients came here if they did not have a home or family to which they might return immediately. The house then acted as a base from which they could work to reestablish their employment and kinship ties. Third, the facility was used as a home for young, unskilled patients involved in a unique rehabilitation program (this is described further on). There were from six to twelve residents at any one time.

The house was located in the district of Sikhay, an area with many Lao addicts. The location of this facility in Sikhay led to its spontaneous use as a social meeting place for addicts trying to resume abstinence. Many returned to the housefather and his wife with a variety of medical complaints, as well as to receive counseling and support.

Any use of drugs led to immediate dismissal from the house. This included such evidence of drug usage as intoxicated behavior, the odor of opium on one's clothes, or possession of drugs. Fighting, loud disruptive arguing, failure to maintain one's bed and personal effects in a neat condition, or failure to cooperate in common tasks (such as cooking and grounds maintenance) could also result in dismissal from the house. Such dismissals were infrequent.

Religious Organizations

Buddhist men in Laos could enter and leave a monastery at various times during their lives. While living in a monastery they had to abide by the rules of the order, wear the orange robes, and shave their heads and eyebrows. They might temporarily enter the monastery as young boys in order to learn reading, writing, and catechism or as adolescents to learn more about Buddhism and Buddhist scripture. As adults they could return to live as monks during a personal crisis, such as the loss of a family member. Similarly, monks who had lived in monasteries for years could apply for dismissal and leave the monastery to resume the secular life.

Infrequently, Lao addicts entered a monastery as monks after going through withdrawal treatment. They remained for several months, living in a supportive environment and examining their lives and values. While this would seem ideal for rehabilitation of drug addicts, relatively few addicts wanted to enter the monastery after treatment. And some monasteries did not want ex-addicts entering directly into the monastery but preferred to give them a special status as individuals seeking help at the monastery. In this role they lived in a separate area and were fed separately. Thus, they did not benefit from the special role and brotherhood of the monks.

Among the several missionary groups whom we contacted regarding addicts, only one group showed interest in helping them. This was the Oblate Order of Catholic missionaries, mostly French and French-Canadian priests and brothers. They had long worked among the Hmong and had been concerned about opium production and addiction among them. Oblate fathers aided some Hmong addicts' travel out of the mountains to NNDC in Vientiane. They provided temporary housing in the city for Hmong addicts who could not yet be admitted to the Center or who had been discharged and were awaiting transportation or gathering strength for the journey home. Oblate missionaries in remote mountainous regions also provided supportive follow-up and counseling for addicts who had been through withdrawal treatment.

Planning an Outreach Program

In 1975 it was planned that an outreach program would be initiated in several sites across northern Laos (i.e., Ban Houei Sai, Long Cheng, Ban Son, Xieng Lom, Luang Prabang). A team from the Center would travel to each site and remain there for several weeks, during which time groups of addicts would be detoxified. The team was to consist of a physician, a few nurses, an administrator, and a pharmacist.

At each location the team members would work with their local counterparts in conducting a detoxification treatment program. The reasons for this were several. First, it would reduce the expense of many addicts traveling to Vientiane. Second, the Center staff would teach local medical staffs in the provinces regarding the assessment, detoxification, and treatment of narcotic addicts. Third, it would establish a relationship between addicts and their local medical personnel, thereby facilitating follow-up care. And fourth, if treatment could be successfully transplanted to the provincial medical centers, this might provide an opportunity of significantly reducing the total number of addicts in Laos.

The last goal was, from a public health perspective, the most important aspect of the proposed outreach program. When both the

Buddhist temple program and the NNDC were most active, they were treating only about 2,000 addicts per year. Even if one were to assume 100 percent success in these endeavors, the number of current addicts being treated would, in all likelihood, not even equal the number of new people becoming addicted. Consequently, there had to be a multi-fold increase in the annual number of addicts treated if there were to be a significant impact on addiction in Laos.

Groundwork for the outreach program was begun in early 1975 by bringing a provincial health worker to the Vientiane center. (An outstanding Hmong medical administrator and a vigorous and effective leader, Her Tou, was the first individual chosen for this project.) This early effort was brought to an end in mid-1975 following the change from a coalition to a communist government.

A VOCATIONAL REHABILITATION PROGRAM

Two businessmen in Vientiane were contacted by Dr. Chomchan Soudaly (director of the National Narcotic Detoxification Center) regarding the training of young, unemployed, unskilled ex-addicts. After lengthy explanation, cajoling, and guarantees of continued medical involvement, the two businessmen agreed to collaborate in the undertaking described here. Over a period of fourteen months, six trainees were placed in this program.

The Ex-Addict Trainees

All six trainees were ethnic Lao. The first four placed were men in their twenties and thirties who were currently separated from their spouses and families. One of them, a twenty-eight-year-old teacher, was unemployed as a result of his having become addicted. Two others, aged twenty-four and thirty-seven, had been truck farmers near Laotian towns; their extended kin groups had evicted them because of sloth, lying, and theft from family members. A twenty-three-year-old had been discharged from a technical vocational school because of failing grades a few years earlier and had been unable to hold a job since that time.

Two other men were placed at a different facility. Both were single students, aged seventeen and nineteen, who had previously attended the same school in Pakse, a Mekong River town in southern Laos.

Five of the men had been smoking heroin at the time of admission to treatment, and one had been smoking opium. Duration of addiction was rather short (one to four years) among five of the addicts. The twenty-four-year-old farmer had been addicted to opium for fifteen years (his family included several alcoholics and addicts).

The common element among these cases was the lack of a current occupation and a home. Their only social support system consisted of other addicts. It was anticipated that discharge from treatment without further rehabilitation would result in early readdiction for all of them. All six of these addicts entered this program voluntarily.

The Businessmen

One shopkeeper was a forty-two-year-old ethnic Chinese born in Cambodia. He had come to Laos at age eleven when his family had emigrated. Later he married a Laotian woman, and they had four children. A mechanic, he operated a successful auto and motorcycle repair business. He maintained the vehicle for the NNDC as well as the motorcycles for several staff members, which provided critical leverage in gaining his collaboration in a program about which he had many doubts.

The other businessman was the owner and manager of a metalworking shop. This forty-three-year-old Lao man had been an acquaintance of Dr. Soudaly for some years. Friendship and the good record of the other businessman with the first four addicts were key elements in gaining his skeptical acquiescence.

Both men were initially quite reluctant to accept the ex-addicts as trainees. They anticipated that the ex-addicts would not work diligently and might steal from the shop. Moreover, they feared that the amount of time required for supervision and the mere presence of ex-addicts in their shops might adversely affect their business. Dr. Soudaly's qualities as a salesman were a key factor in launching this program.

The Agreement

Each businessman and Dr. Soudaly negotiated an agreement acceptable to both parties. The ex-addict trainees had to fully agree to the arrangement in order to be accepted into the training program.

The shopkeepers had the option of discharging the trainees at any time for any cause. Dr. Soudaly agreed to continue to be in regular contact with both the trainees and the businessmen. The trainees would work the regular labor schedule in Laos: ten hours a day, six days a week.

For the first six months of the training period, the trainees would remain at the halfway house (described previously), where they would eat their morning and evening meals. During this time the shopkeeper agreed to provide the subjects with work, supervision, training, and a midday meal. During the second six months, the trainees would move to the shopkeepers' homes and take all of their meals with the family. At the end of the first year, they would begin to receive wages for their work if their employment was continued by the shopkeeper.

Phases in the Rehabilitation Process

During the first six months, grooming and dress improved somewhat, although long hair and a studied sloppiness persisted to some degree. At the work setting, the trainees tended to place themselves relatively close to one another and relatively distant from their businessman-preceptor. They preferred to work at a common task with one another, rather than independently or with the preceptor. Their early industriousness and efficiency was only fair but improved steadily as they acquired skills and worked more collaboratively with the preceptor.

From the beginning they took lunch and tea breaks with the preceptor. These times were important in building the trainee-preceptor relationship. Within weeks, the early silence of these ritual events was replaced by a more lively mutual conversation. Even after several months, however, a social distance prevailed between the trainees and the preceptors' families. The trainees' primary loyalty and affiliation were to one another, and they spent most of their spare time in one another's company. Preceptors also remained measured in their commitments to the trainees, only gradually abandoning their stereotypes about addicted people.

Several changes occurred during the second six months. Hair style and dress became similar to that of other Lao people of their age and sex. At work they positioned themselves close to the preceptor more frequently and showed an increased interest in learning from him. Greater focus on task developed, and they became equally adept at working alone, with the preceptor, or with the entire group. Industriousness and efficiency increased greatly.

Trainees moved their residence from the halfway house to the preceptor's home during the second six months. They then began to relate more closely to the preceptor's family, often serving in the role of older siblings to the preceptor's children. The children sought them out for play, and the trainees became instructors for the children, teaching them to clean motor parts, to garden, or to do other traditional crafts. Trainees remained somewhat more formal in their relationship with the preceptor's wife, although they began to show their appreciation for her cooking by volunteering to make household repairs or improvements that would please her. Concurrently she also began to undertake tasks for them, such as mending clothes. During this time the trainees' loyalty shifted from their peers at the halfway house to the preceptor's family. They spent their evenings and weekends with the family, only rarely venturing out into the community or back to the halfway house. At some point during this time they made their first contact (by visit or by letter) to their family of origin, family of marriage, or both.

During my last trip to Laos in 1975, only two of the six men were well into their third six-month period. Both had recently become involved with activities outside the preceptor's family. One was studying English five evenings a week at a night school. The other was enrolled as a catechumen with a Christian missionary group (unusual among Lao Buddhists) and studied with them in the evenings and over weekends. Both these men were spending gradually more time with their own families, visiting them and staying with them for longer periods. They were also beginning to make plans for the future, one to establish a repair shop elsewhere and the other to return to school. Neither showed any urgent interest in leaving his current dependent and low-paying position in order to strike out on his own. On the contrary, they were planning to spend at least several more months with their preceptor. By the same token, the preceptor was not anxious to evict them, stating that they should leave when they felt ready. The remaining four men, not so far along in the program, remained within the preceptor's family.

The Mentor-Trainee Relationship

The most striking finding of this program was the relationship that evolved between the trainees and their preceptors, who gradually assumed the role of mentors. The businessmen showed a sense of pride in their trainees, as well as a commitment to their futures. This evolved gradually over a long period, preceded by considerable mutual distrust. As this distrust was gradually resolved, both trainees and mentors developed a considerable commitment to one another.

The length of time for this process to occur was prolonged. Similar observations have been made among other self-help groups, such as Synanon, Phoenix House, Alcoholics Anonymous, and Alanon (see Ablon 1974; DeLeon, Skodal, and Rosenthal 1973; Leach 1973; Yablonsky 1965). One mentor explained this by saying that none of his four ex-addicts had had a good relationship with his own father or his own family, and each one was experiencing for the first time a corrective relationship with the mentor and the mentor's family. Both mentors viewed themselves as role-models for the trainees, and they were complimented and pleased by this unanticipated turn of events. The duration and intensity of this trainee-mentor relationship suggested that it was less a rehabilitation than an ensocialization into an adult social role. For the first time, the trainees were learning industriousness and were able to be concerned about others rather than about themselves.

COMMENT

1. Traditional treatment modalities for addiction bore remarkable resemblance to methods developed over recent decades in the United States. "Cold turkey" withdrawal, group process, and community orientation as used by Synanon and other therapeutic communities had its analogs at Wat Tan Kha Bok. The achan's sanitorium, counseling, education, and the weekly follow-up visits were similar to many hospital-based programs. Orally taken opium, with its slow onset and prolonged action (as a substitute for smoked opium, with its more rapid onset), has pharmacologic properties clinically similar to those of methadone. Like narcotic and alcohol addicts around the world, opium smokers in Laos learned to gradually decrease their own dosage to cope with one or another dilemma, such as the need to work or the higher cost of opium. And they often tried other medicines or intoxicants in an attempt to deliver themselves from the growing constraints of their addiction.

2. Addicts by the thousands accepted treatment at Wat Tan Kha Bok despite its involving "cold turkey" withdrawal. Balancing this was the fact that it took place at a traditional and reassuring location (a Buddhist monastery) in the company of fellow villagers. The focus was spiritual rebirth and religious exhortation.

3. After one year of preparation, a medical treatment program for addicts was established in Laos. This program emphasized individual medical assessment, detoxification with methadone, treatment of associated medical problems, education regarding addiction, and individual and family counseling.

4. Follow-up programs reached only a minor segment of addicts after initial treatment. Geographic setting was an important factor, since

follow-up involved access to the clinic in Vientiane or to an Oblate missionary. A halfway house in Vientiane was useful to a limited number of addicts with special needs. An outreach program was in its initial stages, but it came to an end with a major change in the central government.

5. An innovative ensocialization program was useful for several relatively young addicts. The most striking finding in this program was the relationship that evolved between the trainees and the two businessmen. The businessmen showed a sense of pride in the trainees and, after some months of living and working with them, a commitment to them and their futures. The relationship began with their working together at a common task during the sixty-hour work week. During the initial phase the shopkeeper worked along with the trainees, instructing them in new skills. Eventually the trainees moved in with the shopkeeper, virtually as members of the family.

XII

Evaluating Treatment

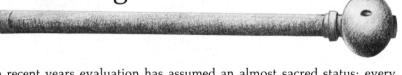

In recent years evaluation has assumed an almost sacred status: every clinician is expected to support and to perform evaluation. Paradoxically, it is a complex and often nebulous area that many shun. As we shall see, they may avoid this complex subject with good reason.

Why go to the trouble and expense of an evaluation? The first step in doing an evaluation is to answer this important question. The goal of the evaluation must be clearly stated. The objective may be to assess whether there is a perceived need for the treatment, to discover if people with the disorder do just as well without treatment, to compare treatments, or to assess cost effectiveness. Framing the "why" question is a critical beginning.

Next, the events to be studied must be determined. Are we interested in percentage of beds filled, number of deaths per year, proportion of addicts abstinent after a period of time? These specifications must be closely linked to the objectives.

Third, the objectives also fix the population of people to be studied and the sampling method to be used. For example, if treatment and no treatment are to be compared, both patients and nonpatients must be studied. In evaluating treatment outcome, if we are only able to find half of our former patients, this seriously undermines the value of the study.

Then we must consider the means and instruments of collecting the data. Do we rely solely on what the drug-dependent person says? Are family members also interviewed? Are withdrawal signs observed or urine tests taken?

And last, there is the matter of the investigators themselves. Are they trained to obtain the data being sought? Is there purpose to clarify the questions under study, to justify expenditures on their treatment program, or some other intent? As quoth the computer analysts, "Garbage in, garbage out."

TREATMENT ACCEPTABILITY

Staff Acceptance

Usually we think only about patients accepting treatment. Just as important is staff acceptance of their treating and healing role. If the staff does not accept this role as a positively valued one, staff-patient conflict is inevitable. Treatment is then compromised before it begins.

A critical factor in staff acceptance is the program director. If the director can empathize with addicted people, that empathy pervades the organization. This was true for both the Buddhist monastery (Wat Tan Kha Bok) and the medical facility described in the former chapter. Both directors had known addicts as individuals and could accept them as people rather than merely stereotyping them. This was also true of the Lao woman who first organized the treatment of Laotian addicts at the Thai monastery.

Abbot Chamroon at the monastery had worked with addicts as a policeman. Dr. Soudaly at the National Narcotic Detoxification Center (NNDC) had grown up in a community where opium addicts lived, and he had cared for their illnesses as a general physician. Both were opposed to addiction as a dehumanizing and debilitating condition. Yet they both could empathize with the problems and foibles, while recognizing the strengths and abilities, among addicts and their families. Initially most of their staff members did not possess these values and attitudes. Based on their stereotypes, they were polarized with extreme opinions. Some stated, "Execute them all," while others stated, "Leave them alone with their pipes." At the beginning of these programs, staff members maintained a distance from their addicted charges. Under the tutorship of their leaders, this gradually changed. In part this was probably due to the role model of their directors and to their emulating their directors' behaviors. In part, also, it was probably related to positive relationships that developed between staff members and addicts under their care. And perhaps most importantly, the changes that they saw occur in the addicts following treatment served to reinforce their own valuation of themselves as treating and healing persons. The involvement of the NNDC staff in their task was reflected in the high level of professional competence that they demonstrated. Effective medical care for a wide variety of infections and nutritional and degenerative disorders, a carefully kept records system, a surprising low mortality rate, and laudatory patient reports—all these pointed toward good staff morale.

Examples of the difficulty in obtaining people with a positive attitude toward working with addicts were given in the previous chapter. Most of the people approached by Dr. Chomchan Soudaly, Larry Berger, or me to aid in follow-up and rehabilitation of treated addicts wanted nothing to do with them. These included the abbotts of several Buddhist monasteries and several Christian missionaries in Laos. Even placing a halfway house for addicts in a neighborhood rife with addiction met with an offended outcry by neighbors. The two businessmen approached by Dr. Soudaly (to act as preceptors for recovering addicts) resisted for months before finally giving their highly tentative agreement. Those who took a risk with the treated addicts—the halfway house neighbors, the two businessmen, the Oblate priests—had mostly positive experiences.

Patient Acceptance

Patients must value the treatment if voluntary programs, such as these in Laos, are to have any chance at success. In this regard, the first patients are crucial to the eventual acceptance of the program. If they speak ill of their treatment, other addicts are not apt to seek admission. After the initial few patients, most later addicts seeking treatment are referred by those treated earlier.

Oddly enough, I discovered that patient evaluation of their treatment experience was not very well correlated with the treatment outcome. As we shall see further on, those who had resumed addiction and had not benefited from treatment sometimes spoke most highly of their treatment experience and advised others to go. Conversely, some who had not resumed opium use and were much improved totally condemned their treatment experience and urged others not to enter it. Establishing rapport and a spirit of collaboration between patient and staff appeared to be the key element in facilitating a positive attitude toward treatment.

As indicated in earlier chapters, those addicts going to Wat Tan Kha Bok were older and included more ethnic Lao as compared to those going to the medical facility. This was an expected finding, since the Lao addicts and the Thai monks shared a common language, history, religion, and culture. The similarities between the Thai and Lao were such that Lao people could feel much at ease in a Thai monastery, with familiar architecture, prayers, clothing, food, etiquette, and so forth. Older Lao were more likely to be illiterate and more religious and traditional. Those choosing the medical facility were younger and included more tribal people, expatriate Asians, and expatriate Caucasians. Thus, it appeared that addicts sought out treatment programs that were most apt to be congenial to their own values and preferences.

During subsequent outcome studies, former patients of the medical center praised several aspects of their treatment. These included the positive attitude of the staff toward them and their individual problems; the relative comfort of the methadone detoxification process; the adequate amounts of nutritious food; the pleasant living arrangements; and the attainment of strength, weight gain, and well-being during the treatment process. On several occasions there was an opportunity to observe the response of former patients to staff members who accompanied me on the outcome study. Staff members were welcomed in a fashion usually reserved for close friends and kin (irrespective of whether the addicts had resumed opiate use).

The most negative patient evaluations came from virtually all tribal addicts going to Wat Tan Kha Bok. They complained of the food, the lodging, the treatment process, the monks' attitudes, and the inability to communicate. Most tribal people going to the monastery spoke little or no Thai-Lao, and the staff did not speak their languages. The tribespeople, many of whom had never been to a Lao town much less in a Lao home, might as well have been attending High Mass in St. Peter's in Rome or listening to the Archbishop of Canterbury holding forth in London as obtaining inspiration from the abbot and his monks. Typical complaints about their treatment were as follows:

The food was not any good. They did not give us enough meat.

They would not take anyone to the hospital, even if they were close to death. [This complaint was accurate; the abbot believed that his curing and outside medical care should not be conjoined under any circumstances.]

We could not understand anything they said; the monks do not speak our language.

They only make the attachment to opium worse. I am more addicted to opium than I was before.

These printed statements fail to communicate the strong negative emotion (ranging from disgust to outright anger) with which most tribal people delivered these remarks. Many said they felt tricked by the Ministry of Social Welfare into going for treatment, and several volunteered that they would die before ever going there again. Even those who were still abstinent condemned the monastery program. Incidentally, in the last case quoted above, we had pretreatment data (provided by the addict himself) to show that his current opium dosage was actually no more than it had been previously. Nonetheless, his perception was that treatment had made his addiction worse.

In light of certain other observations, it is difficult to accept at face value these tribespeople's reasons for disliking the monastery. First, many Lao addicts returning from the monastery complained bitterly of the "cold turkey" withdrawal and emphasized strongly their fear of death from the withdrawal illness. But they generally lauded the abbot, the monks, and the total experience. Expatriate Asians who sought treatment at the monastery (mostly Buddhists and Lao-speakers) also made comments similar to those of the Lao. Conversely, the tribal addicts at the NNDC encountered certain of the same difficulties that occurred at the monastery: a predominantly Lao staff, food somewhat different from their own, medical or administrative procedures that were not familiar to them. Yet they praised their treatment experience highly.

What was operating here to explain this unexpected difference? I think two factors may have been at work. One was the method for sending addicts to Wat Tan Kha Bok. Lao addicts were sent together, along with some expatriate Asians. (There were never enough expatriate Asians wanting treatment at the monastery to comprise a single group of fifty addicts.) Tribal addicts going to the monastery were sent exclusively as tribal groups. Conversely, addicts were never admitted to the medical facility on the basis of ethnicity but rather on a first-come-first-served basis. Thus, there was always a mix of Lao, tribespeople, and expatriate Asians at the medical center. I believe that the exclusively tribal groups at the monastery served to impede the development of rapport between staff and addicts. Further, it engendered polarization between monastery staff and addicts, so that each group could maintain antitherapeutic stereotypes about the other. This resulted in a mutual antipathy.

The other factor involved the differences between the Thai and the Lao vis-à-vis tribal people. The Thai staff lived in an area where there were no tribal people within a few hundred kilometers. They spoke no tribal languages and knew little about tribal people. This was less true in Laos, a country composed of about 50 percent tribal people. Many Lao people (staff and fellow patients alike) could carry on some basic communication with tribal people in a combination of pidgin Lao and fractured tribal dialect. Without fellow Lao patients at the monastery, the tribal addicts could not interact effectively with the Thai staff. Conversely, tribal patients and Lao staff at the medical center could generally find a way to communicate.*

Treating addiction and being treated for addiction are both difficult undertakings that give rise to suffering, pain, boredom, frustration, and doubt. For these feelings to be handled in the treatment setting without polarizing staff and patients, communication and rapport are critical. When the latter are absent, patients assign negative grades to those who treat them and advise other addicts to avoid them.

Gradually over a five-year period, another factor operated more broadly against patient acceptance of the monastery. Mortality among addicts treated there, while never very high, was still consistent. This is covered in greater detail later.

Social Acceptance

New hospitals or monasteries, expensive medical equipment, or new roadways are generally inaugurated with grand fanfare. Not so with facilities serving addicts. Generally they begin among birth pangs and muffled groans. So it was for the Wat Tan Kha Bok program, the medical facility in Vientiane, and the businessmen's rehabilitation effort. Their fanfare had to be earned.

After considerable opposition from various official and unofficial quarters (including the Buddhist hierarchy itself), Abbot Chamroon began to receive accolades and semi-official approval. First it came from family members of the addicts themselves and then from community leaders. Eventually a Thai general, head of one wing of the armed forces, took up his cause. The respected widow of a former American ambassador joined in the effort. As noted previously, Abbot Chamroon eventually received the prestigious Magsaysay Award.

A similar sequence of events occurred at the National Narcotic Detoxification Center. The doors opened inauspiciously one day. Except for a sign in front declaring its identity, there was no public notice of

---

*Eventually translators who could speak both the tribal dialect and Lao-Thai were sent to the monastery. This only alleviated the problem in part since translations were made of formal lectures but not of the many small interchanges that ordinarily occurred between the monks and the suffering addicts. As a result considerable misunderstanding continued.

its existence. As patients began to do well and as their families showed appreciation, word gradually spread. First there were a few articles in the local Lao newspaper and a few mentions on the local radio. Then one day the Minister of Public Health made an official visit. A few months later there was a ceremony, conducted by the prime minister himself, to officially open the program—almost a year after it began receiving patients. Within the next year visitors came from several agencies and governments around the world. Articles appeared in the Hong Kong press and the *New York Times* (see Porter 1974 and Foisie 1973).

Unfortunately, the 1975 change in government did not allow time for the full flowering of the businessmen's rehabilitation program. While they did not receive the national and international attention of the former programs, they did receive the acclaim of their neighbors, the appreciation of the young men with whom they worked, and their own satisfaction in a job well done.

There is a lesson in these historical recountings. Society is not anxious, indeed is typically reluctant, to support services for addicts. Nonetheless, legislatures, ministries, and agencies can sometimes be cajoled into supporting services for addicts and then taking a wait-and-see attitude. And if someone can actually accomplish something with this resistant problem, society can be generous with its support and applause. Without this social acceptance, treatment programs wither and disappear.

MORTALITY

Death during narcotic withdrawal is uncommon. It occurs much less often than death from alcohol or barbiturate withdrawal. Among several hundreds of withdrawing opiate addicts whom I have encountered clinically, only two died in withdrawal. While few deaths were anticipated, data on mortality were collected among addicts at the monastery and at the medical facility. There was a built-in bias in that all addicts going to Wat Tan Kha Bok were first screened by a nurse from the Ministry of Health to ensure that they were in reasonably good health. Conversely, some addicts at the Detoxification Center had been sent from other hospitals and clinics around Vientiane in very poor medical condition with such problems as pneumonia, cor pulmonale, or dehydration secondary to withdrawal. Therefore it was expected that there would be more deaths at the medical facility.

During 1973 and 1974, a nurse from the Ministry of Health collected mortality data among addicts while at the monastery. There were nine deaths among 825 addicts during the time of treatment at the monastery (a mortality rate of 1.1 per 100 admissions). Reports from this nurse and from refugee workers with the Ministry of Social Welfare revealed that another thirty-seven addicts died en route home or soon after arriving home from the monastery, often while they were still in withdrawal (an additional 4.5 percent). Most deaths were among addicts aged sixty years or older, among whom the mortality rate at the monastery approached 5 percent and the mortality soon afterward approached another 20 percent.*

It had been anticipated that the mortality rate at the medical facility would be rather high, since hospitals and clinics in Vientiane often sent critically ill addicts there. Unexpectedly, there were only four deaths among the first 1,000 patients admitted from 1972 through 1974 (a mortality rate of 0.4 per 100 admissions). A fifth man died moments after arrival in the admitting room but prior to admission. All were elderly men with medical complications. I examined two of these five patients and reviewed their medical history. One died on the third day of hospitalization of cor pulmonale, emphysema, and a lower respiratory infection. A Lao man in his late sixties, he was receiving antibiotics and vitamins while being withdrawn very slowly. He died quietly and unexpectedly during the night. The other, a Vietnamese man, was in withdrawal for several days trying to stop addiction "cold turkey" on his own. He manifested agitation and confusion upon arrival. Before he could even be thoroughly examined, he died suddenly. Immediately administered resuscitation was not successful. Death was probably due to dehydration, hypotension, and cardiac arrest. There were no reported deaths en route home from the medical facility, although one young Iu Mien man from Houa Kong committed suicide three weeks after returning home. His family had spent much of their savings to send him by airplane to Vientiane. He reportedly became despondent when he tried to resume controlled opium use but soon found himself readdicted.

These data indicate that the addicts at the monastery had a higher mortality than did those at the medical facility. Virtually all deaths at both places occurred among the aged. Since there were relatively more aged in the monastery group, it is perhaps not surprising that they had a higher mortality. Still, the mortality at the monastery is relatively

*Prior to careful collection of data from these 825 addicts in 1973 and 1974, an informal list of deaths was kept for 2,000 addicts going from Laos to Wat Tan Kha Bok. This unofficial list contained 46 deaths, some at the monastery and some on the way home. This was a rate of 2.3 deaths per 100 addicts.

higher than at the medical facility even when corrected for age. Percentage of addicts over age sixty was 1.2 times greater at the monastery than at the medical facility, while the death rate at the monastery was 2.8 times greater (and several times higher if the posttreatment period is considered). In addition, there were critically ill addicts being sent to the medical facility whereas addicts being sent to Wat Tan Kha Bok were presumably in good enough health to travel a long distance. Overall then, the mortality among the aged or debilitated narcotic addict at the monastery was considerably higher in comparison to those receiving care at the medical facility.

This relatively high mortality was not immediately evident, either to addicts or to officials at the Ministry of Social Welfare. Over time, however, enough people died at the monastery, on the way home, or soon after arriving home to influence the otherwise good reputation of the monastery program even among the Lao and expatriate Asians. If we extrapolate from the data collected on the 825 addicts, perhaps as many as 160 to 170 of the 3,000 addicts who went there died during or relatively soon after treatment. Consequently, by early 1974, fewer and fewer addicts were willing to travel down to the Thailand program. Of interest, addicts did not identify the fact that only older addicts were dying. In their folk wisdom they applied the mortal risk to one and all. It is interesting to note that mortality has not been a significant problem among Thai addicts at Wat Tan Kha Bok, probably because they have had very few Thai addicts aged sixty or older seeking treatment there (see Poshyachinda et al. 1978).

TREATMENT OUTCOME

Abstention Without Treatment

One complication in evaluating treatment is the phenomenon of recovery without treatment, sometimes referred to as spontaneous abstention or recovery. If treatment does not offer an improvement over spontaneous recovery, there is little purpose in expending the time, money, and effort that treatment entails.

How common is spontaneous abstention in substance abuse? While there have been few studies in this area, the spontaneous recovery rate in cases of alcoholism appears to be relatively low. Studies conducted in the United States suggest a rate on the order of 4 to 7 percent, if prolonged abstention after chronic heavy drinking is used as the criterion (Saunders and Kershaw 1979; Kissin, Rosenblatt, and Machover 1978;

Lemere 1953; Smart 1975–1976). It seems likely that prolonged abstention after chronic heavy opium or heroin use is no higher than this and
is probably lower. Over a ten-year period in Laos I tried to locate spontaneous abstainers and was unable to find even one. Eventually I tried
to find cases of long-term recovery without formal treatment through
Hmong friends and associates. Two such people were identified, and
their case reports follow.

Religious Conversion and the District Chief. "My first taste of
opium occurred fifty-three years ago when I was five years old. My
father gave it to me to cure a bad cough. In my family, only my
grandfather smoked opium all the time. My father knew how to smoke
opium, but he did not do so except when a family member was ill.
Then he would use my grandfather's pipe to blow opium smoke under
a blanket so the sick one could inhale it. Opium was used in my family
to cure all kinds of ills: snake bite, bee bite, cough, diarrhea, pains
from any cause. When I was in my early teens, I smoked a few pipes
myself when I was ill but never without my father's permission. Otherwise he would hit me.

"After I was married, I continued to use opium to cure most of
my illnesses. Then at about thirty years of age, maybe thirty-one years,
I was elected to be district chief (*tasseng*). There were many meetings,
many discussions, with planning this or solving that problem. It was
our custom at that time to offer alcohol or opium to honored guests
as a sign of respect. It was at that time that I had many occasions to
smoke opium as an official guest. During that time I developed a liking
for opium and would smoke as many as three to six sets [one set
equals three pipefuls]. I began to develop a hunger for it, just like for
food or water.

"Fortunately around this time I became a Christian. Others in my
clan had converted to Christianity. When I changed my religious belief
and converted to Christianity, I stopped using opium completely and
have not used it since. If I had not changed religion, I would still be
addicted to opium."

That Magnetic Feeling. "I am Tu Neng Lee, and my age is about
fifty-seven years. Opium has always been a part of my life since childhood. My father smoked opium every day until he died. Opium smoking was common at that time. When we visited one another, opium
was offered as a treat. Smoking on the sleeping platform was the main

way of socializing. After one or two pipes, a person felt very good and wanted to talk about everything he knew. One also tended to be more patient than usual after smoking. Opium had a magnetic feeling, for when the same time that you had tasted opium came again, you felt like going back to it and chatting with friends.

"It took ten years before I was addicted to opium. The time of my addiction was from 1950 to 1958. Around 1953 I tried to stop it but failed because my heart was not ready yet. At that time I was in the foothills of the mountain Phou Bia. Then later I moved into Xieng Khouang town and became a meat merchant. I never dared to smoke openly at home as my wife was a fervent Christian. To hide it from her I paid my addicted friends, Hmong and Chinese both, to buy opium for me. At that time I needed it twice a day and was smoking as much as twenty sets [sixty pipes] at one time, which was forty sets or four *bak* [about .015 kilograms] of opium per day. Even my Chinese friends smoked only ten or twelve sets at a time. I spent 200 *kip* each day for opium when it was difficult to make 200 to 300 *kip* a day.

"The expenses for opium became a heavy burden for my family, so I forced myself to stop opium completely without any medicine. During that time I decided that I would succeed even if I had to die. It took me eight days and nights of twisting around to pass through it. I prayed constantly, and the reason I was able to do it was because God helped me. Opium is the worst disease, and it has a spirit of a girl in it. If you do not really pray and trust God completely, that girl-spirit would lure you to being sick again so you would go back to opium."

Timing the Outcome Study

Perhaps no area of psychosocial treatment has so few outcome studies as the treatment of narcotic addiction and alcoholism. Most studies in this field only specify what took place during treatment itself or how many patients opted in or out of the treatment program, with no indication regarding the effect of the treatment process after a follow-up period. Other outcome studies extend for only a few weeks or a few months beyond discharge from treatment. Since many addicts can go several weeks or even several months before relapsing into drug usage, studies soon after treatment are virtually useless. But how long after treatment should outcome studies be done? The extensive review paper by Hunt and Matarazzo indicates that about 90 percent of the recurrence within the first years occurs in the first six months and then begins to level off (see fig. 1). Ideally, then, outcome studies should extend for at least one year, possibly two. Even longer periods are desirable in order to elucidate the course of these phenomena, such as Vaillant's twelve- and twenty-year studies (1966a and b, 1973).

Forty-nine addicts who had successfully withdrawn themselves were questioned about the duration of time at which they resumed addiction. Sampling included twenty nonpatient addicts (i.e., those still using and not seeking treatment) and twenty-nine addicts who had come to be admitted to the medical facility in Vientiane. All were Asians, mostly Lao and Hmong. None of these subjects had been in a treatment

Figure 1. Release Rate Over Time for Heroin, Smoking and Alcohol

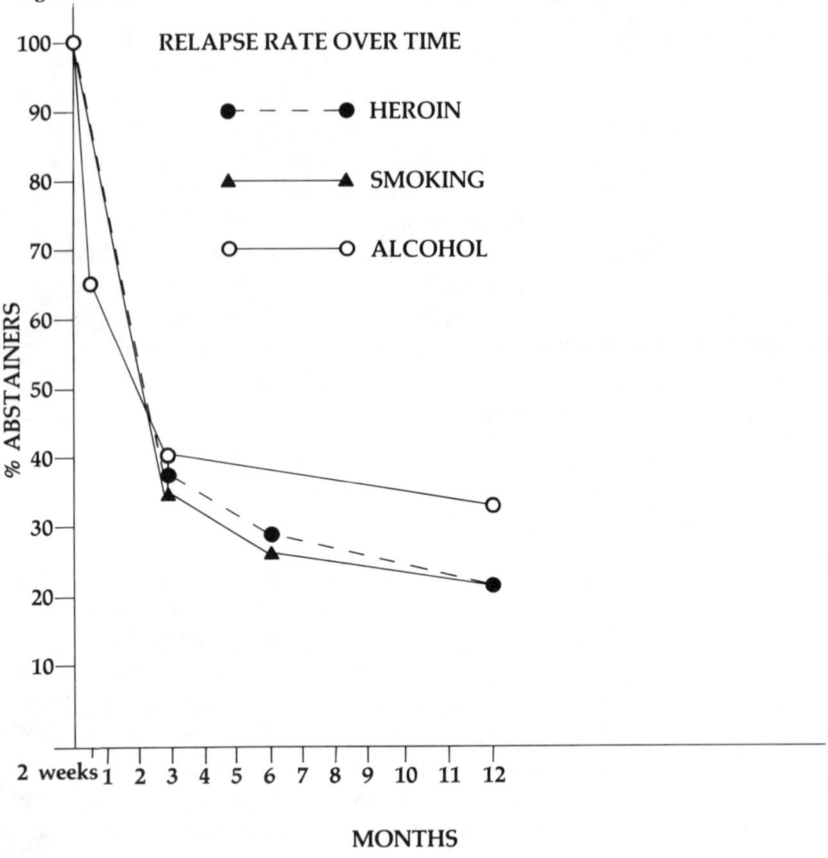

From Hunt, W.A. & Matarazzo, J.D. Chapter in *Learning Mechanisms in Smoking.* Chicago: Aldine, 1970, pp. 65–90; Hunt et al., *J. Clin. Psychol.*, 1971, 27, 455–456; and Hunt, W. A., & Matarazzo, J.D. *J. Abn. Psychol.*, 1973, 81, 107–114.

program designed for addiction but had withdrawn themselves using one or more folk methods described in the previous chapter. Their duration of abstinence before resuming addiction was as follows:

Time	Number of subjects	Percent
0– 6 months	23	(47)
7–12 months	15	(31)
13–18 months	5	(10)
19–24 months	1	(2)
3 years	1	(2)
4 years	2	(4)
5 years	1	(2)
11 years	1	(2)
	49	(100)

The rate of recurrence by six months in these Laotian addicts was somewhat lower than that described by Hunt and Matarazzo, since out of thirty-eight addicts readdicted in the first year, twenty-three (i.e., 61 percent) had relapsed within six months.

These data suggest that outcome studies should be delayed for at least six months, and preferably twelve or even eighteen months, after the addict returns to a setting in which opiate use is a viable option. They also suggest that follow-up treatment or support to aid the recovering addict might best continue for twelve to twenty-four months following discharge from the initial treatment.

Criteria for Assessing Outcome

With a chronic relapsing condition such as addiction, it is misleading to speak of cure. Instead, specific criteria should be used, such as abstinence versus sporadic use versus readdiction, improvement versus no improvement (specifying what comprises improvement), or readmission to treatment. The choice of criteria differs according to the research goals and the population under study. Depending on these various factors, complete abstinence might be considered as improvement, or some return to drugs without recurrence of social or economic problems might be defined as improvement. A patient's merely being alive after one or two years might comprise an acceptable outcome.

Information in addition to self-report by the addict is desirable, such as collateral informants (e.g., family, friends) affirming the individual's abstinence; continued contact by the researcher with the individual, who shows no evidence of intoxication; continued employment; residence with a family; or continued good health. Less reliable as an indication of treatment efficacy is information such as the patient's self-report alone or patient satisfaction with treatment.

Three different outcome criteria were used to evaluate treatment in Laos. One of these was readmission to the medical facility because of relapse. (This method could not be used at Wat Tan Kha Bok, since one of the institutional policies specified that no addict could ever be readmitted.) Another criterion was abstinence at the time of the outcome study. This was always confirmed by someone besides the former patient who was in a position to know whether he or she had resumed use (e.g., family member, close friend). And a third involved the presence or absence of general improvement (e.g., feeling better, being productive, getting along with family) whether or not the subject was using opiates.

In conducting the study, it turned out that abstinence was associated with improvement in about 95 to 98 percent of addicts. That is, they felt better, were more productive, and were getting along better with other people. The issue of abstinence without improvement in the remaining 2 to 5 percent is considered later in this chapter. Conversely, all addicts who had resumed regular opium use after treatment were readdicted by the time of the outcome survey. Controlled or sporadic opium use following treatment for addiction was either a transient or a short-lived phenomenon (lasting only hours, days, or a few weeks in these subjects). Although many of the relapsed addicts were using less opium than they had before treatment, they could not be considered improved from the standpoint of their health, productivity, or family life.

Sampling Methods for Assessing Outcome

One reason for few outcome studies of substance abuse treatment is that they are difficult and expensive to do well. When subjects come to the investigator (as they do in seeking treatment), logistics are relatively simple. When the investigator must later find and go to the subject following a course of treatment, the difficulty and time required by the task increase many times over.

One of the simpler methods for assessing outcome consists of the investigator remaining at the treatment facility and observing the percentage of former patients returning with a relapse. While relatively easy, this method does not identify those patients who relapse but do not return.

The most valid means of conducting an outcome study consists of going to the subjects' residences. Ideally, if one cannot investigate all former patients, then a random sample from the entire patient population should be selected and visited. In Laos, where there were no telephones, mail routes, or roads to the villages where most addicts resided, such a procedure would have required resources well beyond those available. As a compromise, certain villages and districts were selected for the outcome study. Selection of these areas was based on specific variables that were to be studied (e.g., demographic characteristics, ethnicity, cost and availability of opium). The sample was therefore a representative one to permit study of these variables but not a random one.

Four sampling methods were used to evaluate treatment outcome in Laos. First, ex-patients readmitted to the medical facility in Vientiane within 365 days after discharge were compared with addicts not readmitted. Second, twenty-five addicts from NNDC were chosen from rural areas around the country. An extensive interview was conducted at their homes. These twenty-five people were chosen to represent addicts not likely to return to the facility for readmission. Next, addicts treated at Wat Tan Kha Bok were surveyed in four districts. And finally, two towns and eight villages were surveyed to assess the percentage of addicts going to treatment and the percentage remaining abstinent after treatment either at Wat Tan Kha Bok or at the medical facility.

Readmission to the National Narcotic Detoxification Center

Those receiving treatment at the medical facility in Vientiane received no instructions regarding return for treatment in the event of readdiction. Before too many weeks elapsed, ex-patients began returning to the Center, having become readdicted. A policy had been adopted that these patients would be readmitted without prejudice in order to obtain information regarding those at risk to readdiction.

Charts of addicts admitted during the twelve months between September 15, 1972, and September 4, 1973, were reviewed in early 1975 to see if they had been readmitted for readdiction within 365 days from the date of discharge. Their demographic and clinical characteristics were then compared with those of addicts who had not sought readmission.

The percentage of addicts seeking readmission was 10.6 percent (i.e., 51 out of 480). Readmitted patients were slightly more apt to be ethnic Lao or expatriate Asians and addicted to heroin. These differences, however, were not statistically significant (using the .05 level of significance). There were no differences by age, sex, and marital status between those readmitted and those not readmitted. Most readmitted addicts came from metropolitan Vientiane or areas around Vientiane province, suggesting that readmission was primarily associated with proximity to the treatment facility. This proximity probably accounted for the slight predominance of ethnic Lao and expatriate Asians, as well as heroin addicts, among the readmitted addicts.* (See Westermeyer and Bourne 1978, for further details.)

Field Survey of Former Patients from the Medical Facility

Tribespeople and farmer-peasants were underrepresented among the readmitted patients described above. In order to obtain an outcome evaluation of addicts in rural areas, a representative sample of thirty addicts was selected from ten villages in Vientiane and Xieng Khouang provinces. Travel to each of the villages involved aircraft, helicopters, jeeps, and/or lengthy hiking. Five subjects could not be interviewed at the time of the field survey (because of travel, temporary absence at work tasks, change in residence), reducing the number to twenty-five.

---

*Among the first 20 patients admitted to the Center in September of 1972, 9 had been patients there previously. Six of the 9 were readdicted and had returned within days of discharge. The other 3 patients sought care for physical ailments associated with continued withdrawal. This phenomenon resulted from my recommendation—based on experience with heroin, morphine, and Demerol addicts—that methadone detoxification could be accomplished within 7 to 10 days. As it turned out, opium and heavy heroin addicts could not be comfortably detoxified in so short a time. Dr. Chomchan Soudaly, director of the facility, observed that this problem was resolved by lengthening the usual detoxification period to 2 or 3 weeks.

The readmission rate for patients admitted during the first 6 months of operation was somewhat higher: 15.0 percent. The percentage of readmissions fell dramatically in the second 6 months. Subsequently it increased somewhat but not up to the original level. This probably resulted from three factors: (1) the shorter detoxification method described above, (2) a higher proportion of Vientiane addicts among the original patients, with their higher readmission rate, and (3) the later effect of the community factors, which will be discussed further on.

Another early problem was the once-a-day dosage of methadone given in the mornings. Patients then experienced some withdrawal symptoms about 14 to 18 hours later and had trouble sleeping. A few patients left the center for a few hours and purchased a few pipes of opium to relieve their insomnia. This problem was relieved by twice-a-day methadone dosages, splitting the original dose into two equal halves.

Average length of time since discharge was twelve months, although the range was from several months up to almost a year and a half. While more subjects and a uniform postdischarge time would have been desirable, the difficulties and time involved in getting to remote villages in Laos did not allow a larger sample and a uniform twelve-month interval. I obtained the data by lengthy interviews with the former patient, family members, and others who knew the subject (e.g., elder, village chief, local community health worker).

Sixteen of this group were tribal people; the remaining nine were Lao. All twenty-five were opium smokers. Nine of them had become readdicted (i.e., 36 percent).[*] Readdicted and abstinent groups did not differ significantly from one another by age (using Student "t" test), sex, ethnicity, or marital status (using the Chi Square test for statistical significance). Although the sample size was too small to make a definitive statement, the similarity in the two groups (i.e., abstinent and readdicted) suggested that the demographic factors that usually influence outcome in studies elsewhere were not strongly related to outcome in this group.

Of interest, three women (all Hmong) who went to treatment without their addicted husbands became readdicted upon returning home. Two women (1 Hmong and 1 Khamu) whose husbands also went for treatment were both still abstinent. There were only two divorced persons in the field survey sample; both of them were also readdicted during the follow-up study. These findings suggest that the presence of an abstinent spouse favored abstinence, a finding noted repeatedly in the literature on narcotic addiction and alcoholism. (See Westermeyer and Bourne 1978, for further details.)

Field Survey of Patients from Wat Tan Kha Bok

Four rural districts were selected for follow-up studies. All of the addicts in the four districts had been to treatment at least six months earlier. Two of these districts were ethnic Lao located in Vientiane province, and two were tribal areas (Iu Mien and Akha) located in Houa Kong province (sometimes also called Nam Tha) close to the Burmese border.

In the two Lao areas, 107 addicts had gone for treatment; eighty-three of these (78 percent) were abstinent at follow-up. Sixty-two of the

---

[*]Two of the abstinent addicts had had a "slip." That is, they had used some opium but had been able to resume abstention. Both had been cajoled and supported by other abstinent ex-addicts who had been to treatment.

tribespeople had gone for treatment; only eleven of them (18 percent) were abstinent beyond six months following treatment. More data on these widely divergent outcomes, as well as interpretations for them, follow later in this chapter. (See also Westermeyer 1979.)

Comparison of Outcomes: Buddhist Monastery Versus Medical Facility

In some villages and districts, virtually all addicts who sought treatment went to either the Thai monastery or NNDC. In other locations there were chance combinations, with some going to the monastery and some going to the medical facility. The time since treatment was about one year for both the monastery and medical groups (with a range from six to eighteen months). The outcome from the two treatments was as follows:

Outcome	Treatment Program	
	Monastery	Medical facility
Abstinent	24	16
Relapsed	14	17

Note that there was a trend for addicts from the monastery to do better than those from the medical facility although this trend was not statistically significant ($X^2_1 = 1.0338$, $P < .65$).

During the data collection it became evident that, irrespective of treatment program, the addicts from Houa Kong province had done less well than those from the other two provinces. The data appeared as follows:

Location and outcome	Treatment program	
	Monastery	Medical facility
Vientiane and Xieng Khouang		
Abstinent	23	16
Relapsed	3	9
Houa Kong		
Abstinent	1	0
Relapsed	11	8

Again, statistical analysis failed to show a significant difference between the two treatment programs (using the Fisher Exact test for significance). Rearranging these data by location and outcome, these data are as follows:

Outcome	Location	
	Vientiane and Xieng Khouang	Houa Kong
Abstinent	39	1
Relapsed	12	19

This difference between the two locations was highly significant ($X_1^2 =$ 111.5152, P < .0001).

Why should these two regions differ so drastically? In Vientiane and Xieng Khouang, refugee movements out of the northern poppy-producing regions had resulted in decreased availability and increased cost of opium. In Houa Kong, distance from the larger battles and proximity to the still-flourishing poppy fields of Burma and Thailand kept opium availability high and price low. Thus, price and availability factors probably accounted for part of this observed difference. But during this survey, another possible explanation occurred to me. It is elaborated in the next section.

Influence of Community Factors on Outcome

The surveys described above initially focused on (1) outcomes from the two treatment programs and (2) outcomes as related to addicts' demographic and clinical characteristics. In doing these outcome studies it appeared that community factors might also be important, perhaps even more so than treatment variables or patient variables. In order to pursue this possibility, several villages and two towns were studied in 1974. At these locations addicts had been treated an average of twelve months previously (a range of six to eighteen months) either at Wat Tan Kha Bok or at the medical center. The following data were obtained at each site:

1. total population (all ages),
2. total number of addicts,
3. number of addicts who had gone for treatment at the monastery or medical center,
4. number of addicts still abstinent.

Ten sites were surveyed: three in Vientiane province, three in Xieng Khouang province, and four in Houa Kong province. Data were obtained by working closely with several people at each site, including the village chief and elders, addicts themselves, and village health workers. In three locations, the health worker (at our request) had recently collected reasonably complete data regarding addicts, which required relatively brief verification. In two other locations, a careful survey was done. In two larger locations, reasonable estimates were based on reports by village chiefs, elders, addicts, and health workers. In the two largest sites, an estimate regarding the number of addicts could not be made because of the large population and time constraints. And in one district (the Akha villages), a lack of cooperation from village chiefs and elders made a complete addict survey unfeasible. At six sites, the total population of all people in the village was estimated, based on number of houses and average number of people per house; these estimates are believed accurate to within plus or minus 10 percent. Actual counts were made at four sites. (These methodological differences were unfortunately imposed on us by limitations in time and personnel.)

The ten sites were divided into three separate categories depending on the percentage of abstinent persons among those treated. In the high-success group, more than two-thirds of the treated addicts were still abstinent. Middle-success locations had between one-third and two-thirds abstinent rates. And in the low-success areas, less than one-third of treated addicts were currently abstinent. (See Westermeyer and Bourne 1978, for further details.)

a. High-Success Locations. The percentage of abstinent people among those treated in these locations varied from 69 to 100 percent. All four areas were rural towns and villages located in Xieng Khouang and Vientiane provinces, an area where opium production had decreased as a result of refugee movements and the price of opium had increased. Two of the locations were ethnic Lao, and two were tribal (one Hmong and one Khamu). Data were as follows:

Population	Total number of addicts	Number of treated addicts	Number of abstinent addicts	Percentage: treated/ total	Percentage: abstinent/ treated
45	3	3	3	100	100
1,000	53	45	40	85	89
175	16	13	11	81	85
4,000	72	62	43	86	69

Between 81 percent and 100 percent of addicts in all four locations had gone for treatment. They had gone either in one group from the smaller tribal villages or as a few large subgroups over a several-week period in the larger communities. These efforts had been organized by the village leaders (chief and elders) and the addicts themselves. Arrangements had to be made within the village for others to take care of children, farm animals, or gardens. Upon returning home, the treated addicts comprised an informal support group for one another. They socialized together, supported one another's abstinence, chided those who returned to occasional opium smoking, and cajoled untreated or readdicted persons to go for treatment. During our visits to two of these sites, three previously untreated addicts asked to journey back with us to the medical facility for treatment.

The percentage of abstinent addicts one year after treatment in these locations ranged from 69 percent to 100 percent. Among the 123 treated addicts in all 4 sites, 97 (i.e., 79 percent) remained abstinent.

Those who did become readdicted in these villages were using less opium per day than they had been using upon admission to treatment. Their mean daily expenditure was $0.38 at the time of the survey, as compared to $1.05 recorded at the time of original admission to treatment.

b. Middle-Success Locations. The two middle-success areas were Vientiane Prefecture (with 130,000 people) and Ban Son town (with over 10,000 refugees, mostly Hmong). Addict populations in these two locations were large, with thousands of addicts in Vientiane and hundreds in Ban Son. Consequently, given the available treatment resources, all of these people could not receive treatment within a short span of time. Local political leaders had not organized groups of addicts to receive treatment together as they had done spontaneously in the high-success villages. Despite this lack of community organization, hundreds of addicts from Vientiane Prefecture and scores of addicts from Ban Son had gone for treatment, sometimes as solitary individuals and sometimes within a small neighborhood cohort of addicts.

There was no means of determining the precise treatment and abstinence rates in these two large towns. It was possible, however, to estimate the abstinence rate by choosing a representative group of addicts in both locations and assessing the rate of readdiction among them. Ten cases were chosen from areas around Ban Son, and twelve cases were chosen from representative neighborhoods around Vientiane city. Figures were as follows:

Estimated population	Number of treated addicts in survey	Number of abstinent addicts in survey	Percentage abstinent/ treated
10,000	10	5	50
130,000	12	5	42

The percentage of abstinent addicts at these two locations was estimated at about 42 to 50 percent based on the sample. Of the entire 22 treated addicts in the survey, 10 (or 45 percent) were abstinent after an average of 12 months.

Intensive case studies at these sites aided in identifying factors for or against abstinence following treatment. Favorable factors were (1) contacts with other addicts who had been treated and were currently abstinent and (2) frequent contact with a person or institution interested in the addict's continuing abstinence, such as a health worker, clinic, missionary, village or district chief. Unfavorable factors included (1) continued contact with people using narcotic drugs, (2) being single or divorced, (3) dysphoric emotional states in the postaddiction period, (4) recurrence of physical disorders and somatic symptoms, and (5) having an addicted spouse.

c. Low-Success Locations. In these four villages between 0 and 25 percent of the treated addicts were abstinent at the time of the survey. All of these villages were located in the province of Houa Kong, an area at the center of the opium-producing Golden Triangle formed by Laos, Thailand, and Burma. Opium had remained highly available there and was considerably less expensive than in the other provinces of Laos. Data were as follows:

Population	Total number of addicts	Number of treated addicts	Number of abstinent addicts	Percentage treated/ total	Percentage abstinent/ treated
400	39	4	1	10%	25
2,740	approx. 180	58	10	approx. 32	17
2,000	approx. 105	9	0	approx. 9	0
3,000	unknown	3	0	unknown	0

In these locations the majority of addicts did not go for treatment. The highest proportion of addicts seeking treatment in any one place was 32 percent, and the percentages ranged down to 8 percent. Local political leaders did not organize to send the addicts for treatment. Consequently, addicts went off to treatment either singly or in small groups of two or three. Addicts also tended to go for treatment alone or in small groups over a long period of time rather than organizing so that all or most of the addicts went for treatment over a relatively short period. During the collection of data, the lack of village organization was reflected in the dearth of information among village elders regarding how many people in the village were addicted. In a few cases, the district chief did not even know that some villagers from his district had gone for treatment of their addiction.

Percent abstinence in the 4 sites after an average of one year ranged from 0 to 25 percent. Of the 74 treated addicts, 11 of them (i.e., 15 percent) remained abstinent.

The Famous Pig Farmer. Bounme was sixty-nine years old when admitted to the medical facility in Vientiane and seventy years old when interviewed during the outcome study. Prior to becoming addicted, he had been a successful farmer in Vientiane Prefecture. He had eight children, a devoted and charming wife, his health—a good life, one might say. In 1948, when he was about forty-five, he began to smoke opium occasionally with a few friends. In retrospect it is difficult to discern any explanations for it. He wasn't ill, there had been no great losses in his life, and it was a relatively stable, almost tranquil time in Laotian history. Perhaps it was boredom, or maybe he felt he had earned the opportunity to enjoy some pleasurable times with friends. Whatever the genesis, Bounme was addicted a year later.

Over the subsequent twenty-four years, he remained addicted more or less continuously. Several attempts at stopping failed after a few days spent suffering withdrawal. Still, he worked hard at supporting his family and educating his children. All eight children finished elementary school, and five of them attended the French *lycée.* Two obtained scholarships to study abroad. With age, however, his addiction became a greater detriment to the family. Although he went to eating opium (rather than smoking it as formerly) and reduced his daily doses from three down to two, still his opium supply cost $1.20 per day, more than the daily earnings of any one of his children. In addition, his children—all married now with children of their own—needed Bounme's help and support as the clan grandfather; and they wanted him to serve as a good role model for their children.

After pressuring him for some months, Bounme's wife and children finally prevailed upon him to enter treatment at the medical facility.

He complained bitterly of the treatment process, accused the staff of not giving him enough medicine, and had physical complaints referable to every organ and orifice in his body. Soon after his first hospitalization (which lasted twenty-three days) he was back using opium again. Readmitted only twenty-six days after his first discharge, Bounme's second hospitalization was almost the antithesis of the first one. He was more cooperative and less complaining and socialized more with other patients. In particular, he made friends with two other men who were in their early sixties and lived in a village about six kilometers from his own home.

The transformation in Bounme following his second hospitalization was amazing! Almost every day he got together with the two men he had met during treatment; they assembled at one or the other's village or at the outpatient clinic that lay in between the two. Gradually Bounme came out of his former retirement. First he made a number of repairs around the house. Then he planted a vegetable garden. Next he bought several pigs. The animals did so well, and his profits were so considerable, that he was soon raising a few dozen. As Bounme made these changes, his wife underwent a series of changes, too. She regained more of her old energy; and with Bounme doing the repairs and gardening now, she had more time on her hands. So she started looking after several of her grandchildren during the day while their parents were away at work—a day school, Lao style. For both Bounme and his wife entering their seventies, it was a second lease on life.

What does this have to do with being famous? To be sure, Bounme's self-reclamation was well known locally. He also became a national folk hero when a local newspaper ran an article on him. Then a newsfilm, shown nationally, depicted his pig farm and his houseful of grandchildren. From a treatment failure, Bounme had become an inspiring figure to other addicts. When I last visited him at his home in 1975 he was still abstinent and energetic three years following treatment. He and his two friends had become too busy to get together more often than every week or two, but they remained close friends. His craving for opium had disappeared entirely, and he felt strong and well.

A Little Help from Friends. Tshai Mua was a forty-eight-year-old Hmong man who worked as a laborer in Ban Son. I had known him earlier, several years before his addiction, when he had worked in a warehouse at Sam Thong, farther to the north. He smoked opium at that time only when the labor was hard or prolonged and occasionally at festival times like Hmong New Year. Although he had smoked for four years on and off in Sam Thong, he had not become addicted.

In the year that Sam Thong was attacked by the Vietnamese, Tshai had a string of bad luck. His elderly mother, weakened by the long walk out of Sam Thong down to Ban Son, announced one morning that she was not taking to the trail. She was exhausted and ready to join her ancestors, she said. No, she would not let Tshai carry her; he must carry his children. He still saw her in his dreams, waving at him weakly as she became a small dot in the landscape. Then a short way farther along, his six-year-old daughter, the bright, pretty one with the dark flashing eyes, his favorite, came down with the "forest fever" (probably malaria). She died as he carried her along on his back. Later that year, back to work at Ban Son, his opium habit became an addiction.

At the time that he entered treatment, Tshai was smoking twice a day and spending his entire income on opium. His wife, his supervisor at work, and a local village health worker had all urged him to enter treatment. Following discharge from the medical facility, these same three people supported him in the difficult early months of abstinence. His wife complimented him on his healthy appearance and vigor. The village health worker provided reassurance and symptomatic treatment for the myriad somatic symptoms that he experienced during the early months of abstinence. At work his supervisor repeatedly praised his "strong will" in giving up addiction. Two years following treatment Tshai was still abstinent, felt well, and had no craving for opium.

ABSTINENT AND UNIMPROVED

At the time of leaving the medical facility virtually all of the patients reported feeling better than they had in years. They looked better, too: heavier, better color, quicker eye, firmer hand, springier step. The real test lay in the first several months back home. How would they readjust to the indifferent spouse? Or the cold nights alone on a mountainside? Or the first recurrence of malaria or amebiasis? As we have seen above, given a favorable social context, most did run successfully through their own unique gauntlets and, after those early difficult months, resumed satisfying lifestyles. Others, despite months of abstinence, remained miserable. While the latter were in a minority, they did comprise a group for whom social advantages alone did not suffice.

Abstinent and Emotionally Disabled. Among distraught addicts, depression was the most frequent complication of abstinence. Kokeo was a case in point. A fifty-year-old farmer from Vientiane province, he had been smoking opium twice a day for ten years after having smoked episodically for four years. He went through treatment without difficulty and was discharged in good spirits. Upon returning home to his family, he began to feel increasingly sadder—although for no particular reason that he could discern. Gradually he became socially withdrawn and did not want to speak with anyone, even his wife and children. His one continued social contact was with his best friend, an addict who had not entered treatment. At six-months posttreatment he remained abstinent, despite his increasing fatigue, restless sleep, and loss of appetite. "I feel like crying all the time," he said. He was adamant about overcoming his addiction, and his friend never smoked in his presence so as not to tempt him. When I visited him twelve months after discharge, Kokeo looked much better: more relaxed, sociable, and confident. He had resumed opium two months previously.

Songphet, a forty-two-year-old barber from Vientiane Prefecture, had a related but somewhat different problem. Addicted for ten years, he had been eating opium twice a day. He did well at the medical facility but subsequently developed increasingly severe emotional distress at home. At first it was manifested primarily by irritability: "I wanted to hear only pleasant things and have no problems." Then he began to worry and anticipate failure and frustration: "If anybody was unhappy with my family or me or brought a problem to me, I would worry about it constantly and get very upset." Eventually, he developed insomnia, loss of enjoyment, constant dysphoria, and various somatic symptoms: "I began to have severe headaches; I thought I was going to go crazy." When I saw him six months after treatment, Songphet was obviously agitated. Unable to keep from shaking, he could no longer work as a barber. He took odd jobs as an unskilled laborer, but the family had to depend on his wife's taking in laundry. Songphet had several family members and friends supporting his abstinence. Nonetheless, after persisting miserably in abstinence for about a year, he resumed opium use. While his failure at abstinence caused him a notable loss in self-confidence, he felt considerably better emotionally and physically. He was able to resume his work as a barber.

Both Kokeo and Songphet represent typical patients in any psychiatric outpatient clinic or psychiatrist's office. Such patients tend to do well after some weeks or months of psychiatric care. Since this was not available in Laos at the time, these two men (and some others like them) were probably better off going back to opium. They felt better and were able to function at their work after they had become disabled while abstinent.

Abstinent and Physically Disabled

Suwanwela et al. have described a Hmong addict in Thailand in whom they discovered a chronic, painful kidney condition. After treating his addiction, they made arrangements for him to travel out of the mountains to a Thai hospital in the lowlands for a renal evaluation. There he received a skilled and detailed evaluation, which revealed the source of his illness. In order for his problem to be relieved, he would have to visit the clinic regularly for the rest of his life and have his medications closely monitored by a nephrologist. Yet his home and family were in the mountains, and he had no occupational skills to survive in the Thai town. He returned home knowing he had only a few more years to live without treatment. In order to relieve his pain and resume work, he began smoking opium again. Suwanwela and his colleagues appear to have approved and supported his decision.

I concur with my Thai colleagues. In 1965 to 1967, I proffered similar counsel to certain patients in Laos on a number of occasions. One man had a thyroid cancer with metastases, and another had advanced valvular disease from rheumatic heart disease. Recently here in Minnesota I examined a former Hmong addict in considerable pain from a metastasized squamous cell carcinoma of the larynx. After we talked about his dim prognosis, I told him that I wished we could get him some smoking opium. "*Yog kwv!*" he responded, "That's for sure!" Before he died, he had a lot to do for his family, and there were several friends and relatives whom he wanted to see. Instead I prescribed morphine, which he found an acceptable substitute for his familiar opium.

COST EFFECTIVENESS

Working a typical ten-hours-per-day, six-days-per-week schedule, the average citizen of Laos could make about $300 to $360 per year (in 1972–1974 dollars). Compared with these incomes, the costs for one patient at

Wat Tan Kha Bok (i.e., $50) and at the National Narcotic Detoxification Center (i.e., $150) were fairly expensive. Were they worth the cost?

One way of answering that difficult question is to consider the cost per abstinent, improved patient. In Houa Kong where outcome was poorest, the costs per abstinent patient would be about $350 for the monastery and about $1,050 for the medical facility. Conversely, in areas of Vientiane and Xieng Khouang where outcome was optimal, costs per abstinent patient would be $63 for the monastery and $188 for the medical facility. These latter figures look good even for a country with financial resources as limited as those of Laos, while the former costs for Houa Kong are a bit high.

Another way of assessing cost is to ask, "Worth it to whom?" For the family of the abstinent former addict, almost any price might be worthwhile, even the $1,050 in Houa Kong, since the average addict was spending $1.00 to $2.00 per day on drugs over many years. But governments must deal with finances in tougher, more objective terms. Will treating 5,000 addicts for $450,000 over three years (as occurred in Laos) lead to such fiscal improvements for the nation as reduced medical costs, fewer law enforcement costs, higher productivity, more government revenue? Will these expenditures produce such humanitarian benefits as reduced crime, reduced child neglect, greater longevity? No definitive answers to these questions were available when the government changed in 1975, but they were being asked by administrators and legislators in that country at that time.

Another way of assessing cost effectiveness is to look at the projected outcome of the program (projected from firm data, that is, not merely from planners' fantasies). Does the program result in a total decrease in the number of addicts within the nation? By how much? Or does it merely balance the number of new addicts being initiated into addiction? For example, one might make the reasonable assumption that, out of 5,000 addicts treated over three years, 3,000 remained abstinent at one year posttreatment. That would be about 1,000 people removed from the list of addicts each year. It is likely that well over 1,000 addicts alone died each year in Laos. So treatment may not have been as efficient as death in reducing the addict population. We do not know the number of new addicts appearing in Laos each year, but (with a rapidly expanding population) that probably ran about 2,000 each year (plus or minus a thousand). Even if we were to assume that treatment was truly reducing the number of addicts in the country by 1,000 per year, it would not eliminate the addict population in Laos at the current rate of treatment.

In sum, the program at its 1972 to 1975 level was an interesting pilot project and a laudable humanitarian effort but not an efficient public health endeavor that was likely to eliminate narcotic addiction in Laos over a five-, ten-, or even twenty-year period. The outreach program being initiated in 1975 was to be an effort in that direction, but it was not continued by the new government.

ETHICAL CONSIDERATIONS

The Confidentiality Issue

Within the first few months after the medical facility opened, various police, embassy, and intelligence agencies were approaching the medical director for names of patients. This was a major issue for discussion during my 1973 consultation to the medical facility. We discussed the various means by which this would destroy essential features of the doctor-patient relationship. Two key resources were then approached to help in opposing these various pressures: the Ministry of Health and the Public Health Division of the United States Agency for International Development. Once these offices supported the need for confidentiality, pressures to divulge identities ceased.

Medical Records and the Communist Government

Each patient at the medical facility was recorded by name, address, and photo. A small percentage of patients gave pseudonyms and false addresses, so photos aided in establishing the identity of individuals who were suspected of being former patients. They served an important function in record keeping and in assessing readmission as well as outcome. As it turned out, the records and photos later provided a ready means for communist officials to identify and harass former patients.

In retrospect, perhaps those of us associated with the medical facility should have been more alert to this possibility. We had discussed it, but we assumed that there would be sufficient time to destroy the files containing patient information. But the tactics employed by the new government were both disarming and rapid. I repeat them here as told to me by members of the staff who subsequently left Laos as refugees.

Initially the new communist officials came to the medical facility (as to other institutions) in a friendly fashion, reassuring the staff that they should remain and continue as before on their jobs. Several weeks later in the midst of a workday, about fifty armed soldiers appeared at the facility and occupied every section of the two buildings. The director, and only the director, was taken away to a concentration camp in the north. A communist physician was put in charge.

The records at the Center were then used to round up addicts who had been at the facility. They were warned that they were under surveillance and, if known or suspected to be using opiates, they would be sent off to concentration camps. Soon thereafter the medical facility was closed, and all known addicts were sent to concentration camps.

Gradually all of the male staff members and support workers at the center—down to the janitor and jeep driver—were arrested and sent to concentration camps in northern Laos. The medical director eventually escaped after a few years and made his way to Thailand. He now lives in the United States. Later several other staff members escaped and, as of this writing, are in Thai refugee camps. One staff member (an administration/liaison officer) died while he was being herded, along with other officials and officers of the former government, across suspected mine fields to clear them of mines. Another (the jeep driver) escaped but committed suicide when he learned that his wife and four children had all been shot and killed attempting to cross the Mekong River into Thailand. A third (the maintenance man) was shot and killed, along with his wife and three children, while attempting to cross the Mekong. These tragedies are not unique to staff at the medical facility. They also befell other former employees from the Ministry of Health and the Ministry of Social Welfare. But they do indicate the kind of atrocities to which former staff and patients at the medical center have been and are being subjected. It is a burden that we have mourned and that each of us will carry with us through life.

UNSUCCESSFUL PILOT PROJECTS

The medical director, Dr. Chomchan Soudaly, and I both had the opportunity to learn the use of acupuncture for withdrawal. We studied and observed the method employed by Dr. H. L. Wen in Hong Kong (who first described the procedure to physicians) and Dr. Aroon Showanasai in Thailand. The method consists first of placing needles at the proper meridians in both ears, then passing about nine volts of electricity between the two needles. It produces a relief of agitation, pain, and anxiety similar to that produced by electrosleep, a treatment involving the passage of nine to twelve volts across the brain (with or without needles). Either procedure is relatively benign. Patients in discomfort enjoy it, and there is neither loss of consciousness nor convulsion as there is with voltages ten to twenty times higher. While the patients at the medical facility were relieved for fifteen or twenty minutes during the treatment, they were soon as miserable as ever shortly afterward. We did not proceed to a controlled study of it, since addicts in withdrawal would not remain at the NNDC to tolerate it. Dr. Showanasai also abandoned its use. Controlled studies in Hong Kong have failed to demonstrate its efficacy. It is useful for short-term relief or as a placebo in opium users with mild physiological dependence or only psychological dependence.

Another pilot study consisted of assigning some patients to outpatient withdrawal. It did not prove useful to many patients. Those who did best in this modality were employed, living with a family, and had little or no ongoing contact with other addicts. This was continued only for highly selected patients.

Another brief project consisted of permitting a few apparently reliable addicts on outpatient detoxification to take home one of their twice-a-day methadone doses in a solution. Within a few weeks of the Center beginning this, the Lao police brought in a methadone bottle from the clinic that had been sold to another addict. Thereafter all methadone was consumed at the medical facility or at the halfway house.

COMMENT

1. Patient acceptance of an addiction treatment program, while critical to survival of a voluntary program, was not well correlated with successful outcome. Approbation by patients was related to the establishment of rapport and a spirit of cooperation between patients and staff. In turn, staff acceptance of the program was associated with a positive attitude by the director toward addicts and their treatment and with the improvement of patients under their care. Social acceptance was related to favorable outcomes from treatment; it was delayed until programs proved successful.

2. Long-term outcome (as measured by abstinence after one year) was not significantly different between the monastery and the medical facility. There was, however, consistently higher withdrawal mortality at the monastery, especially among older addicts. This led to a declining acceptance of the monastery program among addicts. In retrospect, this might have been avoided by requiring older addicts to enter the medical facility prior to or instead of treatment at the monastery. From a cost

effectiveness point of view, the monastery offered a considerable advantage over the medical facility since it cost only one-third as much per addict. Also, the monastery was able to handle more addicts from Laos per year (i.e., about 1,000 to 1,200) as compared to the medical facility (i.e., about 500, excluding outpatients).

3. Spontaneous abstention by self-care alone was infrequent in Laos; probably well under 5 percent ever achieved one year of abstinence. Any improvement on this figure by a treatment program would indicate some treatment success. To assess treatment success, outcome studies were conducted from six to eighteen months following treatment.

4. Early readmission at the medical facility was alleviated by increasing the detoxification period for most addicts from seven to ten days up to fourteen to twenty-one days. Nighttime "elopements" were eliminated by administering the daily methadone dosage in divided doses twice daily.

5. Readmission to the medical facility for relapse was primarily predicted by the proximity of the addict's residence to the facility. It was not related to other demographic or clinical factors.

6. Best outcomes following treatment (at either the monastery or the medical facility) were associated with the following social factors: (1) increased cost and decreased availability of opium, (2) most or all addicts in the local community going for treatment together or within weeks of one another, and (3) an organized, cooperative effort between local leaders and addicts to arrange for treatment. Individual factors favoring a successful outcome were (1) being married to an abstinent spouse, (2) having abstinent friends, (3) having frequent contact with an authority figure interested in the patient's continued abstinence (e.g., elder, village chief, health worker, missionary), and (4) access to a village health worker or a medical facility for treatment of associated medical conditions or physiological disturbances associated with early abstinence. As demonstrated by the poor outcomes in Houa Kong province, favorable individual factors seldom overcame unfavorable social factors. Conversely, in areas where social factors were optimal, the individual factors were not so critical. Individual resources appeared to be most influential in larger communities where many but not most addicts had gone for treatment.

7. A few percent of addicts remained abstinent for several months but did not improve as gauged by how they felt, their productivity, and their social relationships. Sophisticated medical, surgical, or psychiatric care was needed for this group. In the absence of such care, these few addicts did better, at least temporarily, by returning to opium.

8. Successful as it was as a pilot effort, the treatment program being supported by the Laotian government during 1972 to 1975 was not adequate as an effective public health effort. It had to be either expanded within available resources or abandoned. The previous government in power had opted for the first alternative, while the new government chose the second alternative and then substituted prolonged incarceration for treatment. In the next decade or two, it may be possible to assess whether the latter strategy will have worked as it did in China.

9. Ethical issues inevitably affect this field, as they do all areas of treatment. They are knotty and time-consuming, but they do not go away on their own. They must be addressed.

10. While useful as a placebo or short-term sedative, the acupuncture-electrosleep procedure was not a useful tool in the treatment of severe opiate withdrawal. Outpatient withdrawal was successful only in a small number of highly selected patients. Take-home methadone was diverted into illegal channels and was discontinued.

XIII

Other Drugs

A drug such as opium cannot be considered in isolation from other recreational intoxicants available in a society. Whereas a people may have no problems with opium (such as the Nya Heun in southern Laos), another recreational drug may be used more widely. Conversely, a people with widespread opium addiction (such as the Hmong) may have little or no trouble with other psychoactive substances. Unless the particular drug use patterns of a society are considered in their entirety, false conclusions may be drawn.

Opium is not only a recreational intoxicant, it is also an effective medication. It effectively relieves pain, anxiety, agitation, insomnia, fear, cough, intestinal and other visceral cramps, and diarrhea. Incidence and prevalence of disorders that may produce such symptoms must be assessed. A further crucial factor is the availability of effective methods of preventing, treating, and ameliorating such disorders.

In this chapter, we will first consider common recreational intoxicants and their use among the various peoples of Laos. Then we will address the matter of medical problems and the resources for managing them.

ALCOHOL

The Lao

a. Traditional Lao Patterns. One can conceive of two disparate practices for alcohol consumption among the Lao. One of these was traditional and still held sway among most villagers. The other was a more recent custom that prevailed in a few larger towns and around the larger army camps. To be sure, there was a spectrum of usage between these two extremes among various people depending on time and place. Nonetheless, social contexts clearly demarcated the two types.

Typically, alcohol consumption in villages occurred only at culturally prescribed times. These events included seasonal festivities, such as the Lao New Year, Birth-Death-Enlightenment of Buddha, and end of Buddhist Lent. Drinking also took place on a regional basis at temple fund raisers, or *boun* (merit). Extended kin and friends celebrated changes in a person's life cycle by a *baci*. This consisted of gifts, prayer, feasting, and drinking at such occasions as naming a child, entry into the temple for study and meditation, marriage, school graduation, departure on or return from a trip, and death. Buddhism proscribed the consumption of alcohol by monks. Yet the still-active animist *pam* religion required drinking for the trance and dancing that attended their ceremonies for communion with and exorcism of spirits.

Moderately heavy drinking prevailed on some occasions, such as the New Year, weddings, and the Rocket Festival (a fertility-rainmaking ceremony). Mild, mostly symbolic drinking occurred at funerals and the naming *baci* for infants. Women generally drank less than men, although with some overlap in both directions. Alcohol was consumed only within the multigenerational village or family unit and only on ritual or ceremonial occasions. In remote areas the beverage was a rice wine, sipped through communal bamboo "straws," although rice whiskey had appeared in areas around the larger towns during the 1970s. Hosts urged their guests to imbibe liberally. Some of my fondest memories center on holidays or *baci* that found me in one or another Lao village. Lengthy conversation, welcomes, warmth, joking, and teasing accompanied the feasting. Spontaneous marching bands followed by a file of dancers (with all ages and ranks participating) might snake their way through and around the village.

The Lao paddy farmer was limited in the amount of wine he could make by the number of earthen jars he owned.* Since the farmer must sell or barter some of his rice in order to obtain such necessities as iron tools and cloth, there was a limit to the amount of rice available for rice wine. On the other hand, a constant market for buying and selling

---

*These jars were buried in the ground once rice, water, and yeast had been fermenting for some days. At this point they were sealed, and the ground pressure prevented fracture of the ten-to-forty-gallon jars. This wine was then drunk during the same year. This method was practical if villages were settled or moved infrequently for short distances. Lengthy migrations, as practiced by the Hmong, made distillation a preferable method.

rice existed in Lao towns. The rice whiskey market was limited primarily by the demand for whiskey purchase. No arbitrary restriction limited beer importation; but relative to local rice whiskey, canned or bottled foreign beer was expensive.

During my two years of work in remote Lao villages during 1965 to 1967, I did not encounter one alcoholic person in village settings. In 1975, however, while conducting a survey of mentally disordered persons in Lao villages, I did encounter three traditional villagers who were alcohol addicts in every sense. Two were older men and one was an older woman, all of whom drank about a quart of rice whiskey daily. They lived in villages within fifty kilometers of Vientiane and were able to purchase their supply from nearby merchants. Their use of alcohol was considered to be plainly deviant by their kin and neighbors, but no one confronted them or interfered with their habit.

b. Modern Town Pattern. The town pattern of alcohol consumption was a recent development. It was not described by the first Europeans to visit Laos (Osborne 1975). Traditional drinking also occurred in town though with greater variations on the basic theme. For example, traditional drinking occurred during Constitution Day, which was celebrated by government employees and the military in towns but was hardly known in villages. At the fund raising *bouns* in town, the committee of notable parishioners sponsoring the event sold franchises for alcohol sales. Since a town of only 2,000 or 3,000 people might have a dozen temples, *boun* were regular events at certain times of the year. In the mid-1960s ethnic Lao people rarely frequented the bars and nightclubs that catered to expatriate Asians and Caucasians, but by the early 1970s many young Lao returning from abroad sought their weekend entertainment in these settings.

Whereas rice wine was scarce in towns, rice whiskey was readily available at almost any shop or restaurant. Some of it was made locally as a cottage industry. Mekong rice whiskey, a favorite brand in Thailand, appeared as a franchise operation in Laos around 1970. A quart of 70 proof (35 percent alcohol) could be purchased for about $0.50. Unlike rice wine (which was never used for medicinal purposes), rice whiskey was often used as a medication with or without other substances. Various herbal concoctions were added for maladies such as weakness or arthritis. Whiskey to which recently killed snakes had been added was especially prized for amenorrhea and impotence. Dosage, frequency, and duration of administration were quite variable. A dosage of a few to several ounces of whiskey was a well-known remedy for insomnia.

Imported beer and rice whiskey were found in the markets near army camps and posts, even in remote areas. Like the expatriate taverns and the ever-present *boun*, availability of alcohol to young servicemen away from home served to further undermine traditional constraints concerning drinking. As more people became engaged in wage work (rather than subsistence farming), they had ready cash to purchase alcoholic beverages.

During the mid-1960s I encountered a few older, noncommissioned soldiers who were clearly engaged in an alcoholic drinking pattern. One of these, a Tai Dam man, had been drinking almost daily since the battle of Dien Bien Phu. I encountered no cases of delirium tremens or alcoholic dementia; however, this changed during the early 1970s. At that time I encountered a few Lao soldiers in their twenties and thirties with alcoholic dementia and even an elderly Lao matron from Vientiane with delirium tremens.

Along with the alcohol abuser, another phenomenon was evolving in Lao towns: the alcohol abstainer. Usually women, they did not imbibe even at the socially expected times such as weddings and Lao New Year.

Other new events were the drunken brawling and amok outbursts of indiscriminate assault (typically with hand grenades). Violence was unheard of in the traditional drinking contexts of the village, but it appeared with some regularity in towns. On one occasion in Vientiane I observed several offspring of the Lao elite (including a younger sibling of the medical school dean) break every glass and bottle in reach when a particularly intoxicated comrade was refused service by the tavern's French proprietor. (They also left without paying their bill.) Elsewhere I have shown the relationship of amok outbursts to drinking (see Westermeyer 1972b, 1973d).

In sum, social role and ceremony governed traditional Lao drinking. It was interwoven into other aspects of daily life: rites of passage, animist religion, friendship, seasonal changes, and annual cultural events. Even in towns it remained a core pattern, although supplemented by a pattern introduced from the outside. The latter included individual choice regarding time and amount of drinking, use of alcohol as a medication, and peer drinking. While alcoholism virtually never occurred in association with the traditional pattern, it had begun to accompany the new town-centered pattern.

The Hmong

The Hmong alcohol beverage was corn whiskey and, occasionally, rice whiskey. Since foodstuffs were not generally marketed and each family had to provide its own food, the corn or rice mash necessarily came directly from the family's foodstores. Slash-and-burn technology sharply limited the amount of grain that could be raised in a year. Consequently, the average family's liquor supply consisted of only a few to several liters per year that was neither bought nor sold.

Distillation of the mash was done at home with an ingenious device utilizing available equipment. Its main feature consisted of two shallow, woklike iron pots, one of which was usually borrowed from a neighbor. The lower pot containing the mash was placed over a fire. The upper wok was suspended directly above by means of a wooden frame. After the alcohol evaporated from the lower pot, it cooled and condensed as a liquid on the under surface of the upper pot. The droplets flowing toward the low center of the pot were caught in a hollow bamboo tube and conveyed to a bottle or other container. Typically Hmong whiskey was flammable at room temperature, indicating it was at least 100 proof (i.e., 50 percent alcohol).

Drinking, an integral part of certain Hmong social activities, occurred only in a social context. Three days after the birth of a baby, on the day the child was named, the family and close friends drank a small amount during a household celebration. Again when the child was a month old, as the soul took up permanent residence in the child's body, moderate alcohol drinking accompanied a larger gathering of extended family members and nearby friends. Early in their teenage years, young men and women were invited by adults to drink, usually during New Year or at a wedding. Weddings were noted for heavy consumption of alcohol, which was provided by the husband's clan. Commercial and political relationships sometimes transcended family, clan, and tribal obligations. At an opportune time, such as at leave-taking or during an infrequent visit, the relationship might be cemented by moderate whiskey drinking. At funerals a small amount of whiskey was poured on the ground under the deceased as a spirit offering. The musicians, playing a funeral music played at no other time, also drank small amounts of whiskey between periods of music. Alcohol was taken at two calendrical celebrations. The first was Hmong New Year, a time of merry-making, visiting, and courting lasting about ten days. On the first day of their rice harvest work, the Hmong family might drink a little whiskey with the evening meal. Almost invariably, alcohol and the meat of a domestic animal (as an animistic sacrifice to appease or beseech the spirits) accompanied each other. As among the village Lao, consumption of these two special, near-sacramental nutriments (i.e., meat and alcohol) occurred at rites of passage, calendrical celebrations, and at times of crisis such as illness and death.

Social role, age, sex, and the particular event determined who should drink and about how much should be drunk. The alcohol container and a drinking vessel, usually a bottle and a small glass respectively, were passed around the circle of participants, much like a pipe at an Indian ceremony. Each person poured a small glassful, drank it down in a gulp, and passed it to the next person. Especially for an important or formal ceremony, the host or one of his adolescent daughters might bring the bottle around and pour the drink. Each person was expected to drink his or her share, no more and no less. A rigid etiquette governed host-guest drinking. The host offered a toast and drained his shotglass of whiskey. The guest—regardless of age, sex, or social status —must then match the host shotglass for shotglass. After the first few shotglasses of whiskey, the guest might receive aid from a helper who assumed the obligatory drinking responsibility. This privilege was usually invoked only by younger women who received help from older female relatives not involved in the drinking circle.

Symbolic or mild drinking (two shotglasses or less) did not perceptibly alter behavior. Moderate drinking was accompanied by conviviality, lively conversation, and laughter; the participants usually remained seated in the house. Heavy drinking featured loud talking, mutual joking, uproarious mirth, and shouting. Motor activity increased, and the partying might continue out-of-doors. Should a person imbibe to the point of impaired speech, vision, or ambulation, he quietly went off to sleep before his impaired functions attracted the notice (and badgering) of his comrades.

As among the village Lao, young Hmong people did not drink on their own. Instead they were initiated into the family or clan drinking-circle early in their teenage years as they acquired the other attributes of adulthood (e.g., full adult economic productivity and marriage). Alcohol was not used as medicine or on individual whim. Fairly heavy drinking occurred at particular events (e.g., weddings, Hmong New Year), with lesser amounts taken at other times (e.g., rice harvest, naming a newborn).

During my first two years among the Hmong I never encountered one of them with chronic alcoholism. I may have had the dubious honor of treating the first Hmong person with an acute alcohol-related problem, however. One of the first Hmong in the north to own a motorcycle ran into a tree on the way home from a wedding (under the influence of alcohol) and broke his leg. He survived and now lives as a refugee in the United States.

During the subsequent fifteen years, I encountered one Hmong with chronic alcoholism. He sought me out in the United States for treatment of his poor memory. As a young man, he was a minor official in a remote area. He always enjoyed drinking but never transgressed Hmong drinking customs. In his late thirties, he was summoned to be a minor political leader at the burgeoning Hmong town of Long Cheng. There he had opportunity, in his various official roles, to drink three, four, or five times a week. He never drank alone and always drank in socially acceptable Hmong contexts; but he never passed by an opportunity to drink and even began to initiate meetings and social gatherings for the purpose of drinking heavily himself. After almost a decade of this, he and his wife began to notice that he could not remember recent events in his life (although more remote memories were intact). Subsequently he became a refugee and left Laos. Financial constraints had deprived him of drinking for almost three years when I examined him in 1977. He still had the memory impairment, along with other signs indicating central nervous system damage from long-term heavy alcohol use (i.e., scanning speech and a positive Romberg sign, both of which are associated with central cerebellar injury from alcohol abuse).

I have heard of another Hmong, a military commander at an outpost, who made an occasion of even the slightest visit to drink long into the night. And I have encountered a few Hmong refugees, insomniac with anxiety and depression, who began to drink whiskey while in Thai refugee camps (emulating there the Thai-Lao town pattern of drinking). While none of the latter have shown classical alcoholism signs or symptoms, these few cases and that of the man described above demonstrate the fragility of the traditional strictures against alcohol abuse once new social features (e.g., town life, money economy, exposure to other lifestyles) replace traditional ones.

The case of the Hmong village alcohol pattern also points up the link between social strictures and a particular drug. Just because tradition prevents the abuse of one drug, this is not a guarantee against the abuse of other drugs. Traditional Hmong society provides us with such an example. Despite their highly effective strictures regarding alcohol abuse, they nonetheless had some of the highest opiate addiction rates ever reported.

Other Tribal Groups

My acquaintance with other ethnic groups in Laos was much less than with the Lao and Hmong; however, I have had the opportunity to drink on several occasions with the Iu Mien and Tai Dam and on a few occasions with the Lu, Nya Heun, and Laven. Iu Mien people had a drinking pattern quite similar to their ethnic cousins, the Hmong. The other peoples (from such varied linguistic groups as the Tai-Lao, Tibeto-Burman, Malayo-Polynesian) had patterns similar to that of village Lao.

During my early years in Laos, I observed only a few tribal people in the military who drank heavily. At the time of my last visits to Laos in 1973, 1974, and 1975 I encountered several tribal people with various manifestations of chronic alcoholism. All of them lived in or near Lao towns and were no longer living among their people.

Expatriate Asians

There was considerable variability in the drinking practices of expatriate Asians. Ethnic Chinese and Indians virtually never frequented taverns or nightclubs, although ethnic Chinese often drank Asian beer or European scotch or cognac at formal dinners held in restaurants.*
By contrast, drinking played a quite different role within the Vietnamese and Thai communities. Several nightclubs in Vientiane—with bands, an act or two, and dancing—were owned and largely frequented by the sizable expatriate Vietnamese community. Similarly, Thai workers in Vientiane had particular bars or taverns where they met with their confreres.

As you may recall from an earlier chapter, the Chinese community in Vientiane had a higher rate of opium addiction than did the Vietnamese or Thai. A partial explanation may lie in the relatively effective controls that the Chinese exerted over drinking. This differential stricture over alcohol and opium served the image valued by the Chinese community. Drunken weekend brawls were likely to involve a Thai, and the drunken driver careening about was likely to be Vietnamese (as I discovered when my car was sideswiped one Saturday night). Chinese names never appeared in such news items. Yet the opium addicts going to the downtown den up the street from my favorite Vietnamese nightclub were predominantly Chinese.

Expatriate Caucasians

Europeans, North Americans, and Australians brought their various drinking practices to the towns of Laos. While the expatriate Caucasian community in Laos was never very large, it did tend to be con-

---

*At times there was a conspicuousness or potlatch aspect to this consumption of expensive cognac or similar beverages. The liquor was ingested in quantity along with the meal, much like a table wine, rather than as an aperitif.

centrated into several locations. As one would find in their countries of origin, their drinking practices were secular and individualistic. Some were complete abstainers and would not even join the indigenous peoples in their drinking events.* Others drank regularly or on weekends, with an evening meal or at a cocktail party.

Over a decade of observation, it seemed to me that Caucasian drinking practices had relatively little immediate effect on indigenous drinking. The return of Lao students, trainees, and diplomats from abroad was another story, however. They returned not only with degrees and certificates, but often with new world views, philosophies—and drinking practices.

TOBACCO

The Lao

As with both alcohol and opiates, the Lao demonstrated both traditional and modern tobacco use. There were geographic and demographic similarities among those using the traditional alcohol and tobacco patterns and among those using the modern alcohol and tobacco patterns.

Traditionally, tobacco was grown by farmers themselves rather than imported from abroad. Town users might purchase tobacco grown on the Plateau de Bolovens in southern Laos, whence came tobacco that was highly regarded. Aging and preparation of the tobacco for smoking was entirely a personal task or a cottage industry; there were no major industries devoted to it. It was smoked in a clay pipe, mostly by older men and usually in the evening. Less often a water pipe might be used in some areas. This consisted of a length of bamboo with a few inches of water in the bottom, through which the smoke was inhaled. A few older women also enjoyed the habit. Use was moderate. In two years of general medical work in Laos, I never encountered a case of emphysema or cor pulmonale associated with tobacco smoking by itself—yet both diseases were commonplace among older opium addicts.

The modern form of tobacco consumption was essentially that observed around the world in recent decades: compulsive cigarette smoking. It involved mostly younger men, especially those living in

*In rural areas this had the effect of making them social outcasts to some extent. Certain Caucasian missionaries and technicians whose religion proscribed drinking did not receive invitations to certain events when it became evident that they would not practice the local drinking etiquette.

towns and those in the army. During the early to mid-1960s, most cigarettes used in Laos were manufactured in Thailand and were thus comparatively expensive. By the early 1970s this situation had changed dramatically. Two large and very successful cigarette factories had been established in Laos. (They were two of the first factories there, which included factories making soft drinks, rubber thongs, and matches—the latter to light the cigarettes). Cigarettes were relatively inexpensive, selling for only $0.07 to $0.10 a pack during the early 1970s. The price was kept down because under an American export-aid program (PL 480) American tobacco could be imported into Laos for half-price. Consequently high-quality cigarettes could be manufactured in Laos at a fraction of the cost in the United States. By 1975 even the smallest rural dry-goods stores were selling cigarettes. One could even buy them on the street by the individual cigarette for about $0.01 each.

Like Japanese beer, rice whiskey, and heroin, cigarettes caught on rapidly among male Lao youths. It was a time when literacy, political change, outside influences, and military insecurity were causing great and rapid change in Laos. Young Lao by the thousands were abandoning their eons-old village traditions and birthright. Cigarettes, beer, and whiskey—represented in foreign films and magazines—served as symbols of a new culture that the youth found appealing. In addition to the pharmacological effects and oral gratifications (which the traditional forms already served well), these newly introduced substances represented a turning away from the old and a turning toward the new, the apparently affluent, clever, and informed.

The American obsession against Laotian opium while sloughing excess tobacco into Laos caused me concern. The United States put pressure on Laos to stem its opium produce and export so that the other nations might not suffer such great calamities from heroin addiction. Concomitantly, the United States was supporting the introduction of inexpensive tobacco into a country that did not have a compulsive cigarette smoking problem (with its many and grave public health consquences).

The Hmong

As with the Lao, in addition to the traditional use of homegrown tobacco, there was the recent use of cigarettes predominantly among the young. Regardless of the method, tobacco smoking was much less common than opium smoking.

Farmers who smoked planted a patch of tobacco in a corner of an upland rice or corn field. When the stem was yellowish, the leaves were picked and dried in the sun. Smoking tobacco was prepared by rolling the tobacco leaf into a cylinder, which was forced through a circular hole in a wooden board. As the cylinder was advanced, the tobacco leaf was chopped into small pieces. These pieces were then dried again in the sun and stored in a container. Tobacco thus prepared was smoked in a variety of ways. It could be rolled in a corn husk, in crude rice paper, or in paper of any type or origin. A Hmong favorite for smoking tobacco in some areas was the bamboo water pipe. Some Hmong water pipes were decorated with silver and were painted in different colors. Older men smoked once or a few times daily, when resting or conversing socially. While infrequently an old woman might smoke tobacco in a like pattern, young men rarely smoked tobacco in this way. Some opium addicts took a bit of tobacco to "set" the opium—that is presumably to enhance or to prolong its effects.

Toward the mid-1970s, during the two-year peace interim before the communists assumed control in 1975, commerce increased dramatically across northern Laos. During 1974 in a remote area of Xieng Khouang, several days walk from the nearest road, I encountered a Hmong girl selling Laotian cigarettes and matches to Hmong clientele. While cigarette smoking was still not much in evidence, a few young men were taking up the habit. And some Hmong hosts would provide, besides the traditional oral modes of gratification (tea, whiskey, sometimes opium), a fresh, unopened pack of cigarettes.

The Nya Heun

This relatively small tribe of people lives on the Plateau de Bolovens. Along with the neighboring Laven, they raised tobacco and coffee as cash crops. Neither group used opium; none of the Nya Heun with whom I spoke even knew of its existence. (They had no word for opium, and those able to speak Lao had never heard the word for opium, *dyā fēn.*) Their alcohol drinking pattern was much like that of village Lao.

The Nya Heun were remarkable for their use of tobacco. While a few people used pipes, generally they wrapped their tobacco in a broad leaf (such as a banana leaf) and smoked it like a cigar. Smoking might be observed at any hour of the day, among women as much as among men, and even among relatively small children aged six or seven. Tobacco was widely and readily available. There were no formal ceremonies involving it. Neither social restrictions nor social imperatives governed its use. Some people chose not to use it. Even the decisions of young children to use it were respected without attempts at interference.

I did not observe medical complications from tobacco use among the Nya Heun, but I was not looking for them either. High rates of malaria, intercurrent infections, and a rain forest ecology at once both harsh and plush diminished one's chances of living to an age when the wages of chronic nicotinism might be apparent.

The Nya Heun story is included here to underline the influence of availability on use. Unlike the Lao and Hmong, these people raised tobacco as a cash crop. It was constantly available in their homes, and its use was widespread. The case is parallel to that of the Hmong and opium.

The ethnographer Wall (1975) does not remark on Nya Heun tobacco production and use in her monograph. Yet of seventeen women pictured in such a way that one can assess whether they are smoking, four have cigars in their mouths and two have pipes in their mouths. Her photographs emphasize the prevalence of smoking among these people. The relative absence of comment regarding tobacco in Wall's otherwise detailed ethnography also points to the general paucity of substance use data in most ethnographs. (The works of anthropologists Ruth Bunzel, Dwight Heath, Jack Waddell, and others serve as outstanding exceptions.) This is not to fault ethnographers, since they cannot provide equal time and attention to all aspects of life and behavior. Rather it is to emphasize that total reliance on published ethnographies for substance use data can be grossly misleading.

BETEL

The Lao

Betel chewing (*nyam mak* in Lao) involved the mildly stimulating betel or areca nut. Along with the betel, a piece of porous bark to give substance, lime, and sometimes tobacco were all wrapped in a fresh leaf. More than tobacco or alcohol, betel was dependent on a network of cottage industries: the lime from this place, the betel from that place, the bark from another. Supplies were bought at market and stored in containers made especially for betel. Betel sets might be modestly made of wood and bamboo, but some sets made for serving guests on ceremonial occasions were made of brass or silver.

Lao women used betel much more than did men. Like tobacco smoking, betel chewing was more an individual than a social event. A young woman might be casually introduced to betel by an older friend or relative during a work break from planting or harvesting rice. She was free to accept or refuse as she wished; no pressures were brought to bear (as would occur with drinking alcohol on ceremonial occasions). A woman who accepted might decide she didn't care for it and not use it again. Or she might use it episodically. Rarely would she begin to use it daily until she was in her twenties, thirties, or forties. Habitual users prepared three to five betel cuds per day, spending most of their waking hours with a cud in their buccal pouch. Some Lao men objected to their wives' use of betel, but the women retorted that the men had their tobacco and women thus had a right to their betel.

Habitual betel chewing entailed certain distinctive features that were evident after even brief, casual observation. Besides the bulge from the cud in the lower buccal pouch, chewers episodically spat out a copious amount of blackish-red saliva (much as tobacco chewers do). Early on, the teeth and gums were stained a distinctive dark blackish-red. The lime gradually caused the dissolution of the calcium layer from the teeth, so that only the dentin stumps remained after some years. Chronic inflammation and hyperplasia of the gums took place, leading in later life to gum atrophy and loss of the dentin stumps. Strangely enough, a rationale for chewing betel often heard was "to make the teeth strong," and cuds were sometimes given to young girls for this purpose.

Few Lao men used betel. Those who did were mostly in middle or old age. Typically their wives had introduced them to the habit at home. (Note the similarity here to the female opiate addict in Laos, who had usually picked up the habit at home from a husband or other relative.)

Betel nut chewing was a traditional behavior that, unlike narcotic, alcohol, and tobacco use, had no modern counterpart.* It continued to be practiced by young and old women alike in rural Lao villages, where sometimes the majority of adult women were habitual chewers. It was decidedly on the decline among younger women in towns. Among elite Lao families in which even women up to age fifty were literate, the only betel chewers were grandmothers in their sixties and older. The reason given for the decline was always an aesthetic one: the omnipresent cud, the spitting, and the staining of teeth and gums were considered *baw ngam* (not beautiful).

Betel has been described as having properties similar to nicotine (Burton-Bradley 1966). Oral cancer has been associated with betel nut chewers (Orr 1933), although I can neither defend nor question that

---

*I suppose the coffee or tea breaks that were practiced by women in the offices of Laos might be a parallel activity, since they also involved the communal use of a stimulant during a brief respite from repetitive work.

theory from my own observations. One report from Malaysia remarked that, as in Laos, women started betel earlier than men (Ahluwalvia and Ponnampalam 1968).

The strength of the habit was indicated by one of my Lao refugee patients in Minneapolis. A sixty-five-year-old woman, she had used betel daily since her thirties. Upon first arriving in the United States, her supply was interrupted for the first time in over thirty years. After considerable shopping about, she found a Chinese foodstore where the proprietor would order betel from Taiwan. Due to the expense, she cut her habit back to three cuds a day (which cost $2.50 daily in 1981).

Other Ethnic Groups

Women in several Lao Theung groups, along with a smaller number of men, used betel much as did the Lao. These included the Khamu, Tai Dam, and Lu of northern Laos. Among the Hmong, betel chewing was infrequent. The few who did use it were usually men who had acquired the taste during trading forays into lowland Lao towns. A few expatriate Asians used it, especially the older Vietnamese women (who considered a show of white teeth to be doglike and barbaric). I never observed a Caucasian chewing, although a few told me that they had tried it out of curiosity.

Relative poverty among some Lao Theung groups forced certain accommodations in supplies and equipment. For example, a special root was used by some in place of lime. Instead of the special containers and utensils possessed by many Lao, everyday household containers and utensils (e.g., knife, mortar and pestle) were used.

CANNABIS

In the mid-1960s and until 1972, cannabis could be purchased at town markets in bulk form along with areca, rice whiskey, opium, tobacco, tea, and coffee. Its use seemed to be favored mostly by expatriate Asians, especially the Thai, Vietnamese, and Indians. Lao familiarity with it centered in those Mekong River towns with numerous expatriate Asians. Until the obsession with drugs in 1971 and 1972, it was not considered dangerous or illegal.

Only relatively small plots of cannabis were grown in Laos and then primarily to meet the gardener's own weekend recreational needs. Market supplies of it probably came from Thailand, where there was a larger market for it. Two varieties of cannabis were known to the Lao: a stronger variety called tea (*sa*) or red tea (*sa deng*) and a less powerful variety known as red tobacco or red medicine (*dya deng*). The Thai and Lao were said to prefer the stronger cannabis, while Chinese and Vietnamese were said to prefer the weaker. Cannabis was grown in gardens along rivers and streams during the dry season.

In addition to its use as a recreational intoxicant, cannabis was also used as a condiment, particularly by the Vietnamese. In 1973, when foreign pressures against cannabis (along with opium) were being felt, cannabis was no longer available. Around that time I discovered that my favorite Vietnamese soup vendor (from whom I had for years purchased a bowl of chicken noodle soup on those days when I was in downtown Vientiane) had always sprinkled fresh cannabis along with other greens on his product. Martin (1975) refers to this practice in Laos, although she attributes it to Chinese soup and records that small quantities of green tea had replaced cannabis as a soup condiment in 1973. Some expatriate Asians attributed medicinal values to it.

I never observed cannabis use among village Lao or the tribal groups in Laos, although I was not specifically looking for it. Aside from its personal use for enjoyment, there was no medical or sociocultural function for cannabis in Lao society. No social rules or etiquette governed cannabis use. Only a very small proportion of Lao people smoked it. Those who did use it were thought likely to become narcotic addicts subsequently. (I have no data to confirm or deny this popular opinion.) There are no references to cannabis as a folk medicament in Sassady's list of the Lao folk pharmacopoeia.

A Case of Cannabis Psychosis. Luong was a twenty-two-year-old single Lao man. He had been discharged from the army four months previously and had returned home to live with his widowed mother and five younger siblings on the outskirts of Vientiane. An adept student, Luong had completed five years of primary school before joining his father in running a small store. Following the death of his father three years ago, his mother had relied primarily on her male relatives rather than on the nineteen-year-old Luong. She admitted Luong had always been a favorite of hers, and she had never placed much expectation on him.

After his father's death Luong began a period of heavy cannabis use, sometimes with friends but often alone. After some months of this he suddenly became *bā* (crazy, insane) and began indiscriminately destroying property and assaulting anyone nearby. Luong was placed in jail for some weeks, where he continued to manifest eccentric and disorganized behavior. An aunt made a trip to Thailand where she described Luong's symptoms to a Thai psychiatrist and returned with a supply of chlorpromazine (an antipsychotic medication). Within a few days of receiving this drug, Luong began to recover. After several weeks of treatment with the medicine, he returned to his former self.

Soon after his release from jail, Luong joined the army. While there he drank with army buddies from time to time, and he tried opiates on a few occasions. He never had the difficulty with these drugs that he had experienced with the cannabis. His military discharge was an honorable one.

Within several days of his returning home, he was again smoking cannabis with his old friends. Soon he was smoking all day long, frequently by himself. Our paths then crossed about four months later (in early 1975) while I was conducting a study of bā people. Three days prior to my seeing him, Luong began to show rapid changes in mood, from hilarious laughter to tears to sudden anger. After a few days, this emotional lability flowed into a growing rage. First he began striking furniture around the house. Next he began throwing the furniture out of the windows of their house-on-stilts, damaging most of it, and ripping the family's clothes and bedding. When he began to demolish the home itself, tearing down an entire wall, his mother asked for help from neighbors. They had considerable trouble subduing him, since Luong had armed himself with a board. Finally they managed to tie him with a rope. During the night he got free and armed himself with a knife. At that point the police were called and, after disarming him, they handcuffed him and left him in the care of his family and neighbors.

During these three days Luong had slept and eaten very little, and he had lost considerable weight with his almost constant assaults and struggles. At the time that I interviewed him he was still hyperalert, constantly on the move, and chain smoking. (The family was able to cajole and to calm him somewhat with cigarettes.) He expressed his belief that we were all trying to kill him. His attention span was short, and he was confused by open-ended questions or requests. Luong knew his own name and those of his relatives, his current location and the year, but not the month, day, season, or time of day. His thinking was mostly concrete, with little ability to abstract. While he glared suddenly around the room on several occasions as though he were having auditory hallucinations, he denied that he was hearing voices.

As with the previous episodes, Luong again recovered following several weeks of treatment with chlorpromazine.

PHARMACEUTICALS: FOLK AND MODERN

Medical Problems

Laos provided examples of almost the entire spectrum of tropical diseases. During my two years of general medical work I encountered the following among my patients: malaria, tuberculosis, amebic and bacillary dysenteries, tetanus, leprosy, typhoid, typhus, lung and liver flukes, trichinosis, noma and oriental sore, various nutritional deficiencies (e.g., keratomalacia, beri-beri, pellagra, marasmus, and kwashiorkor) and all manner of intestinal parasites (ascaris, hookworm, and giardia being perhaps most common). Many of these disease entities produced symptoms such as pain, cough, and diarrhea for which opium provided excellent symptomatic relief. The journalist Wolfkill, captured and held prisoner in Laos, attributed his recovery from chronic dysentery, and indeed his survival, to draughts on the opium pipe (1966).

While my experience with opiate therapy was not so dramatic as Wolfkill's, I also came to appreciate the respite provided by opiates during acute illness. Of some six malaria attacks that I had in Laos, two were particularly severe. They were due to the falciparum strain of malaria, which can persist for some days without respite and cause more severe symptoms than the other strains. During one of these I experienced 102° to 104° fevers for three days, hypotension with a blood pressure of 80/0, and confusion. Diarrhea and white blood count of 28,000 suggested that bacillary dysentery might also be present, perhaps precipitating the recurrence of malaria. After two days of sleeplessness, an injection of one-quarter grain of morphine brought four hours of welcome slumber and the beginning of my recovery. On a subsequent and similar recurrence, a single fifty milligram Demerol injection had the same effect. (Subsequently chloroquin-resistant falciparum malaria was reported in Indochina, so the chloroquin that I was taking at the time was not effective. A two week regimen of quinine eventually eliminated my malaria.) While there are no medically controlled studies regarding the beneficial effect of opium on malaria, I can vouch that opiates certainly can make such attacks more endurable from the sufferer's perspective and thereby sustain the will to survive.

Medical Resources

A paucity of medical resources was another feature of Laos. At any one point during 1965 to 1967 there were never more than forty physicians and even fewer registered nurses in noncommunist areas of Laos, a country with about three million people that was at war. In such a setting only the most severe and life-threatening disorders received medical attention.

People were primarily dependent on home self-care, folk medications, and traditional healers. As documented by Sassady (1962), Lao tradition contained notions about anatomy, physiology, diagnosis, and herbal medication. Interestingly, opium was not included in Sassady's volume (probably because herbal healers rarely recommended it— I know of no such prescriptions by Lao herbalists). This system of care— along with parallel, if less sophisticated systems among tribal groups —was effective in self-limited diseases as a familiar aid to sufferers. It probably had relatively little effect on mortality, however.

The decision to use opium, as documented in the case histories presented in this volume, did not evolve in either a traditional or modern healing context. Rather, individuals and sometimes families made this decision. To be sure, some of these decisions were based on medical indications, such as the tubercular Haw merchant, the arthritic Lao farmer, and the Hmong woman with chronic pelvic inflammation. In this sense, then, the matter of opium use in Laos cannot be considered apart from local medical problems and resources. Suwanwela and his colleagues in Thailand have similarly made this point in their description of a Hmong man with a chronic renal disease.

This is not to say that most opium addiction in Laos stemmed from medical problems or that the availability of medical services could remove the prime reason for opium addiction. As life histories indicate, opium addiction more commonly grew out of recreational use and emotional dysphoria than out of infectious or degenerative diseases. Of course, many addicts ascribed their continued opium use to illness when first asked their reasons for smoking. But further interviewing usually elicited that they were referring to the withdrawal illness that ensued if they stopped current use, not to the circumstances associated with their originally using opium.

Earlier I said that an opium den existed a stone's throw from Sam Thong Hospital where I worked for about eight months during 1965 to 1967. Some addicts who might have benefited from medical treatment of their maladies voted every day with their feet, preferring the den to the hospital. Simply making medical resources and preventive health programs available, while they might be a crucial part of a total intervention program against addiction, cannot alone comprise a total solution for opium addiction.

COMMENT

1. While an ethnic group may have virtually no problem with one potentially addicting substance (e.g., the Hmong and alcohol), that does not guarantee that they will not have problems with another addicting substance (e.g., the Hmong and opium).

2. Some of the ethnic groups in Laos with the lowest rates of opium addiction (e.g., the Lao, Vietnamese) were most apt to drink heavily and even show indications of an evolving alcoholism problem.

3. Traditional use patterns existed in Laos for opium, alcohol, and tobacco. These began to be replaced in the 1960s and 1970s by other patterns that appeared in towns and primarily involved young men. While a substance might not have been abused when used in its traditional form (e.g., rice wine among the Lao), the same substance might be abused in nontraditional forms (e.g., beer and rice whiskey among the Lao). Ecological changes (such as the development of a large Hmong town at Long Cheng) also influenced traditional patterns.

4. The high prevalence of tobacco smoking among the Nya Heun (who grew tobacco as a cash crop) further implicated the role of availability in substance use.

5. As in the biological world, substance use may also have its diminishing or extinct species. Over the years 1965 to 1975 betel chewing was diminishing, especially among young town-dwelling women. Coffee and tea breaks served similar functions to some extent.

6. Unlike other drugs, betel was predominantly a woman's drug. Lao men usually acquired the habit from their wives—the converse of opium, in which men tended to introduce women.

7. Among opium and the four recreational substances considered here, only alcohol was subject to strict social controls in traditional culture. Opium, tobacco, betel, and cannabis were not subject to required social use (i.e., social imperatives); decisions on whether to use and with what frequency were made individually.

8. Despite their proximity to one another, no two cultural groups in Laos possessed the same pattern for using these five substances. Certain aspects of these patterns were linked to ecological considerations. For example, the Hmong went to the trouble of producing whiskey, while

virtually all of the other village peoples produced rice wine. This may be linked to the tradition of mobility among the Hmong, who tend to travel widely and move their villages. Poppy culture was favored in the Hmong's mountains; and tobacco, on the Nya Heun's plateau.

9. Drug use can change rapidly in a society, as exemplified by tobacco and alcohol use among the young. Foreign beer and factory-made cigarettes became the symbols for new attitudes, values and behaviors.

XIV

Social Considerations

Social issues play as important a role in addiction as the pharmacology of opiate drugs or the psychobehavioral characteristics of addicts themselves. In this chapter we will amplify the social data presented earlier. The perspective will be that of the social observer rather than the clinician or epidemiologist.

EFFECTS OF AN ANTIOPIUM LAW

Origins of the Law

After considerable pressure by the United States* and by other national governments as well as international organizations, the Royal Lao Government passed an antinarcotics law on August 10, 1971. This law was not implemented until November 15, 1971. During the interim there were various decrees and procedures regarding the following: the formation of an Interministerial Commission to devise a national plan; creation of a Narcotics Suppression Commission composed of representatives from the police, military, and customs; creation of a Narcotics Prevention Sub-Commission composed of the Ministries of Public

---

*In the early 1970s the United States was plagued by a rapid increase of heroin addiction, both among its youth at home as well as its soldiers in Vietnam (Siegel 1973; Robins, Davis, Nurco 1974; Robins, Helzer, and Davis 1975). Much of the heroin in Vietnam during the 1960s probably came from opium produced in or transported through Laos, since Vietnam had been a traditional market for Laotian opium production. In response to this problem the United States began to pressure Laos, then its ally, to bring opium production and commerce under legal control.

Health, Interior, Social Welfare, and Education; a policy of rewards for arrests in connection with narcotics suppression; and a procedure for disposing of confiscated drugs. The law that provided for the initiation of these various governmental activities is in appendix 1.

There were not enough police in Laos to enforce an antiopium law. Much of Laos at the time was a no-man's-land, under the control of neither the central government nor the communist Pathet Lao.* Were it theoretically possible to cover the country with enough police to suppress opium, there was still the issue of police attitudes toward opium, which were parallel to those of police toward alcohol in the United States during prohibition (i.e., a widely varying and ambivalent attitude). Even among the police, known opium users and addicts continued in their jobs so long as they were able to maintain their responsibilities.

Paramount in such a situation are the will and tradition of the people. The people of Laos had produced, traded in, and used opium for centuries. Prohibition against alcohol in the United States demonstrated that laws alone do not root out deep-seated traditions. The experience of mainland China showed that it requires careful preparation of the populace through the mass media, complete political control, the threat of long-term incarceration, even occasional use of the death penalty to effectively dislodge such traditions. To further complicate matters, Laos by 1971 was probably importing opium for its own consumption rather than exporting it, since many poppy-producing farmers from the north had become refugees in the lowland areas where efficient poppy growing was not feasible.

Why then did the leaders of Laos pass an antinarcotics law? They probably did so in part because the local attitude toward opium, especially among most leaders of the country, held that it was a social evil. It corrupted people, undermined families, and destroyed the addict's health and character. (Among the very same people, as some evidence of their ambivalence toward opium, one could obtain positive opinions regarding its value as an economic export, its solace in terminal illness and old age, its occasional use as a relaxant or medication.) Lao officials were also astute enough to realize that they would receive a few more jeeps, a few more boats, a few more helicopters, a few more guns, and a few more dollars if they passed such a law. Regrettably, they were not

*The fact that the central government could, with apparent seriousness while fighting a civil war, pass a law that it had no hope of enforcing is a telling statement on the quality of its leadership. The result was further deterioration in the status of government and in the people's respect for law.

astute enough to comprehend the effects of antiopium laws in other countries around the region. (See Westermeyer 1976b, for further details.)

Proheroin Effects of an Antinarcotic Law

Opium is bulky and has a characteristic odor that cannot be effectively masked by ordinary containers. Since it gradually loses its potency beyond a year or two, it should be shipped to market expeditiously. While being smoked, it emits a strong and characteristic odor that can be readily perceived even at a distance by a knowledgeable passerby. (I have often noted it while passing by a house in Laos or Thailand or an apartment in Hong Kong.) All of these attributes discouraged illegal transport and sale of opium to the population centers of Asia, since it is so difficult to ship, sell, and use covertly. Opium can only be used in an open fashion within a society not prohibiting its use.

Heroin lends itself to varied packaging and precise division into exact doses since it is a powdery substance unlike the sticky, tarlike opium mass. It occupies less than 10 percent of the weight and space of the opium from which it is derived. Heroin does not deteriorate so rapidly as opium and can thus be stored for longer periods. It takes twenty to forty minutes to smoke opium while an equivalent amount of heroin can be injected in seconds or smoked within a few minutes. While opium traffic and use are virtually impossible to hide, heroin lends itself to surreptitious supply and consumption.

Economic Effects of the Change to Heroin

Prior to the antiopium laws, the production and supply of opium to the consumer was essentially a cottage industry. Farmers who grew opium also processed it from its crude form to its smoking form, using only simple equipment available in the home for food preparation. Small entrepreneurs, engaged primarily in nonopium business activities such as dry goods or rice commerce, managed the transport and sale of opium to the consumer.

The change from opium to heroin meant a shift from a cottage industry, where profits were kept primarily by farmers and small merchants, to a large industrial complex, in which the largest profits were made by middlemen, organizers, and government officials. In contrast to the modest profits made by the farmers and small merchants in the cottage industry, the heroin organizers made much larger profits. For the addict, the economic effect was a higher price for a similar narcotic effect.

274

Law Enforcement Effects of Antiopium Laws

Legal, political, and law enforcement difficulties in controlling heroin supply and consumption have been described in the earlier chapter on heroin use. Whereas the police previously had no jurisdiction over narcotic trade and use, the new laws gave them the right to interfere with it. Opium use did not offend many police officials in these areas, and they did not object to its continuance. For some, the offer of a bribe was too tempting to resist. For others, the passage of the law provided them with the opportunity to harass individual addicts or small shopkeepers for protection money. Consequently, addicts had to contribute to the support of a new group of people, the police. For law enforcement and the society at large, the result was increased corruption.

REPERCUSSIONS OF WAR

Reduced Supply and Increased Cost

Between 1965 and 1972, the intensification of armed conflict forced many poppy farmers down from the mountains of northern Laos onto the flood plain of the Mekong River where opium poppy could not be grown (Dommen 1965, Langer and Zasloff 1970, Burchett 1967). The Hmong, pushed out of their mountainous poppy-growing areas, could no longer produce opium (see fig. 2). Addicts in Laos dependent on Hmong opium production had to rely on opium produced elsewhere, leading to an increase in the cost of the drug. Military insecurity impeded transportation throughout the area, thus exacerbating the problem of obtaining opium from distant areas still growing poppy. As a result, addicts had to contend with an inconstant availability of opium, which further increased the cost.

Due to these events, farmer-addicts, who had never previously comprised a national problem, became a major social problem in refugee camps and resettlement villages around Laos. Addicted patriarchs deprived their families of food and clothing in order to purchase opium. Theft became a daily event in refugee camps as addicts sought to obtain money for opium. It was in this context that the government of Laos passed a law proscribing the transport and sale of opium. In areas of effective police control (i.e., mainly the area round Vientiane), opium trade was effectively controlled. This in turn led to heroin importation.

Figure 2. Social Changes

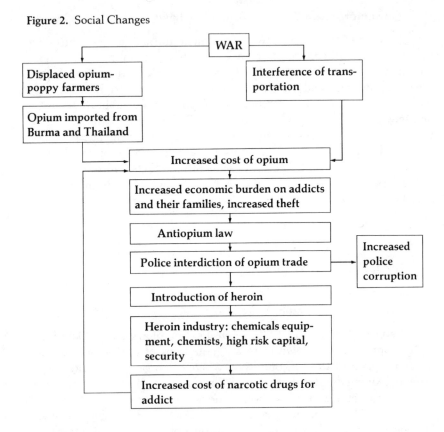

From J. Westermeyer, "Social Events and Narcotic Addiction: The Influence of War and Law on Opium Use in Laos," *Addictive Behaviors* 3 (1978):57–61.

Effects on Addicts and Their Families

These changes in the price and availability of narcotic drugs had major effects on addicts themselves. Perhaps most important was the economic effect: formerly most tribal addicts grew their own opium supply, and nontribal peoples could barter rice or other goods for opium. Town dwellers might support large addictions on fairly small sums of money ($8 to $15 per month). By the early 1970s narcotic habits were relatively expensive: from $12 to $20 per month in areas closer to supply routes to $30 to $60 per month in Vientiane.

As indicated earlier, addicts had several means to deal with this problem (see fig. 3). These included lower dosages, fewer doses per day, eating rather than smoking opium, sale of accumulated wealth, deprivation of other needs (e.g., food, clothes, household necessities), and theft. Initially many opium addicts avoided heroin whenever possible, the general consensus being that it was too intoxicating and caused withdrawal symptoms too soon. Unable to obtain opium, those in Vientiane substituted heroin. Pressured on all sides, addicts were also more apt to enter treatment.

Refugee moves and higher opium costs compounded the financial problem of opium addiction for families. Whether or not they were addicted, many refugee farmers were not able to obtain work. Their

Figure 3.   Effects on Addicts

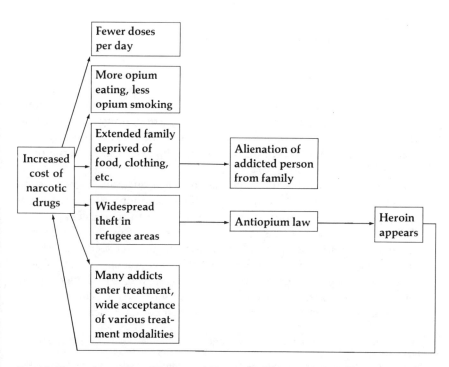

From J. Westermeyer, "Social Events and Narcotic Addiction: The Influence of War and Law on Opium Use in Laos," *Addictive Behaviors* 3 (1978):57–61.

need to buy food and replace lost cooking and farming implements depleted their scarce resources. Since most refugees functioned within an extended kin group, an addicted kinsman could cause financial strain on a large group of people. Understandably, some addicts previously accepted within the family became alienated from them.

Addicted Soldiers

I have no way of knowing how many soldiers in the Royal Lao Army were opium addicts. The number was not an insignificant one, as indicated by the occupations of addicts detailed in earlier chapters. A few of the case reports in this book involve soldiers. During one major battle in 1966, opium had to be dropped by parachute to the Lao and Hmong forces who were fighting the Vietnamese in northern Laos. Unable to obtain their opium supplies through usual channels, a significant minority of these soldiers were in withdrawal and unable to fight.*

RELIGIOUS CONCOMITANTS

As addicts progressed into the chronic stages of addiction, their religious practices were usually discontinued. Animists no longer attended to their house shrines or paid their respects to the ancestor spirits. Buddhist addicts did not participate actively in the community or contribute toward maintenance of their local temple or monastery. Christians abandoned their practice, except insofar as they might extract material benefits from their local missionary.

In contrast to this functional agnosticism during addiction, some addicts were influenced by religion in their abandoning opium. In one case report of spontaneous recovery described in a previous chapter, the man ascribed his cure to his religious conversion. Many more recovered addicts who did not give credit to religion for their recovery nonetheless became quite active in their subsequent religious practice. Whereas prior to recovery they had seldom attended quasi-religious social events (e.g., religious holidays, marriages, funerals), many recovered addicts became devout and religiously active members of their communities.

---

*Eventually the Lao and Hmong lost that battle, which was the beginning of their eventual defeat in the north several years later. This defeat probably resulted more from overwhelming numbers of Vietnamese troops, although addicted soldiers on the Laotian side did not help the situation. At the time, I treated several wounded soldiers who went into withdrawal during hospitalization. I treated a few score captured Vietnamese and Pathet Lao soldiers and encountered no addiction among them.

POLITICAL RELATIONSHIPS

Politics intersected with opium at every turn in Laos. Poppy farmers viewed the mountains as their homeland over which they had complete usufruct so long as they resided in them. Opium production had been their birthright for generations, virtually their only means of achieving some semblance of comfort and security. They thought no less of themselves for growing poppy than do Carolina tobacco farmers, Bolivian coffee growers, or Scottish rye farmers for growing their respective psychoactive crops. That anyone might interfere with their productivity was an alarming thought. Raids by Americans on Hmong poppy fields in Laos during 1973 caused considerable resentment. Educated Hmong friends who had strongly antiopium sentiments expressed extreme discontent to me that Americans should be so brazen as to damage poppy on Hmong land. (There were apparently a number of instances during the early 1970s in which helicopters made forays into Hmong fields to burn or otherwise destroy poppy.)

The Lao saw the world through somewhat different eyes, however. To them Laos was the country of the Lao. Swidden agriculture and poppy culture decimated an important resource of their nation: timber. It also impaired the watershed, although that was a less substantial argument. From their point of view, the poppy farmers were intruders, unwanted guests, wasters of natural riches that belonged to the Lao.

Opium influenced the relationship between poppy growers and Chinese merchants. Poppy trade was the source of several Chinese fortunes in Laos. Similarly, tribal people relied on the Chinese to supply them with silver, iron, various trade goods, and sometimes credit. In the Chinese-Lao and Chinese-mountaineer relationships—an admixture of love, hate, dependence, and admiration—opium trade often played a major role.

The United States and other allies of Laos took another tack. They wondered why they should assist Laos when Laotian heroin was running in the veins of their youth.

Throughout the 1965 to 1975 era, the situation in the political arena was further complicated by the absolutely righteous and consistent stand taken by the communist Chinese, Vietnamese, and Pathet Lao. They did not trade in opium, did not permit its production in lands under their control, and would not allow their party members and soldiers to consume it.* Compared to the RLG military and political lead-

*Poppy has been grown in Laos and in Vietnam over the last several years, according to several reputable sources (including inhabitants of both countries). This has not been

ers, the communist side was steadfastly moral and correct in relation to opium—a notable phenomenon since the North Vietnamese and Pathet Lao often showed little concern for human life and other moral matters in the midst of their military and political struggles.

While relatively few of the Lao elite were intimately involved in the opium trade, there were sufficient numbers of them to besmirch the name of the royalist and neutralist Lao. They included the following: a police colonel whose home, when raided by Lao narcotic agents, contained over two tons of opium; a senior Lao general who in 1972 admitted to being the central coordinator of opium exports from Laos for over a decade; an ambassador to France who was stopped in the Paris airport with several kilograms of the purest type of heroin in his personal luggage and who was never even arraigned for his crime upon returning to Laos. Opium corruption no doubt played a role in the overthrow of the constitutional monarchy in Laos, although it was only one factor among many. In my view it was not a major factor in and of itself; rather opium merely reflected and exacerbated other, more basic social, political, military, and economic problems.

OPIUM AS SYMBOL

As indicated above, opium came to be symbolic of corruption and weakness: in the moral crisis of the Royal Lao Government, in the use of opium by Laotian army personnel, and in the use of heroin by American forces in Southeast Asia. It has continued to possess that symbolism in Asia. (See Sapira 1975, for an exposition that historical precedent supports this symbolism.)

For the Hmong, the Iu Mien, and some other tribespeople, opium could be viewed as possessing different meanings. It represented their independence, their freedom from constraint and tyranny by lowlanders, their means of attaining wealth and a good life for themselves. While many of them would not fight for the abstract notion of a nation-state, they would fight or migrate to retain their right to raise poppy. A Hmong village chief, talking to Garrett (1974) about his clan's migration out of China, exemplified this attitude when he stated, "Our clan came to Laos to grow opium. We had to, because Chinese opium growers,

---

officially approved, however, but rather grows out of political exigencies that the communist governments have encountered since assuming authority.

fearing our competition, cut down our poppies." It is not likely that Chinese communists were trying to edge the Hmong out of the opium market, but rather they were eliminating poppy culture (except as condoned by the government). Still, the force of the Chinese against Hmong poppy fields caused the Hmong to migrate elsewhere in the hope of retaining autonomy over their own lives. This control by the national government over Hmong opium fields broadcasted the intent of the new Chinese government to alter traditional Hmong autonomy.

COMMENT

1. The antinarcotic law in Laos provides an example par excellence for establishing an unenforceable ordinance. The initial stimulus for the law originated outside the country. The law countermanded traditional behaviors and established agroeconomic production and trade. While an Interministerial Commission was established to implement the law, this was done hastily. The commission had no funds or personnel to undertake its recommendations. Consequently, the law was unevenly applied, police were corrupted, heroin was introduced, and the price of narcotic drugs around Vientiane Prefecture went up.

2. The war in Laos, beginning in the early 1950s and continuing for twenty years, did not have much effect on opium production until the late 1960s. By that time Vietnamese forces, assisted by some Pathet Lao units, had overrun much of northern and northeastern Laos, in particular the provinces of Phong Saly, Luang Prabang, Sam Neua, and Xieng Khouang. These comprised the main poppy-producing areas inhabited by the Hmong. Some opium continued to be produced in areas of Houa Kong and Sayaboury provinces, but it is likely that opium began to be imported from Burma and Thailand. These events led to increased prices for opium. Theft and family discord increased as a result. In this context, large numbers of addicts voluntarily sought treatment.

3. It is difficult to assess the effects of opium on the military proficiency of Lao and Hmong soldiers. In the short run, it helped some individuals cope with the rigors and boredom of soldiering (although that is not to say that they could not have coped without it). Chronic use and addiction undoubtedly did not help the progovernment forces, although it is difficult to assess opium's role in the eventual defeat of the Royal Laotian Government forces.

4. Functional agnosticism and opiate addiction tended to accompany each other. Conversely, religion often played an important role in attaining and/or maintaining abstinence. This was variously manifested as conversion experiences to new religions or a vigorous resumption of once-indolent religious practices.

5. Opium and politics in Laos were inseparable. The drug affected the relationships among the Lao, certain tribal people, and the Chinese. Depending on the nature of ethnic assumptions and interactions, opium facilitated or impeded political alliances. Eventually Laotian opium and international politics became bedfellows, giving rise to the antiopium law.

6. Opium symbolized many things to the people of Laos. It could represent wealth or poverty, pleasure or degradation, corruption or independence, waste or security—all depending on the context, the individual, the purpose. Like sex, money, life itself, opium both attracted and repelled, created and destroyed.

XV

Opium Reconsidered

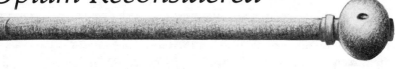

The Nonaddictive Use of Opium

These data from Laos are not sanguine about the nonaddictive use of opium, whether as a recreational intoxicant or as a self-prescribed remedy. While nonaddictive use of opium can continue over months or even years, addiction ensues frequently—certainly more often than is the case for alcohol. These data do not demonstrate what percentage of opium users are apt to eventually become addicted. But the high age-specific prevalence of addiction among the Hmong (i.e., up to 40 or 50 percent in later middle age, with about 20 to 25 percent among women and 60 to 75 percent among men at that age) suggests that many, if not most users eventually become addicts in a context of high availability and low cost.

Nonproblematic Addiction to Opium

The point is validly made that many addicts appear to have no problems with their addiction. They work hard, meet their social obligations, enjoy life, and appear to be healthy. It can even be cogently argued that opiate addiction can enhance one's productivity, enjoyment, sociability, and health, at least for a time. These points are based on cross-sectional observations, however. As one studies addicts over time or relates current clinical status to duration of addiction, the argument falters. To be sure, the onset of problems associated with addiction varies widely. One can find a few cases in which severe problems ensue within four months, whereas in a few others cases only mild problems exist even after four decades. In my interviews with addicted persons in both field and clinical settings, however, rare was the addict who had experienced even minor drug-related problems before four months or who had not experienced some major drug-related problems within four years of becoming addicted.

Cash Crop Replacement

After some experience with poppy farmers, it becomes evident that most of them will readily abandon poppy for more lucrative cash crops. The difficulty lies not in teaching them the means for growing other crops; this can be done easily and inexpensively. Rather the dilemma lies in transporting produce to markets. As one Hmong poppy farmer in Laos said, "Build us roads, and we will sell rice or pigs. We realize the dangers of opium, but now it is our only source of money" (Garrett 1974). Yet building roads through the karsts and ridgebacks and across the streams and valleys of the poppy-producing mountains requires tremendous capital investments. Maintaining them against the monsoon's annual torrents similarly runs dear. The billions of dollars that would be required run well beyond the resources of the countries involved. Lack of security also poses a problem. Mountaineers do not want to invest years of hard labor in terracing or in growing long-term products such as coffee if the chances of being driven off the land are high.

Poppy Cash Crop: Asset or Liability?

The outsider's perspective on poppy growing is usually that the farmers of Laos aggrandize their profits at the cost of increased heroin addiction in Singapore, Paris, or New York. Like all stereotypes, there is a half-truth to it. Poppy culture does permit remote mountaineer farmers to participate in the iron age while many of their neighbors must rely on nonmetal implements to a greater extent. Poppy farmers can also enter the world marketplace, buying cloth from Korea, needle and thread from Japan, tea from China, and sugar from Thailand.

Poppy-growing villages also pay dearly for participating in the opiate market. They have the highest prevalence rates ever recorded for opiate addiction, with crude rates of 8 to 10 percent and age- and sex-specific rates ranging even up to 30 to 50 percent among middle-aged males. Not even alcohol addiction occurs so commonly in societies with high rates of alcoholism.

Opium commerce centers encounter the same fate but to a lesser extent. Their crude rates of addiction are down around 5 percent, and it is mostly males who become addicted. Nonetheless, this is a high cost to pay for profits that are distributed so narrowly in the community. At least in poppy-producing villages, almost every household benefits from the cash crop profits. On the contrary in the commercial centers, only a few central organizers, police officials, and traffickers profit. Yet the burden of the 5 percent addiction rate on the local population is heavy.

The Wealthy, Old Chinese Addict

As indicated in these data, most opium addicts in Laos were not wealthy, old, or Chinese. Why is this stereotype so widely supported in Asia and in the West? I believe there are several sources for it. First, it does describe the situation in which most people would approve of addiction, namely for the person no longer productive and now close to death. All of the nations in the world today currently approve of medically prescribed opiate use, even opiate addiction, for painful, terminal illness. Second, since this is the socially approved image of an addict, anyone falling outside of this image is a deviant. The addicted young father, woman, and destitute beggar have no claim on social support since they stand outside the approved role characteristics. Third, it permits people to ignore the problems associated with addiction, since the stereotype describes opium as a solution (i.e., respite in the face of infirmity and illness) rather than as a problem (i.e., the cause of infirmity and illness). Fourth, it allows everyone who is not a Chinese to define the problem as a Chinese one and to write off their addicted ethnic peers as "acting like a Chinese" and thus as being beyond their concern.

The Chinese stereotype raises the question of culture and addiction. To what extent do cultural factors cause or at least predispose people to addiction? These data from Laos suggest that availability determines addiction rates to a large extent, and cultural factors can influence availability to a considerable degree. Cultural barriers can be as strong as geographic distance in affecting addiction, as exemplified by the Chinese and Vietnamese in Vientiane. (Recall that both communities had geographic access to Chinese opium dens and Vietnamese nightclubs but that members of each group generally preferred to intoxicate themselves among their ethnic peers.) Within ethnic groups, rates of addiction varied with access to opiates (e.g., the Iu Mien in poppy villages and commerical centers). And across ethnic groups, rates tended to remain constant with a given availability (e.g., Hmong and Iu Mien in poppy villages; Iu Mien, Lao, Chinese, and Cambodians in opium commercial centers). This is an example of pharmacological-environmental factors proving more powerful than cultural factors. By the same token, cultural factors also influenced prevalence rates but through their influence on availability rather than through sociocultural factors per se.

Opium Versus Heroin

These data indicate that heroin is neither more nor less "addicto-genic" than opium. The duration of use prior to addiction is the same for the two drugs. And the type of difficulties associated with the two drugs does not differ, at least when heroin is taken by smoking rather than by nonsterile injection. The primary difference between the two drugs is the time at which the addict wants to seek treatment. That probably happens sooner for heroin than for opium. It is not clear whether this phenomenon occurs for economic reasons (i.e., heroin is more expensive and may lead to financial problems sooner) or for pharmacological reasons (i.e., heroin has a shorter duration of action, so there are more frequent episodes of intoxication and withdrawal with heroin). The types of problems to which each drug gives rise were similar in Laos.

Based on this difference between heroin and opium, it could be argued that heroin is worse since it causes problems more quickly than opium. Conversely, it might be argued that heroin is better, since the person mired in heroin addiction will struggle to get out of it sooner than the person addicted to opium. Thus, heroin addicts (if successfully treated) would waste less of their lives stranded in an addiction limbo as compared to opium addicts. Neither argument is obviously more persuasive than the other, so the matter is not a clear one.

Of interest, heroin addiction spread in Vientiane Prefecture in a way similar to that observed for infectious disease. That is, it began in a few focal areas and spread. Indigenous contacts, rather than foreign influences appeared to predominate. This mode of spread resembles that described by Hughes, Brakes, and Crawford (1972), Dai (1937), and others in North America. While we must avoid making simplistic analogies between infectious disease and substance abuse, at the same time we should not ignore the parallels between them.

The chronological relationship between heroin and expatriate addicts, especially youthful Caucasians and some youthful Asians, suggests that heroin attracted the former to Laos. This has implications for countries that fear an influx of expatriate addicts. This is not a negligible concern, since such countries become deluged with any number of international problems: overdose deaths, crimes, embassy pressures, foreign inquiries about missing youth, undesirable public images. Reducing heroin availability, particularly in places where expatriates concentrate, aids in preventing or reducing this problem. From the standpoint of the foreign traveler in areas with endemic opiate addiction, preventive measures include traveling with companions, entry into the indigenous society as a student or worker, avoiding opiate use, and attending to one's own mental health.

Narcotic Addiction: Illness or Pastime?

I have heard the viewpoint often stated that opium addiction is merely a habit or pastime in Asia and that the notion of addiction as an illness is a concept superimposed on the East by Western minds. There is more than a grain of truth in this statement. Opium addiction is viewed as a habit or pastime, especially in its early stages. As the psychological, social, and biomedical sequelae of addiction develop, however, addicts themselves commonly seek treatment in an effort to rid themselves of addiction or at least of the problems associated with it. Insofar as addicts collaborate in their own treatment, families and healers commonly assign them the sick role. Folk modalities used to treat opium addiction include the entire array of available healing methods in Asia. These attitudes and behaviors with regard to treatment are traditional and indigenous; they were not imported from the West.

That which has been imported from the West is the use of modern medical and social institutions against widespread addiction. These methods have been successfully applied in Japan, the Koreas, China, Taiwan, the Philippines, and Indonesia. They have not proven successful (at least as of this writing) in Southeast Asia, Malaysia, and parts of south Asia.

The Social Role of Opium Dens

In many societies, the locus of drug consumption (i.e., the den, the tavern) is often viewed as the problem. This simplistic view suggests that society need only get rid of this locus and the problems of substance abuse will disappear. This opinion was popular among leaders in Laos, as it has been among leaders elsewhere.

Studies of den attenders and den society in Laos did not support these views. Virtually no rural addicts had ever been in a den. Most urban addicts did not frequent them, either. Dens were primarily a supportive social institution for those addicts alienated from or abandoned by other social institutions (in particular the family and the small face-to-face community).

Natural Course or Multidimensional Phenomenon?

Some observers aver that the notion of natural course (i.e., the sequence of events in an illness over time without treatment) originated with infectious diseases and should remain there. In fact, the notion of natural course was around long before Pasteur and others demonstrated that some diseases were due to specific infectious agents. None of the infectious diseases (or any of the noninfectious diseases, for that matter, regardless of their origins) runs a unidimensional course. For example, typhoid can produce a rather mild illness in some, a severe illness of several weeks' duration for others, and a fatal outcome for yet others. Some recover completely without residuals, others are left disabled for months, and a few become chronic carriers who later infect others. Diversity is nature's way. The concept of a natural course, for typhoid as an example, applies to the usual or typical courses of typhoid, with its major manifestations.

Some students of addiction debate convincingly that addiction's manifestations are so variable and myriad that they defy reduction into a natural course. I disagree with their point of view, since addiction seems no more variable to me than tuberculosis, arteriosclerosis, or hypothyroidism. But admittedly, I speak as a clinician, as one schooled in clinical method and steeped in a clinical tradition. For those unfamiliar or uncomfortable with clinical method, whether in an applied or a research context, I am loath to urge its use. It is a concept, a method, an approach—and that is all. If it is useful or aids in structuring one's perceptions, employ it. If not, abandon it.

There is work yet to be done in detailing the natural course of addiction. Abstracting from my own earlier work (Westermeyer 1976a) and that of others (Jellinek 1952 and 1960, Wikler 1961), the concomitants of early, middle, and late phases of this course are as follows:

Characteristic	Early phase: problematic use	Middle phase: chronic dependence, addiction	Late phase: deterioration
1. Behavioral factors			
a. Drug use	Increases dose and frequency	Uses chronically, heavily; attempts abstinence	Uses emergency or substitute intoxicants

Characteristic	Early phase: problematic use	Middle phase: chronic dependence, addiction	Late phase: deterioration
b. Control	Attempts to reduce dose or frequency	Loses partial control (uses higher doses or more often than intended)	Loses almost complete control (cannot cease or reduce dosage)
c. Drug-related behavior	Seeks occasions to use; chooses friends who are heavy users; may begin secretive use	Uses compulsively at specific times and places; centers life on obtaining and using drug	Uses continuously despite increasing drug-related problems and decreasing enjoyment from drug
2. Psychological factors			
a. Motivation	Uses to enjoy, build up confidence, relieve insomnia, anxiety or depression	Uses to feel normal	Uses to dull perceptions of self and reality
b. Emotional concomitants	Has mood swings; feels anger or shame regarding use; feels defensive, weak	Exhibits personality change; feels guilt, remorse, ambivalence about drug use	Is erratic, suspicious; feels alone; may be apathetic
c. Cognitive processes	Is obsessive regarding use	Denies nature of problem; projects blame onto others	Is confused
d. Judgment	Is able to extricate self from problems	Makes decisions leading to more problems	Is unable to solve problems
3. Social factors			
a. Interpersonal relationships	Changes friends to heavy users	Alienates and embarrasses others	Manipulates others in passive-aggressive manner
b. Family	Argues with family	Abuses family	Leaves family (or vice versa)

Characteristic	Early phase: problematic use	Middle phase: chronic dependence, addiction	Late phase: deterioration
c. Employment, work	Shows stable or increased productivity	Shows decreased productivity	Is nonproductive
d. Residence	Has stable home	Moves from place to place	Lives alone
e. School	Participates less	Has falling grades	Drops out; is suspended
f. Finances	Takes on a second job to support drugs	Spends all income on self, assumes debts, squanders family resources	Is destitute, dependent on others
g. Social affiliations	Discontinues nondrug-related affiliations	Has short-lived companionships	Is client of social or charitable institutions

This model is not suggested as a rigid road down which all addicted persons must trek. One might be at an early phase of one characteristic and at a late phase of another. Research done among substance abusers has shown that a variety of characteristics influence the course of addiction in myriad ways. Such characteristics include early versus late onset of substance abuse (Bahr 1969); individual substance use patterns (McNamee, Mello, and Mendelson 1968); intercurrent events such as death, recovery, incarceration, or psychiatric disorder (Vaillant 1973); personality (Walton 1968); gender (Wanberg and Horn 1970); the biological effects of the drug or drugs being abused (Mendelson 1970); superimposed courses from biomedical or socioeconomic complications (Rao, Nicastri, and Friedman 1974); and the effects of treatment (Romond, Forrest, and Kleber 1974). To reinforce my earlier point, the concept of natural course is just that—a concept. Given the considerable variability from a central theme, it might be better to speak of natural courses.

Clinical Concomitants of Pharmacological Variables

A strictly pharmacological model would state that the appearance of clinical problems is a function of increased opiate dosage. To some extent that no doubt is true, since a certain minimum dose and duration are required to produce addiction. Beyond that level, however, the relationship between dose and disability appears poorly correlated. Some of the most disorganized addicts are those who appear early in the course of their addiction while still on rather low dosages. The relationship between dose and duration of addiction also shows no direct correlation. Indeed, there was a trend among these Laotian addicts for those with the longest addictions to be taking somewhat lower doses.

Part of the confusion may lie in assessing the actual pharmacological variables for any one addict. The percent of active alkaloids varies from one sample of opium to another. Many addicts vary their own dose from one week to the next. Different routes of administration produce variable pharmacological effects per unit of drug. Even quantifying the detoxification dose of methadone has its drawbacks, since addicts vary in their tolerance to withdrawal symptoms, nurses and physicians diverge in their dosing practices, and the nuances of the patient-clinician relationship can influence prescribing habits. In short, we may not yet have the tools that permit a valid assessment of pharmacological factors in the addict. Until we do, the burden of proof must lie with those who hold that increasing disability follows inevitably on the heels of increasing dosage.

Other Drugs

Through drugs and their use, the various ethnic groups in Laos expressed their history, traditions, values, politics, and economics. All of the peoples in Laos had an etiquette governing alcohol use, although this was weakening as contemporary socioeconomic factors undermined traditional social and religious forms in favor of rural-to-urban migration and universal literacy. Betel nut and pipe smoking were giving way to coffee and cigarettes. Drug use served as a barometer for change.

Among the various drugs, opiates were not necessarily the most habit forming. Tobacco and alcohol were probably as habit forming. Habitual tobacco use may have been as widespread among the Dya Heun as opium use among the Hmong, although there are no data to support that notion. It does not stretch the imagination to suppose that the rates of alcohol and opiate dependence, if combined, would add to sums that would be similar among the Chinese and the Vietnamese in Vientiane. Firmer epidemiological data are necessary to test these ideas.

Still, there were certain features of opium that suggested that opium dependence was more detrimental personally and socially as compared to the other drugs. The effect of opium was more attractive than that of other drugs, dependence became established more readily, and drug abstinence produced more untoward consequences. Compared to other drugs, addictive levels of opiate drug use were relatively much greater than recreational levels so that the economic burden of addiction was considerably greater. Alcohol dependence, even in the early stages, could produce gastritis, hangovers, and other unpleasant sequelae that favored moderation or abstinence. The early stages of opiate addiction tended to bring few biomedical complications. Betel and tobacco dependence did not precipitate financial and family crises, while opiate dependence routinely did so.

CLINICAL VERSUS PUBLIC HEALTH APPROACHES

The Clinical Model

This approach presumes that the individual clinician or clinical facility can, in isolation, manage the problem of addiction. Corollaries of this theme hold that other social helpers or agents—psychologists, social workers, nurses, police, attorneys, judges, teachers—should similarly deal with addiction as independent entities. A strategy parallel to starting a clinical program would be passing an antinarcotic law, with delegation of addiction problems to law enforcement officials and the judiciary.

This approach can be effective in managing addiction when it occurs in an occasional and isolated case. Typical examples are the addicted health worker (e.g., physician, dentist, nurse, pharmacist), the iatrogenic addict (i.e., person inadvertently addicted by one or more physicians), or the addict returning home after becoming addicted in another country. These cases are infrequent and can usually be managed within existing resources and programs.

This approach was adequate for the occasional alcohol-dependent person in Laos. The numbers were few and there was no alcoholic subculture. It was not adequate to address the problem of opiate addiction, however. Even if 3,000 opiate addicts could be treated and cured on an annual basis, this would probably not even balance the annual crop of newly addicted persons. Over a period of years, large resources would be devoted to clinical treatment without any hope of eventually reducing opiate addiction or eliminating it from the population.

The Public Health Model

In this model a large number of disciplines, institutions, and agencies collaborate in a concerted effort against addiction. These include

hospitals, clinics, mental health facilities, social agencies, law enforcement personnel, jails, prisons, courts, customs agents, teachers, the
mass media, political leaders, neighborhood associations, family and
parents' groups, religious organizations, unions, employers, industries,
and others—in short, virtually any and all segments of the society. It
assumes that their total power and influence working together are greater
than the sum of their individual strengths. This approach is built on
communication and cooperation among many individuals. Leadership
may be multifocal, central, or a combination of both.

In the face of widespread addiction, the public health approach
is the only method that both is cost effective and offers some hope of
success. That is not to say that it is readily undertaken. It is expensive
and time-consuming. Other pressing needs must be set aside temporarily
while high priority is assigned to addiction. Individuals and agencies
without a tradition for cooperating with one another must come together in order to set common goals and work toward them in an integrated fashion. Disparate value systems, jargon, and *modus operandi*
among various professionals and organizations constantly pose obstacles
to this approach. Extra effort is required on all sides.

Such a concerted effort cannot continue indefinitely on a widespread basis. Consequently, the goal of this approach must be the virtual
elimination of all addiction within a specific span of time. Subsequently,
sporadic cases can be managed on a parochial or clinical level without
this massive intervention system.

This society-wide approach to addiction had been begun in selected
areas of Laos, such as Vientiane and Xieng Khouang provinces. Despite
corruption of the police and heroin introduction among urban youth,
this approach was having some successes. Traditional opium addiction
was declining and almost disappearing in certain villages. Whether these
successes could have been sustained during a prolonged period of peace
was never ascertained. If poppy farmers returned to their mountains
and resumed poppy production, widespread addiction would likely
return.

Special Aspects of the Public Health Approach to Addiction

There are certain similarities between the public health approach
to both infectious disease and addiction. Clinicians, epidemiologists,
and others in the infectious disease field must deal with a wide variety
of disciplines to overcome certain disease outbreaks. For example, the
services of the mass media may be necessary to alert the populace re-

garding preventive measures. Police authority has been exercised against tubercular, typhoidal, and other carriers not cooperating with medical treatment. Immunization against infectious disease has been undertaken in schools and at work places. Customs agents have prevented the importation of certain insect vectors and unsafe foods.

There are also certain differences between infectious disorders and addiction. Few people ever choose to become infected with a virus or parasite, while almost all addicts first use drugs voluntarily (although virtually none of them counts on eventually becoming an addict). This element of voluntary choice inevitably involves certain difficult social issues that have little relevance to most infectious diseases (although they do exist for venereal disease). Matters of individual freedom and choice, the rights of society, the role of moral standards and religion, complex ethical and legal considerations must all be fully voiced and carefully weighed. In addition, such decisions are always influenced by political, social, and economic factors that may not bear any direct or even discernible relationship to addiction.

These social issues were never broached in Laos (at least beyond the decision to maintain patient confidentiality from the police and other government agencies). It was not necessary to consider them because there were always large numbers of addicts willing to enter treatment voluntarily. Eventually, however, such hard questions would have to be faced. First, there would be the problem of the chronic, recurrent addict coming back repeatedly to treatment. Recurrent patients displace other addicts who have a better prognosis. They also consume large amounts of scarce societal resources. Over time, this "revolving door" syndrome results in what has been referred to as lifetime institutionalization on the installment plan. Second, there would be the problem of addicts who did not want treatment. Their continued presence, even in a community with few remaining addicts, would serve as a continuing nidus for introducing new people to opiate use. By 1975 both of these problems were on the horizon as future difficulties.

Another problem not considered in Laos was the female addict. To be sure, many women were treated and did well. But a comparison of the epidemiological data and clinical data indicated that relatively fewer women benefited from treatment as compared to men. And among the treated women, there was a trend for them to do less well—probably because of the presence of an addicted husband in many cases. These gender-related treatment problems are by no means unique to Laos, but effective means for dealing with them did not evolve out of the Laotian experience.

Social Interventions as a Two-Edged Sword

An antiopium law led to a scourge that Laos had avoided for decades: the introduction of heroin. A culturally insensitive treatment program for tribal addicts at a lowland Buddhist temple alienated a large segment of the population from any government-sponsored treatment. Sporadic treatment seeking by a few addicts in some areas led to a very high rate of treatment failure and subsequent disenchantment with treatment. A high mortality among older addicts at a Buddhist temple undermined public faith in that program.

These untoward consequences emphasize the need for careful evaluation prior to widespread adaptation of any legislation, intervention, or treatment program. Once an attempt has ended in failure, it may be impossible to begin again as though nothing had happened. Personal bias and a do-gooder intent (both rife in the field of substance abuse) do not suffice. One has to know what one is doing. As in any area of health, there is a need for a high level of expertise and professionalism.

FACTORS AFFECTING TREATMENT OUTCOME

Development of a treatment program for addicts will be necessary in either the public health approach (for widespread addiction) or the strictly clinical approach (for the sporadic cases). What do these data from Laos tell us about planning treatment for addicts?

First, they tell us that an important aspect of treatment is that it should be at least acceptable, and preferably attractive to addicts. There are always numerous pressures on addicts to seek treatment (although these pressures can be enhanced by public education, reduced drug availability, and other public health efforts). In order to conduct treatment acceptable to addicts, we as clinicians need to provide services that are humane, confidential, in keeping with the societal expectations of healing, and professional. The example of tribal minorities at Wat Tan Kha Bok teaches the importance of communication and rapport between staff and patients. Especially where staff and patients belong to different ethnic groups, special efforts must be made to welcome patients, to help them participate in the treatment process, and to pay particular attention to translation and communication. This was done with optimal effect at the National Narcotic Detoxification Center. Despite the all-Lao professional staff, expatriate Asians and tribal peoples enthusiastically presented themselves for admission throughout the Center's brief two-and-a-half years of existence.

Second, we should not be fooled into thinking that a particular treatment mode offers some inherent advantage over another mode. At our present state of knowledge, no one modality is clearly superior. We have seen here that the monks at the Thai temple made virtually no individual assessments, employed "cold turkey" withdrawal, and gave religious exhortations. Yet the record of addicts' social function and abstinence from drugs was as good six to eighteen months later as it was at the National Narcotic Detoxification Center, with its individual assessments, methadone withdrawal, and a two-to-three-week residential program that was on a par with those in North America at the time. To be sure, the patients at these two programs were self-selected rather than randomly assigned. Conclusive evidence that such programs show no difference at outcome must ultimately rest on random distribution of patients from the same pool of addicts. In the meantime, these experiences in Laos suggest that the activitites at a treatment program may not be very important. If that proves to be true, we might then focus our attention on other, possibly more important variables. Currently much attention is focused at the transactions and/or programmatic aspects of treatment, although many of our "modern" treatment methods have their parallels in folk treatment modalities.

More critical may be such factors as the addict's decision to seek treatment, the attraction of the addict to a treatment program, the social expectation that the addict can and might change, access to follow-up treatment, decreased drug availability, family support, or other as-yet-unknown factors. If and when these critical factors can be identified (and perhaps even quantified), treatment staff can expend their efforts and resources in a more efficient and effective manner.

Third, clinicians treating addiction must provide a high level of professional service. An inordinate morbidity or mortality will ultimately be self-defeating. The high mortality of elderly Laotian addicts at Wat Tan Kha Bok is a case in point. Eventually it led to a pariah status for that treatment resource. The conventional wisdom was not discerning in its evaluation of the *wat*, however. While the high mortality was restricted to elderly addicts, this fact was only discovered through careful record keeping. Evaluation of treatment must receive high priority, especially when new methods are being tried.

Fourth, treatment staff must establish rapport with their addicted patients just as they would with any patient. This rapport must be built on empathy and effective communication. Out of this clinician-patient relationship, one can expect most addicts to collaborate with treatment. Those addicts unable to work cooperatively with staff at one time will often return at a future time if rapport has been established and if the parting takes place on a positive note. The successful pig farmer presented earlier, who did not respond to his first treatment but did well after his second admission, is such a case. At the same time, policymakers and treatment personnel must address the problem of the ever-returning addict-patient who does not respond to repeated treatment. All societies seeking to reduce or eliminate widespread substance abuse must face this issue. Not choosing to deal with it is one type of response, with its own special consequences. At this time there does not appear to be a single highly desirable, cost-effective, humanitarian, and efficient means of coping with this dilemma. Rather there are a number of less-than-optimal alternatives (e.g., laissez-faire and ever-returning addicts, with institutionalization on the installment plan; incarceration; mandatory treatment; long-term residential supervision; community shelters; halfway houses; quarterway houses). Another clinical dilemma is the single or divorced, unemployed, unskilled addict with inadequate ensocialization.

Fifth, the outcome from treatment is probably more strongly influenced by subsequent events in the addict's home and community than by treatment events. Our major efforts at improving treatment outcome should be focused on helping the addict in reestablishing a social network free of addicts insofar as possible, establishing a follow-up program, working in an ongoing fashion with the recovering addict's family or other significant people, being alert to the development of incapacitating emotional or psychophysiological disorders, and reducing drug availability. The comparable long-term results at a Buddhist temple and a medical facility suggest that programmatic events during a brief period of residential treatment are not so critical. Programmatic events probably serve important functions in (1) attracting addicts to treatment, (2) accepting the addict as a valuable person capable of change, and (3) serving a rebirth or ritual function, by which addiction becomes part of the person's past and abstinence becomes part of the future.

Sixth, in communities with a high prevalence of addiction, interventions must take place on a community basis. Returning addicts to a community that has widespread addiction merely sets up the addict-patient and the clinician for failure. Community leaders—clergy, teachers, merchants, elders, and others—must feel some investment, power, and support by the society at large if they are to cope effectively with addiction at the grass-roots level. The power of community factors was demonstrable in refugee areas experiencing a crisis. Villages that organized to support and to send their addicts to treatment had astounding treatment outcomes, while those without such organization had atrocious outcomes. This disparity occurred whether treatment was at the temple or at the medical facility—strongly suggesting that posttreatment community factors were considerably more powerful than residential treatment factors in predicting outcome. Other community variables favoring improvement were low drug availability, high cost of drugs, stable marriage, and a nonkin helping person (e.g., missionary, health worker, clinical worker). Patient satisfaction with treatment does not seem to be associated with outcome, although it may influence treatment seeking among the patient's peers. Following treatment, social competence and abstinence tended to occur together, but there were remarkable instances of little or no correlation between the two. A particularly common syndrome associated with abstinence was disabling depression.

PUBLIC HEALTH INTERVENTION OR LAISSEZ-FAIRE?

At times the most judicious public health alternative is to do nothing. Public health approaches to widespread addiction require resources: time, personnel, money, and material. More than that, they need strong commitment throughout all levels of leadership and from the populace at large. And they need support over a sufficient period of time to be effective. Unfortunately, this usually occurs only after the social repercussions of addiction have become widespread and severe.

Before getting to the point where an all-out move against addiction can be made, considerable infrastructure must be laid. People must be trained to new tasks. Those accustomed to working only within their own discipline or agency must learn to communicate with those from other fields and disciplines. Pilot projects must be tried on a limited basis and abandoned when they prove ineffective or too expensive.

Short of initiating a major effort, serious consideration should be given to avoiding establishment of special clinical programs. Special clinical services are notoriously expensive. If they offer no hope of ever eliminating or reducing a problem with a high prevalence, it may be better not to initiate them. This is particularly true if indigenous, folk, or general medical services are already available for treating addiction. Similarly, the failure of a half-hearted or inadequate public health program serves to undermine subsequent efforts even before they get underway.

Timing is extremely important in undertaking a major public health effort. Prematurely foisting an extensive program on an unenthusiastic populace can lead to a dismal outcome, with failing addicts and their disappointed families the biggest losers of all. Conversely, letting addiction remain at a high level for a long period also has its risks. As shown by these data from Laos, communities can and will accommodate extremely high prevalence rates of addiction—up to 40 or 50 percent of middle-aged adults. (This is not so different from accommodations to 50 percent childhood mortality or to the constant threat of nuclear annihilation.) Once the social accommodation is made, subsequent public health programs against addiction may only be possible within a total social reorganization.

By the same token, general medical facilities can and should make diagnoses, provide assessments, and—within available resources—treat substance abuse. Attending only to the sequelae of substance abuse (e.g., injuries, depression, infections) is like treating a headache from a subdural hematoma with aspirin rather than with definitive surgery. This treatment of epiphenomena alone is frustrating for clinicians if community factors continually undermine the clinicians' treatment efforts. Appreciation that community factors are critical can lead to effective collaboration between clinicians and other key community members, however. This approach can be thought of as a micro-level public health intervention, an essential skill in the compleat clinician's armamentarium.

Appendix

(Unofficial translation of the Lao Presse *version of September 27, 1971)*

ANTINARCOTICS LAW

Kingdom of Laos
National Assembly

Law

No. 71/5 dated August 10, 1971, pertaining to prohibition from cultivation, flavoring, smoking or consumption, purchase, sale and having
in possession of opium or opium compound or opium tailing, including
morphine and heroin, in the Kingdom of Laos.

The National Assembly has deliberated on and adopted a draft law
pertaining to the prohibition from cultivation, flavoring, smoking or consumption, purchase, sale and having in possession of opium or opium
compound or opium tailing, including morphine and heroin, in the
Kingdom of Laos, the provisions of which are the following:

Article 1: Absolute prohibition is imposed on the cultivation of opium
poppy throughout the Kingdom of Laos.

On a temporary basis, however, members of the tribes whose native
villages are located in the mountains and jungles where, for genera-

tions heretofore, opium poppy has been cultivated, and those who have been authorized to grow opium poppy may carry on this cultivation or smoke the opium grown and produced by themselves subject to the conditions stipulated in the following paragraphs:

Permit to grow opium poppy or to smoke opium thus produced shall be issued by the Chao Khoueng to individuals whose age is over forty years, effective upon the promulgation of this law.

The Provincial Advisory Committee, under the chairmanship of the Chao Khoueng, and the representatives of the Ministries of Public Health, of National Education, and of Finance shall fix the amount of land for the cultivation of opium poppy in favor of the applicant as appropriate.

Article 2: Flavoring, possession, consumption or smoking, and transportation of opium or opium compound or opium tailing, including morphine and heroin, in the Kingdom of Laos are absolutely prohibited.

Purchase and sale of opium or opium compound, including morphine and heroin, are prohibited to the general public and also to those who have been issued special permits to grow opium poppy and to smoke or consume opium produced by themselves.

Article 3: The importation or exportation, passage in transit, storage in warehouse, and movement of opium or opium compound, either opium tailing or opium mixture, powdered opium or remainder of opium flavoring, including morphine and heroin, are also prohibited, except for the medicine which is mixed or flavored with opium for the purpose of treating disease and prepared in whatever form under commercial practices in connection with the use of poisonous narcotics.

Article 4: Persons who grow opium poppy or consume or smoke opium or opium compound or opium tailing or opium mixture, powdered opium tailing or remainder of opium flavoring, including morphine and heroin, without permit as stipulated in Article 1, or encroach on the border of the land area specified in the certificate authorizing them to grow opium poppy duly issued to them, shall be liable to a fine from 5,000 *kip* to 200,000 *kip* and an imprisonment from three months to three years, or either of the above.

In case of recurrence of the offense, the fine shall be increased to the maximum of the penalties set forth hereabove.

Article 5:

   a) A fine from 10,000 *kip* to 500,000 *kip* and an imprisonment from six months to five years, or either of the above, shall be imposed on any persons in the following cases:

     1) Issuance of an inaccurate permit for the cultivation of opium poppy or for the smoking of opium, or falsification of a permit already issued by the Chao Khoueng by changing name and surname or photograph or by giving false or erroneous information in the certificate of birth;

     2) Acting as accomplice in the falsification of a permit as stated above;

     3) Issuance of a permit free of charge or sale of a permit;

     4) Acceptance of a permit free of charge or purchase of a permit;

     5) Having committed an offense or having an intention to commit an offense in the issuance of a permit.

In case of offense as stipulated in Items 1, 2, 3, 4, and 5 hereabove, the permit must be confiscated by the Court of Justice for disposal.

In case of recurrence of an offense, the fine shall be increased to the maximum of the penalties set forth hereabove.

   b) A fine equivalent to five times the price of the confiscated items, the assessment of price thereof being in conformity with the provisions of the Royal Decrees which shall be established in this regard, and an imprisonment with hard labor ranging from five years to twenty years shall be imposed on:

     1) Persons who produce opium or opium compound or opium tailing of any type whatsoever or compound made of opium tailing or flavored with opium tailing, including morphine and heroin, except the cases stipulated in the provisions of Article 1 hereabove;

     2) Persons who grant to others free of charge or with payment, transport or possess or leave or purchase or accept opium or opium compound or opium tailing of any type whatsoever or compound made of opium tailing or flavored with opium tailing, including morphine and heroin;

     3) Persons who bring opium or opium compound or opium tailing of any type whatsoever or compound made of opium tailing or flavored with opium tailing, including morphine and heroin, into Laos, or store it in any place or move it or transport it in transit in Laos.

The Court of Justice is prohibited from granting a reduction of the penalties. The penalty or a fine shall be in conformity with the provisions set forth in Item b) hereabove.

In case of recurrence of an offense, the Court of Justice is prohibited from granting a reduction of the penalty to an imprisonment with hard labor; the sentence hereto shall conform to the provisions set forth in Item b) hereabove.

Article 6: Any persons who set up an opium den shall be liable to a fine from 10,000 *kip* to 1,000,000 *kip* and an imprisonment from six months to five years, or either of the above.

In case of recurrence of an offense, the fine shall be increased to the maximum of the penalties set forth hereabove.

Article 7: The offenses with penalties therefor fixed in this law shall form the subject of legal action in the Court of Justice by the Public Prosecutor.

In all cases, the opium or opium compound or opium tailing of any type whatsoever or compound made of or flavored with opium tailing, including morphine and heroin, must be confiscated and destroyed. Likewise, the transportation means and containers used in this connection shall be confiscated and put on auction sale, and the proceeds obtained therefrom shall be deposited in the National Treasury, provided that it can be proved that the owner of said transportation means or containers is himself the offender or acts as an accomplice of the offender.

Opium or opium tailing of any type whatsoever or opium compound or compound made of or flavored with opium tailing, including morphine and heroin, if found, shall be confiscated and destroyed upon request of the Public Prosecutor.

Household materials and other items accessory to opium smoking found in the house of the owner of the opium or in the opium den, such as: bed, lamp, opium pipe and others, shall be confiscated and destroyed.

Article 8: All laws and regulations contrary to the present law are hereby abrogated.

It is hereby certified that this Law has been deliberated on and adopted during the general meeting of the National Assembly on August 12, 1971.

Vientiane, August 12, 1971
President of the National Assembly
/s/ Phagna Houakhong
(Phoui Sananikone)

Glossary

Abscess the walling off of an area of inflammation, containing infectious agents and pus.

Achan (Lao) an honorific title given to an older person who has studied and read for many years (usually Buddhist tracts in Pali).

Addiction daily use of an addicting drug (e.g., opium, barbiturates, alcohol) over a period of weeks, months, or years, such that sudden cessation of the drug produces a withdrawal illness; addiction ranges along a spectrum, with mild to severe withdrawal resulting from it.

Alveolus a microscopic unit within the lung where oxygen enters the blood and carbon dioxide leaves the blood.

Anemia a condition in which an individual's circulating blood volume contains abnormally low hemoglobin within the red blood cells.

Arthritis inflammation of the joint capsule between bones.

Baci (Lao) a ritual usually held at home to celebrate rites of passage, such as naming a newborn, marriage, entering a monastery, graduation, honoring a visitor or friend; the process consists of a lengthy speech and/or prayer, individual prayers by each of the guests while tying a string around the wrist of the person(s) being honored, and a festive meal usually accompanied by alcohol drinking.

Betel a stimulant plant widely used in parts of Asia and Oceania.

"Binge" use consumption of an addicting or dependency-producing drug, such that the daily intake of drug varies widely from day to day or week to week.

Boun (**Lao**) a temple festival for raising money to maintain and improve the monastery or *wat*; the term *boun* itself refers to "merit," which is believed to accrue to a person during life and which serves to enhance the person's life after death (leading either to a higher status in the next life or progression into nirvana); sponsoring activities at the festival is believed to increase one's *boun*.

Bride price a marriage custom in which the bridegroom's family provides recompense to the bride's family; it both formalizes the marriage bond and serves as a "quit claim" allowing the woman's children to become members of the husband's clan.

Bronchial tree the subdivisions of the main bronchus in each lung into the larger bronchi subdivisions and then down to the smaller bronchioles.

Bronchitis inflammation of the bronchi within the lung.

Buccal pouch the space between the teeth and gums on one side and the cheeks on the other.

Cannabis a hallucinogenic plant; marijuana.

Cheilosis ulceration or cracking of the mucocutaneous junction at the angles of the mouth, sometimes associated with vitamin deficiency.

Chipping episodic use of an opiate drug but without addiction.

Collateral informant a person (usually a relative or friend) who provides information about a patient or research subject.

Cor pulmonale heart disease secondary to hypertension in the pulmonary vessels.

Cyanotic bluish discoloration of the skin and/or mucous membranes.

Dehydration excessive loss of fluid from the body, leading ultimately to vascular collapse and death.

Demerol Trade name for a synthetic (i.e., man-made) opiate drug; generically called meperidine.

Dermatitis inflammation of the skin; it can be caused by malnutrition, poor hygiene, allergy, and various infections and infestations.

Diacetylmorphine the chemical name for heroin.

Diaphragm the sheet of muscle and connective tissue that separates the abdomen from the chest; its contractions can aid the chest muscles during breathing.

Dyā fēn (**Lao**) literally "opiate medicine"; opium.

Dysphoria a vague feeling of emotional discontent or dis-ease but without the more specific characteristics associated with fear, anxiety, depression, or other more "formed" emotional states.

Emphysema a chronic condition of the lung characterized by fibrosis, scarring, and inefficient or inadequate exchange of oxygen and carbon dioxide between the blood and air in the lungs.

Enzyme a molecular structure that enables a chemical reaction or transformation to occur.

Epidemiology the study of the distribution and correlates of health problems in populations.

Exhalation the phase of breathing in which air is expelled out of the lungs.

Exogamous a culturally determined marriage pattern in which a group does not permit two of its members to marry (e.g., clan members with the same family name).

Gastrointestinal tract the organs through which food is taken into the body, including the stomach, small intestine, colon or large intestine, and rectum.

Gingivitis inflammation of the gums, often associated with poor oral hygiene.

Glottis the structures within the larynx that can be voluntarily closed before coughing, during a Val Salva maneuver, or during smoking to increase intrapulmonary pressure.

Iatrogenic caused by a physician; it usually refers to a pathological condition.

Inhalation the phase of breathing marked by taking air into the lungs.

Intoxication the state of an individual who has sufficient drug or alcohol in the body to interfere with neurophysiological functioning (e.g., slurred speech, incoordination). It can occur in either addicted or nonaddicted persons. Intoxication ranges along a spectrum from quite mild intoxication, to stupor, to death from overdose. Addicts may show no or only mild intoxication with doses that could prove severely intoxicating or lethal to a nonaddict.

Intrapulmonary within the lung.

Keratitis inflammation and/or ulceration of the cornea, sometimes associated with vitamin A deficiency.

Kha (**Lao**)   literally "slave"; it refers primarily to those Lao Theung tribal groups from whom the Lao, Thai, and Cambodians once took slaves; some Lao still used the term when speaking of Lao Theung peoples during 1965 to 1975.

Khon tēt dyā fēn (**Lao**)   literally "person attached to or next to opium"; it refers to those opium users who take opium daily and go into withdrawal if they try to stop (i.e., opium addicts).

Lingua franca (**Latin**)   a common or market language in a region where many languages are spoken (e.g., Lao was the lingua franca in Laos, even though many residents of Laos could neither speak nor understand it since they had their own dialects).

Lao hai (**Lao**)   rice wine.

Lao lao (**Lao**)   rice whiskey.

Lao Lum (**Lao**)   literally "the low Lao"; refers to ethnic Lao people who reside in the lowest altitudes of Laos.

Lao Sūng (**Lao**)   literally "the high Lao"; it refers to the Hmong (Meo) and Iu Mien (Yao) who live at the highest altitudes in the mountains of northern Laos.

Laotian   a citizen of Laos; this term applies to both ethnic Lao people and citizens of other ethnic groups.

Malaise   a feeling of being ill, usually accompanied by weakness, bodily aching, and sometimes fever.

Matrilocal   a culturally approved residence pattern in which a married couple lives with or close to the wife's parents.

Menses   intermittent vaginal flow of blood from the uterus of a woman, occurring approximately monthly and lasting a few to several days; menstrual period.

Morbidity   refers to illness, disease, disability.

Mortality   refers to death.

Naiban (**Lao**)   village headman or chief, popularly chosen by the family heads and elders.

Neeng hao yeeng (**Hmong**)   literally "person who ingests opium"; opium smoker.

Neolocal   a culturally approved residence pattern in which a married couple lives in a place close to neither the wife's nor the husband's parents.

Nyam mak (**Lao**)   chewing betel.

Pali   an archaic Sanskritic language; it is the written and spoken language for some Buddhist sects (as Latin is for certain Christian sects).

Pathet Lao (Lao)   literally "the Lao country"; for a time it referred to the Lao communist party.

Pathogenic   capable of causing pathology.

Patrilocal   a culturally approved residence pattern in which a married couple lives with or close to the husband's parents.

Paum (**Lao**)   any diluent added to opium in order to increase its weight and dishonestly obtain a higher price; it usually consists of the chopped or ground poppy stalks, certain barks, or other plant materials.

Pharmacopoeia   a list or collection of drugs.

Physiological   refers to the physical and physiochemical phenomena within living organisms.

Physiological dependence   this indicates the presence of a withdrawal illness when drug use is stopped. It occurs with addiction to drugs.

Placebo   a nonspecific treatment method that does not have a demonstrable therapeutic effect (e.g., fructose-containing capsules).

Polygyny   a culturally accepted marriage form in which a man is permitted to have more than one wife.

Process model   a theory with multiple cause-effect relationships, with branching alternatives and feedback mechanism.

Psychological   refers to such mental phenomena as thought, memory, intelligence, emotions.

Psychological dependence   the person uses psychoactive substances often, usually daily; however, physiological dependence may or may not be present. This phenomenon may occur with addicting drugs (such as opium) or with nonaddicting drugs (such as cannabis or betel).

Psychosomatic   refers to the mutual effects of mind and body upon each other.

Pulmonary hypertension   increased pressure within the blood vessels of the lungs.

Pyorrhea   an advanced stage of gingivitis characterized by gum and bone resorption, purulent discharge, loose teeth, and fetid or foul breath.

Register collection of clinical data for a population at a central office; nonclinical events collected for substance abuse often include certain causes of death, drug-related arrests and incarceration, and other drug-related phenomena that are surveyed by social agencies.

Rite of passage a ritual or ceremony marking an individual's change in status, such as graduation, marriage, birth, death, investment into office.

Sanskrit an ancient language of India; it is the classical language of India and of Hinduism.

Stethoscope an instrument for listening to body sounds.

Stochastic model a theory with a single cause-effect relationship.

Subsistence farming an economic endeavor in which farmers consume all or most of their produce and meet all or most of their own needs.

Swidden a system of agriculture in which land is alternately left fallow for some years or decades and then farmed for a few to several years; also referred to as slash-and-burn agriculture, since the forest or brush is slashed (i.e., cut down) and then burned prior to being planted.

Tasseng **(Lao)** the leader among a group of village headmen who meet at intervals to discuss matters of mutual concern; the position is popularly chosen, but usually then endorsed by the central government's representative in the area (i.e., the *chao mouang*).

"Titer" use consumption of an addicting or dependency-producing drug, such that the daily intake of drug tends to remain fairly stable over a prolonged period.

Tolerance as an individual uses addicting doses of an addicting drug over time, he or she discovers that increasing doses are required to achieve the same perceived effect. Eventually, the addicted person can safely take a dose level that might kill a nonaddicted person, or show no intoxication effects whereas a nonaddicted person would show severe intoxication.

Trachea the pipelike structure between the larynx and the bronchi; it carries air to the lungs.

Val Salva maneuver contraction of the abdominal and thoracic muscles against a closed glottis; it increases the pressure within the abdomen and chest.

Wat (**Lao**) the grounds and associated buildings for Buddhist study and worship; it usually includes a temple, quarters for monks, a gong for announcing prayer times, and sometimes a pavillion for meetings and study.

Withdrawal the illness that develops in an addict when the drug is suddenly stopped. It can be comparatively mild (e.g., runny nose, irritability, bodily aches, loss of appetite) or severe (e.g., diarrhea, vomiting, dehydration, hypotension, or shock).

Yen chai (**Lao**) literally "cool heart"; it refers to the traditional Lao value for remaining calm and avoiding direct, overt expression of strong emotion.

References

ABLON, J.
    1974.   Al-Anon family groups. *Amer. J. Psychotherapy* 28:30–45.

AHLUWALIA, H.S., and PONNAMPALAM, J. T.
    1968.   The socioeconomic aspects of betel-nut chewing. *J. Tropical Med. Hygiene* 71:48–50.

ALLISON, R. S.
    1965.   On nervous disease in Thailand. *Ulster Med. J.* 34:74–92.

AMERICAN PSYCHIATRIC ASSOCIATION
    1980.   *Diagnostic and Statistical Manual of Mental Disorders.* 3d ed. American Psychiatric Assoc., Washington, D.C.

ANDIMA, H., KRUG, D., BERJNER, L., PATRICK, S., and WHITMAN, S.
    1973.   A prevalence estimation model of narcotics addiction in New York City. *Amer. J. Epidem.* 98:56–62.

ANNIS, H. M.
    1979.   Self-report reliability of Skid-Row alcoholics. *Brit. J. Psychiatry* 134:459–465.

ARNOLD, C. B.
    1967.   Culture shock and a Peace Corps field mental health program. *Community Mental Health J.* 3:53–60.

ARNON, D., KELINMAN, M. H., and KISSIN, B.
    1974.   Psychological differentiation in heroin addicts. *Internatl. J. Addict.* 9:151–159.

ASTRUP, C., and ODEGAARD, O.
    1959–   Internal migration and mental disease in Norway. *Psychiatry Quarterly*
    1960.   *Suppl.* 33–34:116–130.

BAGLEY, C., and BINITIE, A.
    1970.   Alcoholism and schizophrenia in Irishmen in London. *Brit. J. Addic.* 65:3–7.

BAHR, H. N.
    1969.   Lifetime affiliation patterns of early- and late-onset drinkers. *Quart. J. Stud. Alc.* 30:646–656.

BARNEY, G. L.
  1967.   The Meo of Xieng Khouang Province, Laos. In *Southeast Asian Tribes, Minorities, and Nations,* ed. P. Kunstadter, pp. 271–294. Princeton: Princeton Univ. Press.
BECKMAN, L. J.
  1975.   Women alcoholics: A review of social and psychological studies. *Quart. J. Stud. Alc.* 36:797–824.
BENEDICT, R.
  1934.   Anthropology and the abnormal. *J. of General Psychology* 10(2): 59–82.
BERGER, L. J., and WESTERMEYER, J.
  1977.   "World traveler" addicts in Asia: II. Comparison with "Stay at Home" addicts. *Am. J. Drug Alc. Abuse* 4:495–503.
BERKSON, J.
  1946.   Limitations of the application of fourfold table analysis to hospital data. *Biometrics Bull.* 2:47–53.
BERNATZIK, H. A.
  1970.   *Akha and Miao: Problems of Applied Ethnography in Farther India.* New Haven: HRAF Press.
BIRLEY, J. L. T., and BROWN, G. W.
  1970.   Crises and life changes preceding the onset or relapse of acute schizophrenia: Clinical aspects. *Brit. J. Psychiatry* 116:327–333.
BOURNE, P.
  1974.   Issues in addiction. In *Addiction,* pp. 1–19. New York: Academic Press.
  1975.   The Chinese student—Acculturation and mental illness. *Psychiatry* 38:269–277.
BROWN, G. W.
  1976.   Berkson fallacy revisited: Spurious conclusions from patient surveys. *Amer. J. Dis. Child.* 130:55–60.
BROWNING, F., and GARRETT, B.
  1971.   The new opium war. *Ramparts* 9:30–39.
BURCHETT, W. G.
  1967.   *Mekong Upstream.* Hanoi: Red River Publishing House.
BURTON-BRADLEY, B. G.
  1966.   Papua and New Guinea transcultural psychiatry: Some implications of betel chewing. *Med. J. Austral.* 2:744–748.
  1979.   Arecaidinism: Betel chewing in transcultural perspective. *Canad. J. Psychiatry* 24:481–488.
BUTTERFIELD, F.
  1972.   Laos's opium country resisting drug law. *New York Times,* Oct. 16.

CARSTAIRS, B. M.
  1954.   Daru and bhang: Cultural factors in the choice of intoxicant. *Quart. J. Stud. Alc.* 15:220–236.
CAVAN, S. E. G.
  1965.   "Social Interaction in Public Drinking Places." Ph.D. dissertation, University of California at Berkeley. University microfilms No. 66–3559.

CHAMBERS, C. D., HINESELY, R. K., and MOLDESTAD, M.
   1970.   Narcotic addiction in females: A race comparison. *Internatl. J. Addic.* 5:257–278.
CHIEN, I., GERALD, D. L., and LEE, R. S.
   1964.   *The Road to H: Narcotics, Delinquency, and Social Policy.* New York: Basic Books.
CHOPRA, R. N.
   1928.   The present position of the opium habit in India. *Indian J. Med. Res.* 16:389–439.
"Clean living" without drugs in Laos. *Medical Tribune* (Jan. 26, 1972), p. 2.
COMMITTEE ON ADDICTION PRODUCING DRUGS
   1957.   *World Health Organization Report, Series 116.* Geneva: World Health Organization.
COPELAND, J. R. M.
   1968.   Aspects of mental illness in West African students. *Social Psychiat.* 3:7–13.
COX, T. J., and LONGWELL, B.
   1974.   Reliability of interview data concerning current heroin use from heroin addicts on methadone. *Internatl. J. Addict.* 9:161–165.

DACOSTA, J. L., TOCK, E. P. C., and BOEY, H. K.
   1971.   Lung disease with chronic obstruction in opium smokers in Singapore: Clinical electrocardiographic, radiological, functional, and pathological features. *Thorax* 26:555–571.
   1972.   Chronic obstructive lung disease in Singapore. *Amer. Rev. of Respiratory Disease.* 106:246–259.
DAI, B.
   1937.   *Opium Addiction in Chicago.* Shanghai: Commercial Press Limited.
DELEON, G., SKODAL, A., and ROSENTHAL, M. S.
   1973.   Phoenix House, changes in psychopathological signs of resident drug addicts. *Arch. Gen. Psychiatry* 28:131–135.
DESSAINT, A. Y.
   1971.   Lisu migration in the Thai highlands. *Ethnology* 10:329–348.
   1972.   The poppies are beautiful this year. *Natural Hist.* 81:31–36.
A detoxification center in Laos. 1975. *ICAA News* 3:2–7.
DOMMEN, A. J.
   1965.   *Conflict in Laos: The Politics of Neutralization.* New York: Praeger.
DUMONT, M. P.
   1967.   Tavern culture: The sustenance of homeless men. *Am. J. Orthopsychiatry* 37:938–945.
DUPONT, R., and GREENE, M. H.
   1973.   The dynamics of a heroin addiction epidemic. *Science* 181:716–722.
DURRENBERGER, P.
   1976.   The economy of a Lisu village. *Amer. Ethnologist* 3:633–643.

EDWARDS, G.
   1973.   Epidemiology applied to alcoholism: A review and an examination of purposes. *Quart. J. Stud. Alc.* 34:28–56.
EDWARDS, G., HENSMAN, C., and PETO, J.
   1972.   Drinking in a London suburb; III/Comparisons of drinking troubles among men and women. *Quart. J. Stud. Alc. Suppl.*, no. 6:128.

ELLIS, W. G.
  1901.   Some remarks on asylum practice in Singapore. *J. Trop. Med.* 4:411–
          414.
EVERINGHAM, J.
  1975.   The Gold Triangle trade. *Asia Magazine* 15 (Mar. 23):24–30.

FEINGOLD, D.
  1975.   Constraints on opium production. In *Proposal to Control Opium
          from the Golden Triangle and Terminate the Shan Opium Trade*, pp.
          223–239. Washington, D.C.: U.S. Govt. Printing Office.
FOISIE, J.
  1973.   U.S. helping Laos to fight drug addiction. *New York Times* (Mar. 4),
          Part VIII, p. 4.
FONG, S. L., and PESKIN, H.
  1969.   Sex-role strain and personality adjustment of China-born students in
          America. *J. Abnormal. Psychol.* 74:563–567.
FORT, J.
  1975.   Giver of delight or liberator of sin: Drug use and "addiction" in Asia.
          Bull. on Narcotics 17:1–11.
FROST, I. F.
  1938.   Home-sickness and immigrant psychosis: Austrian and German
          domestic servants the basis of study. *J. Mental Sci.* 84:801–847.

GARB, S.
  1969.   Drug addiction in physicians. *Anesthesia and Analgesia—Current
          Researches* 48:129–133.
GARETT, G. R., and BAHR, H. M.
  1973.   Women on Skid Row. *Quart. J. Stud. Alc.* 34:1228–1243.
GARRETT, W. E.
  1974.   The Hmong of Laos: No place to run. *Natl. Geographic* 143 (Jan.):
          78–111.
GEDDES, W. R.
  1976.   *Migrants of the Mountains.* Oxford: The Clarendon Press.
GERMAN, G. A., and ARYA, O. P.
  1969.   Psychiatric morbidity amongst a Uganda student population. *Brit. J.
          Psychiatry* 115:1323–1329.
GILMAN, A. G., GOODMAN, L. S., and GILMAN, A.
  1980.   *The Pharmacological Basis of Therapeutics.* New York: Macmillan.
GLATT, M. M., and HILLS, B. R.
  1968.   Alcohol abuse and alcoholism in the young. *Brit. J. Addic.* 63:183–191.
GOODWIN, D. W., SCHULSINGER, F., HERMANSEN, L., GUZE, S. B., and
WINOKUR, G.
  1973.   Alcohol problems in adoptees raised apart from alcoholic biologic
          parents. *Arch. Gen. Psychiatry* 28:238–243.
GORDON, E. G.
  1965.   Mentally ill West Indian immigrants. *Brit. J. Psychiatry* 111:877–887.
GRAY, D. D.
  1977.   Laotians bent on changing Meos' traditional way of life. *Bangkok Post*
          (Mar. 16).

REFERENCES

GREENE, M. H.
    1974.   An epidemiologic assessment of heroin use. *Amer. J. Publ. Health Suppl.* 64:1–10.

HAHN, E.
    1969.   The big smoke. *New Yorker* (Feb. 15), pp. 35–43.

HALIKAS, J. A., and RIMER, J. D.
    1974.   Predictors of multiple drug abuse. *Arch. Gen. Psychiatry* 31:414–418.

HALPERN, J.
    1961.   Observations on the social structure of the Lao elite. *Asian Survey* 1:25–32.
    1961–   Cultural change in Laos and Serbia: Possible tendencies toward uni-
    1963.   versal organizational patterns. *Human Organization* 20–21:11–14.
    1964a.   *Economy and Society of Laos.* New York: Inblinger.
    1964b.   *Economy and Society of Laos: A Brief Survey.* Detroit: Cellar Book.

HALPERN, J., and KUNSTADTER, P.
    1967.   Laos: Introduction. In *Southeast Asian Tribes, Minorities, and Nations,* ed. P. Kunstadter, pp. 233–258. Princeton: Princeton Univ. Press.

HARLPIEU, H. R., and HAGAR, R. N.
    1958.   The alcohols. In *Pharmacology in Medicine,* ed. V. Drill. New York: McGraw Hill.

HENDLER, H. I., and STEPHENS, R. C.
    1977.   The addict odyssey: From experimentation to addiction. *Internatl. J. Addict.* 12:25–42.

HES, J. P.
    1958.   Hypochondriasis in Oriental Jewish immigrants. *Internatl. J. Soc. Psychiatry* 4:18–23.
    1970.   Drinking in a Yemenite rural settlement in Israel. *Brit. J. Addic.* 65:293–296.

HO, K.
    1977.   "Heave-ho" for heroin. *South China Morning Post* (Nov. 12), p. 15.

HOLMES, T. H., and RAHE, R. H.
    1967.   The social readjustment rating scale. *J. Psychosomatic Res.* 11:213–218.

HOLZNER, A. S., and DING, L. K.
    1973.   White pearl dragons in Hong Kong: A study of young women drug addicts. *Internatl. J. Addict.* 8:253–263.

HORTON, D.
    1943.   The functions of alcohol in primitive societies: A cross-cultural study. *Quart. J. Stud. Alc.* 4:199–320.

HOWARD, H.
    1927.   *Ten Weeks With Chinese Bandits.* London: John Lane, The Bodley Head Ltd.

HUGHES, P. H., BRAKER, N. W., and CRAWFORD, H. A.
    1972.   The natural history of a heroin epidemic. *Amer. J. Publ. Health* 62: 995–1001.

HUGHES, P. H., and CRAWFORD, G. A.
    1972.   A contagious disease model for researching and intervening in heroin epidemics. *Arch. Gen. Psychiatry* 27:149–155.

317

1974.   The high drug use community: A natural laboratory for epidemio-
         logical experiments in addiction control. *Amer. J. Publ. Health Suppl.*
         64:11–15.

HUGHES, P. H., CRAWFORD, G. A., and BARKER, N. W.
1971.   Developing an epidemiologic field team for drug dependence. *Arch.
         Gen. Psychiatry* 24:389–393.

HUGHES, P. H., and JAFFEE, H. H.
1972.   Heroin copping area. *Arch. Gen. Psychiatry* 24:394–400.

HUGHES, P. H., PARKER, R., and SENAY, E. C.
1974.   Addicts, police, and the neighborhood social system. *Amer. J. Ortho-
         psychiatry* 44:129–141.

HUGHES, P. H., SENAY, E. C., and PARKER, R.
1972.   The medical management of a heroin epidemic. *Arch. Gen. Psychiatry*
         27:585–592.

HUMAN, M. M., HEBRICH, A. R., and BESSON, G.
1972.   Ascertaining police bias in arrests for drunken driving. *Quart. J. Stud.
         Alc.* 33:148–159.

HUNT, L. G.
1974.   Recent spread of heroin use in the United States. *Amer. J. Publ. Health
         Suppl.* 64:16–23.

JAFFEE, J. H.
1980.   Drug addiction and drug abuse. In *The Pharmacological Basis of
         Therapeutics*, 6th ed., pp. 535–584. New York: Macmillan.

JELLINEK, E. M.
1952.   Alcoholism: Phases of alcohol addiction. *Quart. J. Stud. Alc.* 13:
         673–684.
1960.   *The Disease Concept of Alcoholism.* New Haven: Hillhouse Press.

KAY, L.
1960.   *Alcoholism in Twins: Studies on the Etiology and Sequels of Abuse
         of Alcohol.* Stockholm: Almquist and Wiksell.

KIM, K. I.
1969.   Epidemiology of addictive or habit-forming drug use in Korea. *Korean
         Med. Assoc. J.* 14:207–209.

KISSIN, B., ROSENBLATT, S. M., and MACHOVER, K.
1968.   Prognostic factors in alcoholism. *Amer. Psychiatric Assoc. Res.
         Reports* 24:22–43.

KNUPFER, G., and ROOM, R.
1967.   Drinking patterns and attitudes of Irish, Jewish and White Protestant
         American Men. *Quart. J. Stud. Alc.* 28:676–699.

KOX, T. J., and LONGWELL, B.
1974.   Reliability of interview data concerning current heroin use from heroin
         addicts on methadone. *Internatl. J. Addict.* 9:161–165.

KRAMER, J. C.
1978.   Social benefits and social costs of drug control laws. *J. Drug Issues*
         8:1–7.
1979.   Speculations on the nature and pattern of opium smoking. *J. Drug
         Issues* 7:247–256.

REFERENCES

KRUPINSKI, J.
  1967. Sociological aspects of mental ill-health in migrants. *Soc. Sci. Med.*
         1:267–281.
KUNITZ, S. J., LEVY, J. E., ODOROFF, C. J., and BOLLINGER, J.
  1971. The epidemiology of alcoholism in two southwestern Indian tribes.
         Quart. J. Stud. Alc. 32:706–720.
KUNSTADTER, P.
  1972. Spirits of change capture the Karens. *Natl. Geographic* 141:267–284.

LANGER, P. F., and ZASLOFF, J. J.
  1970. *North Vietnam and the Pathet Lao: Partners in the Struggle for Laos.*
         Cambridge, Mass.: Harvard University Press.
LEACH, B.
  1973. Does Alcoholics Anonymous Really Work? In *Alcoholism: Progress in
         Research and Treatment,* ed. P. Bourne and R. Fox. New York:
         Academic Press.
LEBAR, F., and SUDDARD, A.
  1960. *Laos: Its People, Its Society, Its Culture.* New Haven: Human Relations
         Area Files Press.
LEBAR, F. M., HICKEY, G. C., and MUSGRAVE, J. K.
  1964. *Ethnic Groups of Mainland Southeast Asia.* New Haven: Human Rela-
         tions Area Files Press.
LEMERE, F.
  1953. What happens to alcoholics. *Amer. J. Psychiatry* 109:674–767.
LEMOINE, J.
  1967. *Un Village Hmong Vert du Haut Laos.* Paris: Centre National de la
         Recherche Scientifique.
LEONG, H. K., POH, S. C., and GANDEVIA, G.
  1970. Ventilatory capacity in a group of opium smokers in Singapore. *Singa-
         pore Med. J.* 11:75.
LESSA, W., and VOGT. E.
  1965. *Reader in Comparative Religion.* New York: Harper and Row.
LEUTGERT, J. J., and ARMSTRONG, A. H.
  1973. Methodologic issues in drug usage surveys: Anonymity, recency, and
         frequency. *Internatl. J. Addict.* 8:683–689.
LONG, G.
  1952. Indochina faces the dragon. *Natl. Geographic* 102 (Sept.): 287–328.
LUKE, J. L., and HELPERN. M.
  1968. Sudden unexpected death from natural causes in young adults: A
         review of 275 consecutive autopsy cases. *Arch. Pathology* 85:10–17.
LURIE, N. O.
  1970. The world's oldest on-going protest demonstration: North American
         Indian drinking patterns. *Pacific Historical Rev.* 40:311–332.

MADDUX, J. F., and DESMOND, D. P.
  1974. Obtaining life history information about opium users. *Am. J. Drug
         Alc. Abuse* 1:181–198.
  1975. Reliability and validity of information from chronic heroin users.
         J. Psychiatric Research 12:87–95.

REFERENCES

Malloy, M. T.
 1973.   Laos, Burma, and Thailand are the three sides of heroin's golden tri-
          angle. *Natl. Observer* 12 (Feb. 10):1–20.
Malzberg, B.
 1964.   Mental disease among native and foreign-born whites in New York
          state, 1949–1951. *Mental Hygiene* 48:478–499.
Mandelbaum, D.
 1965.   Alcohol and culture. *Current Anthropology* 6:281–294.
Marks, T. A.
 1973.   The Meo hill tribe problem in north Thailand. *Asian Survey* 13:929–
          944.
Martin, M. A.
 1975.   Ethnobotanical aspects of cannabis in Southeast Asia. In *Cannabis
          and Culture*, ed. V. Rubin, pp. 63–75. Hague: Mouton.
McKinnon, J. M.
 1978.   The Jeremiah Incorporation. Mimeograph report. Chiengmai, Thai-
          land: Tribal Research Center.
McNamee, H. B., Mello, N. K., and Mendelson, J. M.
 1968.   Experimental analysis of drinking patterns of alcoholics; Concurrent
          psychiatric observations. *Amer. J. Psychiatry* 124:1063–1069.
Meeker, O.
 1959.   *The Little World of Laos.* New York: Chas. Scribner.
Mellsop, G. W.
 1969.   The effect of distance in determining hospital admission rates. *Med. J.
          Austral.* 2:814–817.
Mendelson, J. H.
 1970.   Biological concomitants of alcoholism. *New Engl. J. Med.* 283:24–32.
Merrill, T. F.
 1942.   *Japan and the Opium Menace.* New York: Institute of Pacific Relations.
Mezey, A. G.
 1959.   Psychiatric aspects of human migrations. *Internatl. J. Soc. Psychiatry*
          5:245–260.
Miles, D.
 1979.   The finger knife and Ockham's razor: A problem in Asian culture
          history and economic anthropology. *Amer. Ethnologist* 6:223–243.
Miller, J. S., Sensenig, J., Stocker, R. B., and Campbell, R.
 1973.   Value patterns of drug addicts as a function of race and sex. *Internatl.
          J. Addict.* 8:589–598.
Moore, W.
 1882.   Opium smoking. *J. Amer. Med. Assoc.* (Mar. 5).
Murray, R. M.
 1974.   Psychiatric illness in doctors. *Lancet* 1:1211–1213.
Musto, D. F.
 1973.   *The American Disease.* New Haven: Yale Univ. Press.

Na Champassak, S.
 1961.   *Storm Over Laos.* New York: Praeger.
Nicol, A. R.
 1971.   Psychiatric disorder in the children of Caribbean immigrants. *J. Child.
          Psychol. Psychiat.* 12:273–287.

Ninety-six kilos of opium and heroin burned at national stadium. *Vientiane News*, Nov. 21, 1971, p. 1.

ODEGAARD, O.
  1932. Emigration and insanity: A study of mental disease among the Norwegian population in Minnesota. *Acta Psychiatrica et Neurologica Suppl. IV*, 1–206.

O'DONNELL, J. A., BESTEMAN, K. J., and JONES, J. P.
  1967. Mental history of narcotic addicts. *Internatl. J. Addict.* 2:21–38.

ORR, I. M.
  1933. Oral cancer in betel nut chewers in Travancore: Its aetiology, pathology, and treatment. *Lancet* 2:575–589.

OSBORN, G. M. T.
  1967. Government and the hill tribes of Laos. In *Southeast Asian Tribes, Minorities, and Nations*, ed. P. Kundstadter, pp. 259–270. Princeton: Princeton Univ. Press.

OSBORNE, M.
  1975. *River Road to China: The Mekong Expedition, 1866–73*. New York: Livermore.

PARK, W. H.
  1899. *Opinions of 100 Physicians on the Use of Opium in China*. Shanghai: American Presbyterian Mission Press.

PARKER, S., KELINER, R. J., and NEEDELMAN, B.
  1969. Migration and mental illness: Some reconsiderations for further analysis. *Soc. Sci. Med.* 3:1–9.

PATTISON, E. M., COE, R., and DOERR, H. C.
  1973. Population variation between alcoholism treatment facilities. *Internatl. J. Addict.* 8:199–229.

POPULATION REFERENCE BUREAU, INFORMATION SERVICE
  1969. "1969 World Population Data Sheet." Washington, D.C.

PORTER, J.
  1974. Drug addiction in Laos: Authorities trying to cope with serious problem. *Asia Magazine* 14 (Feb. 10):12–14.

POSHYACHINDA, V., ONTHUM, Y., SITTHI-AMORN, C., and PERNGPARN, V.
  1978. *Evaluation of Treatment Outcome: The Buddhist Temple Treatment Center, Tam Kraborg*. Bangkok: Chulalongkorn University Institute of Health Research.

PRANGE, A. J.
  1959. An interpretation of cultural isolation and alien's paranoid reaction. *Internatl. J. Soc. Psychiatry* 4:254–263.

RACHIKUL, O.
  1970. Studies Regarding Subjugation of Planting of Opium in Kingdom of Laos. Mimeograph report, Vientiane, June 1.

RAHE, T. H., MEYER, M., and SMITH, M.
  1964. Social stress and illness onset. *Psychosomatic Res.* 8:35–44.

RAO, T. K. S., NICASTRI, A. D., and FRIEDMAN, E. A.
  1974. Natural history of heroin-associated nephropathy. *New Engl. J. Med.* 290:19–23.

RIMMER, J., PITTS, F. N., REICH, T., and WINOKUR, G.
    1971.   Alcoholism: II. Sex, socioeconomic status and race in two hospitalized samples. *Quart. J. Stud. Alc.* 32:942–952.

ROBERTS, B., and MYERS, J.
    1954.   Religion, national origin, immigration and mental illness. *Amer. J. Psychiatry* 110:759–764.

ROBINS, L. N., DAVIS, D. H., and GOODWIN, G. W.
    1974.   Drug use by U. S. Army enlisted men in Vietnam: A follow-up on their return home. *Amer. J. Epidem.* 99:235–249.

ROBINS, L. N., DAVIS, D. H., and NURCO, D. N.
    1974.   How permanent was Vietnam drug addiction. *Amer. J. Publ. Health Suppl.* 64:38–43.

ROBINS, L. N., HELZER, J. E. and DAVIS, D. H.
    1975.   Narcotic use in southeast Asia and afterward: An interview study of 898 Vietnam returnees. *Arch. Gen. Psychiatry* 32:955–961.

ROLNICK, H.
    1974.   Buddhist drug cure. *Asia Magazine* 14:18–25.

ROMOND, A. M., FORREST, C. K. and KLEBER, H. D.
    1974.   Follow-up of participants in a drug dependence therapeutic community. *Arch. Gen. Psychiatry* 32:369–374.

ROOM, R.
    1968.   Cultural contingencies of alcoholism: Variations between and within nineteenth-century urban ethnic groups in alcohol-related death rates. *J. Health Soc. Behavior* 9:99–113.

SAPIRA, J. D.
    1975.   Speculations concerning opium abuse and world history. *Perspectives in Biology and Medicine* 18:379–398.

SASSADY, K.
    1962.   Contributions a l'étude de la medecine Laotienne. Ph.D. dissertation, University of Paris.

SAUNDERS, W. M., and KERSHAW, P. W
    1979.   Spontaneous remission from alcoholism —A community study. *Brit. J. Addic.* 75:251–255.

SCHMIDT, W., and DeLINT, J.
    1969.   Mortality experiences of male and female alcoholic patients. *Quart. J. Stud. Alc.* 30:112–118.

SCHUCKIT, M. A., GOODWIN, D. A., and WINOKUR, G.
    1972.   A study of alcoholism in half-siblings. *Amer. J. Psychiatry* 128:1132–1136.

SEELYE, H. N., and BREWER, M. G.
    1970.   Ethnocentrism and acculturation of North Americans in Guatemala. *J. Soc. Psychol.* 80:147–155.

SHIPLER, D. K.
    1974.   Opium in Laos: It's hard to stop. *New York Times* (Nov. 7).

SIEGEL, A. J.
    1973.   The heroin crisis among U. S. forces in southeast Asia: An overview. *J. Amer. Med. Assoc.* 223:1258–1261.

SILLETT, R. W., WILSON, M. B., MALCOLM, R. E., and BALL, K. P.
    1978.   Deception among smokers. *Brit. Med. J.* 2:1185–1186.

Singer, K.
1974. The choice of intoxicant among the Chinese. *Brit. J. Addic.* 69:257–258.
Skinner, G. W.
1957. *Chinese Society in Thailand.* Ithaca, N. Y.: Cornell Univ. Press.
1958. *Leadership and Power in the Chinese Community in Thailand.* Ithaca, N. Y.: Cornell Univ. Press.
Smart, R. G.
1975– Spontaneous recovery in alcoholics: A review and analysis of available
1976. research. *Drug Alc. Depend.* 1:277–285.
Srisavasdi, B. D.
1963. *Hill Tribes of Siam.* Bangkok: Bamrung Jukoulit Press.
Stephan, W. G., and Stephan, C.
1971. Role differentiation, empathy, and neurosis in urban migrants and lower-class residents of Santiago, Chile. *J. Pers. Soc. Psychol.* 19:1–6.
Sutker, P. B., and Allain, A. M.
1973. Incarcerated and street heroin addicts: A personality comparison. *Psychol. Rep.* 32:243–246.
Sutter, A. S.
1969. Worlds of drug use on the street scene. In *Delinquency, Crime, and Social Process,* ed. D. R. Cressy and D. A. Ward, pp. 802–829. New York: Harper and Row.
Suwanwela, C., Poshyachinda, V., Tasanapradit, P., and Dharmkrong-at, A.
1977. *The Hill Tribes of Thailand: Their Opium Use and Addiction.* Bangkok: Institute of Health Research.

Ulmann, A.
1958. Sociocultural backgrounds of alcoholism. *Ann. Amer. Acad. Political and Social Change,* pp. 48–54.

Vaillant, G. E.
1966a. A twelve-year follow-up of New York narcotic addicts: I. The relation of treatment to outcome; IV. Some characteristics and determinants of abstinence. *Amer. J. Psychiatry* 122:727–37; 123:573–584.
1966b. A twelve-year follow-up of New York narcotic addicts: II. The natural history of a chronic disease. *New Engl. J. Med.* 275:1281–1288.
1973. A twenty-year follow-up of New York narcotic addicts. *Arch. Gen. Psychiatry* 29:237–241.

Wade, N.
1972. Role of technology in curtailing supply. *Science* 177:1083–1085.
Wall, B.
1975. *Les Nya Hon: Étude Ethnographique d'Une Population du Plateau des Bolovens (Sud-Laos).* Vientiane: Editions Vithagna.
Wall, H. H.
1973. A study of alcoholism in women. *Amer. J. Psychiatry* 93:943–952.
Wallace, A. F. C.
1959. The institutionalization of cathartic and control strategies in Iroquois religious psychotherapy. In *Culture and Mental Health,* ed. M. Opler, pp. 63–96. New York: Macmillan.

REFERENCES

WALTON, H. J.
 1968. Personality as a determinant of the form of alcoholism. *Brit. J. Psychiatry* 114:761–766.
WANBERG, K., and HORN, J.
 1970. Alcoholism symptom patterns of men and women; A comparative study. *Quart. J. Stud. Alc.* 31:40–61.
WANBERG, K. W., and KNAPP, J.
 1970. Differences in drinking symptoms and behavior of men and women alcoholics. Brit. J. Addic. 64:374–375.
WARD, J. T.
 1967. U. S. aid to hill tribe refugees in Laos. In *Southeast Asian Tribes, Minorities and Nations*, ed. P. Kundstadter. Princeton: Princeton Univ. Press.
WARD, T. F.
 1961. Immigration and ethnic origin in mental illness. *Canad. Psychiatr. Assoc. J.* 6:232–332.
WAY, E.L.
 1965. Control and treatment of drug addiction in Hong Kong. In *Narcotics*, ed. D. M. Wilner and G. G. Kasselbaum, pp. 278–289. New York: McGraw Hill.
WESTERMEYER, J.
 1969. The Use of Alcohol and Opium among Two Ethnic Groups in Laos. Master's thesis, Univ. of Minnesota, Minneapolis. Abstract in *Transcultural Psychiatr. Res. Rev.* 6:148–151.
 1970. Cash crop raised by northern tribes. *Medical Tribune* (June 8), p. 3.
 1971a. Traditional and constitutional law: A study of change in Laos. *Asian Survey* 11:562–569.
 1971b. Use of alcohol and opium by the Meo of Laos. *Amer. J. Psychiatry* 127:1019–1023.
 1972a. Chippewa and majority alcoholism in the Twin Cities: A Comparison. *J. Nerv. Ment. Dis.* 155:322–327.
 1972b. A comparison of amok and other homicide in Laos. *Amer. J. Psychiatry* 129:703–709.
 1972c. Options regarding alcohol use among the Chippewa. *Amer. J. Orthopsychiatry* 42:398–403.
 1973a. Assassination in Laos: Its psychosocial perspectives. *Arch. Gen. Psychiatry* 28:740–743.
 1973b. Assassination and conflict resolution in Laos. *Amer. Anthropologist* 74:123–131.
 1973c. Folk treatment for opium addiction in Laos. *Brit. J. Addic.* 68:345–349.
 1973d. Grenade-amok in Laos: A psychosocial perspective. *Internatl. J. Soc. Psychiatry* 19:251–260.
 1973e. Lao Buddhism, mental health, and contemporary implications. *J. Health and Religion* 12:181–188.
 1973f. On the epidemicity of amok. *Arch. Gen. Psychiatry* 28:873–876.
 1974a. Alcoholism from the cross cultural perspective: A review and critique of clinical studies. *Amer. J. Drug Alc. Abuse* 1:89–106.
 1974b. Opium dens: A social resource for addicts in Laos. *Arch. Gen. Psychiatry* 31:237–240.

REFERENCES

1974c. Opium smoking in Laos: A survey of forty addicts. *Amer. J. Psychiatry* 131:165–170.

1976a. *Primer on Chemical Dependency: A Clinical Guide to Alcohol and Drug Problems.* Baltimore: Williams and Wilkins.

1976b. The pro-heroin effects of anti-opium laws. *Arch. Gen. Psychiatry* 33:1135–1139.

1977a. Narcotic addiction in two Asian cultures: A comparison and analysis. *Drug Alc. Depend.* 2:273–285.

1977b. Psychiatry in Indochina: Cultural issues during the period 1965–1975. *Transcultural Psychiatric Review* 15:23–38.

1977c. Opium addiction in Laos: An overview. In *Current Perspectives in Cultural Psychiatry,* ed. E. F. Foulks, R. M. Wintrob, J. Westermeyer, and A. R. Favazza, pp. 191–202. New York: Spectrum Publ.

1978a. Indigenous and expatriate addicts in Laos: A comparison. *Culture, Medicine and Psychiatry* 2:139–150.

1978b. Social events and narcotic addiction: The influence of war and law on opium use in Laos. *Addictive Behaviors* 3:57–61.

1978c. Ecological sensitivity and resistance of cultures in Asia. *Behavior Science Research* 13:109–123.

1979. Medical and nonmedical treatment for narcotic addicts: A comparative study from Asia. *J. Nerv. Ment. Dis.* 167:205–211.

1980. Sex ratio among opium addicts in Asia: Influences of drug availability and sampling method. *Drug. Alc. Depend.* 6:131–136.

1981a. Opium availability and prevalence of addiction in Asia. *Brit. J. Addic.* 76:85–90.

1981b. Three case finding methods for opiate addicts among the Hmong in Laos: A comparison. *Internatl. J. Addict.* 16:173–183.

WESTERMEYER, J., and BERGER, L. J.
1977. World traveler addicts in Asia; I. Demographic and clinical description. *Amer. J. Drug Alc. Abuse* 4:479–493.

WESTERMEYER, J., and BOURNE, P.
1977. A heroin "epidemic" in Laos. *Amer. J. Drug Alc. Abuse* 4:1–11.
1978. Treatment outcome and the role of the community in narcotic addiction: A case study from Laos. *J. Nerv. Ment. Dis.* 166:51–58.

WESTERMEYER, J., and HAUSMAN, W.
1974a. Cross cultural consultation for mental health planning. *Internatl. J. Soc. Psychiatry* 20:34–38.
1974b. Mental health consultation with government agencies: A comparison of two cases. *Social Psychiatry* 9:137–141.

WESTERMEYER, J., and PENG, G.
1977a. Opium and heroin addicts in Laos; I. A comparative study. *J. Nerv. Ment. Dis.* 164:346–350.
1977b. Opium and heroin addicts in Laos; II. A study of matched pairs. *J. Nerv. Ment. Dis.* 164:351–354.
1978. A comparative study of male and female opium addicts among the Hmong (Meo). *Brit. J. Addic.* 73:181–187.

WESTERMEYER, J., SOUDALY, C., and KAUFMAN, E.
1978. An addiction treatment program in Laos: The first year's experience. *Drug Alc. Depend.* 3:93–102.

WESTERMEYER, J., and WALZER, V.
　1975.　Sociopathy and drugs in a young psychiatric population. *Dis. Nerv. Syst.* 36:673–677.
WHITAKER, D. P., BARTH, H. A., and BERMAN, S. M.
　1972.　*Area Handbook for Laos.* Washington D.C.: Superintendent of Documents.
WIKLER, A.
　1961.　On the nature of addiction and habituation. *Brit. J. Addic.* 57:73–79.
WILLIAMS, C. L., ENG, A., BOTWIN, G. J., HILL, P., and WYNDER, E. L.
　1979.　Validation of students' self-reported cigarette smoking status with plasma cotinine levels. *Amer. J. Publ. Health* 69:1272–1274.
WINOKUR, G., and CLAYTON, P. J.
　1968.　Family history studies. IV. Comparison of male and female alcoholics. *Quart. J. Stud. Alc.* 29:885–891.
WINOKUR, G., REICH, T., RIMMER, J., and PITTS, F. N.
　1970.　III. Diagnosis and familial psychiatric illness in 259 alcoholic probands. *Arch. Gen. Psychiatry* 23:104–111.
WINTROB, R.M.
　1967.　A study of disillusionment: Depressive reactions of Liberian students returning from advanced training abroad. *Amer. J. Psychiatry* 123:1593–1598.
WOLFKILL, G., and ROSE, J. A.
　1966.　*Reported to be Alive.* London: W. H. Allen.
WOODRUFF, R. A., GUZE, S. B., CLAYTON, P. J., and CARR, D.
　1973.　Alcoholism and depression. *Arch. Gen. Psyciatry* 28:97–100.

YABLONSKY, L.
　1965.　*Synanon: The Tunnel Back.* New York: Macmillan Co.
YABLONSKY, L., and DEDERICH, C. E.
　1965.　Synanon: An analysis of some dimensions of the social structure of an antiaddiction society. In *Narcotics,* ed. D. M. Wilner and G. G. Kaselbaum, pp. 193–216. New York: McGraw Hill.
YANG, D.
　1975.　*Les Hmong du Laos: Face au Developpement.* Vientiane: Edition Siaosavath.
YIH-FU, R.
　1962.　The Miao: Their Origin and Southward Migration. *International Association Historians of Asia, Second Biennial Conf. Proc.* Taipei, Taiwan.
YOGACHANDRA, N.
　1978.　Nature against nature. *Bangkok Post* (Apr. 9), p. 8.
YOUNG, G.
　1962.　*Hill Tribes of Northern Thailand.* Bangkok: Siam Society.

ZASLOFF, J. J.
　1973.　*Pathet Lao: Leadership and Organization.* Lexington, Mass.: Lexington Books.

Index

Treatment expectations. *See* Expectations of treatment
Treatment outcome. *See* Evaluation of treatment
Treatment outreach. *See* Outreach program
Treatment, phases of. *See* Phases of treatment
Treatment program, 196–197, 200–201, 206–210
Tribal. *See* Mountaineers
Tropical disease. *See* Infectious disease; Malaria; Malnutrition
Trust, 94
Tuberculosis. *See* Pulmonary disease

Union of Soviet Socialist Republics, 18, 34, 205
United Nations, 152
United States Agency for International Development, 5, 7–8, 10–11, 107, 175, 200, 203–205, 247
United States of America, 12, 46, 63–64, 82, 84, 151–153, 168–187, 206, 257, 261, 272, 279
University of Minnesota, 7, 11
Urine analysis, 104, 107

Validity, 83–84, 88, 91
Valliant, George, 85
Val Salva maneuver, 57, 58
Variability, 89–91
Veteran, 139, 144, 197–198
Vientiane, 10–12, 17, 33–34, 43, 47, 64, 65, 76, 84, 89, 108–109, 113–117, 132–133, 134, 137–139, 143–144, 146, 147, 148, 150, 153, 155–158, 164, 178, 185–186, 198, 199, 204, 210, 211, 233, 234–237, 239–240, 255, 259, 266
Vietminh, 17, 32, 95
Vietnam, 12, 17, 21, 32, 52, 64, 66, 95, 112, 125, 132, 147, 150–151, 167, 169–170, 192, 194, 226, 259, 265–266, 272
Village, 19, 23–24, 48–49, 52, 64, 107–112
Violence, 23, 255, 267. *See also* Suicide, War

Visa restrictions, 169, 174
Vitamin deficiency, 96, 208. *See also* Malnutrition
Vomiting, 69, 190, 201

Walker, Anthony, 42
Wall, Barbara, 263
War, 17–18, 32, 51, 155, 275–278. *See also* Military; Soldier
Wat. *See* Monastery
Wat Than Kha Bok, 196, 199–203, 220–224, 225–227, 235–237
Weakness, 69–70
Wealth, 29, 39, 43, 48, 143, 191. *See also* Silver
Weather. *See* Climate; Monsoon; Season
Weddings. *See* Marriage
Weldon, Charles (Jigs), 202, 203
Wen, H. L., 248
Whiskey. *See* Alcohol
White House, 8, 12
Widowed, 139–140, 266
Wine. *See* Alcohol
Withdrawal, 1, 69–71, 80–81, 86, 90, 97–99, 102–103, 106, 126, 149, 161, 178, 181, 183, 186, 190–193, 196, 201, 207, 225–227, 269, 278
Wolfkill, Grant, 55, 64, 268
Woman. *See* Female
Work, 58, 70, 89–92. *See also* Employment; Labor; Occupation
World Health Organization, 8, 10–12, 34, 102, 205
World travelers, 35, 62–63, 158–159, 164–187. *See also* Caucasians
World War II, 36, 49, 149

Xieng Khouang, 10, 12, 25, 32, 36, 38, 43–44, 47, 70, 82, 109, 111, 117, 138, 197–198, 203, 229, 234

Yang, Dao, 118
Yao. *See* Iu Mien
Yen chai, 23
Young, Gordon, 106
Yunnan, 49, 93, 139, 141

Designer: Linda Robertson
Compositor: Freedmen's Organization
Printer: Braun-Brumfield
Binder: Braun-Brumfield
Text: Palatino
Display: Palatino

4/04   Y/R/121 UCP

Westermeyer